To uhm

Regulating a New Economy

To what extent does tech change
drive regulation

why is US. antitrust response so much more inter
than Europe?

⇏ teller misses point that gov'ts role is to hammer
out agreements between conflict'g interests

? Antitrust: where is the public?
(∞ Emergence of Puc - service us. rates)

Regulating a New Economy

*Public Policy and Economic Change
in America, 1900–1933*

Morton Keller

Harvard University Press
Cambridge, Massachusetts, and London, England

First Harvard University Press paperback edition, 1996

Library of Congress Cataloging-in-Publication Data

Keller, Morton.
  Regulating a new economy : public policy and economic change in America, 1990–1933 / Morton Keller.
    p. cm.
  ISBN 0-674-75362-3 (cloth)
  ISBN 0-674-75363-1 (pbk.)
  1. United States—Economic policy—To 1933. 2. Industry and state—United States—History—20th century. I. Title.
HC106.K45 1990   89-78193
338.973'009'041—dc20   CIP

For Barney, Jacob, Jared, and
Gabriel—the next wave

Preface

This book is part of a larger study of American public life from 1900 to 1933, a sequel to my *Affairs of State: Public Life in Late Nineteenth Century America* (1977). It is to be followed by a volume that will treat the realms of social policy—family, education, and religion; civil liberties and civil rights; crime and social mores; race and gender; public health and social welfare; immigration and citizenship—as economic policy is dealt with here. A third and final volume will examine the structure of politics, government, and law that provided the setting for the public policy response to the emergence of modern America. The collective title of this enterprise, "Persistence and Pluralism: Public Life in Early Twentieth Century America," signifies its underlying, unifying themes.

I should say something about the research technique on which my work rests. I concluded early on that to rely on traditional primary sources—manuscript collections, government documents, statistical data, and the like—in a synoptic study such as this would be the scholarly equivalent of trying to empty the sea with a slotted spoon. Yet to depend solely on the work of other historians would imprison me in their sense of what mattered and what it meant, and remove me from the freshness and immediacy of contemporary observation. So I immersed myself not only in the very substantial body of historical writing on early twentieth-century American economic policy, but also, and most especially, in the periodicals of the time that described and analyzed the political, governmental, and legal response to economic issues from 1900 to 1933. The Harvard College and Law School libraries made it possible for me to examine this very large and diverse body of materials. I am very grateful to these institutions, and to the Brandeis University Library.

*   *   *

Finally, it is a pleasure to indulge in that most satisfying of authorial rites, thanking those who gave me the benefit of their expertise and critical acumen: Lawrence M. Friedman, James Kloppenberg, Roy Lubove, Thomas K. McCraw, Stanford Ross, and Stephan Thernstrom.

Contents

The only people who treasure systems are those whom the whole truth evades, who want to catch it by the tail; a system is like truth's tail, but the truth is like a lizard; it will leave the tail in your hand and escape: it knows that it will soon grow another tail.

—*Turgenev*

All the truth, and all the pleasure, lies in the details.

—*Stendhal*

Introduction

An English traveler is supposed to have observed after a visit to Mayor Daley's Chicago in the early 1960s: "I have seen the past, and it works." Indeed it does: ceaselessly, pervasively, on all our lives and institutions.

But aren't twentieth-century Americans in fact the darlings of the new? Isn't ours above all others and above all else the Century of Change? Certainly we think so: we dilate endlessly on the uprootedness, transience, impermanence of our way of life.

And there are grounds for holding that around the turn of this century, much of Western society experienced change at a pace, and on a scale, far beyond what had been seen before—or, arguably, since. It was then that modernity came with a rush. The historian Eric Hobsbawm reminds us that "so much of what remained characteristic of our times originated, sometimes quite suddenly, in the decades before 1914." Norman Stone makes the same point more dramatically: "In 1895 the novelist Henry James acquired electric lighting; in 1896 he rode a bicycle; in 1897 he wrote on a typewriter; in 1898 he saw a cinematograph. Within a very few years, he could have had a Freudian analysis, travelled in an aircraft, understood the principles of the jet-engine or even of space-travel." Mark Sullivan recalled some of the words unknown in 1900 but very much part of the American language a quarter-century later:

> The newspapers of 1900 contained no mention of . . . jazz, nor feminism, nor birth-control. There was no such word as rum-runner, nor hijacker, nor bolshevism, fundamentalism, behaviorism, Freudian, . . . Rotary . . . cafeteria, automat . . . they would not have pictured boy scouts . . . nor traffic cops, nor Ku Klux Klan parades . . . nor one-piece bathing suits, nor advertisements of lip-sticks, nor motion-picture actresses, for there were no such things.[1]

But the hegemony of the new did not go uncontested. Much more so than we normally recognize, institutions adapted to or coopted the forces of change. Describing this complex interplay between old and new is the major challenge facing historians of twentieth-century America.

This book takes on the challenge in the realm of economic policy: that is, the response of American politics, law, and government to the new economy that came into being after 1900. The distinguishing features of that new economy were the rise of big business, large-scale technological change, and a shift of emphasis in production and distribution from capital goods to consumer goods.

Chapter 1 examines contemporary perceptions of this economic transformation. Chapters 2–4 deal with the most conspicuous and contentious economic issue of the time: the appropriate public policy response to large enterprise. They reflect the fact that big business was not a homogeneous, single-interest economic entity. Capital goods industries such as coal, oil, and steel—the classic trusts—differed profoundly in character and function from railroads, mass urban transit companies, and other public utilities (Chapters 2 and 3). And technological change generated a host of new enterprises—trucks and buses, autos and planes, electric power and telephones, motion pictures and radio—each of which called for its own regulatory response (Chapter 4).

Supervision of the modern business economy included as well the more general framework of commercial organization and practice: the law of corporations and the licensing of occupations, commercial and bankruptcy law, contract and tort law, and—increasingly important in the new consumer economy—regulating the prices, ownership, and sale of goods (Chapter 5).

Chapters 6–9 survey the regulation of what economists would call the factors of production: labor, land, trade, capital, and taxation. Labor-management relations and the status of unions came under increasing legal and political scrutiny (Chapter 6). So too did the use of land: in the city, where housing regulation and zoning became important public policy matters (Chapter 7), and in the countryside, where the marketing of agricultural products and the conservation and use of natural resources made ever larger demands on the polity (Chapter 8). Finally, old American public policy concerns—trade and the tariff, capital (banking and securities), taxation—came under new public pressures (Chapter 9).

This was indeed a changed world of economic issues and policy responses. Large corporations, new technologies, and a mass consumer market called for new forms of regulation. But the polity's response was deeply, inexorably conditioned by preexisting values, interests, procedural and structural arrangements. The importance of institutional and ideological *persistence* in the regulation of the new economy emerges as one of the two major themes of this book.

Its second major theme is that *pluralism* best describes the configuration of early twentieth-century public policymaking. The coming of a new economy did not produce a concentration of authority in ever-fewer, more-powerful corporate or public hands. Instead, modern American economic regulation emerged from an expanding, roiling aggregate of interests, issues, institutions, ideas: in sum, an increasingly pluralist American polity.

Economic modernity added substantially to the range of material goods and to the prevailing forms of getting, making, and spending. True, big business came into its own. But so too did new modes of labor, enterprise, production, technology, marketing, distribution, and consumption, resulting in a far more complex and variegated economic order than Americans had ever experienced before. The public policy response reflected that fact.

This is not the currently fashionable view of historians of early twentieth-century America. The prevailing opinion is that just as the rise of big business was the primary economic fact of the time, the political power of large corporations was the primary determinant of economic policy.

The predominance of corporate power was an important theme of contemporary radicals and reformers: Populists and Socialists, progressives, old-fashioned liberals. And substantial historical treatments of Progressive politics along these lines—John Chamberlain's *Farewell to Reform* (1932), Matthew Josephson's *The President Makers* (1940)—appeared in the wake of the Depression.[2] These books argued that the dominant political reality of the early 1900s was an unholy alliance between big business and big politics, in which Presidents Theodore Roosevelt, William Howard Taft, and Woodrow Wilson were prominent coconspirators.

But the apparent revival of anti-big-business reform in Franklin Roosevelt's New Deal, the triumph of liberal democracy in World War II, and the relative economic prosperity of the postwar years weakened the appeal of this view. Eric Goldman's *Rendezvous with Destiny*

(1952), Arthur Link's *Woodrow Wilson and the Progressive Era* (1954), and George Mowry's *The Era of Theodore Roosevelt* (1958) made Progressivism progressive again. Richard Hofstadter's *The Age of Reform* (1955) moved the argument still further from the Marxist framework of exploited workers and exploitative capitalists by locating the sources of the Progressive movement in a status-afflicted middle class fearful of both the radical threat from below and the plutocratic threat from above.[3]

The historiographical wheel turned a vigorous half-circle in the 1960s, when the traumas of that decade fed a widespread disillusion with the American liberal-reform tradition. The pacesetting work was Gabriel Kolko's *The Triumph of Conservatism* (1963).[4] Echoing Chamberlain and Josephson, Kolko held that economic policy during the early years of the century was neither progressive nor liberal, but rather conservative, in the sense that it served the interests of large corporations seeking through public policy to protect themselves from the vicissitudes of an uncertain market.

Kolko's corporative thesis—of a polity actively intervening to serve big business interests—was extended by others who shared his Marxist inclination. Stuart Ewen's *Captains of Consciousness* (1976) and David F. Noble's *America by Design* (1977) went furthest in arguing that corporate power shaped major aspects of modern American life. Ewen argued that mass consumption was primarily the product of corporate manipulation through advertising and its allied arts. Noble found a similar process under way in science and technology: "The spirit of standardization thus promised to weld science to power, and to lend to the weight of legal and moral authority the legitimacy of scientific truth; the creation of the Bureau of Standards [replacing the more easygoing Office of Weights and Measures] was a symbolic and actual step in that direction."[5]

Another, more moderate, neo-Marxist line of interpretation sees the early twentieth-century relationship between big business and the state not as corporatism but as corporate liberalism. Private corporations administered the market and their own affairs with a minimum of reliance on the state. The role of public policy was to smooth the way for business self-governance rather than to enter into a more active, corporatist relationship. James Weinstein's *The Corporate Ideal in the Liberal State* (1968) was the first substantial presentation of this view, followed most recently by Martin Sklar's major work, *The Corporate Reconstruction of American Capitalism* (1988).[6]

Most influential of all has been the organizational interpretation of early twentieth-century American public life. This approach emphasizes the growing new reliance, in both the private and the public spheres, on managerialism, administration, and bureaucracy. Its major exposition, Robert Wiebe's *The Search for Order* (1967), is a neat counterpoise to Hofstadter's *The Age of Reform*. Hofstadter characterized the Progressive movement as "the complaint of the unorganized against the consequences of organization"; Wiebe proposes in effect that the main thrust of public policy was the spread of the organizational impulse against the consequences of disorganization.[7]

This rich and evocative body of historical writing has done much to broaden our understanding of modern American life and institutions. But I question what I take to be its underlying assumption: that the central reality of the early twentieth century was the inexorable concentration of economic power in a few powerful organizations, and a concomitant narrowing of the lines of policy and authority. What, for instance, are we to make of a description of corporate "concentration" that notes that in every year from 1904 to 1939, "the top 184,230 plants accounted for at least 99 percent of the aggregate value of manufactured products, and . . . of these, the top one-tenth, or 18,423 plants, accounted for over 75 percent of the aggregate value of manufactured products"?[8] Is this testimony to the concentration of economic power—or to its diffusion? Are they always the same plants? the same products? the same companies?

And then there is the plethora of interpretations of the public policy response to economic change. Was it anti-big-business reformist—or pro-big-business conservative? Was it corporative (the state doing the bidding of big business) or corporate liberal (the state getting out of the way of big business)? Did progressivism serve the interests of the unorganized or of the organized?

Surely the parable of the blind men and the elephant is relevant here. None of these interpretations is necessarily wrong. But each unduly slights the persistence of the existing structure of politics, government, and law. And each, because it seeks to subject early twentieth-century American public policy to the confines of a particular overview, takes insufficient account of the intimate relationship between modernity and pluralism.

Persistence and pluralism: isn't this just another system? a theory as appropriate to the Reaganite 1980s as Mowry and Link and Hofstadter were to the confident 1950s and Kolko & Co. to the alienated

1960s and 1970s? Perhaps so. But in defense I would argue that I seek here to portray more than to explicate; that persistence and pluralism, the organizing themes of this book, are descriptive more than they are theoretical terms.

It is necessary to justify this wariness of theory at a time when the humanities and the social sciences wallow in a welter of *Weltanschauungen*. The trouble with all social theories, William James once observed, is that they leak at every joint. And the trouble with historians who bind themselves to theory is that they run the risk of forgetting the novelist L. P. Hartley's reminder: "The past is a foreign country; they do things differently there."[9] My ultimate purpose is (or should be) every historian's purpose: to apply present insight and perspective not to make the past more usable but to make it more comprehensible.

So what follows is not so much an argument from theory as an argument by example. I have tried to describe the very complex interplay between the economy and the polity as comprehensively as I could, not limiting myself to the usual playing field of antitrust. I have sought also to compare the American experience with analogous European ones (particularly that of Great Britain) whenever it seemed appropriate to do so. My assumption is that historical understanding emerges from the rich, complex texture of social experience more than from a predetermined theoretical pattern. Charles Beard's observation comes appropriately to mind: "Writing any history is just pulling a tomcat by its tail across a Brussels carpet."[10]

Have I fully succeeded? Of course not.

Is the game worth the candle? Indeed, is it the only historian's game worth playing? Of course.

1 · A New Economy: Patterns and Perceptions

This book examines the governmental, legal, and political response to the economic transformation of the early twentieth century. Before plunging into those turbulent currents of public policymaking, we shall take a look at how some contemporary observers saw and responded to the coming of the new economy. What follows is partial, discursive, impressionistic. But insofar as its leitmotifs are the persisting weight of received tradition, and a wide variety of views as to what was happening and what should be done about it, then it properly sets the stage for the chapters that follow.

New Views in a New Century

A striking conjunction of events around the turn of the century compelled public opinion and public policy to confront the reality of substantive economic change. Consider:

A burst of corporate consolidation, unique in its suddenness and scale, made it clear that big business was the primary instrument of American industrial capitalism. From then on, widespread, politically potent fears of bigness and consolidation interacted with a no less influential desire to foster the efficiencies of scale, and of service to a massive consumer market, that only large enterprise could provide. And it became necessary for politics, law, and government to adapt to the onrush of new technologies, each bringing with it novel problems and intricate new regulatory solutions.

At precisely the same time agriculture emerged from a long, debilitating depression. A palpable shift in policy resulted, in Richard Hofstadter's phrase, from pathos—the pathos of farmers responding to powerful, shadowy forces with emotive movements of protest such as

Populism—to parity—the public policy of agriculture as business.[1] A no less substantial change occurred in thinking about natural resources: from how most rapidly to exploit them, to how most usefully to conserve them.

Meanwhile, the growth of the industrial work force, fed especially by massive immigration, gave a new edge to labor relations. The nature of work, forms of labor and of managerial organization, the role of public opinion, politics, and law: all became far more complex, and more complexly intertwined, than before.

It would be a mistake to assume that disequilibrium, a sense of loss of control, dominated the initial response to these winds of change. Anxiety there was; but the predominant tone in public discussion at the turn of the century was an expanded sense of American power. European analysts spoke of "the American peril," "the American invasion." When National City Bank president Frank A. Vanderlip, with a banker-salesman's hyperbole, wrote a series of articles in 1901 on "The American 'Commercial Invasion' of Europe," they were shown to Kaiser Wilhelm II, who had them translated and widely distributed in Germany.[2]

This new economic vigor was frequently attributed to the beneficent consequences of American public policy: in particular, sound money and the protective tariff. "In no other country does business prosperity depend so much upon politics as in the United States," commented one observer. Brooks Adams saw things in a different light. In 1900 he forecast an inexorable flow of wealth and power from Britain to the United States, drawn by the larger scale and superior organization of American industry. Yet he feared that the government of the United States was not keeping pace: "in America there is no administration in the modern sense of the word . . . Every progressive nation is superior to us in organization." The nation, he concluded, soon would have to "abandon the individual for the collective mode of life."[3]

Adams was not alone in his views. A belief in the promise of bureaucratic modes of organization, the concentration of resources (economic, political, social), and the doctrines of managerial efficiency and social control became a significant theme in public discourse during the early twentieth century. This mind-set would have important regulatory consequences. But it was not the prevailing view. As we shall see, in field after field of regulatory policy traditional values (of laissez faire, of individualism and competition) yeastily coexisted with the new stress on corporate efficiency and corporatist control.

Neither perspective had a single ideological provenance. Hostility to the state was shared by antediluvian capitalist George F. Baer, labor's chief spokesman Samuel Gompers, and anarchists. Nor was a particular social commitment necessary to conclude that the capacity of workers to deal with labor-saving machinery would be enhanced by better working conditions, profit-sharing plans, and other ideas that now came into vogue. Corporation lawyer William C. Redfield thought and spoke in terms not far from most Progressives: "The modern spirit in America, progressive and therefore truly conservative . . . has set its face to the task of correcting the things that here and now are wrong"—which would be done by putting an end to "The Days of the Rule of Thumb." When moderate socialist Laurence Gronlund argued that as collectivism replaced competition the likelihood of class war would decline, he was not too far from the view of trusts defender Arthur J. Eddy.[4]

The German talent for organization had similarly wide appeal. Waldemar Kaempffert, managing editor of *Scientific American*, reported in 1911 and 1912 on the wonders of Germany's systematic, scientific approach to education and welfare. Admirers called Julius Kruttschmitt, who rose to head the Southern Pacific Railroad, "the von Moltke of transportation." Charles P. Steinmetz learned his socialism as a young man in Germany, belonged to the American Socialist party—and was General Electric's resident scientific guru. He found in bigness both virtue and hope for the future, and in the integrated corporation a model for the cooperative society of the future. (But Finley Peter Dunne's Mr. Dooley voiced a persisting popular skepticism: "I wisht I was a German and believed in machinery.")[5]

Frederick W. Taylor's theory of scientific management of industrial production also battened on the new passion for efficiency. Taylorism, said one disciple, was "large enough to form the basis of a philosophy and hopeful enough to have won the designation of a gospel . . . There is today a more direct tie between individual, corporation and national efficiency, and individual, family, and social well being." The attractions of Taylorism reached beyond the captains of industry to whom it was directed. Lenin was much taken with it; *Izvestia* discussed—and praised—Taylor's doctrines in 1919. But the degree to which Taylorism in fact shaped the character of America's industrial workplaces remains uncertain.[6]

While discussion focused on how best to manage an economy of large-scale production, awareness of another economic reality steadily grew. This was the appearance in the United States of the first mass consumer economy. True, much of the economic growth of late nineteenth-century Europe took place in consumer-based industries and occupations. But the scale and range of American consumerism in the early twentieth century, the degree to which it was based not on "luxury" but on mass-produced items, was unique.[7]

Consumer interests first became a significant element in American economic regulation with the general increase in prices that began around 1900, after decades of stagnation or decline. Articles on the cost of living in popular magazines increased from 89 in the years 1905–1909 to 247 between 1910 and 1914. Walter Lippmann observed in 1914: "The real power emerging to-day in democratic politics is . . . the mass of people who are crying out against the 'high cost of living.' That is a consumer's cry. We hear a great deal about the class-consciousness of labor; my own observation is that in America to-day consumers' consciousness is growing very much faster."[8]

Consumption thus took a place beside production as a major new concern of economic policy. So too did the distribution of wealth and income. Economist Willford I. King in 1915 made the first large-scale attempt in eighty years to calculate American wealth and income. Since 1896 there had been a marked increase in the concentration of income among the very rich; the poor had lost relatively little ground; the chief sufferers were the middle class. His major policy recommendation: eliminate the lower classes through eugenics and immigration restriction. But others saw economic growth linked to—indeed, emerging from—the maldistribution of wealth. Great wealth was "one of the unwholesome fruits of progress."[9]

Questions and answers such as these fed a growing interest in welfare economics. Doyens of the field such as A. C. Pigou in England and John B. Clark in the United States argued that society as well as individuals set a value on things, and that social value might—should—be included in the calculus of classical economics. This expanded concept of utility helped to legitimate the social welfare role of the state.[10]

So it was that a widening range of concern about basic economic issues—production, consumption, distribution—unfolded in pace with the increasingly diversified economy of pre–World War I America. Thought and action, experience and perception, had a common quality: ever more variety. The new did not displace the old, but mixed with it in fresh and varied ways. Looked at in this light, the relationship between economic development and public policy from

1900 to 1914 cannot be subsumed within either the "interests versus reform" framework of traditional Progressive historiography or the more recent stress on corporate liberalism. Rather, a pluralist perspective, less satisfying in its theoretical (and emotional) payoff perhaps, but closer to historical truth, is most appropriate to the task of describing and explaining the public policy response to the new American economy of the early twentieth century.

Coming to Terms with Prosperity

Differences in the character of politics and the tone of culture between the Progressive years and the 1920s have led most American historians to draw sharp distinctions between the two periods. But in the realm of economic experience, perception, and policy, continuity is more evident than change.

Far more than in the United States, English critics questioned the social desirability of the new economic order. Postwar disillusion spawned anti-industrialism, even talk of postindustrialism. The *New Statesman* warned lest industrial modernization come to Britain in the uncontrolled and planless American way. Sydney and Beatrice Webb spoke for many intellectuals when they blamed the Great War on capitalism and looked to the Soviet Union as a more promising alternative.[11]

But the more insistent note during the 1920s was admiration for American industrial efficiency. Two British engineers found the American "Secret of High Wages" not in the size of the country's natural resources or her home market, but in the development of labor-saving machinery and hence increased labor productivity, coupled with the creation of mass markets through advertising and price reductions. Britain's Liberal *Nation* agreed; and party leader Ernest J. P. Benn hopefully predicted in 1928: "Students of the English language will in later years discover that about the beginning of the year 1927 the word 'Industrialism' reappeared in the English vocabulary . . . It surely cannot be denied that the whole force of public opinion in this country is directed to teaching our people to lean, whereas on the other side of the Atlantic the whole force of public opinion is directed to encouraging the people to push." Even a *New Statesman* writer was convinced that "the United States has flung overboard our old concerns of capital, profits, and wages." America had returned to the idealistic socialism of William Morris—updated by machinery: "I affirm that there is throughout America an entirely new attitude towards social and industrial problems, and that, perhaps for the first time in the history of the world . . . there is a general recognition that prosperity depends on the well-being and wealth of the worker."[12]

American commentators in the 1920s, like their prewar counterparts, celebrated not the promise but the performance of technology and organization. One overheated (but typical) celebrant called on "Efficiency"

> to forward the new morality, to extend the dominion of man over incarnate energy and its use, to substitute highly paid thinkers and supervisors for devitalized toilers, to help each individual, each corporation, each government to meet its part of the obligation, above all to inspire those executives on whose skill all progress and all wise performance depends.[13]

The prewar amalgam of morality, efficiency, and prosperity continued to weave its spell over right and left alike. Stuart Chase attacked "The Tragedy of Waste" in 1925. His views closely followed those of Herbert Hoover, whose *Waste in Industry* had appeared in 1921. And indeed the left-leaning Chase admired Hoover and especially Henry Ford, as did Lenin. Chase inveighed against the fact that 8 of 40 million working Americans produced "illth": war material, luxuries, advertising. But he fondly recalled how "war control lifted the economic system of the country, stupefied by decades of profit seeking, and hammered it and pounded it into an intelligent mechanism for delivering goods and services according to the needs of the army and the working population."[14]

Perhaps the purest expression of the marriage of progress, technology, efficiency, and prosperity appeared in the writings of Boston department store head Edward A. Filene. In 1930—a bit late in the day, to put it mildly—he celebrated "The New Capitalism," the product of a labor-capital concordat on shared prosperity through high productivity, low prices, and high wages. He had little use for "the spiritualist critic . . . forever lamenting the passing of the 'simple life' . . . He has gained an automobile, they say, and has lost the reverence with which he once tramped through his native hills." Filene equated this with "opposing the sunrise because the beautiful bats have flown. It is like opposing the development of language and literature because it encroaches so much upon one's baby talk. It is like arraying ourselves staunchly against the idea of our children's growing up."[15]

But not all was sanguinity. The 1920–21 depression kicked off a spate of analyses as to what ailed the economy. One pointed to the cutoff of immigration, first by the war and now by restriction: "constant additions of new labor are indispensable for America." Others dwelt on structural distortions. Although new technology and the organizational revolution of the war period greatly spurred production, the system of distribution did not keep pace. The railroads had been allowed to decay; capital costs for these and other utilities had risen too high; excess manufacturing capacity led to overstocked inventories and high unemployment: "Our so-called 'prosperity' is like a weed with an enormous flowering growth but a very inadequate root system."[16]

The Harvard Committee on Economic Research spectacularly mispredicted that prices would be high for a decade after the war, and that the American standard of living would decline. More perceptively, the committee denied that the war had stimulated American productivity: almost all the supposed gains were an illusion created by inflation. And of course the problems of agriculture—the decline in farmer purchasing power, the continuing downward pressure on crop prices—were obvious to everyone.[17]

But by the late 1920s it appeared that higher per capita productivity—on the farm, in the factory—was the greatest change in the economy. By one contemporary estimate, output per person increased 50 percent from 1899 to 1925, with most of this occurring after 1921. The sharpest productivity gains appeared to be not in producers' goods—the growth sector of the nineteenth century—but in recreation and "luxuries" (including products such as automobiles, phonographs and cameras, silk goods, and packaged foodstuffs). More power-driven technology in the production of goods, modern distribution and marketing techniques, increased purchasing (and borrowing) power by an ever-larger consuming public: these were the most vibrant new facts of American economic life.[18]

Optimistic or pessimistic, commentators during the 1920s had to come to terms with an economy uniquely, unprecedentedly given over to servicing a vast domestic consumer market. Competition now took on new meanings, not only among makers of the same goods, but between products seeking the same consumer dollar. Production yielded primacy of place to distribution and marketing. The traditional perception of the worker as producer now also had to make room for the worker as consumer.

Comprehension of this new state of affairs did not come easily. An observer complained in 1923 that no important field of business statistics was so neglected as retail and wholesale merchandising. When it estimated the income of occupational groups, the National Bureau of Economic Research classified workers in that area with professionals and "all others." One reason was that they were widely distributed, and employed in relatively small firms. Still, there were about 4 million wholesale and retail employees in 1920, more than 6 million in 1929. From 1920 to 1928, according to one estimate, 150,000 automobile repairmen, 100,000 insurance agents, 250,000 teachers, 125,000 movie operators, 170,000 barbers, 525,000 hotel and restaurant employees—and 100,000 bootleggers—joined the work force.[19]

Ralph Borsodi's *The Distribution Age* (1927) explored the character and import of this new economic reality. And the substantial 1929 report by Herbert Hoover's Committee on Recent Economic Changes paid due attention to the rapid rise of power-assisted productivity and "optional consumption." The first Census of Distribution was conducted in 1930. An economy of production now might better be termed an economy of consumption. Its ramifications ran through the culture at large: "Our social psychology of today is entirely different from that of pre-war times." It became acceptable to speak of saving as a vice, of spending as a virtue.[20]

Even after the inflation of the war period came to an end, concern over the cost of living persisted, fed by a rising sense of what constituted an acceptable standard. Installment buying was one outlet for consumers whose wants were bigger than their pocketbooks. Outstanding consumer credit climbed from $2.6 billion in 1919 to $7.1 billion in 1929, when almost 20 percent of the total was for automobiles. The General Motors Acceptance Corporation had over $30 million in capital by 1927, more than all but about twenty of the nation's 30,000 banks. The expansion of personal credit joined farm mortgaging and "blue sky" stock speculation as a source of concern.[21]

The orgy of self-congratulation over American prosperity that preceded the Depression has long been a staple of historians with a taste for irony. By common consent the chief malefactor was Yale economist Irving Fisher. Typically, he declared in 1927 that the Federal Reserve Board "has definitely abolished financial panics" and had all but eliminated the risk of a major business depression.[22]

But respectable opinion did not wholly echo this view. One of Fisher's epigones conceded that "hard-headed, close-fisted and old-fogy business men" foresaw a panic and depression. The National City Bank warned in 1927: "Repeatedly since 1922 a wave of pessimism has spread over the country, having its origin each time apparently in apprehension that capacity to produce is so much in excess of our ability to consume that, after a brief 'spell' of prosperity, we must of necessity have a period of depression while an accumulated surplus is being worked off." Economist Gustav Cassel took due note of the factors threatening prosperity: tariff and other restrictions on the international exchange of goods, constraints on the free movement of labor, limits on purchasing power, the concentration of enterprise.[23]

Stuart Chase discussed "Prosperity—Believe It or Not" in a *Nation* series that began on October 23, 1929, six days before the market's Black Friday crash. Fortunately for his reputation, Chase stressed the reasons for disbelief: sluggish wholesale prices; numerous business bankruptcies; the fact that only a small portion of the American people enjoyed economic security, leisure, or an abundant life. But it cannot be said that in any significant way economic perceptions of the 1920s—right or left—prepared Americans for the Great Depression any more than did public policy. The sense that a new economy had come into place during the early twentieth century, and that it had deep roots in American life, was too strong and widespread to allow for any substantial prevision of what was to come.

Making Sense of the Depression

Over time the Depression changed prevailing views of the American economy. But only gradually, and with recurring reference to the accumulated perceptions of decades, did attention shift from prosperity, new technology, and consumerism to an economic crisis that, month by month and year by year, became deeper, more intractable, less like anything known before.

Most contemporary observers saw the stock market crash that began on October 29, 1929, as a speculative panic, not as a manifestation of fundamental problems in finance or business or agriculture. "Future historians, it is freely predicted," said one of them, "will speak of it as 'the prosperity panic of 1929.'" Irving Fisher assiduously added another blot to his reputation: "unless I am wrong about the factors underlying the plateau to which the stock market has risen, there will be further tendency to rise rather than to fall as soon as present conditions are stabilized." The British *New Statesman* was no more acute: "The 'break' will probably do American industry little harm; for, while the panic is now reacting on many good stocks as well as on bad, this will soon readjust itself; and, as the speculative boom, however exaggerated, had a real basis in economic prosperity, these forces are likely to reassert their influence as soon as the panic passes." [24]

Prevailing ways of thinking about the economy and public policy had great inertial force. In November 1929 the *New Republic* praised Hoover for convening a conference of industrial, agricultural, trade, and labor leaders charged to maintain production in the wake of the stock market crash. Although an "Economics General Staff" might have responded more quickly, "Fortunately, the present breakdown is not likely to be serious in any case. But it warns us that we need, not industrial playboys, but skilled engineers." The Democratic *World* likewise welcomed Hoover's response as "a significant expansion of the processes of conscious social planning." [25]

Indeed, much as the sudden entry into war can lead to a rush of relief, a release from tension and uncertainty, so did the coming of the Depression. Reports of 2 million unemployed by January 1930 led to the Panglossian observation that, after all, it might result in the removal of that number of child laborers from the work force. The *Wall Street Journal* viewed the years before the crash as a period when "a new industrial revolution based upon a virtually new discovery of the possibilities of power machinery and a variety of literally new chemical and technical processes irresistibly swept the country past anything that might have been recognized as a normal state of affairs," and confidently predicted that more normal, stable conditions would return in 1930. [26]

Early on, however, the possible effect of the market collapse on the consumer economy evoked concern. One observer warned that "just as the stock-market profits stimulated the buying of all kinds of comforts and luxuries, so will stock-market losses inevitably have an opposite effect." And Stuart Chase spoke of "the chance that this explosion of a balloon composed solely of speculative optimism will set psychological fears in motion which, spiraling downward, will attack the solid corpus of commercial prosperity itself." [27]

As the Depression persisted, analysts began to try to come to terms with this ugly new fact of American life. Overproduction—the classic cause of past maladjustments—continued to get most of the blame for the slump. Experts, however, looked increasingly to underconsumption or maldistribution of income and wealth. The *Washington*

Post among others dwelt on people's inability to afford the new demands for expenditure imposed by a consumption economy. A uniquely percipient Swiss banker warned that "the present crisis will be but a prelude to a dark period to which the historian of the future will give the name 'Between Two Wars.'"[28]

British economist John Maynard Keynes offered the most profound and wide-angled contemporary explanation of the Depression. He observed in 1931: "The world has been slow to realize that we are living . . . in the shadow of one of the greatest economic catastrophes of modern history." He called the Depression "not a crisis of poverty, but a crisis of abundance." Its basic cause was "the lack of new enterprise due to an unsatisfactory market for capital investment," with international capital sources asking for too high a return and the unsettled state of the world diminishing their readiness to invest. Production and prosperity would revive only if profits were restored by a mix of public spending, decreased saving, and a larger proportion of production in capital goods—in short, reversing the major postulates that had grown up around the economic development of the early twentieth century. This *echt*-Liberal was ready even to repudiate free trade: most countries could undertake modern mass production with equal efficiency, and producers and consumers were better off interacting within a national economy.[29]

At the same time Keynes resisted the statism that enraptured so many of his contemporaries. National economic planning and direction readily fell prey to silliness, haste, and intolerance: "Russia exhibits the worst example which the world, perhaps, has ever seen of administrative incompetence and the sacrifice of almost everything that makes life worth living to wooden heads . . . Let Stalin be a terrifying example to all who seek to make experiments."[30]

American perceptions of the Depression's causes, consequences, and cure were more superficial. The old national belief in progress and prosperity, so strongly reinforced by the experience of the early twentieth century, was not readily overridden. Progressive ideas of social engineering, comparatively free of the right/left ideological connotations that infused European policy, enjoyed a new popularity. A 1931 plea to replace "the largely sterile ideas of our inherited social science" with "those of a more dynamic, instrumental and creative character," to recognize that society "is essentially and historically disorderly and incongruous, and that order, system and regularity are not given, but must be achieved," could as well have been made in 1910.[31]

Howard Scott's Technocracy movement, which ascribed the Depression to the price system and proposed to cure it through economic rule by engineers and technocrats, harkened back to Thorstein Veblen and the early twentieth-century belief in the beneficent power of technology and engineers. One prescriber suggested that banks add engineers to their staffs, thus improving their capacity to seek out new technologies and new industries in which to invest. The degree to which both Hoover and the early New Deal relied on the World War I experience of national mobilization is a familiar story.[32]

An old American skepticism—toward authority, expertise, theory—was as important as newly popular ideologies of left and right in eroding the influence of existing prescriptions for recovery. Newspaperman Elmer Davis wryly said of President-elect Franklin D. Roosevelt: "I am not a passionate admirer of the incoming president, but one thing about Mr. Roosevelt enlists my confidence—he does not seem to know what to do about the tariff."[33]

Nevertheless the depth of the collapse put ever-greater weight on deep analysis and systematic, planned recovery. In this sense economic discussion during the early 1930s resembled the attempts of the early 1900s to understand the sudden appearance of a new economy—with this difference: in the earlier case the argument for social and economic planning rested more on nonpublic economic models (corporations, engineering) than on political or ideological agendas. Now planning was much more explicitly linked to the role of the state.

But *was* there an American state? Certainly not in the European sense. Not the least striking aspect of the response of American politics, government, and law to the new economy was the degree to which the new wine of economic change was contained within old bottles of regulatory ideas and institutions.

Many writers, intellectuals, social scientists, and others ignored or discounted this record. Soviet (for some, Fascist) models—or at least a collectivist approach—shaped their prescriptions for recovery. Theodore Dreiser's *Tragic America* (1931) echoed the muckrakers of the early 1900s in attacking the corruption and greed of banks, corporations, and political leaders. His remedy—"an executive power for the American working masses not unlike the Communist Central Committee in Moscow, but composed of American men and women (if there are such) who have made a thorough study of the social and economic ills that today engulf America"—typified the view of many intellectuals.[34]

But the ambivalent character of the New Deal that followed, and indeed of American economic policy since, suggests how weighty, how precedent-setting was the policymaking experience of the early twentieth century. The forms of economic regulation adopted during those years would persist. The sequence of economic mobilization and then of sharp policy contraction played out during World War I set the tone for the New Deal and World War II. And a political culture characterized by the pluralist interplay of interest groups, the complexities of a pervasive legal system, and an administrative state shot through with political and legal constraints, is with us still.

2 · Regulating Trusts

The large business enterprise is a distinguishing feature of the modern age. By the turn of the century, the giant corporations of the United States, the major firms (still most often partnerships) of Great Britain, the cartels of Germany, the *syndicats* of France, had become major facts in those countries' economic lives.

Observers on both sides of the Atlantic saw that a profound change in the character of industrial organization was under way. "The tendency towards combination in all countries seems to be substantially the same. The difference in the laws, and in the business habits of the people, seem to change only the form of organization," American economist Jeremiah Jenks observed in 1900. "After a century of conflict we find that a new motive is gripping the industrial world, the desire to put an end to competition while maintaining the private ownership and direction of industry," echoed British publicist Henry Macrosty in 1901.[1]

The power of big business to control the market, to set prices, and to force out lesser competitors stirred public concern everywhere. But history and culture gave a distinctive cast to each nation's response.

Comparative Perspectives

The number of large-scale firms abruptly expanded in turn-of-the-century Great Britain as they did in America. About 650 British companies were absorbed in 198 mergers from 1898 to 1900, leading to much discussion about "trusts." But the scale of the British merger movement was much smaller than its American counterpart. And it was concentrated in consumer goods (brewing and distilling, textiles, hotels), not the capital goods combines (coal, iron, steel, oil) that aroused public concern in the United States.[2]

The legal responses to the rise of large enterprise also differed. British unlike American courts gave legal standing to cartel agreements—as long as they reflected the rigors of competition and had a clear contractual basis. One study concluded that "during the course of the nineteenth century the English courts became so obsessed with the theory of *laissez faire* that the doctrine of conspiracy in restraint of trade, whether as a part of the criminal law or of the law of torts, appears to have been entirely abandoned." The Companies Consolidation Act of 1908 limited government restrictions on combination to cases of demonstrable fraud. A look backward in the mid-1920s concluded that "as a practical matter, [British] law does not forbid monopoly at all."[3]

Modern British cartel policy emerged in two major cases, *Mogul v. McGregor* (1891) and *Maxim v. Nordenfelt* (1894). The *Mogul* decision upheld rebates to favored customers by a steamship cartel. *Maxim* enforced an ancillary covenant between an arms cartel and the defendant, which required the latter not to sell munitions anywhere for twenty-five years. Though close in time to the Sherman Antitrust Act, these decisions were far removed in spirit from that law and its interpretation by American courts. One of the *Mogul* justices declared that it was not "the province of judges to mould and stretch the law of conspiracy in order to keep pace with the calculations of Political Economy. If peaceable and honest combinations of capital for purposes of trade competition are to be struck at, it must, I think, be by legislation, for I do not see that they are under the ban of the common law."[4]

The dictates of an imperial economy and international competition encouraged British judges to take an expansive view of permissible cartel practices. Indeed, the very character of the society seemed to foster arrangements of this sort: "Combination has been accepted without regulation in England because the entire English social system is a series of closed groups ... English society is stratified and cellular."[5]

In stark contrast with the American experience, only a handful of cases challenged cartel and combine practices. And although Edwardian Liberals paid some attention to business malpractice and the political influence of business groups such as the brewing industry, there was little concern with structural issues (except to worry about the growing economic challenge posed by American trusts and German cartels). Asked in 1908 what was to be done about cartels and trusts, Prime Minister Herbert Asquith replied that this was less of a question in Britain than elsewhere, and that he saw no need for an inquiry.[6]

Extensive cartelization was part and parcel of Germany's spectacular late nineteenth-century economic growth. By 1902, 450 cartels embracing some 12,000 firms dominated industries such as coal, iron, chemicals, textiles, rubber, timber, chemicals, and drugs; by 1912, the number of cartels was 600.

True, the German Civil Code of 1896, echoing the French Code Napoléon of 1804, declared that "a transaction in violation of good morals is void" and imposed liability on anyone "who designedly injures another in a manner violating good morals." And the same year saw the passage of a Statute against Unfair Competition based on several articles of the French Commercial Code. But a powerful German corporatist tradition persisted under this appliqué of nineteenth-century liberalism. American ambassador Andrew White correctly called the cartels rising in Germany during the 1870s "some new form of guilds." The Wilhelmine courts readily legitimated cartels and their practices. Late nineteenth-century German judicial decisions held cartel price and production agreements to be not only legal, but contributions to the public good. "It lies in the interest of the whole community," said Germany's highest court in 1898, "that immoderately low prices shall not exist permanently in any industry."[7]

Anticartel sentiment did exist: among socialists protesting the control exercised by the major banks, agrarian conservatives fearful of industrial-commercial power, and wholesalers and retailers suffering from cartel pricing and distribution policies. There were attempts in 1908 and 1912 to subject cartels to more stringent regulation; 1909 legislation toughened the 1896 statute forbidding unfair competition. Industrialists Hugo Stinnes and August Thyssen criticized cartels as outdated and inefficient in comparison with America's horizontally integrated corporations. Thyssen warned in 1905: "The time of syndicates is actually past and we must move on to the time of trusts."[8]

But law and regulation dwelt on fraudulent business practices, not on the cartel system itself. A 1912 American study observed: "The men who in other countries are sometimes called muckrakers, feel themselves estopped in Germany from attacks on capital except in the orthodox socialistic way." Mainstream public opinion accepted cartels as the most rational form of economic organization; and even many socialists welcomed them as a step in the direction of a planned economy.[9]

Imperial commissions in 1902–03 and 1906 concluded that no regulatory action was necessary. The German shipping magnate Albert Ballin noted that although the American government might require the dissolution of a syndicate, such an action would be punishable under German law. Indeed, the German state became a major participant in potash and coal cartels: *raison d'état* figured ever more in the economy as in other aspects of German life. "Cooperative nationalism" was held to be more beneficent, efficient, and honest than the private oligopolism of the American economy.[10]

Trusts: The Progressive Years

Nowhere did large enterprise take root so readily or flourish so luxuriantly as in the turn-of-the-century United States. And in no other country was there so strong a political, legal, and regulatory response. James Bryce observed in 1905 that the leading issue in American public life "is the one least discussed in Europe: I mean the propriety of restricting industrial or mercantile combinations of capitalists."[11] The land of the trust was also the land of antitrust.

Because of the scale of the domestic market, the strong tradition of an autonomous private sector, and the limited agenda of government, American industry's links to *raison d'état* were much weaker than those in Europe. For all the rhetoric of grand national purpose indulged in by the more megalomaniacal capitalists and politicos, in fact there was no sweeping government-corporate American scheme of empire, of international domination through economic hegemony. Theodore Roosevelt's dreams of American world power rose (and fell) quite apart from—indeed, often in conflict with—the diverse interests and expectations of big businessmen and financiers.

The polity's response to the rise of big business is often described in similar terms. One influential interpretation holds that big business sought in federal regulation surcease from the uncertainties of an expanding, explosive new economy and of varied regulation by the states. In this view the public record of the early twentieth century should be read as "The Triumph of [Corporate] Conservatism." A more sophisticated version of this view ascribes antitrust and the regulatory system to "corporate liberalism." It holds that "the institutionalization of the modern corporate—capitalist order" did not mean the end of the nineteenth-century liberal state. Rather, the regulatory system allowed corporated capitalism to regulate the market.[12]

The present analysis hardly questions the power of corporate self-interest. Nor does it hold to the older view that popular fear of the trusts alone explains the rise of antitrust. Instead it suggests that both antitrust and corporate liberalism—in Thomas McCraw's classification, "public interest" and "capture"—were elements of an expanding congeries of ideas and interests, including but hardly limited to these explanatory warhorses, that went into the formation of early twentieth-century American public policy toward big business.[13]

The interplay between big business and regulation is best understood in terms of the realities of a pluralist polity: great variety of input and consequence. To speak of manufacturers, merchants, railroads, shippers, farmers, middlemen, retailers, unions, lawyers, judges, economists, publicists, and politicians as active participants in regulatory policymaking is only to scratch the surface. For each of these categories includes and to some degree obscures complex subdivisions of interest and attitude.

factors

Regulatory policy took form in a polity that was responsive to established values of competition and free enterprise, to a new linkage of bigness and efficiency, to the demands of particular interests, to the reality of a larger, more consciously defined "public interest," and to the sheer scale and complexity of the new industrial economy. This explains why "in the old world [the trusts'] presence seems to cause little troubling of the waters of politics; in the United States, the problem of the Trusts is recognized as one of the greatest problems of the day."[14]

The passage of the Sherman Antitrust Act in 1890 made it clear that the problem of corporate power had a conspicuous place on the public agenda. But it was the turn-of-the-century burst of corporate consolidation that brought the issue of "the trusts" into the forefront of American public life. From 1895 to 1904, 157 holding companies absorbed more than 1,800 existing firms. The great majority of these new corporations—the "big business" of the early twentieth century—controlled 40 percent or more of the market shares of their products. Together they held more than one-seventh of the nation's manufacturing capacity; their capitalization exceeded $4 billion, better than four times the value of all industrial combinations created from 1860 to 1893.[15]

This merger movement had more than economic importance. Like the Bryan-McKinley election campaign of 1896, the Spanish-American War and the controversy over imperialism, and the rise of a new adversarial journalism, it was part of the matrix for a new generation in American public life: the generation of Progressivism.

Public discourse, politicians, law, and legislation tried to respond to this disturbing new economic reality. Congress in 1898 created the United States Industrial Commission to examine the changing economic structure. In 1901 the commission produced a report concluding that the merger movement was both natural and beneficent. Jeremiah Jenks, the commission's leading staff economist, found that wages paid by the new big businesses as yet showed no decrease, indeed possibly were increasing. Similar in tone was the report of the Chicago Civic Federation's 1899 conference on trusts. Defenders argued that big business was the logical, inevitable product of modern markets and technology.[16]

But before assuming that big business captured the American polity, it is necessary to keep in mind the claims—and the power—of other interests and viewpoints. Senator William E. Chandler of New Hampshire gave voice to a widespread attitude when he warned that trusts (the generic term for big business) tended to destroy competition, crush individualism, and put the control of society into the hands of opulent oligarchs.[17] The strength of antitrust in national politics and government, the courts, and the states abundantly testifies to the depth of this sentiment.

The British Liberal economist J. A. Hobson offered a particularly acute interpretation of big business in America. He recognized that large enterprises had come to dominate key areas such as oil, sugar, iron and coal, tobacco, and transportation. But competition between fields of industry, decentralization in areas such as agriculture, and most notably a constant flow of new products and technology also flourished. These were not unrelated developments. The economy of scale in capital and labor provided by consolidation, said Hobson, "liberates large masses of industrial energy to apply themselves to new experimental industries for the supply of new wants."[18]

From this perspective, American antitrust policy sought to keep (indeed, to foster) the benefits of bigness but to avoid the inhibiting effects of monopolies and cartels on new technologies and products. It relied on an expanding economy to keep open the prospect for competition. Critics then and since have held this to be a Faustian bargain, in which the failure to secure social democracy or a welfare state—even the decline of democracy itself—was the price paid for the big business product-machine. But perhaps a truer judgment is that, given the character of the polity, and its need to respond to the conflicting American commitments to the greater material affluence promised by the trusts and to the preservation of entrepreneurial freedom proffered by antitrust, no other resolution was likely. Or even possible.

The argument that the rise of big business was national in character, and thus required a national government response, had much appeal. Some took it to its logical conclusion and called for public ownership of railroads and the telephone and telegraph systems. "Governmental passiveness means national death," warned one such advocate. Another put the case for public ownership in even larger terms: "The grand political movement that has swept over the civilized world in our own age is the revolt against political despotism and the effort to establish political democracy. Individual aggrandizement has now taken refuge in the industrial world, and a new revolt is already in progress that must in the end establish industrial democracy and emancipate the nations from the despotism of wealth." [19]

More attractive was federal incorporation of big business, an idea whose appeal ranged across the ideological spectrum from William Jennings Bryan to James B. Dill, the attorney chiefly responsible for the trust and the holding company. Corporation lawyer Bruce Wyman wanted "the law of public callings"—previously limited to public service companies such as railroads—to be extended to all large enterprises with substantial market control. [20]

But neither the nationalization or tight control sought by radical critics, nor the beneficent federal oversight sought by sophisticated big business spokesmen, was to be. Potent constitutional and practical obstacles stood in the way. One major difficulty was the distribution of power between the nation and the states. The Supreme Court's *E.C. Knight* decision of 1895 held that the structure and activities of a corporation came under the jurisdiction of the state that chartered it—a serious legal stumbling block to federal regulation under the Sherman Act. [21]

Indeed, in counterpoint with (and sometimes at cross-purposes to) federal policy, state antitrust actions continued to be vigorous and frequent. As big business more and more directly dealt with masses of consumers, the politics of antitrust expanded beyond its traditional constituency of aggrieved producers and shippers. Ice, books, insurance, and farm machinery joined oil, steel, coal, and freight rates as objects of concern.

The first persons sent to jail for violating an antitrust law were defendants in an Ohio action against an ice combine. New York City's dominant ice distributorship (in which Tammany leaders were involved) became the object of a state antitrust suit in response to an exposé in the Hearst press—and because New York's Republican administration had an obvious political interest in the action. As the number of policyholders in large life and industrial insurance companies grew, so did state regulation of that business, and state actions against the large New York companies.[22]

New oil finds and a consequent increase in the number of independent producers joined with the explosive growth of petroleum products and thus of consumers to fuel state assaults on that Ur-trust, Standard Oil. The Texas supreme court in 1909 levied a $1.6 million fine on Waters-Price, Standard's clandestine Texas branch, for suppressing competition and for price-fixing, and turned over the company to a federal receiver. This was part of a general assault on national firms doing business in the state, during which International Harvester and a number of insurance companies were temporarily expelled.

Some 500 oil companies sought to exploit Kansas' new oil fields. But Standard Oil subsidiary Prairie Oil and Gas owned the state's only refinery, as well as the pipeline that fed it. The cost of shipping oil out of state rose while the price of crude broke, in effect forcing Kansas independents to sell to Prairie Oil. Pressure mounted for a state-owned refinery to force down Standard's refinery rates. With the governor's support the legislature passed a state refinery bill, which justified its constitutionality by declaring that its purpose was to provide employment for state convicts.[23]

But the states could do relatively little to regulate an increasingly national economy. After the near-quiescence of the McKinley years, federal suits under the Sherman Act markedly increased. Theodore Roosevelt's administration initiated forty-four antitrust actions and secured twenty-six indictments; during William Howard Taft's four years, the record climbed to forty-six suits and forty-three indictments.[24]

Much has been made of the varying approaches of Roosevelt, Taft, and Woodrow Wilson to trust regulation. Roosevelt was openly skeptical about the effectiveness of the Sherman Act. "The successful prosecution of one device to evade the law immediately develops another device to accomplish the same purpose," he observed. He dwelt on the distinction between "good" and "bad" trusts and preferred "continuous administrative action" to "necessarily intermittent lawsuits." Federal incorporation attracted him; and his Bureau of Corporations (established in 1902 within the new Department of Commerce and Labor) promoted licensing and other relatively interventionist approaches to corporate regulation. These ideas came together in the proposed Hepburn amendments to the Sherman Antitrust Act, developed by the National Civic Federation and other sophisticated corporate spokesmen. But "almost universal opposition to the bill" assured its death in the Senate Judiciary Committee.[25]

Taft shared Roosevelt's disbelief in the economic soundness of the antitrust law, and like him for a time favored federal incorporation of large enterprises. But this quintessential lawyer-judge ultimately saw no alternative to strict judicial enforcement of the Sherman Act. In his January 1910 message to Congress he held that the public should rid itself of the idea that there was a choice to be made between good and bad trusts or between reasonable and unreasonable restraints of trade: "Certainly under the present anti-trust law no such distinction exists." The active enforcement of the Sherman Act during Taft's administration stemmed more from his belief in the obligation to uphold the law than from a well-developed view of the proper relationship of state power to corporate enterprise. With Taft as with his predecessor, a conception of the character of government (and responsiveness to the politics of antitrust) took precedence over economic policy.[26]

Wilson had close political and emotional ties to the antimonopoly, small-is-good tradition of the Democratic party. But as a thoroughly modern academic intellectual, he was influenced by the "promise of bigness" theme that flourished side by side with Louis D. Brandeis's "curse of bigness" beliefs.

During his brief term as governor of New Jersey, Wilson fostered the passage of strict new state corporation laws, including an act—repealed in 1917—outlawing holding companies, the basic legal form of big business. In his 1912 presidential campaign he sought to secure "the destruction of monopoly not by regulation, but by the enactment of specific legislation."[27]

Yet as president Wilson did much more than his predecessors to expand the administrative regulation of big business, most notably in

the Federal Trade Commission Act of 1912. This was not necessarily
a sign that he sought an accommodation of government with corporate capitalism. Brandeis, who both influenced and gave voice to Wilson's views on the trust question, wanted the normal forces of the
market to dictate the size and shape of enterprises. But no less than
Roosevelt, Wilson believed in a forceful executive branch of government, and thus turned to regulation by federal commission.[28]

Roosevelt sought to harness his taste for strong leadership to the
dual (and in some ways contradictory) tasks of fostering social fairness
and the efficiency of big enterprise. Taft tempered his more probusiness leanings by a tender solicitude for upholding what he took to be
a strict law of antitrust. Wilson sought to fulfill his Democratic commitment to a society of small competitors by expanding the role of
the administrative state. For all the differences in their approaches to
the problem of the trusts, a revealing common denominator emerges:
the necessity to respond to policy demands that in themselves were
diffuse and ambiguous.

The three presidents were part of the Progressive generation. All
were touched by its stress on efficiency, organization, and the active
state as ways of dealing with a new industrial society. At the same
time each had commitments (though of varying intensity) to older
American beliefs: an economy of small competitors, limited government or a government of law, privatism and localism. The variety of
their responses to the rise of large enterprise accurately reflected the
prevailing diversity of views regarding the place of big business in
American life.

Antitrust policy in practice unfolded by judicial decision rather than
by executive fiat or legislative enactment. The Supreme Court's interpretations of the Sherman Act in effect constituted government policy
toward big business before 1914. The contrast with Britain is marked:
eleven of the fifty leading American industrial companies faced lawsuits in appellate courts during the early 1900s; none of the fifty leading British firms did.[29]

The early judicial response to the rise of big business rested heavily
on established common law precepts. Indeed, the inability of pools,
trusts, and cartel agreements to secure legal standing strongly spurred
the turn-of-the-century movement to consolidate firms into holding
companies. The persistence of traditional assumptions in the face of
new conditions is evident in the Supreme Court's *Northern Securities*

decision of 1904. Northern Securities was a holding company designed to end the long transcontinental railroad rivalry between James J. Hill and Edward H. Harriman. Its potential impact on the freight rates paid by agrarian and other interests in the Northwest made the merger a politically explosive development, and the Roosevelt administration hurriedly brought suit under the Sherman Act.[30]

Because the defendants so literally engaged in interstate commerce, the Court had no problem with the federal government's intervention. A majority concluded that Northern Securities violated the Sherman Act, leading some to fear that holding companies, like pools and trusts, might not be legal. Appropriately enough John Marshall Harlan, the Court's most eloquent spokesman for individual freedom, wrote the majority opinion. Oliver Wendell Holmes dissented—not on the basis of a modern efficiency-minded apologia for big business (although he did warn against allowing the Sherman Act to outlaw all combinations), but because he thought that contract rather than restraint of trade was the key issue.[31]

The diversity of common law precedents, the ambiguities of the Sherman Act, and the varying fact situations of antitrust suits, allowed the courts to interpret corporate consolidations either as exercises in freedom of contract and survival of the competitive fittest, or as illegal restraints of trade. Not surprisingly, a 1910 review of two decades of judicial interpretation of the Sherman Act concluded that "great uncertainty exists as to its meaning and legal effect." If any discernible policy seemed to be emerging, it was that "under a complex civilization the lawfulness of acts often must be made to depend upon complex considerations and cannot be determined by simple rules that can be applied without the exercise of discretion and in a mechanical manner."[32]

The Supreme Court's *Standard Oil* and *American Tobacco* decisions of 1911 underlined the truth of that observation. Notable scale and complexity by now characterized antitrust litigation: the government's case against Standard Oil rested on twenty-three volumes of evidence totaling 12,000 pages. The two cases involved 1,198 holding companies, with 8,110 subsidiaries and a capital of $10.6 billion.[33]

Chief Justice Edward D. White's "rule of reason" dictum in these cases—that a "standard of reason" was the proper measure for determining whether or not the Sherman Act had been violated—had consequences for future antitrust law comparable to the rise of Fourteenth Amendment procedural due process. His was a statement of economic as well as legal policy: in effect, a declaration that big business had come to stay. By modifying the previous assumption that the Sherman Act prohibited restraint of trade regardless of its utility, the court "justified those who believed that the logic of facts was stronger than the logic either of theories or even of tolerably well-settled law."[34]

Whatever the future implications of the rule of reason, the Court concluded that the business practices of Standard Oil and American Tobacco demonstrated a clear intent to monopolize, and ordered their dissolution. But then the realities of a modern consumer economy intruded. Standard Oil was not to be enjoined from doing business during the dissolution period because, said an observer, "of the possible serious injury to result to the public from an absolute cessation of interstate commerce in petroleum and its products by such vast agencies as are embraced in the combination."[35]

Breaking up American Tobacco proved to be no less complicated. Each of its sixty-five American and two British subsidiaries "made brands owned by some other concern, or had made for it by some one of the other companies a brand or brands which it owned," for a total of 1,500 brands of tobacco, 200 of cigarettes. What was more, the interests of American Tobacco bondholders, preferred stockholders, and common stockholders often conflicted and had to be treated separately. An elaborate dissolution plan was worked out by company officials and lawyers, federal circuit court judges, and the attorney general's office. The new companies had to have the brand names, factories, distribution facilities, and earning power necessary to compete on reasonable terms. Even so, it seemed evident that "the business itself offers insuperable obstacles to the creation of perfect competitive conditions under any method of distribution."[36]

Neither decision resulted in the kind of dissolution that antitrust advocates wanted. Attorney Samuel Untermyer percipiently predicted that investment bankers would do as well from the process of divestment as they had from the creation of the companies, and that community of interest and gentlemen's agreements would diminish the effect of the breakups. An antitrust expert summed up the episode: "In the extent of the business affected, in the learning displayed in the decisions and the lack of results obtained, the Standard Oil and American Tobacco cases are fairly representative and fully convincing of the futility of injunction and dissolution suits."[37]

The rule of reason became the accepted judicial standard after 1911.

And the flow of antitrust litigation continued, embracing not only major capital goods combines but also the producers of widely used consumer or consumer-related products: bathtubs, window glass, watches, breakfast cereal, cash registers. But regulation by judiciary did not clarify antitrust policy. By 1915, according to one authority, about 1,200 large combinations still were of doubtful legality. Lawyers confessed to confusion; the Court divided five to four on important cases. The rule of reason appeared to reduce antitrust to questions of fact, to produce not predictability but case-by-case administration.[38]

Rising dissatisfaction with judicial oversight and the growth of a consumer economy spurred demands for new forms of regulation, designed to deal with marketing and distribution as well as with corporate structure, control, and competition. This widening base of discontent led to the Federal Trade Commission (FTC) and Clayton Antitrust Acts of 1914.

The FTC was to be an "expert machinery" continually monitoring business practices to prevent "unfair methods of competition in commerce." It had considerably greater administrative flexibility and a broader regulatory mandate than its predecessor, the Interstate Commerce Commission. The FTC could issue cease-and-desist orders to the firms it regulated, and it could act as a special master in chancery, carrying out a court's dissolution order.[39]

Recommending the FTC Act to Congress, Woodrow Wilson declared: "The business men of the country desire something more than that the menace of legal process in these matters be made explicit and intelligible. They desire the advice, the definite guidance and information which can be supplied by an administrative body, an interstate trade commission." He later announced that the FTC "has transformed the government of the United States from being an antagonist of business into being a friend of business."[40]

Wilson had in mind not the giant companies but the great body of firms that were not "big business." Ninety-nine percent of American corporations in 1915 were capitalized at less than $5 million; 95 percent for less than $1 million. When one adds to this the increasing pressure on the FTC to respond to the concerns of a consumer economy—price discrimination, resale price maintenance, false and misleading advertising—it becomes even more difficult to ascribe the commission primarily to big business influence.

Given the range of interests and expectations represented, it is not surprising that both political parties, the United States Chamber of

Commerce and almost all trade associations, the New Freedom's Louis Brandeis, and the New Nationalism's Herbert Croly supported the FTC Act. It won unanimous approval in the House; only five senators opposed it. Was its creation a milestone of American corporatism? of corporate liberalism? of the active state? It might well appear to be any of these things to sufficiently tunnel-visioned observers. But surely a larger view must stress the range and diversity of the expectations surrounding the FTC.[41]

The Clayton Act also testified to the expanding cast of interests participating in the *ronde* of antitrust. It singled out those practices endemic to modern large enterprises—price discrimination, exclusive dealer and tying contracts, intercorporate stockholding, interlocking directorates—that fostered restraint of trade. And it recognized the presence of new political interest groups. Clayton exempted labor unions and farmer associations from the Sherman Act as long as their goals and actions were legitimate.

The FTC and Clayton Acts are often portrayed as Congress's response to the arrogation of regulatory power by the Supreme Court and its "rule of reason." But from a broader perspective, all the branches of government appear to have been caught up in a common effort to adjust the regulatory system to an increasingly complex corporate economy. The FTC Act modernized the procedural component of antitrust, the Clayton Act its substantive component. With these laws Congress "recognized . . . that the trust problem was not a single problem but a large number of problems," requiring legislative and administrative as well as judicial oversight.[42]

This is not to deny that for some, FTC and Clayton were two more arrows in the quiver of sophisticated corporate capitalism—as additions to a regulatory apparatus designed to assure a more ordered market and to avoid more intensive state control or the specter of nationalization. One can readily imagine the proscriptive resonance for corporate leaders of Elihu Root's observation that from 1909 to 1913, 62,000 state laws and 45,000 appellate court decisions dealt with business regulation.[43] But this was not the primary purpose of those laws. Rather, their legislative history reinforces the larger historical truth: that antitrust, like so much else that concerned the early twentieth-century American polity, reflected a growing diversity of interests, issues, and ideas.

America's entry into World War I put a temporary halt to antitrust as a public issue. Sherman Act prosecutions ceased; the *Political Sci-*

ence Quarterly's "Trust Problem" column, a staple since 1902, ended in 1917. Wilson fostered a policy of government—big business cooperation that came close to fulfilling the boldest hopes of sophisticated corporate leaders and of Theodore Roosevelt's New Nationalism. The Webb-Pomerene Act of 1918 in effect allowed cartel-like arrangements among export associations. Price-fixing, the expansion of trade associations, and voluntary and government controls flourished in the hothouse environment of the war years.[44]

Would this turn out to be little more than wartime expediency? Or did it mark the beginning of a new age of corporatism?

Trusts and Antitrust: Prosperity and Depression Years

In every major Western country World War I led to government-industry arrangements that strengthened the economic hand of large enterprise. At the same time the wartime experience in state controls quickened the expectations of those who advocated a larger government role in their nation's economic life. It was reasonable to expect that the postwar situation of big business would be very different from what it had been in 1914.

The war, observed Britain's *New Statesman* in 1916, "forced upon us the beginnings, at any rate, of the same sort of industrial revolution that the Germans and the Americans had been busily working out for the past thirty years and more." A postwar "nationalization movement" flourished, focusing on railroads and coal mining.[45]

The British Ministry of Reconstruction created a Committee on Trusts, whose 1919 report was the first instance of a British concern over business combination comparable to that of the Americans. The Profiteering Act of 1919 created a Standing Committee on Trusts with some resemblance to the FTC. From 1919 to 1921 it issued forty-seven reports on trusts and pricing. But then it faded away, its chief legacy having been to show how difficult it was to establish an American-style regulatory system in a different political culture. In postwar Britain as in the United States, "there arose a cry for the relaxation of government controls in all directions," and wartime restrictions were quickly dropped. But trade associations flourished. The Federation of British Industries (founded in 1916) and the British Employer's Confederation (1919) were influential industry spokesmen during the postwar years.[46]

The American economic miracle of the 1920s came in for considerable, admiring attention. Much was made of how the Americans attained both high wages and high productivity, and of the need for Britain to do so too by modernizing its industrial plant and managerial system. The Liberal party's "Yellow Book" of 1928, *Britain's Industrial Future,* called for industrial "rationalisation" and state control. Conservatives hoped that the Board of Trade might emulate Herbert Hoover's Department of Commerce by helping British industry join the worldwide movement for economic "federation, cooperation, and combination." The Finance Acts of 1927 and 1930 made it easier and cheaper to merge firms; the Companies Act of 1929 made it possible to force a resistant minority of stockholders to give up their shares.[47]

Yet all in all the British government in the 1920s did little more to promote trusts than it did to bust them. The legal standing of cartels did not erode: as of 1932 the British high court had not yet refused to enforce a contract between firms because it created a monopoly or hurt the public interest. When a judge voided one arrangement with the observation "You will never convince me that any combination of manufacturers puts down competition for the benefit of the public. Such combinations are against public policy," the Court of Appeal reversed him two days later. In sum, the established relationship between the British state and large enterprise did not significantly change.[48]

Defeat in 1918, revolution, and economic chaos dealt powerful blows to the German cartel structure. Fritz Thyssen and Hugo Stinnes created vertical combinations during the 1920s—a development that sociologist Ernst Troeltsch called the "Americanization" of German industry. At the same time, the Weimar government sought to regulate cartels in the American antitrust tradition. A Cartel Court was established in 1923, to which the government and cartel members (but not competitors or customers) could bring complaints. The court had the power to void cartel agreements that "endanger the welfare of the people." This German analogue to the Federal Trade Commission heard more than 2,000 complaints during the 1920s.[49]

But after the currency stabilization of 1923, traditional German cartelization revived. The Cartel Court did little to slow the process: there were 1,500 cartels in 1923, 2,500 in 1925. No organized political counterforce of competing business interests, no public tradition of antitrust or free market competition, was in place to alter German economic policy in the 1920s.[50]

A review of American antitrust decisions during the 1920s concluded that judicial policy toward business consolidation "appears now to have become fairly well crystallized." Acceptance of large enterprise with little regard for the extent of its market control came to be the norm: the courts dissolved no functioning corporate merger during the decade.[51]

The Supreme Court's *United States Steel* (1920) and *International Harvester* (1927) decisions sustained combines that dominated the bulk of their markets. Their business behavior, the judges concluded, did not constitute an abuse of power. In another major case Justice Joseph McKenna held that United Shoe Machinery's control of more than 90 percent of its market did not violate the antitrust law: "The Company, indeed, has magnitude, but it is at once the result and cause of efficiency, and the charge that it has been oppressively used is not sustained." It appeared that "judicial interpretation of the anti-trust laws has had the effect of legalizing almost any degree of concentration of economic power if certain legal formalities are observed."[52]

The Justice Department's Antitrust Division almost never met a trust it didn't like. William J. Donovan, its head from 1925 to 1929, concentrated on proposed rather than existing mergers; but hardly with great intensity. Almost 1,300 combines, absorbing about 7,000 firms, appeared from 1919 to 1928; of these, 60 were challenged by the government and only one was blocked. Antitrust enforcement expenditures fell from more than $270,000 in 1914 to $81,000 in the inflation-ridden year of 1919.[53]

Consent decrees rather than antitrust suits—few before 1917, 112 by 1932—became the favored instrument of regulation. Once the litmus test had been "the existence of power"; now it was "the abuse of power." As one commentator put it, "We are no longer implicated in a conflict of economic orders, but are considering what we shall do with the one we have."[54]

But this static regulatory order had to deal with a dynamic economy. One of the few areas in which the Justice Department showed some vitality was the politically sensitive one of market control in the food industry. The government challenged the legality of the newly formed National Food Products Corporation, an investment trust designed to control a number of chain store and dairy combines. Other suits reflecting sensitivity to consumer interests were brought against a merger of bread manufacturing companies, the American Can Corporation, and a combine of furniture manufacturers.[55]

The five largest meat-packers' dominance over their industry led to numerous antitrust suits before the war. By 1917 interests other than small packers and livestock raisers had concerns about their power. The big companies had accumulated a large inventory of refrigeration equipment, which led them to enter massively into poultry and dairy distribution. Their use of profits to acquire grain elevators, cold storage plants, hotels and hotel supply companies, and a number of other enterprises raised a storm of complaints. An FTC investigation led to a 1919 consent decree, in which the packers agreed to divest themselves of most of the "unrelated lines" of business that they had entered. The rapidly changing character of the food business led the packing companies to have second thoughts by the end of the decade. They asked the Supreme Court in 1928 and again in 1930 to vacate the decree, arguing that the rise of chain stores, and of agricultural cooperatives doing their own marketing, reduced the danger of monopolistic control over food distribution. But the Court refused to do so.[56]

Recent examinations of business-government relations during the 1920s tend to dwell on the theme of cooperation between big business and the government; to find in effect a (milder) American equivalent of the prevailing corporatism in postwar Europe. Certainly it is true that during the war the Wilson administration fostered intraindustry price and production agreements on a scale previously unimaginable. And from 1921 to 1928 Secretary of Commerce Herbert Hoover pursued the goal of an "associative state" seeking to make the productive process more efficient and to lessen destructive competition.[57]

Hoover's preferred instrument was the trade association. These bodies flourished in the benign atmosphere of the 1920s. By 1926 there were about 1,000 of them, covering a range of goods and services—indeed, the cycle of life—stretching from the National Association of Baby Vehicle Manufacturers to the Casket Manufacturers' Association of the United States. Their activities included not only sub rosa price and production agreements but also—and more importantly—services keyed to the demands of an increasingly complex economy: labor relations and arbitration; traffic bureaus monitoring freight rates; promotion of research, development, and standardized products; patent pools and the interchange of patent rights; education in cost finding; advertising to stimulate consumer demand; information on customers' credit standing; and representation before legislative and administrative bodies.[58]

But corporatism made heavy way in a pluralistic, decentralized polity. The Department of Commerce set up a price-fixing Industrial Board in the spring of 1919. Within a few months it fell victim to the hostility of other government agencies such as the Railroad Administration, to the political appeal of antitrust, and to the sheer diversity of interests with which it had to deal. A similar fate befell efforts by the United States Chamber of Commerce and the National Association of Manufacturers to "liberalize" the antitrust laws.

Hoover's attempts to make the Commerce Department the core of his "associative state" faced similar problems. And even at the height of his power in the mid-1920s, he was hardly a spokesman for cartels or corporatism in the European sense. "Probably the most compelling reason for maintaining proper trade associations," he argued, "lies in the fact that through them small business is given facilities more or less equivalent to those which big business can accommodate for itself." Like the antitrust and business regulation movement of the prewar years, Hoover's policies in the 1920s were not only compatible with but supportive of small enterprise, competition, a level playing field, and individual initiative.[59]

Similar values prevailed in the Supreme Court. For all its subservience to the "rule of reason," the Court of the 1920s only marginally modified its traditional hostility to price and production fixing. Into the early 1920s a majority of the justices resisted information pooling (to say nothing of direct price, production, and marketing constraints) by trade associations. The Court dealt with the issue most substantially when it reviewed the efforts of the lumber industry to meet the competition posed by cement, steel, and other building materials.

Holmes and Brandeis—the latter, in particular, hardly an advance agent of the corporate state—prepared the way for a more lenient view of trade association activities in their *American Column & Lumber* (1921) dissents. They argued not for the virtues of bigness but for the free exchange of information and a hard-pressed industry's right to cope with competition. Holmes observed: "I should have supposed that the Sherman Act did not set itself against knowledge . . . I should have thought that the ideal of commerce was an intelligent interchange made with full knowledge of the facts as a basis for a forecast of the future on both sides." Caustically he observed that the government's attempt to prohibit information sharing in the hardwood industry was "surprising in a country of free speech that affects to regard education and knowledge as desirable." Brandeis, too, held on Hoover-like grounds that the shared activities of the industry were designed "to make rational competition possible," and warned: "May not these hardwood dealers, frustrated in their attempts to rationalize competition, be left to enter the inviting field of consolidation?"[60]

In its 1925 *Maple Flooring* and *Cement Manufacturing* decisions the Court sanctioned information sharing. Harlan Stone's *Maple Flooring* opinion rested on an argument very much like White's "rule of reason" rationale for corporate consolidation a generation before:

> It is the consensus of opinion of economists and of many of the most important agencies of Government that the public interest is served by the gathering and dissemination, in the widest possible manner, of information with respect to the production and distribution, cost and prices in actual sales, of market commodities, because the making available of such information tends to stabilize trade and industry, to produce fairer price levels and to avoid the waste which inevitably attends the unintelligent conduct of economic enterprises . . . Competition does not become less free merely because the conduct of commercial operation becomes less intelligent through the factor of free distribution of knowledge of all the essential factors entering into the commercial transaction.[61]

But in the *Trenton Potteries* case (1927), trade association price-fixing was overt. And here Stone refused to accept so flagrant a violation of antitrust law: "Whatever difference of opinion there may be among economists as to the social and economic desirability of an unrestrained competitive system, it cannot be doubted that the Sherman law and judicial decisions interpreting it are based on the assumption that the public interest is best protected from the evils of monopoly and price control by the maintenance of competition."[62]

The practical importance of trade associations and other forms of interfirm cooperation was very considerable; though how successfully they coped with technological change, depression, and war is questionable. The fact remains that they had a limited impact on the frame of public policy.

The rulings of the Federal Trade Commission, like those of the Interstate Commerce Commission, were supposed to create a "new common law" governing business practices. But in both cases the clash of diverse economic and governmental interests, and the deep constraints on active government, dictated otherwise.

The chief concern of the FTC was not with corporate ownership and control, but with those activities that most directly affected pricing and sales. Of the 1,318 FTC rulings issued by mid-1925, 59 percent dealt with fraudulent or deceptive trade practices; by the early 1930s, more than 90 percent did so. By then the FTC's primary role was to prevent "false and misleading advertising in reference to hair-restorers, anti-fat remedies, etc.—a somewhat inglorious end to a noble experiment." (Even this was too sanguine a judgment. The Supreme Court held that ads trumpeting the scientific worth of fat-reducing tablets, to which the FTC took exception, were opinion not fact and threatened no substantial injury to competitors or consumers.)[63]

The general entropy afflicting regulation in the 1920s left its mark on the FTC as well. For years it was housed, with appropriate symbolism, in a World War I "temporary" building. The furor over the appointment of the resolutely probusiness William E. Humphrey to the commission in 1925 added to its desuetude. It was weakened too by endless conflicts among economic interests and their political advocates: "it is not uncommon for the Commission to be under fire in the Senate for exercising its powers too gingerly and in the House for daring to use them at all."[64]

Judicial decisions also did much to reduce the effectiveness of the FTC. The Supreme Court refused to accept a broad definition of the commission's powers. Justice James McReynolds held in 1920 that when it came to defining unfair methods of competition, "it is for the courts, not the commission, ultimately to determine as a matter of law what they include." Brandeis in dissent sought to justify the FTC's power to issue cease-and-desist orders as a "prophylactic" function, aimed not at "the commission of *acts* of unfair competition, but the pursuit of unfair *methods.*" But McReynolds's belief that the FTC was "certainly not intended to fetter free and fair competition as commonly understood and practiced by honorable opponents in trade" prevailed.[65]

Not surprisingly, one FTC commissioner concluded that the Court's rulings "completely devitalized" the commission, "reduced it to terms of a futile gesture." Clashing branches of government and a complex and dynamic economy made effective administrative regulation of big business all but impossible.[66]

The Great Depression swept over a nation with more than forty years' experience in the legislative, judicial, and administrative regulation of large enterprise. From that perspective it is, perhaps, not surprising that even the unparalleled economic disaster of the Depression and the political upheaval of the New Deal did not fundamentally alter the prevailing indeterminate, ambiguous regulatory policy.

Hoover did little to change course during his term in office. He tried to foster voluntary restraints on production and price-cutting much as he had tried to encourage cooperation for greater productive and marketing efficiency during the 1920s. At the same time his administration could not ignore the anti-big-business sentiment stirred by the Depression. Justice Department proceedings against trade associations increased; and the FTC sponsored fewer conferences on trade practices. In any event, industries struggling to deal with the economic slide had little interest in cooperation; *sauve qui peut* prevailed.[67]

Growing acceptance of the view that the Depression was a national emergency led the Supreme Court—for a while—to set aside its traditional hostility to price and production agreements. In *Appalachian Coals* (1933) the Court accepted price-fixing by 137 mine owners, calling it "an honest effort to remove abuses, make competition fairer, and thus to promote the essential interests of commerce."[68] Its 1934 *Nebbia* decision permitted price-fixing by New York milk producers. But in each case the economic situation of the affected group was exceptionally severe, justifying emergency steps. And the parties involved—coal operators with a smallish share of the market, dairy farmers—hardly came under the rubric of big business.[69]

The New Deal's National Industrial Recovery Act of 1933 was something else again. The boldest attempt since World War I to institute large-scale price and production controls, it sought to break the deflationary spiral of the Depression by allowing the industries themselves rather than the government to set production and prices. Hundreds of industry codes were worked out under the auspices of the National Recovery Administration (NRA), most of them dominated by the views of the largest firms—a triumph of corporatism achieved, ironically enough, by an administration elected in protest against a business civilization gone sour.

This was cartelization with a vengeance. But the NRA had a shaky grounding in American law and custom. The government's wartime industrial controls provided the only precedent; and indeed the NRA's rationale rested on the ground that the Depression, like the war, was a national emergency. It soon became clear that the NRA presaged no new era of regulatory policy. The administration declared that it had no intention of superseding the antitrust laws; the Recovery Act itself piously proclaimed that the individual codes were "not designed to promote monopoly." And in its *Schechter* decision of 1935 the Supreme Court held that the NRA improperly delegated legislative power to the executive branch and interfered with the flow of interstate commerce: this last argument eerily reminiscent of the Sugar Trust case of 1895, when the regulation of big business was in its infancy.[70]

It is doubtful whether NRA codemaking had much of a future even without *Schechter*. In short order a familiar cloud of conflicting interests made the codes as difficult to enforce as had been pooling and other earlier attempts to fix production and prices. The NRA had to take account of the interests of small and medium-sized firms and of organized labor as well as of big business. And the old hostility to large enterprise, fueled by the Depression, led to a recrudescence of government antitrust activity—which in turn proved to be no more permanent than the corporatist venture of the NRA. Through decades of economic, technological, and cultural change, the lineaments of a pluralist polity stubbornly persisted.[71]

3 · Regulating Utilities

Antitrust was the primary public policy response to the rise of big business. More than anything else, the impact of large enterprises on competition—their capacity to restrain trade—seized the attention of the polity. By the same token, issues relating to service—rates charged, functions performed—became the major concern of public policy toward those enterprises that in twentieth-century America came to be called public utilities. Law, opinion, and policy made an increasingly sharp distinction between businesses that operated in, by, and for the market and those—such as railroads and municipal utilities—that were "affected with a public interest."[1] Once again, the new economy fostered an increasingly complex, multiform regulatory response.

Railroads

The railroads were America's oldest, largest, and most powerful enterprise by 1900. And none operated within so dense and well-established a regulatory structure: state railroad commissions dating from the 1870s; the Interstate Commerce Commission from 1887; and a massive body of state and national laws and judicial decisions.

The early twentieth-century experience of the railroads serves as a case study of the impact of economic change on public policy: growing pressure for efficiency and order on one hand, and for democratic control and public accountability on the other; ever-more-numerous and assertive interests seeking a policy voice; and beneath it all, the roiling impact of new technology on an old enterprise.

British railroad regulation bore some resemblance to the American system. A British Railway and Canal Commission functioned from

1888 on as a specialized court, hearing disputes between railroads and shippers. Parliament set maximum rate schedules; controversies came before the Board of Trade. Major conflicts broke out over the lines' service to particular ports of entry—not unlike the disputes over long- and short-haul rate discrimination that dominated the politics of pre-1900 American railroad regulation.

Pressure from shippers for lower rates grew in turn-of-the-century Britain as in America. More than 1,700 complaints came before the Board of Trade in 1894 and 1895; and a parliamentary act froze rates at their 1892 level. After 1900 the British authorities (like the ICC) began to deny rate increases. A 1913 cabinet inquiry found problems all too familiar to American regulators: rising public unhappiness over service and rates, a regulatory structure inadequate to the power of increasingly consolidated lines. It concluded that "the public interest probably needs to be guarded not merely negatively by access to a judicial tribunal, but positively by a large measure of administrative control."[2]

Railroads also figured prominently in the public life of other countries. German lines were state owned and run; the major French railroads were private (except for one bought by the government in 1908). The government offered financial concessions, including dividend guarantees, in the late nineteenth century. But it forbade competition, and rates had to be approved by the Ministry of Public Works. Like their American and British counterparts, the French lines by the eve of World War I found the costs of operating an increasingly expensive technology to be mounting much more rapidly than the rates they were able to charge.[3]

American railroads had business and regulatory concerns very much like those of their British and French counterparts. But the scale and importance of the American rail network, the variety and complexity of interested groups, and the character of its regulatory milieu were unique.

No industrial trust matched the railroads' size, wealth, and political power. The American "Railway Empire" in 1905 had a capital worth of $13.2 billion, one-seventh of the national wealth. The roads participated in the turn-of-the-century surge of corporate consolidation: from 1897 to 1903 the major groups—Vanderbilt, the Pennsylvania, Morgan-Hill, Gould-Rockefeller, Harriman—substantially expanded their mileage. They also extended their interests in allied enterprises: coal mines, oil wells and pipelines, urban and rural landholdings, steamship companies, docks, hotels, banks. And for decades railroad influence and corruption penetrated—indeed, suffused—state and national politics and government.[4]

An imperial presence indeed! Yet all this wealth and power did not secure a stable regulatory environment. The railroads' very centrality in the nation's economic life fed a public concern that politicians and courts could not ignore.

Calls for public ownership came from a variety of sources.[5] But this was never a politically viable option before World War I. Instead, a yeasty mix of new political and legal approaches to railroad regulation became the order of the day.

The history of railroad regulation confirms that modern times brought not consolidated, corporate domination of the polity, but rather an increasingly pluralistic public life. The late nineteenth-century struggle between railroads and (primarily agricultural) shippers over rates and markets gave way in the early twentieth century to a far more complex regulatory *ronde* of railroads, shippers, farmers, manufacturers, unions, politicians, judges, regulators, and a better-informed and more articulate "public interest."

The creation of the Interstate Commerce Commission in 1887 did little to bring clarity and order to the realm of railroad regulation. True, ICC commissioner Thomas M. Cooley expected that he and his colleagues would be "a new court," whose task was "to lay the foundations of a new body of American law." And from 1887 to 1892 almost 1,300 ICC decisions on rates and other issues sought to do just that.[6]

The Supreme Court had other views as to who would be the final arbiter in these matters. Its *Trans-Missouri* (1897) and *Joint Traffic* (1898) decisions struck down cartel-like rate agreements among the roads, thereby bringing them under the same pressure to consolidate that weighed on other large enterprises. In its *Minnesota Rate* (1890) and *Smyth v. Ames* (1898) decisions, the Court stripped the ICC of rate-setting powers and ruled that a "reasonable" rate schedule should be based on the "fair value" of the railroad's property. This was an approach whose openness to interpretation put it in a class with those other milestones of judicial creativity, substantive due process and reasonable or unreasonable restraint of trade. By the early 1900s the courts had reversed well over half the ICC decisions that came before them for review.[7]

But after 1900 neither judges nor ICC commissioners nor the

lines—indeed, no single voice—called the tune of railroad regulation. The relative political clout of the railroads ineluctably declined in the face of an ever-larger and more complex industrial economy. Andrew Carnegie in 1908 welcomed the ICC's efforts to create a more balanced rate structure because it added to the security of corporate investments in general. Senator (and millionaire mine owner) Stephen B. Elkins of West Virginia, chairman of the Senate Committee on Interstate Commerce, declared: "My interest on the side of the shipper is ten times greater than on the side of the railroads."[8]

Muckraker Ray Stannard Baker excoriated the major roads' financial influence and their attempts to influence public opinion. But railroad leaders did not in fact speak with a single voice on regulatory policy. Some officials from the larger lines saw the advantages of government rate setting or at least of constraints on rebates and other self-destructive competitive practices. Paul Morton, secretary of the navy under Theodore Roosevelt and a former Santa Fe Railroad executive, welcomed the end of rebates and warned that banning railroad pools increased the tendency of the lines to consolidate, thereby raising the risk of government ownership.[9]

But other railroad men, especially from the relatively crowded East, where competitive pressures were strong, opposed state intervention. These included the president of the Delaware & Hudson and the egregious George F. Baer of the Philadelphia & Reading, ready as always with some *mots malséant*:

> The owners of these railroads are practically to be denied the privilege of managing their own property . . . The trained experts, the men of genius, who have built up this wonderful system of American railroads, and through it have developed the wealth and the population of this country to a degree unheard of in the annals of history, are to be declared incompetent and dishonest.[10]

Chicago, Milwaukee & St. Paul head A. J. Earling warned that an ICC rate schedule based on mileage would have disastrous consequences for midwestern agriculture, and claimed that the railroads themselves were engaged in a "scientific effort—to overcome the effects of distance." Another opponent of government rate setting recounted a variety of horror stories about the constricting effects of government regulation on the development of transportation in other countries, and held that rate discrimination was the source of the efficiency of the American railroad network.[11]

A substantial increase in state supervision added to this open-ended regulatory environment. Legislatures passed more than 800 railroad laws from 1902 to 1907, often in response to pressure from local job-bers and shippers. State railroad commissions increased from thirty-one to thirty-seven; Wisconsin's had rate setting-authority.[12]

A number of states tried to legislate reductions in passenger fares as the size—and political clout—of that constituency grew. Resistance by the railroads in North Carolina led to a ticket agent's spending thirty days on a chain gang, threats by the governor to use the state militia to enforce the passenger fare law, and, finally, compliance by the roads. George F. Baer's objections to a Pennsylvania two-cents-a-mile bill had a predictable effect on the legislature. "Who is Baer? Are we for him? No!" the members chanted as they enacted the law by a 175–0 vote.[13]

The federal government, too, busily crafted new railroad regulation policy. The antirebate Elkins Act of 1903, a response to widespread shipper anger over rebates to Standard Oil and other large companies, passed unanimously in the Senate and with only six negative votes in the House. But the law also served the interests of the Pennsylvania Railroad (whose attorneys had helped to draft it) by enabling the line to resist the demand for rebates from ever-larger corporate shippers.[14]

The movement for stronger railroad regulation culminated in the passage of the Hepburn Act of 1906. This law emerged from a dense, complex clash of interests and ideologies—the pluralist polity fully manifest. Most railroads opposed further regulation; Hepburn was the product of a coalition of regulators seeking a strengthened ICC, small shippers, merchants, farmers, and businessmen. One observer thought that a "feeling of impotency" over the task of proving in the courts that prevailing rates were unreasonable was "the moving cause in the present agitation, far more than the existence of general or spe-cific schedules of rates which are in themselves unjust."[15]

The solution was a strengthened Interstate Commerce Commis-sion. ICC chairman Martin Knapp tirelessly pressed in classic bureau-cratic fashion for an administrative approach to railroad regulation. Theodore Roosevelt asked Congress to give the ICC rate-setting pow-ers, and the Hepburn Act provided just that. Passed by a vote of 347–7 in the House with only three nays in the Senate, it empowered the ICC to set "just and reasonable" maximum rates and widened the commission's jurisdiction over the ancillary instruments of an ever-widening transportation system: express and sleeping-car companies, oil pipelines, switches, yards, terminals. But the precise role of judicial review remained unclear.[16]

The commission expanded in size and authority after this congressional vote of confidence. Its staff grew from 178 in 1905 to 527 by 1909; it inspected and set rates not only for the railroad, telephone, and telegraph systems but also for the District of Columbia's public utilities and the parcel post system; it even determined time zones and daylight savings. The ICC could lay fair claim to being the strongest and most interventionist of American regulatory agencies in the early twentieth century. The courts deferred more and more to its findings, and the commission's membership expanded to include the proshipper Franklin K. Lane and Edgar E. Clark of organized labor. But this hardly meant that the ICC responded effectively to the changing economic situation of the railroads.

Rapidly evolving railroad technology and a massive increase in freight and passenger traffic put great pressure on the lines to rebuild their roadbeds and trackage and to replace their moving stock. But past overcapitalization and the reluctance of an increasingly shipper-influenced ICC to agree to rate increases made it difficult for them to secure the capital they needed.[17]

Nor could the ICC effectively oversee rapidly changing corporate structures and practices. Increasingly complex railroad holding companies, not subject to ICC regulation, were expensive and unwieldy institutions, divorced from the operating problems of the lines they controlled.

The roads tried to pay for construction by floating new securities. A favored device was the collateral trust bond, based not on tangible property but on mortgage bonds or corporate shares. Very much like the oil companies of the 1970s, the railroads invested heavily in real estate and other ancillary enterprises. But the ICC had little or no control over this increasingly important aspect of the railroad business.[18]

Another coping device was that venerable instrument the railroad receivership. In 1916 court-appointed receivers had charge of lines with about 40,000 miles of track—one-sixth of the national total—and $2.25 billion in capitalization. In practice the existing management continued to run things, avoiding the full weight of its company's debts and able through the sale of receivers' certificates to raise new capital for road improvements. The Rock Island's board chairman explained in 1915: "A receivership at the present time is merely to obtain the protection of the court that the company's physical condition and equipment may be improved, its temporary loans continued, and an opportunity be given for working out a comprehensive and permanent plan for financing to preserve for the shareholders the valuable equity which it is believed there is in the property."[19]

The scale and complexity of the interests involved—1,000 formal complaints came before the ICC in 1909 alone—fueled a continuing search for new regulatory approaches. Proposals abounded to valuate the railroads for rate-setting purposes, to regulate the railroad securities market, to permit ICC-regulated traffic associations with cartel-like powers, to secure federal incorporation or even ownership.[20]

Discontent with the cumbersome and unpredictable federal court review of ICC decisions led to the Mann-Elkins Act of 1910. This law established a Commerce Court composed of five federal circuit court judges and additional members appointed by the president. Its sole task was to hear suits brought against ICC rate and other findings. President Taft strongly favored the Commerce Court: it embodied his judicial-administrative approach to governance. Mann-Elkins opened the Commerce Court not only to the parties in a particular dispute, but also to interested communities, associations, corporations, and individuals—testimony to the expanded, pluralistic impulse in Progressive public policy.[21]

Controversy immediately arose. How, precisely, did the Commerce Court fit into the American judicial system? The limited terms of its members raised the prospect that it would be more an instrument of the legislature than an independent judicial body. The Supreme Court countered this threat to its authority by announcing (three days after Taft proposed the Commerce Court) a narrow review policy toward ICC rate decisions. Thus it undercut the argument that a more responsive review body was needed. During its brief life the Commerce Court frequently reversed the ICC; but the Supreme Court in turn reversed four of its five decisions that went up for review. In 1913 Congress ended this lame, ill-fated extension of the administrative state.[22]

Congress's Valuation Act in the same year ordered the ICC to determine the worth of all railroad, telegraph, and telephone property, the cost of its reproduction, and the value of franchises and goodwill. This information was supposed to provide a rational basis for rate setting. The ICC (quite rightly, as it turned out) held that it could not do what the act required. But the Supreme Court said that it was bound to comply. Thus began a decades-long exercise in futility by the ICC's

Bureau of Valuation: an emblematic Progressive attempt to find fixed grounds for regulating an enterprise whose prime reality was flux.

The ICC continued to be busy, busy, busy. From October 1914 to October 1915 it conducted 1,543 hearings and churned out more than 200,000 pages of testimony. But for all its enlarged power, the commission remained subject to significant congressional direction and judicial review.[23] Meanwhile, litigation over ICC rate decisions sharply declined; only twelve cases came before the courts between 1915 and 1921. "The litigation phase of the whole subject is passing into the economic phase," one expert hopefully concluded. But the Court continued to be an unpredictable participant in important rate and merger decisions. And in disturbingly contradictory decisions in 1913 and 1914, it first strengthened and then weakened the power of state railroad commissions to fix intrastate rates.[24]

In sum, the early years of the new century saw not the creation of a rational, efficient national railroad policy—the Progressive ideal—but rather a new regulatory chaos that differed from the old one primarily in the ever-greater diversity and complexity of the interests, issues, ideas, and instruments of government participating in the regulatory game.

By the time America entered World War I in 1917, the condition of the railroads was as unsatisfactory as their regulatory milieu. Fewer miles of new track—only 718—were built in 1915–16 than at any time since 1848. A decade of ICC resistance to rate increases, along with the roads' mismanagement and earlier overcapitalization, impeded the modernization of trackage and rolling stock. The Wilson administration's Adamson Act of 1916, which set an eight-hour day for railroad workers, added substantially to labor costs. And the system began to buckle under the strain of the great increase in freight traffic heading to East Coast ports.[25]

This state of affairs added more spice to the already pungent stew of railroad policy. Pressure grew for a more substantial federal presence—by railroads seeking refuge, by Progressives seeking more rationalized control of the business. According to one estimate, 84 percent of the roads wanted federal incorporation, as did many chambers of commerce and boards of trade. Rail spokesmen hoped that this would weaken control of intrastate rates by state commissions and strengthen their ability to raise money in the capital market: "The railroads have got to have money to keep up with the growth of the nation in population and commerce, but money they cannot get. The investor is afraid of regulation." Even bolder plans were afoot. One was for a public corporation, modeled on the Federal Reserve system, that would oversee four regional railroad corporations: "The Government has not gone into the banking business, but it has utilized the corporation to control the banking business. Why not consolidate the railroads in the same way?"[26]

After the United States entered the war, the Wilson administration took over the railroads—not in accordance with a preconceived plan, but *défaute de mieux*. Would this clear the way for a new era in railroad policy—government ownership, legalized pooling, or federal incorporation—after the war? Many expected that wartime unification into one system would put an end to "making a fetish of competition." But past experience offered ample warning that the roiling diversity of interests and the ambiguous place of regulation in the American polity made so seductively clean-limbed a solution unlikely indeed.[27]

In Britain as in America, the wartime state ran the railroads. And there too, lively controversy erupted over their postwar disposition. Difficult questions of compensation had to be answered: operating costs rose substantially above revenue; heavy wartime use badly eroded tracks and rolling stock; railroad securities were worth half their 1914 value. It was no great help when a Rates Advisory Commission recommended a settlement of not less than cost and no more than value. The Labour party and other advocates of nationalization wanted the government to buy the lines at their 1913 valuation (less 30 percent for depreciation) and put them under the new Ministry of Transportation. But the Lloyd George government turned instead to a mix of private ownership and tighter regulation.[28]

The purpose of the Railways Act of 1921 was to implement "a policy of rationalization." It sorted out the lines into four closely regulated regional groups. The old system of statutory maximum rates, with the companies free to charge less, gave way to a Railway Rates Tribunal setting standard rates for each regional network. A National Wages Board, in principle representing the public, had the final voice in wage disputes. Controversies over company consolidation would come before an Amalgamation Tribunal drawn from the railroad, shipper, and legal communities.[29]

In France, too, the state operated the railroads during the war. Mounting deficits and large-scale strikes plagued the lines there as elsewhere in the postwar years, and nationalization schemes emerged from organized labor, the Socialists, and the Ministry of Public Works. But the final disposition closely resembled Britain's: a return to private ownership, but oversight in the hands of a Superior Council made up of management, labor, and public representatives vested with rate, wage, and other regulatory powers.[30]

On the face of things, postwar American railroad policy followed the same course. It appeared that the oldest of big enterprises had come to the same stage of development in each of the three nations, and that the regulatory response was—had to be—structurally similar. But once again the distinctive character of America's economic and public life put its stamp on regulatory policy.

The politics of railroad regulation, complex enough before the war, became even more convoluted. Organized labor, which like its British and French counterparts had done relatively well under wartime nationalization, now joined investors, shippers, regulators, and the railroads as a major player. Glenn Plumb, general counsel for the Railroad Brotherhoods, proposed a plan of government ownership that combined the principles of scientific management with a Guild Socialist vision of worker control borrowed from the British coal miners. Plumb attributed his scheme to a "moral reawakening" of American society: "I claim no credit for the framing of the plan which bears my name, for it is not my plan nor is it the creation of the brain of any one man. It is rather God's plan."[31]

A number of more secular-minded Progressives also wanted public ownership to continue after the war. ICC commissioner Joseph B. Eastman held that the war experience demonstrated the advantages of government ownership and operation; William G. McAdoo, who headed the wartime Railroad Administration, wanted it to continue for another five years. Frederic C. Howe saw in public control not only more efficient management, but also an opportunity to bring talented people into public life: "The real trouble is that we have made it almost impossible for strong men and capable men to be identified with the state."[32]

But other schemes jousted for acceptance as well. The Senate passed a bill providing for a Transportation Board, a consolidated rail system, and mandatory arbitration of labor disputes. The Association of Railway Executives and investor groups banked on federal incorporation to reduce ICC (and hence shipper) power over rates. Shippers of course wanted to return to the *status quo ante bellum*; and, as *Traffic World* observed, "The Commission is the friend of the shipper."[33]

The Transportation Act of 1920 settled the issue. It restored the prewar system of private ownership but also drew on the wartime experience of government involvement. The law set up a Railway Labor Board, made up of employer, employee, and public representatives, to hear labor disputes. It gave the ICC considerable new power over railroad rates, corporate structure, profits, and financing. Most important, through its recapture clause the act authorized the ICC to divide the country into four districts, calculate reasonable rates of return in each, and distribute the earnings of lines making more than 6 percent to their less profitable fellows.

The Transportation Act appeared thus to signify an important change in railroad regulation, from the restrained, reactive prewar style to a more interventionist policy. The old issue of federal versus state railroad regulation now led only rarely to litigation; the act had "undeniably reduced the power of the states over traffic charges to a shadow." Railroads were regarded less as private enterprises than as public utilities. Chief Justice William Howard Taft upheld the recapture clause on the ground that this was a public service industry. The ICC began to issue certificates of public convenience and necessity (the prevailing instrument of utilities licensing) for new construction and to pass on the abandonment of existing trackage.[34]

It seemed to some observers that the railroad regulation wars finally had come to an end. One saw a "practical withdrawal of the railroads from political activity since the World War, yielding place to administrative control by the Federal government." The rise of a consumer economy, according to another, made rate conflicts "a struggle for existence between competing groups of producers or shippers and their consumers . . . The railroads in much of the present-day litigation before the Commission are frequently mere bystanders . . . taking the frank position that it is a rate fight between producers or shippers."[35]

But for all the change of regulatory ambience, the railroads' economic position was no more secure. The Railroad Labor Board lowered wages by 12 percent in July 1921, setting off a major rail strike. Shippers continued to bombard Congress with complaints about the roads' rate scales; the rate zones set up by the Transportation Act fueled intersectional political controversy. And the sudden, sweeping growth of trucking wrought havoc with the railroads' short-haul traffic, opening up a major new area of political and regulatory conflict.[36]

An important source of tension was the ICC's inclination to treat the railroads as a regulated public utility, in contrast to the older view of them as a big business subject to the dictates of antitrust. The commission accepted rate pooling and other cartel-like practices and favored the consolidation of competing lines. It dropped its former hostility to higher rates for short than for long hauls on the same line. Instead it favored a "reasonable compensatory" principle that took market factors into account: "a rigid long and short haul rule would threaten the nice adjustment to the needs of shipper and railroad which the present flexible clause permits." But this led to growing shipper (especially agricultural) criticism from spokesmen in the Departments of Agriculture, Commerce, and Interior, the Maritime Commission, and Justice's Antitrust Division.[37]

Midwestern agricultural interests led by the Grange and the Farm Bureau secured the Hoch-Smith Resolution from Congress in 1925, which instructed the ICC to set rate differentials "to the end that commodities may freely move." Commission rate setting inevitably evoked counterattacks—by the highly organized fruit growers of California seeking to preserve their long-haul rate advantages; by competing coal shippers from Pennsylvania and Ohio on the one hand, and from West Virginia and Kentucky on the other—as red in tooth and claw as anything in the past. The expanding economy of the 1920s and the constant vigilance of congressional and judicial overseers hardly simplified the ICC's regulatory milieu. As before, it was "distinctly one of special interests, and the regulatory body lives in an environment of conflicts. . . Producers desiring to reach the same markets, markets desiring to reach the same producing fields, intermediate gateways desiring to divert traffic through their routes, all have come to the Commission to improve their positions at the expense of their competitors."[38]

The core issue of railroad regulation in the 1920s was the ICC's valuation of the roads and their equipment, mandated by Congress in 1913. This required constant hearings and a flood of data in pursuit of those elusive grails "reproduction cost," "cost value," "present value," "fair value," "value of the service," and the like. A wholly appropriate skepticism rose as to "the conclusiveness or ultimate usefulness of the figures so expensively secured and so elaborately presented." By the mid-1920s the tedious process appeared to be nearing its end. The 260,000 miles of track had been examined, ties counted, bridges and terminals inspected, the age and condition of masonry determined, elaborate depreciation tables prepared. The cost of the exercise approached $100 million.[39]

As far back as 1898, William Jennings Bryan had argued on behalf of agricultural shippers that "the present value of the roads, as measured by the cost of reproduction, is the basis upon which profit should be computed." But now that standard nicely suited the railroads and their bankers, who expected that the inflation of the war would make it seem that the roads were not overcapitalized.[40]

As was so often the case, the choice between the reproduction cost and the original (or "historical") cost basis for rate setting lay with the courts. Justice Louis D. Brandeis tried to sell his colleagues on a more realistic "prudent investment" standard of valuation. The ICC sought to apply that yardstick. But the Supreme Court's *O'Fallon* decision of 1929 made it clear how little had changed in the realm of railroad regulation. The majority held that the ICC had overstepped itself: value was an inherent property right, not subject to modification by public policy. Still, just what the railroads' "value" was remained as vague to the Courts as to everyone else. And after 1929 the Great Depression again sharply altered the terms of the debate and the positions of the parties. As the value of the railroads' property collapsed, so did their desire for rates based on reproduction cost: for these would hardly suffice to cover their high fixed obligations.[41]

The Depression wiped out the modest prosperity attained by some lines during the 1920s, and intensified old problems of overcompetition, labor conflict, insufficient rate income, overcapitalization and underfinancing. Once again the regulatory mill groaned and ground. The Emergency Transportation Act of 1934 created a National Railroad Adjustment Board, empowered to hand down judicially enforceable decisions in labor disputes. It also provided for a coordinator of transportation: Joseph B. Eastman, the ICC commissioner most favorably disposed to government ownership. He had the (temporary) power to merge the nation's roads into three large regional systems and to eliminate duplicate lines.

But the attempt to supersede the seven-member ICC with a single permanent administrator failed, as did the surprisingly scant calls for government ownership. By the mid-1930s a regulatory system half a century old was fundamentally unchanged in its relationship to the interests that it served (or disserved), and to the polity of which it was a part.[42]

Municipal Utilities

In many respects water, streetcar, subway, gas, and electric companies resembled the big businesses that produced steel, mined coal, extracted oil, or made consumer products. But the nature of their output and their relationship to their customers were special. They provided a steady, continuous flow of service—transportation, power, water— very different in character from the distribution and sale of discrete, material commodities. And they dealt with the public at large, without middlemen such as shippers, distributors, wholesalers, and retailers.

Enterprises that by their very nature had special public responsibilities—to serve all comers, to charge reasonable and nondiscriminatory rates, to provide adequate service—were as old as the common law. The common carrier and the business affected with a public interest were established legal categories. But the scale and technological novelty of the municipal utilities that rose to serve a modern urban society raised a host of new political, legal, and regulatory issues. The very terms *public service company* and *public utility* were born with the new century; the latter had not yet appeared in the 1904 edition of *Words and Phrases Judicially Defined*. They had no place in European law and practice. The large, privately owned and operated municipal utility was a peculiarly American institution.[43]

The growing European experience with publicly owned utilities attracted much American attention around the turn of the century. Prominent Progressive Frederic C. Howe praised the efficiency and freedom from corruption of British and Continental municipal services. Legal theorist Christoper G. Tiedman, an influential advocate of limits on the states' police power, nevertheless saw no constitutional bar to (and much good sense in) government-operated utilities. An American advocate of public ownership thought that it would foster a public sense of social obligation: "In these last days of the nineteenth century, we have a new light upon the possibilities of the commonwealth."[44]

But aside from municipal waterworks, publicly owned utilities were *rarae aves* in turn-of-the-century America. Only 20 of 981 cities (Philadelphia, Louisville, Richmond, Duluth, and Wheeling were the five largest) had municipal gasworks in 1900; only 193 of 1,471 urban electric systems were publicly owned. Almost all municipal public transit was privately owned, and private utilities consistently produced well over 90 percent of the nation's electricity after 1900.[45]

Criticism of public ownership flourished on both sides of the Atlantic. Exposés in 1900 and 1901 unveiled the corrupt management of utilities in a number of British towns, and the London *Times* in a widely noted series of articles sharply attacked "Municipal Socialism." Critics charged that publicly owned utilities were costly and inefficient. Thomas Edison said of the British government's role in the nascent electric industry: "Why, they've throttled it!" In 1907 a Commission on Public Ownership and Operation sponsored by the National Civic Federation reported on municipal ownership in the United States and Great Britain. It concluded that success depended on the capacity and honesty of municipal government: in effect, a declaration that in the United States it was bound to fail.[46]

There were grounds for this skepticism. The Philadelphia and Wheeling gasworks failed in part because those cities' political machines used them as patronage catchpools. In the early 1890s the Massachusetts legislature enacted a Municipal Lighting Act that authorized cities and towns to purchase privately owned gas and electric plants. But its consequence was hardly encouraging: a turmoil of politics and litigation, and a number of forced municipal purchases at excessive cost.

American advocates of public ownership appeared "to be animated rather by the feeling that company ownership of public utilities is irredeemably sordid and corrupt than by a conviction of the excellence of public management." British towns, "partly by organization we shall not imitate, partly by habits we cannot borrow . . . come nearer than our own to a business corporation"; hence the label "municipal trading" applied to their utilities operations.[47]

No legal obstacle impeded municipal ownership and operation. Indeed, the Supreme Court held in 1919 that San Francisco's private transit combine could not keep the city from building competing tracks. But the predisposition against public ownership persisted until the Great Depression. The political power of the utilities, the ever-more-daunting financial cost of municipalization, and distrust of government's capacity to run these enterprises prevailed.

The major impetus to public ownership came not from ideology but from the economics of the utilities business. A number of small communities relied on revenue from their plants; and at times real estate associations in search of lower property taxes backed publicly owned utilities. Most important were the pressure of a rising price level on fares politically difficult to raise, and the competitive challenge of motor transportation. By 1919 companies holding one-tenth of the nation's street railway mileage were in receivership.[48]

The Depression reinvigorated the cause of public ownership—and increased the readiness of hard-strapped utilities to sell out at a comforting profit. New state laws allowed municipalities to purchase, condemn, or enter into competition with existing private utilities. To relieve the cost burden on consumers, many cities relied on tax revenues to pay for acquired plants. This led to consumer-taxpayer disputes that often wound up in court. In general, as long as there was no clear discrimination in the distribution of costs, municipalities could finance their new acquisitions as they thought best. But municipally owned utilities still were subject to state regulation. And substantial public ownership of urban transit came only gradually, as the Depression, the automobile, and the suburb eroded its profit potential.[49]

The politics of municipal gas, electric, and especially traction companies had an ascendant place in state and local public life. Disputes abounded over franchises and rights of way, fares and financing, private or municipal ownership and operation. Major players in the transit game—Charles Tyson Yerkes in Chicago, Peter Widener in Philadelphia, Thomas Fortune Ryan in New York—were important figures in their cities and states. Chicago politics in the early 1900s often hung on the issue of public ownership of the transit system; New York's subways (built by the city, leased to transit companies) added spicily to the city's political life; Philadelphia's gas and traction rings defined—and disfigured—that town's political reputation.[50]

Transit, gas, and electric companies had extensive, and corrupt, influence in state legislature and city councils. But by no means did they always have their way. Transit unions, local businessmen with a stake in a low fare structure and efficient service, bankers and others drawn to reforms that promised to block municipal ownership, politicians well aware of the benefits of an anticompany stand—together these constituted a powerful political counterforce.

Every city had its utilities wars; the politics of gas in Minneapolis may stand for the rest. In 1907 the General Electric Company sought a new franchise to replace those of recently acquired lesser firms. Democratic mayor James C. Haynes made this the major issue of his 1908 reelection campaign and won by a small plurality in that normally Republican city. After a fierce political and legal struggle (Mayor Haynes had a breakdown, GE's chief counsel went south to soothe his nerves), a settlement favorable to the city was secured—in great part because Minneapolis bankers and business interests intervened in order to avoid municipal ownership.[51]

Utilities politics reflected rapid technological change as well as the play of interest. Street railways burst the bounds of their cities, and a web of interurban trolleys spread over the countryside. Conflicts broke out over who would bear the costs of the burden imposed on streets and highways. One judge declared that "the interurban car, which tends more than almost any other material influence to make the residents of country and city a homogeneous people, is a proper vehicle on the city street." Others disagreed. The interests of cities and suburbs, abutting owners, rival steam railroads, and an expanded public generated intense legal and political controversy. Often this took the form of confrontations between "experts" who championed municipal home rule and "experts" who advocated state regulation. Interurban trolleys soon became an interstate system of public transportation, raising the old question of state versus federal control in a new context. Should—could—the ICC be the regulator? The commission thought so. But this form of interstate transportation was very different from the railroads; and soon the rise of bus transportation further complicated the issue.[52]

Even more unsettling in its regulatory implications was the unique character of what the public utilities did: "transportation or transmission as distinguished from the sale of commodities which pass from hand to hand." The continuous use of street railways, subways, gas, and electricity by hundreds of thousands of customers, paying fares and rates measured in pennies per unit of service—a single ride, a kilowatt hour—was very different from railroad freight and passenger haulage, or indeed from most other major business transactions.[53]

The immediacy of the utilities' relationship to the public fostered a new management style. William G. McAdoo, later to be Woodrow Wilson's son-in-law and secretary of the Treasury, headed the Hudson & Manhattan commuter railroad, which ran through the new Hudson Tubes from northern New Jersey to lower Manhattan. In sharp contrast to the prevailing style of corporate management, McAdoo championed a "public be pleased" policy. In 1909, at the behest of the Women's Municipal League, his company set aside a separate car for female passengers. There was much male ridicule of "The Adamless Eden" and the "Jane Crow Car" (and indeed it was the last coach on each train). The experiment came to an end after three months because of limited patronage—and because a male passenger brought a charge of discrimination to the ICC.[54]

Government and law had to come to terms with these technologically complex, mass consumer-oriented public services. In 1907 Wisconsin and New York created the first state public utilities commissions (PUCs). By 1914 all but three states (Delaware, Utah, and Wyoming) had commissions; New York, Massachusetts, and South Carolina had two. Twenty were elected; twenty-eight were appointed, almost always by the governor.

European states had no precise counterpart to the independent, autonomous public utilities commission. British regulatory bodies such as the Railway Rates Tribunal, metropolitan transport committees in London and twelve provincial districts, and the Central Electricity Board were made up of representatives of interest groups: management, labor, the public. Appropriate state ministries oversaw Continental utilities.[55]

Although they were modeled on the state railroad commissions of the late nineteenth century, the public utilities commissions faced a very different regulatory ambience. For one thing, their primary clientele was not a relatively limited number of shippers, but the community at large. Thus New York's PUC emerged not from the politics of rate setting—the primary source of nineteenth-century railroad regulation—but from public dissatisfaction with the service provided by upstate railroads, by New York City's trolleys and subways, and by Edison Electric.[56]

Not until the 1920s and the 1930s were there federal regulatory agencies like the ICC with which the utilities commissions had to interact. Meanwhile they set and monitored rates and service for a continuous flow of service, very different from the discrete contractual arrangements and business practices regulated by the ICC, the FTC, and antitrust law. As Felix Frankfurter observed, "in their range and complexity these commissions constituted a new political invention responsive to the presence of new economic and social facts."[57]

Utilities regulation went hand in hand with utilities politics. Governor Charles Evans Hughes favored a commission as an alternative to municipal ownership of New York City's transit system—a cause championed by his 1906 gubernatorial opponent, William Randolph Hearst. Democratic governor John A. Dix attacked "government by commission" in 1911 and appointed Tammany men to the body who clashed with Hughes's more conservative majority over the awarding of subway contracts.[58]

The PUCs often had a cosy relationship with the utilities under their surveillance. As in other realms of regulation, their advocates included those interested in a sophisticated—and amenable—business-government relationship. The National Civic Federation's Department of Public Utilities drafted an influential model state PUC law. In a familiar mode the companies, initially skeptical, came to favor the commissions:

> the public utilities have found that state regulation serves their purposes admirably; that it protects them from unreasonable rates, assures them liberal dividends, imposes no unreasonable service obligations, by means of the indeterminable permit assures the permanency of their investments with opportunity to get out in the event of purchase by the city at a price considerably above the legitimate investment in the property, increases the market value of their securities, and finally, in effect, through state supervision of bond and stock issues, guarantees the integrity of their securities.[59]

PUCs rarely engaged in conspicuous regulatory muscle-flexing. The New York Commission relied on publicity to coax its charges into upgrading their service. A 1915 review concluded: "The catchwords of this new movement are 'co-operation' and 'publicity.'" It is not surprising that the commissions became ever more captive to massive and rapidly growing utilities companies in the 1920s. A 1930 list of commission members who had gone to work for the companies stretched over four pages of footnotes.[60]

But there were other aspects to utilities regulation that complicated the picture. Its complexity put a premium on legal and other expertise. A 1929 survey of the backgrounds of state utility commissioners found that 79 were lawyers, 13 engineers, 29 businessmen and bankers, 17 farmers, 12 industrial workers, and 9 government employees. Although political considerations figured prominently in these appointments, the commissions tended to see themselves as fact-finding, quasi-judicial bodies, charged with securing good service, fair returns, and honest financing. And in fact the overwhelming majority of PUC activity involved technical and administrative matters. From 1921 to 1928 the commissions of twenty-one states handed down 142,704 separate orders.[61]

The extent and public importance of the utilities' services, and the collective clout of economic interests with a stake in low rates and reliable service, significantly affected their regulation by PUCs. But there was yet another regulatory dimension, one not readily absorbed in the ambit of companies, commissions, and politicians: the legal system.

The courts initially treated public utilities companies much as they did private corporations in general. They held that a utilities franchise, like any corporate charter, was a contract rather than an application of the state's police power. This meant that the utilities frequently had recourse to Fourteenth Amendment due process and other corporate legal security blankets. And on occasion courts faced down PUCs in familiar judicial-administrative turf tussles. Thus after the Connecticut supreme court upheld the New Britain Gas Light Company's appeal of a state PUC order that it extend its service to a nearby area, the commission adopted a more cautious administrative stance.[62]

During World War I a Columbus, Ohio, street railway company tried to abandon its franchise on the ground that wage increases ordered by the War Labor Board were confiscatory. The court held that its franchise contractually bound the utility to performance. But during the 1920s transit companies with increasing frequency sought to withdraw from lines rendered unprofitable by automobile and bus competition. Unless its franchise held the company to provide service for a specific period, the courts permitted exit, holding that enforced unprofitability was an unconstitutional taking of property.[63]

At the same time they adhered to the established principle that the states had substantial regulatory power over public service companies. And over time, as the PUCs became a fixture of utilities regulation, the courts became less inclined to interfere in their decisions.

The utilities' primary economic function—the provision of continuous service—worked against prevailing legal categories. Theorists wrestled with the problem. One argued for a distinction between utilities whose business came to them (transit and telegraph companies) and those that had to make special arrangements with each patron (water, gas and electric, and telephone companies). Others held that the utilities' obligations to the public went beyond the classical contractual relationship to become "the involuntary ones of a legal status, not the defined ones of a specific assumption." In consequence, the regulatory response to public utilities—the requirements that they file their rates and serve all equally—harked back to earlier doctrines such as the law of public callings. Roscoe Pound wryly noted: "It is significant that progress in our law of public service companies has taken the form of abandonment of nineteenth century views for doctrines which may be found in the Year Books."[64]

As in the case of the railroads, the courts came to concentrate not on the public power to regulate utilities but on how the regulators set rates. Their fairness, according to the prevailing view, could be determined only by information "of a kind to be established mainly by the testimony of experts and the most careful, complicated, and elaborate investigation of a mass of data generally technical and difficult to understand."[65]

Problems both novel and familiar inevitably arose. The peculiar nature of the utilities enterprise led to early speculation about the place of "social welfare in rate making"—that is, the degree to which utility rates might be fixed to achieve purposes such as relieving congestion, promoting community and industry development, fostering education, or raising the standard of living. The Supreme Court in 1892 permitted a transit company to sell reduced-rate commuter tickets (in effect, rebates), in part because it would relieve urban congestion. Similarly, courts accepted reduced rates for schoolchildren and for small—or large—consumers of gas, electricity, and water.[66]

But generally the courts restricted themselves to a cost-of-service approach—"an arithmetical determination of value and proportionate returns"—that left little room for considerations of social welfare. When North Dakota tried to fix a low rate on the sale of coal to attract more of that fuel into the state, the Supreme Court found this confiscatory. And in 1909 the Court allowed intangibles—the value of its franchise, goodwill—to be included in the rate base of New York City's Consolidated Gas Company.[67]

So rate setting for utilities was drawn ineluctably into the same black hole of valuation into which the railroads had plunged. Prevailing doctrine had it that rates should allow for a reasonable return based on the "fair value" of the property. As with the rule of reason in antitrust law, this was a highly subjective standard. Each of the interests involved—public utilities commissions, tax assessors, the utilities, the investment market, consumer spokesmen—had its own method of measurement, its own definition of "value."[68]

This esoteric issue, borne along by greatly varying valuation and accounting procedures, was fought out in endless commission hearings and court reviews. PUC hearings on the New York Telephone Company's rates yielded a bumper crop of 625 witnesses, good for 37,000 pages of testimony. Estimates of the company's fair value ranged from $367 to $615 million. With understandable skepticism, one judge observed that estimates within 10 percent of each other suggested collusion.[69]

The primary point of conflict was whether fair value should be based on initial cost, current reproduction cost, or what the "prudent investment" of its assets would bring. The rise in prices during World War I led utilities (like the railroads) to reverse their prewar position and to argue for reproduction rather than for original cost. Consumer advocates of course held out for initial cost. Charles Evans Hughes, serving as referee in a Brooklyn Borough Gas Company case in 1918, concluded that the war-inflated price level of the moment was not a proper base for rate valuation. His decision induced a number of PUCs and courts to seek some more reasonable way of determining a utility's worth. But state and federal courts often struck down the commissions' rate decisions on the ground that they gave insufficient weight to reproduction cost.[70]

So did the Supreme Court. During the early 1920s federal appeals courts found for the utilities in twenty-eight of thirty-four cases; of the six decisions that went against them, the Court reversed three. In *Southwestern Bell* (1922) and *Bluefield Water Works* (1923) the majority criticized PUCs for taking insufficient account of higher wage and equipment costs, and seemed to be opting for current reproduction cost as the preferred standard. In 1926 Justice Pierce Butler defined "fair return" as what a utility's assets invested at the moment would bring. In effect, he made "spot" reproduction cost the determinant of rate setting. The *New Republic* thought that this would lead to state legislation, to new franchises' setting a more acceptable rate base—or to public ownership. Constitutional law expert Thomas Reed Powell offered a sarcasm-drenched description of the Supreme Court's approach: "notwithstanding occasional lapses to common sense, the court had clung to its formula of present fair value . . . Fair value has been fixed with reference to some compound of contradictory considerations concocted by the alchemy of uncontrolled and changeful compromise."[71]

Brandeis dissented in these cases, arguing for his more eclectic "prudent investment" standard over the "legally and economically unsound" fair value rule. At times his approach prevailed. But valuation remained a dark and bloody ground of conflicting interests and interpretations. By 1930 what constituted fair return was no closer to resolution than what constituted reasonable restraint of trade. Utilities regulation, said one expert, was "admitted almost unanimously to require a new deal."[72]

The Depression made that new deal a possibility. A regulatory system that so intimately linked rates to value was deeply affected by the cataclysmic price decline, economic stagnation, and consequent excess utilities capacity of the early 1930s. The courts became less sensitive to how PUCs set rates or what those rates were. Hughes in 1933 refused to set aside a commission rate order even though it had a historical cost rather than a present fair value basis.[73]

The costly, time-consuming, quasi-mystical process of formal valuation and rate hearings hardly seemed appropriate now. The Depression "greatly stimulated the use of the negotiating functions of the commissions," and in 1932 Wisconsin's PUC came up with a "value of the service" standard to reduce telephone rates. Stricter PUC regulation of the utilities' capital-raising and accounting procedures spread rapidly, though with little uniformity. A wave of state laws tightened the regulation of public utilities holding companies and raised their taxes—a prelude to the national Public Utilities Holding Companies Act of 1935.[74]

By the early 1930s municipal utilities, like the railroads, operated within a dense regulatory framework of legislation, commission oversight, and court review. Perhaps the major consequence of this regulatory infrastructure was enough oversight to prevent an effective movement for municipal ownership and operation.

4 · Regulating New Technologies

Economic change in early twentieth-century America is generally described in the language of either Marxism or managerialism: as the replacement of industrial by finance capitalism, or as the rise of big business and an organizational revolution. But Americans were less directly affected by these structural changes than by the flood of new technologies—motor vehicles and airplanes, electricity and telephones, the movies and radio—that entered and altered their lives. The rapidity with which these devices spread through the social fabric, and the rich variety of regulatory problems that they brought with them, posed a major additional challenge to the American polity.

Trucks and Buses, Automobiles and Airplanes

The most prodigious newcomer was of course the motor vehicle. Trucks, buses, taxis, and above all automobiles altered the life styles of tens of millions of Americans and (more slowly) the flow of commerce (see Table 1).

This second American transportation revolution, more rapid in its spread and more pervasive in its economic and social consequences than the coming of the railroad a century before, imposed a bewildering variety of new demands on public policy. A horse-and-buggy road system had to be transformed; millions of dangerous machines and their no less dangerous drivers had to be certified and overseen; safe and adequate public service by commercial vehicles had to be assured; the endlessly complex issues of entry into a new transportation industry and of its impact on existing goods carriers had to be faced.

Commercial as distinct from private vehicle regulation came slowly. By 1914 municipal ordinances licensed and regulated the taxi-

Table 1. Motor vehicles sales and registrations, 1900–1929 (thousands)

Year	Sales		Registration	
	Autos	Trucks and buses	Autos	Trucks
1900	4.1	—	8.0	—
1905	24.2	.7	77.4	1.4
1910	181.0	6.0	458.3	10.1
1915	895.9	74.0	2,332.4	158.5
1920	1,905.5	321.7	8,131.5	1,107.6
1925	3,735.1	530.6	17,481.0	2,569.7[a]
1929	4,455.1	881.9	23,120.8	3,674.5[b]

Source: U.S. Bureau of the Census, *Historical Statistics of the United States, Colonial Times to 1970* (Washington, D.C., 1975), p. 716.
 a. Bus registrations: 17.8.
 b. Bus registrations: 33.9.

cab ("automobile hack" or "jitney bus") business. Street railways used their political influence to confine these new competitors to specific routes and termini. But the Supreme Court complicated state and local truck regulation in 1912 by holding that a New York City licensing ordinance interfered with the flow of interstate commerce when applied to vehicles delivering goods sent from other states.[1]

Only seven states (but among them New York and Pennsylvania) regulated commercial vehicles by 1917. A rush of others followed after the war. The National Association of Railroad and Utilities Commissioners drafted a model statute in 1923; and by 1927 forty-two states had motor vehicle regulation acts, supervised by railroad or public utilities commissions: all of this widely upheld by the courts as a valid exercise of the states' police power.[2]

Truck and bus regulation differed substantively from the regulation of railroads. The latter rose primarily in response to shippers' concern over rates; only after the Transportation Act of 1920 did the ICC's attention shift to the effects of competition on the railroads. But from its earliest days "the regulation of competition, if not its elimination [was] the main reason advanced for the regulation of common carrier motor vehicles": so rapid and easy was entry into the business. Bus operators—and the railroads and street railways feeling their competition—were the major proponents of regulation. Truckers, more numerous and independent, and shippers favoring the rate-cutting effects of competition, were less favorably inclined.[3]

An issue of some weight was how (and whether) to distinguish between common carriers available to all, and private carriers who contracted with a limited number of customers. So rapid and helter-skelter was the growth of motor transportation that the distinction raised "troublesome constitutional and administrative problems of first importance." In its *Duke* (1925) and *Frost* (1926) decisions, the Supreme Court held that private carriers were not public utilities, and in the related case of *Buck v. Kuykendall* (1925) it invalidated state licensing of motor transport in interstate commerce. Justice Louis D. Brandeis acidly commented that this "is not regulation with a view to safety or to conservation of the highways, but the prohibition of competition."[4]

These decisions sowed "consternation and confusion" among regulators and carriers alike. In their wake a large number of bus companies sprang up in the profitable New York–New Jersey and Philadelphia–New Jersey interstate markets, their termini often straddling state lines and thus avoiding state regulation. One observer complained in 1931 that the concept of the common carrier, like that of the public utility was "now little more than jargon." In *Stephenson v. Binford* (1932) the Supreme Court in effect reversed its *Frost* decision, reaffirming the power of the states to certify motor carriers in order to secure highway maintenance and safety.[5]

The rapidity with which motor transportation spread across state lines led to proposals for national bus and truck licensing and regulation, or for regional boards similar to the Federal Reserve system. But the sheer number and diversity of motor carriers (so different from railroads and municipal utilities) and the presence of a substantial structure of state supervision blocked national regulation. Not until the Motor Carrier Act of 1935 did the ICC get the power to license and otherwise regulate interstate trucks and buses. Thereafter, federal and state regulation coexisted in a complex and uneasy relationship.[6]

The number, variety, and elusiveness of trucks, buses, and taxis and the pressure to restrict entry into the business made licensing the basic instrument of commercial vehicle regulation. Public utilities commissions issued certificates of convenience and necessity—permits to operate that, unlike railroad charters or streetcar franchises, were granted for relatively short periods. Their most obvious purpose was to limit the number of competitors where entry costs were low and highways were endangered by congestion and overuse. But these certificates did more than protect established carriers. They obligated bus companies to serve less as well as more profitable routes; and they had a more flexible regulatory potential than the franchises of street railways.

Certificates of convenience and necessity had no common law counterpart. They differed significantly from charters or franchises; they were not contracts; they did not confer property rights; and they were not assets in terms of goodwill. One authority concluded that they were "nothing but a revocable license or a license to serve the public for a limited period of time." Licensing—a form of regulation that had fallen into disfavor during the nineteenth century because it smacked of privilege and monopoly—now reemerged as the best way to deal with new technology.[7]

Of the inventions that changed the face of early twentieth-century American life, by far the most consequential was the automobile. From its beginnings (and to our own day) it evoked moral and cultural disapproval. An early commentator predicted that cars would not replace horses for pleasure driving because "the cold and heartless mechanism of the automobile furnishes a poor substitute" for the "companionship of the horse." Woodrow Wilson worried that these expensive playthings of the rich might foster a socialist spirit among an American people deprived of them. A 1915 Indiana church conference resolved: "Whereas we realize the difficulty and unpleasantness in dealing with the automobile spirit . . . we advise all churches not to allow their members to own or operate an automobile, auto-truck, motorcycle or any motor vehicle, at least until such time as they become in general use, or until we get more light on the subject."[8]

But of course autos quickly became a major part of modern life. And governments everywhere had to register cars and drivers, define and regulate dangerous driving, and develop rules of liability and compensation for the multitude of harms produced by this potent new machine.

The British cabinet took up the subject as early as 1903, impelled not by public opinion but by car owners who feared that without protective legislation "the feeling against these vehicles will become so strong as practically to prevent their use altogether." One M. P. predicted in 1904: "Future generations in all civilized countries will laugh at the cumbrous and illogical efforts their forefathers made to restrict the use of the automobile, and smile at their assumption that it was a dangerous and uncontrollable vehicle."[9]

In 1905 a Royal Commission on Means of Locomotion and Trans-

port in Greater London examined the traffic problem of the metropolis and (without mentioning the automobile) recommended the creation of a Traffic Board. Parliament in that year raised the national
speed limit to twenty miles per hour and provided for auto licensing
and taxation. By 1909 the British Automobile Association was send-
ing out scouts to flush out police in wait for speeders, and a debate
broke out over the need for a speed limit "in this singularly congested
and motor-infested country."[10]

Two facts shaped the American public response to the coming of
the automobile: regulation was in the hands of the states and localities, not of the federal government; and very quickly the country had
a massive number of cars and drivers.

State laws, local ordinances, and court decisions quickly created a
dense and diverse body of auto regulation. Speeding attracted attention early on. "Scorching" became a California pastime, and twenty-
two drivers were arrested for speeding in San Francisco in one year; all
the charges were dismissed. New York's 1901 law prohibiting speeds
in excess of what was "reasonable and proper" seems to have been the
first specifically designed to control motor travel. New York and Massachusetts in 1902, followed by several other states over the next decade, set absolute speed limits (often about nine miles per hour in "en-
closed places"). The courts generally upheld speed restrictions,
although a few warned that it was unlawful to distinguish the automobile from other vehicles. The Illinois supreme court refused to
strike down the state's 1903 auto law, even though its requirement
that a driver stop when his vehicle frightened a horse came under fire
as class legislation.[11]

Twenty-five states required license plates and auto registration by
1906. Fines, taxation, and drivers' licenses also spread, though more
slowly: as late as 1906, no state tested drivers. New York City adopted
the first comprehensive traffic code in 1903. A state Highways Act
followed in 1904, but it left most regulation to the municipalities.[12]

New technology and rapid growth far outstripped the pace of regulation. By 1907 it seemed that "automobile legislation is about as far
behind the mechanical progress of the vehicle as a one-cylinder car is
behind a high-powered racer." Local speed limits and state regulations
varied widely; indeed, several places abolished previously imposed
speed limits, relying instead on a "reasonable and proper" standard. A
driver going from New York City to Washington needed separate licenses for New York, New Jersey, Pennsylvania, Maryland, and the
District of Columbia. Registration fees ranged from fifty cents in Ala-

bama to fifty dollars in Texas. Nine states imposed additional levies on out-of-state drivers; twenty-one others allowed localities to impose them.[13]

In 1922 more than twenty different speed regulations segmented the 149 miles of the Boston Post Road. Even by 1933, laws setting absolute speed limits existed only in Georgia, Nevada, Pennsylvania, South Carolina, and West Virginia. When New York in 1910 instituted state registration of (and license fees for) cars, a thirty-mile-per-hour speed limit, and driver tests, only Massachusetts and the District of Columbia had comparably thorough regulations. But by the early 1920s the modern structure of automobile regulation was pretty much in place.[14]

The national government had little or nothing to do with these developments. A bill sponsored by the American Automobile Association did come before Congress in 1907, providing for federal registration and a federal bureau of automobiles. But the local, private nature of vehicle use cast doubt on the constitutionality of a federal role. And auto regulation remained the province of the states and localities.

The primary federal response to the rise of motor transportation came in highway building. The Federal Highway Act of 1916, appropriating $75 million to be spent on road building for five years, began a commitment that became one of the most consequential government policies of the century. By 1932, $191 million, 82 percent of all federal intergovernmental expenditure, assisted state highway construction.[15]

Would federal highway spending be a massive pork barrel, or a grand national effort comparable to the transcontinental railroad or the Panama Canal? Legislation proposed in 1911 called for an ocean-to-ocean highway along the thirty-fifth parallel, with feeder lines to every state and a right of way a mile wide, combining a macadam road for cars, tracks for electric cars, and a fast railroad. But political reality dictated rather that federal highway funds go to the states on a matching basis—in itself a new phase of American federalism. The states in turn left the bulk of road-building responsibility to counties and municipalities. A whole new realm of governance, embracing massive highway funding, accountability, and safety and construction standards, suddenly came into being. Complex new political and administrative relationships sprang up, involving the federal Bureau of Public Roads, Congress, state highway departments, and local interests as varied as stone quarries, brick kilns, asphalt plants, and materials carriers.[16]

In most sectors of the economy, the major regulatory issues involved competition, production, and distribution: the demands of competing firms, middlemen, and consumers; price and product regulation; labor relations; the relationship of "the industry" to "the public." But in the case of the automobile, by far the most frequent appeals to public authority stemmed from the physical and material harm that drivers inflicted on themselves, on each other, and on third parties. As a result the law—more particularly, the law of torts—became the area of public authority on which the automobile had its greatest impact.

After nearly a century, during which tort law dealt increasingly with unequally situated parties—employers and employees, manufacturers and customers—the classic scenario of one individual inflicting harm upon another once again demanded the attention of courts and legislatures. Automobile tort law became the chief setting for endless, never-resolved conflict between the view that personal liability reinforced the social obligation to exercise due care, and the view that the individual should not be held to strict accountability for fault in a complex, mechanized society.

By 1915, automobile-related cases were the major category in the docket of a Wisconsin county trial court. Personal injury cases stemming from automobile accidents swamped the civil courts during the 1920s, accounting for about 75 percent of the cases before the state's lower court in New York County.[17]

Yet for all the scale of the new machine's impact, the courts to a striking degree crafted automobile liability law within the traditional torts framework. As with nineteenth-century industrial and railroad development, they inclined at first not to subject an infant industry to too strict a measure of liability. Judges held that the automobile was not inherently dangerous: not to be classed with explosives, inflammable substances, vicious animals, and the like. Rather, human behavior—the actions of the driver and the victim—bore the brunt of responsibility.

As the power, speed, and number of cars inexorably increased, so did the death, injury, and property damage they inflicted. Motor vehicle deaths averaged 6,700 a year in the period 1913–1917, 30,900 a year in 1928–1932.[18] It became necessary to adjust automobile tort law to new realities. But how? By slow, rules-laden, case-by-case adjudication.

At first a driver's liability for an accident depended on clear evidence of negligence or fault. But as accidents mounted, and the courts remained reluctant to treat the automobile as an inherently danger-ous instrument, they put greater stress on the standard of care exer-cised by the driver. The inclination to hold drivers to a strict standard of liability led to a Pennsylvania law that a driver coming to a railroad crossing had to stop as well as look and listen for an oncoming train. Justice Oliver Wendell Holmes in 1927 held that if the driver could not otherwise determine whether or not a train was dangerously close to a crossing, he had the obligation to get out of his car and examine the situation more closely before proceeding.[19]

The manifest unworkability of this "stop, look, and listen" rule led juries increasingly to find exceptions, and most states did not follow Pennsylvania's lead. In 1934 Justice Benjamin Cardozo explicitly re-jected Holmes's guideline: "Standards of prudent conduct are de-clared at times by courts, but they are taken over by the facts of life." Getting out of one's car to check for an oncoming train could be not only futile but dangerous. At the same time, state laws imposed crim-inal sanctions on drivers for failing to stop at railroad crossings.[20]

Insurance came to be the solution to automobile accidents as work-men's compensation did for industrial accidents. The courts were an inadequate forum not only because of the time and expense involved, but also because of considerations peculiar to the automobile: the im-munity of state vehicles, the frequency with which the car causing the accident could not be identified, the fact that all too often the defendant had little or no property. Compulsory insurance laws spread, Massachusetts pioneering in 1925. A 1932 Commission to Study Compensation for Automobile Accidents called for a limited right of recovery without regard to fault. But no-fault was still decades away from implementation. And when it did finally come into use, it hardly ended the conflict over whether or not fault should figure in determining liability.[21]

Perhaps the most novel legal impact of the automobile was its gen-eration of issues involving members of a family. One of these had to do with the owner's liability for torts committed by family members using his car. Traditionally, the relationship between the owners and the users of equipment was defined in economic terms: master-servant, principal-agent. These hardly seemed appropriate when, say, a son took the family car out for a pleasure drive and ran into trouble. Still, the need to define some form of obligation was there, and the result was a new twist to the law of agency. A number of courts in the South and West (but not the more conservative East) developed the "family purpose" or "family car" doctrine during the 1920s. This held that the purpose—the "business"—of a family's car was pleasure; thus when a family member drove it, he was acting as the agent of the car's owner. In this way the father-owner could be held liable for his agent-son's tort.[22]

More dramatic was the automobile's impact on the traditional common law rule that no tort relation was possible between husband and wife or parent and child. The automobile posed the first challenge to the rule—not because of judicial compassion, but because of the character of auto insurance. Often an injured family member had to file a damage suit against the parent or spouse who drove the car in order to recover under an insurance policy. The need was compelling—and frequent—enough to induce some courts to begin to accept these intrafamily suits.[23]

In comparison with the automobile, the airplane had only a marginal place in early twentieth-century American life and law. Nevertheless, aviation came far and fast enough to add significantly to the rich variety of regulatory demands imposed by new technology.

Scientific American warned in 1911: "The flying machine and the airstrip have brought us face to face with new legal problems, that affect not only local conditions, but interstate and international politics as well." In fact this new invention raised familiar regulatory issues: the conflicting desires to encourage a new enterprise and to prevent or compensate for the harm it caused; and the character and interrelationship of local, state, and national regulation. Still, in the most literal sense law and public policy had to deal now with a new medium: the air.[24]

What rights did users of airspace have to the atmosphere through which they flew? To what degree did landowners have claims on the use of the air above them? How far did the liability of pilots and plane owners go? Judges as always sought answers in analogy: with the law of the sea and the three-mile-limit rule (though a federal court held in 1914 that airplanes were not subject to admiralty jurisdiction), with users of navigable streams or those whose cattle grazed on unenclosed land.

At first the courts assumed that property rights extended indefinitely upward, and that airplanes were comparable to wild animals and dangerous instruments. Thus an aviator might be liable for damage caused by the attention he attracted. In a 1933 case, a pilot who crashed into a transmission tower was charged with negligence and trespass. The court refused to accept the defense arguments that aviation still was in its infancy and that the mere fact of the accident was not sufficient proof of negligence. It held rather that the inherent riskiness of aviation placed a heavy duty of care on the pilot.[25]

The decision, according to one commentator, "synchronizes with the realization that America is no longer a frontier country in which productive activities are needed to develop latent and unlimited resources and that, therefore, the proper distribution of what we have is of more importance than the production of a surplus." He concluded that the development of aviation should be aided by grants and subsidies, rather than (as in the case of the railroads and manufacturing) by letting those who suffered from the resulting harms bear the cost.[26]

The novel concept of "property in the air" required new approaches. By the 1920s pilots had to be able to fly without running trespass risks: air routes with a clear right of way were a necessity. (The advice of an anxious parent to a son about to solo—"Fly low and fly slow"— clearly misunderstood the character of flight.) The Massachusetts Supreme Judicial Court tried to clarify the matter by proposing that flights below 100 feet ran the risk of trespass and above 500 feet came under the police power of the state. And a federal circuit court relied on the "reasonable use" doctrine to limit the degree to which landowners could interfere with the use of the sky above them.[27]

Alongside this nascent common law of aircraft rights and obligations, a public law of the air took form. First municipalities and then the states assumed regulatory responsibility. In 1922 the Commissioners on Uniform State Laws promulgated a Uniform Aeronautics Act, and by 1925 nineteen states had laws regulating civil aviation. The Air Commerce Act of 1926 (just a year before the Federal Radio Act) established federal sovereignty over airspace and a Bureau of Aeronautics in the Department of Commerce. Thus "the last 'free domain' may be said to have passed out of existence." But the argument persisted that aviation was essentially a form of intrastate commerce, and thus beyond federal law: Arkansas, Connecticut, Florida, Kansas, Massachusetts, and Pennsylvania refused to give control over local flying to the federal government. Committees dealing with the law of public utilities in a number of states held that air travel was in its pioneer stage and needed to be free of close regulation.[28]

Both state regulation and the Air Commerce Act sought "to secure individual initiative and effect a large freedom of action." The Interstate Commerce Commission was reluctant to extend its jurisdiction in this area; and whether or not an airplane was a common carrier (in the sense of trucks or buses or taxis) or a private carrier remained unresolved. But once again, established modes of regulation proved to be highly adaptable to new technology. When in 1938 a federal Civil Aeronautics Authority was created with the power to certify planes and pilots and to oversee the use of the nation's airways, it drew on a rich tradition of railroad, bus, and public utilities regulation.[29]

Electricity and Telephones, Movies and Radio

Still other new technologies became important parts of the American economy—and American society—in the early years of the century. Massive telephone and electric grids were constructed, and two unprecedented media of mass entertainment—the movies and radio—suddenly became accepted parts of American life.

Although each of these technologies quickly entered the province of big business, they had distinctive features—the nature of their product or service, the character of their distribution and marketing, their relationship to consumers—that raised new and often-unprecedented regulatory problems.

The growth of the electric power and light industry followed the classic course of big business in America: initial exploitation of a new technology by a large number of small firms, followed by an inexorable process of consolidation into a few giant enterprises. The need to provide a steady stream of electric power to an enormous number of consumers—57,125,000 kilowatts to almost 35 percent of American dwellings in 1920, 115,783,000 kilowatts to over 60 percent in 1930—made this enterprise an exceptionally appropriate setting for economies of scale. It also made the provision of electricity a natural public utility. There was, of course, the theoretical alternative of public ownership and operation; but it remained just that—theoretical. Privately owned utilities generated 92 percent of the nation's electric power in 1902, 95 percent in 1912, 94 percent in 1932.[30]

A familiar sequence of headlong consolidation and reactive public concern played itself out in the electric power and light industry as it had before in railroads, oil, and steel. J. P. Morgan & Company sought in the United Corporation, a superholding company designed to foster "close relations among the greater [electric and gas] utility systems of the East," to repeats its earlier triumphs in railroads and steel—but with a capitalization twenty times that of United States Steel. Electric Bond and Share was one of Wall Street's high fliers during the bull market of the late 1920s. There was even a devil figure who attained a notoriety comparable to that of John D. Rockefeller in his prime: Samuel Insull, the central figure in the rise of the Midwest's major electric utility holding companies.[31]

The electric utilities' use of money to influence politics, regulation, and public opinion stirred public concern in the late 1920s. Governors Gifford Pinchot of Pennsylvania and Franklin D. Roosevelt of New York made "the power trust" a prime political issue, a reprise of earlier antitrust crusades. The FTC investigated the electric light and power industry in 1928; Senator James Couzzens conducted an inquiry that led to a bill calling for federal regulation of all electric power transmission in interstate commerce. President Hoover backed the idea of an ICC-like commission on communications and power.[32]

The most pressing regulatory need was to oversee natural monopolies whose dealings with the public were essential, massive, continuous, and direct. In 1924, as secretary of commerce, Hoover worried about how to get rapid, widespread development and distribution of electric power at the lowest possible cost. The problem, he thought, lay in the fact that there were too many independent power systems— about 60,000 by one count—and that fewer than 10 percent of them were interconnected. "Unless we have a liquid flow of power into national channels of consumption," he warned, "we shall have permanently a larger cost, less reliability of service, and an imperfect utilisation of our coal and water resources." The solution lay not in federal regulation, but in power districts: groups of states overseeing the industry, with assistance from the national government. "The Government can best contribute," Hoover believed, "through stimulation of and co-operation with the voluntary forces in our national life."[33]

But industry resistance to new forms of regulation and the inertial pull of the existing state-centered structure of public utilities regulation were too strong. A Federal Power Commission (FPC) had been established in 1920 with the goal of fostering and regulating the development of hydroelectric power. However, the commission's members were the secretaries of war, interior, and agriculture, the departments with the largest claims to a stake in water power development—a guarantee that the FPC's major activity was bureaucratic infighting. In any event oil and coal, not water, turned out to be by far the chief sources of electric power.[34]

The securities flotations that underwrote the expansion of electric utilities (by 1928 they were greater than those of any other corporate group) went on with little or no oversight by state public utilities commissions. Only in New York, Massachusetts, New Jersey, and Alabama was there direct regulation of public utilities combines. Elsewhere the courts denied the jurisdiction of PUCS on the ground that holding companies were not public utilities.

In 1930 the Supreme Court "extended the jurisdiction of the state commissions to the very doors of the holding company." But this still was far from national regulation of the sort provided by Britain's new Central Electricity Board. Only after the passage of the Public Utility Holding Company (Wheeler-Rayburn) Act of 1935 could the Federal Power Commission regulate the interstate transmission of electric power. And to this day—for nuclear as for electric power—relations among private power companies, state PUCs, and federal authority are convoluted and imprecise, a fecund source of public controversy.[35]

After some halfhearted provision for private service (especially in Great Britain), the European response to the telephone was to put it under government operation: most often to combine it with the telegraph in the postal service. One consequence of joining this new technology to its natural competitors was to assure its laggard development.

The American story was a very different one. Like motor transportation and electric power, telephone service rode into American life on wings of competition. This reached its peak in 1907, when independent companies accounted for half the telephones in use. But here as elsewhere, the pressure for consolidation of ownership and operation was very great—all the more so because of the character of the enterprise. American Telephone and Telegraph became the dominant holding company in the early 1900s.[36]

Technological limits initially made telephoning a local matter, as were early regulatory issues such as municipal controls on the number and placement of telephone poles and wires. The problem of streetcars' electrical interference with telephone wires came before the New York and Ohio courts. They upheld the streetcar companies on the ground that transportation, not communication, was the primary function of the streets.[37]

But the telephone was quickly defined as a public utility, "a common carrier [of news] in the sense in which the telegraph is a common carrier, . . . [with] certain well-defined obligations of a public character." Wisconsin's supreme court in 1913 approved an agreement between two local telephone companies not to compete, on the ground that a regulated monopoly was preferable to ruinous competition. In the same year New York's Public Utilities Commission decided that local telephone rates should be regulated on a statewide basis.[38]

The manifest importance of the telephone and the rise of AT&T as a national utility spurred interest in federal regulation. In 1910 Congress gave the ICC authority over interstate telephone and telegraph communication. A 1914 Senate resolution called on the Post Office Department to do a comparative study of government ownership of telephone and telegraph systems, which led the postmaster general to recommend public ownership and operation directed by—the postmaster general. AT&T vigorously and successfully resisted. Company president Theodore N. Vail argued for regulation instead, warning: "Government administration is more or less a game of politics; and while with government operation it may sometimes be possible to have efficiency, it will always be impossible to have economy."[39]

An amendment to the Transportation Act of 1920, adopted by a party vote with little debate, committed the government to eliminate dual service and foster consolidation of the nation's telephones into a single system. By 1930 fewer than 5 percent of the 21,000 exchange points in the American network of 20 million telephones reaching 41 percent of American households were served by non–Bell System companies. AT&T assumed its dominant position with far less political controversy than did the electric utility holding companies, in part because telephone technology brought down the cost of service far more rapidly, in part because of AT&T's more skillful management, financing, and politicking. But the regulatory bottom line was the same for both utility networks: a dual system of local regulation by state PUCs and interstate federal oversight (for telephones, by the FCC instead of the ICC after 1934). Once again, a new technology of breathtaking social consequence was absorbed with relatively little fuss into the existing regulatory framework.[40]

The two great new media of entertainment, motion pictures and radio, affected the lives of Americans as substantially as the other major technological innovations of the time. And like the others, they posed peculiar and particular new problems of regulation.

By 1931 the product value of the movie industry was the third largest in the United States and the fourth largest in the world. Very much like the auto industry, it had come to rest on intense, consumer-oriented competition among a limited number of large producers. And the major studios sought to control distributors and exhibitors just as the major automobile companies sought to control their dealers.

The consolidating impulse was a powerful one, reaching its peak in the late 1920s with the formation of Radio-Keith-Orpheum (RKO), a merger of radio, motion picture, and vaudeville interests: the Radio Corporation of America (RCA), supplying technical facilities for the production of talking pictures, radio broadcasting, and eventually television; and the Keith-Albee-Orpheum (RKO) combine, which provided theater outlets and entertainers. David Sarnoff of RCA and Hollywood entrepreneur Joseph P. Kennedy played key roles in this merger.

The industry's trade association, the Motion Picture Producers and Distributors of America, headed by Will Hays, dealt primarily with problems of censorship. But it sought also to mediate disputes among its members. The Allied States Association of Motion Picture Exhibitors (headed by former FTC attorney Abram Myers) represented the thousands of theater owners in the constant litigation brought by these interests.⁴¹

In part because this was an industry purveying not steel or oil but pictures and ideas, the government was slow to respond to these developments. True, there were numerous state and local attempts to censor the content of movies, and a bill for a Federal Motion Picture Commission came before Congress in 1931. But no federal regulatory body emerged.

Instead, the industry's structure and practices were challenged in the courts. Although the Supreme Court in 1915 found the movies to be a medium of entertainment rather than one of information and opinion, unlike vaudeville or baseball it also was held to be an industry substantially engaged in interstate commerce, and thus subject to the antitrust laws. In 1917 the Supreme Court decided that the Motion Picture Patents Company was a conspiracy in restraint of trade. More successful was Paramount Pictures, a merger of three leading producers that secured national preeminence in distribution and theater ownership by 1919. FTC attempts to strike at block booking, an important part of Paramount's power, failed in the courts. But the Clayton Antitrust Act's prohibition of stock acquisitions that substantially lessened competition prevented a merger of Fox and MGM in 1931.[42]

Another fecund source of litigation was the chaotic relationship of distributors with exhibitors. Conflicts between these groups led to about 4,000 lawsuits in the early 1920s. A Standard Exhibition Contract, with a binding arbitration clause, was devised to bring order to the business. But in 1930 the Supreme Court held that the arbitration clause constituted a conspiracy in restraint of trade. Justice James McReynolds observed: "It may be that arbitration is well adapted to the needs of the motion picture industry; but when under the guise of arbitration parties enter into unusual arrangements which unreasonably suppress normal competition their action becomes illegal."[43]

Judicial policy and the explosive popularity of the movies combined to keep the industry relatively open. More than 300 companies still were making motion pictures in the early 1930s. Massive, complex litigation over patents and legal battles among producers, distributors, and exhibitors continued to be the norm. One observer summed up the situation in the mid-1930s: "The anti-trust laws . . . have been largely instrumental in preventing national monopoly of production and distribution, and in curbing joint action to regulate trade practices. But they seem not to aid the small exhibitor in his struggle against circuit competition and allegedly oppressive distribution tactics."[44] In the long run, macroeconomic conditions and economies of scale, and not the dictates of regulatory policy, determined the shape of the movie industry. The growing dominance of the major studios during the 1930s owed far more to the Great Depression than to the vagaries of antitrust.

In its rapid technological development, its breakneck growth into a mass-consumer, highly profitable industry, and its inexorable evolution from a large number of small competitors to a few large ones, radio strikingly resembled the movies. Yet its regulation followed a very different course.

Radio's dependence upon a frequency band that was a public not a private resource meant that from its beginnings the medium fell subject to government regulation on a scale unknown to movie distribution and exhibition. However, the character of radio distribution—release of its product into the atmosphere, where it might be received at will—and the nature of its output—talk, music—meant that traditional forms of regulation did not readily apply. In many respects radio was most closely analogous to public utilities such as electricity and the telephone. But to set standards of service entailed a degree of control over program content that might well violate the First Amendment.[45]

The British experience differed instructively from the American one. The Sykes Report of 1923 called for the postmaster general to license broadcasters—the same policy adopted in the early days of the telephone. The British Broadcasting Company, wholly owned by radio manufacturers, at first dominated the field. But in part because the company had an exclusive license from the government, in part because its director, John Reith, had a powerful vision of radio as a force for lifting the intelligence and the cultural aspirations of the people, public policy came to override private gain in the development of British radio. The British Broadcasting Corporation, a quasi-public corporation chartered by the crown and free of commercial interests, was created in 1927, precisely when in America the Federal Radio Act guaranteed the dominance of private radio networks. Under Reith's leadership the BBC developed its special cachet of independence and creativity. But as in the case of the British telephone system, this came at some cost in technological innovation and popular appeal.[46]

Radio transmission came into use in the United States before World War I, primarily for maritime and military purposes. The Wireless Ship Act of 1910 vested regulatory power in the Commerce Department's Bureau of Navigation and Bureau of Standards. The Radio Law of 1912 empowered the secretary of commerce to license radio operators and stations but allowed no discretion in granting licenses. The government took over radio transmission during the war, with the navy in charge of a medium still regarded as primarily a navigational aid. A bill allowing the navy to continue its control came before Congress in 1918, but failed because of interservice rivalry and congressional fear of executive power.

Commercial radio transmission and reception exploded in the postwar years. Commerce Secretary Hoover tried to take control of broadcast policy. His department staged a series of radio conferences, and he struck an alliance with RCA, the largest equipment firm in the industry. Hoover took it upon himself to set broadcasting standards and to give or deny licenses. But the courts in the mid-1920s checked this power play.

The relative ease and cheapness of entry into the industry, the rapid growth of the market, and the lack of clear federal regulatory authority fostered a spectacular expansion of radio stations: from about 8 in early 1921 to 529 in July 1926 and 734 in March 1927. Chicago, Dallas, and New York had municipal stations, as did trade associations (Boston's WEEI of the Edison Electric Institute), labor unions (Chicago's WCFL of the Chicago Federation of Labor, whose "purpose is to serve the labor movement"), churches (WCBQ—We Can't Be Quiet— of Nashville's First Baptist Church), and 129 schools and colleges.

But only 189 frequencies were available on the broadcast band, and the airwaves in large cities fell into Babel-like confusion. The resulting regulatory situation, as civil liberties lawyer Morris Ernst observed, was unique: "For the first time in history the problem of free speech becomes an administrative problem, for the Government controls the licensing of stations and the distributing of wave lengths."[47]

Meanwhile industry consolidation continued. RCA was created in 1919 as a merger of leading radio manufacturers (and with the collaboration of key navy personnel). Patent fights involving RCA, Westinghouse, General Electric, and AT&T were settled in 1925; the National Broadcasting Company, the first large network of radio stations, appeared in 1926.

A coalition of anti-Hoover Republicans, Democrats, and radio industry interests not close to Hoover induced Congress to pass the Radio Act of 1927. The bill created a Federal Radio Commission (FRC) with the authority to grant licenses but no censorship power over content. These licenses were revocable grants based on the familiar public utilities standard of public interest, convenience, and necessity.

But radio differed in basic ways from utilities such as electricity and telephones. State and local regulation, a commonplace in the other public service industries, had little relevance to a medium that so readily overleapt government boundaries. Some analogized broadcasting stations with common carriers and held that anyone who could afford to open a station should be allowed to do so. Attempts were made to pass congressional legislation enforcing this view. But a federal court in 1930 rejected the classification of radio as a public utility or a common carrier.[48]

The FRC brought the headlong expansion of radio licenses to a halt by favoring stations with the longest continuous broadcasting records and the broadest listener appeal—usually outlets linked to the developing national networks—at the cost of the smaller religious, educational, and municipal stations. Many FRC decisions were challenged in the courts, but the federal judiciary sustained the vast majority of them.[49]

By the end of the 1920s there was much discontent with this regulatory system, and considerable—and considerably justified—talk of a "radio trust." The Senate Interstate Commerce Committee held hearings in 1929–30, coterminous with a congressional inquiry into the movie industry. In 1929 the attorney general sought an injunction against RCA and several other companies, alleging that their patent agreements constituted a violation of the antitrust laws. RCA Executive Committee chairman Owen D. Young welcomed the suit as a way of getting the issue out of the political arena: like the AT&T's Vail he saw the virtues of supervision analogous to that of public utilities, concentrated in the administrative and legal sectors of the polity.[50]

But a medium as pervasive as radio broadcasting could not be so neatly removed from public scrutiny. The Federal Communications Act of 1934 stemmed in part from discontent with the FRC's failure to influence the character of commercial advertising and programming. The act replaced the FRC with a more powerful Federal Communications Commission, charged with overseeing radio, telephone, and telegraph communication.

Predictably, the regulatory consequences did not meet these expectations. Indeed, the presence of a federal regulatory agency discouraged antitrust actions against RCA or the radio networks on the scale experienced by the movie industry. The courts (still unsure of the appropriate regulatory theory under which to classify broadcasting) generally deferred to FCC decisions. And the FCC itself turned out to be a toothless tiger indeed in its licensing and oversight of stations. The combination of big business clout and the cloak of the First Amendment made broadcasting a most favored industry. Through the years—and decades—since, into the age of television, the composite of network broadcasting and federal regulation that emerged in the late 1920s has changed little.[51]

The interplay between new technology and regulation during the early twentieth century is a revealing example of the capacity of the American polity to absorb change. Motor vehicles and airplanes, telephones and electric power, movies and radio, transformed the American economic, social, and cultural landscape. Inevitably they raised a host of new regulatory problems and led to a number of new regulatory concepts, approaches, and instruments.

And yet the larger impression—the historical bottom line—that emerges from this experience is one of persistence and continuity. As with antitrust and public utilities regulation, the regulatory response to these new technologies was preservative, not transforming. It sought to encourage development and broad product diffusion through private not public means; to provide enough of a regulatory presence to ease public concern over the dangers of big business, but not to challenge the efficiencies of scale that bigness brought.

5 · Regulating Business

Along with trusts, utilities, and new technologies, the American regulatory system oversaw the infrastructure and practices of business in general. Less conspicuously but no less importantly, courts, legislators, and administrators had to respond to rapidly changing conditions in corporation law and occupational licensing; business practices as reflected in commercial, contract, and tort law; and the marketing structure of prices, products, and sales.

The result was an ever more complex, detailed body of rules and regulatory instruments, reflecting the shift from a nineteenth-century economy centered on the production of capital goods to a twentieth-century economy driven by marketing, mass consumption, and new technology.

Corporation Law and Occupational Licensing

The corporation was the instrument of choice for most substantial American business enterprises. There were 341,000 of them in 1916, 455,000 in 1926, 516,000 in 1931. But their significance went beyond their numbers. In 1904 noncorporate enterprises (partnerships, proprietorships) produced one-third of the nation's manufactured product; by 1927, 93,415 corporations accounted for 97.6 percent of the total.[1]

The Federal Trade Commission estimated in 1928 that corporations controlled almost 30 percent of the nation's wealth of $350 billion and conducted four-fifths of its business. In 1939, the first year for which such figures are available, the United States had almost 1.8 million business enterprises, with receipts of $172 billion. Proprietorships, 59 percent of this number, accounted for 14 percent of business receipts.

Fifteen percent were partnerships, garnering 8 percent of receipts. The remaining 77 percent came from the corporations that made up the remaining 26 percent of enterprises.[2]

The accountability of business enterprises, corporate or noncorporate, was a matter of widespread concern in Western nations at the turn of the century. Germany's Commercial Code of 1900 set up an elaborate system of compulsory registration of trading firms and partnerships. Britain's Companies Act of 1900 had much in common with its German counterpart. It significantly tightened disclosure and other requirements in securities flotations. It distinguished between the formal act of incorporation and what was required to do business and raise money from investors. And it tried to prevent overcapitalization, while American law continued to rely on punishment after the fact.[3]

Corporations were far more common in the United States than elsewhere, and regulatory policy focused on this form rather than on proprietorships and partnerships. The primary tension in nineteenth-century corporation law was between the traditional Anglo-American conception of the corporation as a creature of the state, and the increasingly widespread view that in a legal sense the corporation was a person. At the turn of the century, the by-now-widespread assumption of corporate personality (with all the implications of freedom from regulation that that implied) came under growing theoretical and practical challenge. Critics and defenders alike looked more to public authority than to the play of the market for support.[4]

The venerable argument over the precise juristic nature of the corporation now gave way to a new and more explicitly public, even political, policy concern: what was to be done with an institution strong enough to pose a challenge to the state itself? The laws of New Jersey, and then of Delaware and West Virginia, were revised to allow corporations to hold the stock of other firms. Out of this came the holding company, the predominant legal form of American big business in the twentieth century.

New Jersey attorney James B. Dill, who bore the major responsibility for this development, was quite frank about its intent. He observed in 1899: "Since 1875 it has been the announced and settled policy of the State of New Jersey by the enactment of laws first wise and then liberal to attract incorporated capital to the State, and by like legislation to protect capital thus invested against attacks from within and from without." The 1896 revision of the state's corporation law sought, as he delicately put it, "simplicity of organization, freedom from undue publicity in the management of the private affairs of the company, and facility of dissolution without recourse to judicial proceedings." Further liberalization took place in 1899, so that "the conduct and condition of [a corporation's] business are treated as private and not public affairs."[5]

A model business companies act, drawn up by Dill and trust expert Jeremiah W. Jenks, was considered (but not adopted) by the New York legislature in 1900. The Massachusetts legislature, out to "consider and determine whether the corporation laws of other states or countries are not more favorable than those of this Commonwealth," passed a revised corporation act in 1903 based on the "modern . . . theory . . . that an ordinary business corporation should be allowed to do anything that an individual may do."[6]

But this tinkering did not clarify the ambiguous legal position of the corporation. From one perspective it was a legal person and the embodiment of free enterprise; from another, the creature of the state and the embodiment of untrammeled economic power. A 1913 review concluded: "American corporation law has not yet been formulated with any clear purpose of fixing and localizing corporate responsibility, but rather [of] dissipating or concealing it."[7]

The antitrust movement was of course the most obvious expression of this concern. But it cropped up in more subtle ways as well. Thus in Massachusetts and other states, old fears of mortmain—of land permanently vested in a corporation—led to laws forbidding corporations from holding real estate. As with the holding of corporate securities, the trust device provided an alternative. Small-enterprise trusts for real estate and other forms of property (variously called common law trusts, voluntary associations, express trusts, or Massachusetts trusts) multiplied. More than 6,000 were created in Massachusetts from 1907 to 1911. An investigating committee looked into them in 1912; an observer in 1918 predicted that the Massachusetts trust would replace the corporation because of its freedom from regulation and taxation. But it was precisely for those reasons that the state-chartered corporation prevailed.[8]

Similar considerations worked against federal incorporation. One advocate argued that "there can be no effective corporate regulation until the Federal Government has broader constitutional power. Until then, incorporations will seek the state giving the greatest freedom if convinced of the reasonable stability of its legislative policy." Proponents held that a national common law, based on the commerce power and the legal status of corporations as citizens, provided the constitutional basis for federal incorporation.[9]

Presidents Roosevelt and Taft proposed a federal incorporation law to Congress. Some big businessmen, most notably in the state-regulated life insurance industry, wanted federal incorporation. But the interests—corporate, legal, and regulatory—committed to state chartering were too well entrenched, and federal incorporation remained stillborn.[10]

Instead, the Supreme Court continued its late nineteenth-century policy of limiting the states' power to regulate foreign (out-of-state) corporations in an increasingly national economy. *Allgeyer v. Louisiana* (1897) struck down a Louisiana attempt to keep its citizens from doing business with a New York life insurance company. In 1910 the Court voided a Kansas law that required out-of-state corporations to pay a charter fee benefiting the state school fund. And in 1917 the Court for the first time held that stopping the local business of a corporation interfered with its interstate activity. But as before, the states' taxation and regulation of their own corporations met with little judicial resistance.[11]

It was in the 1920s that the modern corporate economy, dominated by large, publicly financed companies servicing a massive consumer market, came of age. Did corporation law develop in pace with this new reality? Or did the inertial power of vested interests and established legal ways prevail?

The relationship of a company's stockholder owners to its management now became a matter of substantial concern in a number of Western nations. German industrialist Walter Rathenau observed in 1918: "The depersonalization of ownership, the objectification of enterprise, the detachment of property from the possessor, leads to a point where the enterprise becomes transformed into an institution which resembles the state in character." The English Companies Act of 1929 sought to protect small shareholders by reducing the traditional secrecy of British company practices and the power of its directors and management, as well as by tighter regulation of the issue and sale of securities. A new German Company Law in 1930, modeled on the British act, also sought to do something about the declining rights of individual stockholders and to address the problem of concentration of financial power.[12]

Nowhere did these issues loom as large as in the United States. Arthur Deming's five-volume work, *The Financial Policy of Corpora-*

tions (1920), was a monument to the steady increase in the complexity of corporation law, to the importance of corporate finance, and to the widening gulf between investors and managers. The sale of corporate securities to the public at large began before World War I and became an accepted part of American middle-class life during the 1920s. The estimated number of book stockholders in American corporations grew from 4.4 million in 1900 to more than 14 million in 1922 and to 18 million in 1928.[13]

Adolf Berle, specializing in the law of corporate finance during the 1920s, took note of "the phenomenon of one group with a relatively small beneficial interest [managers], controlling large amounts of property beneficially owned by others [stockholders]." He thought that the courts rather than the state were best situated to deal with management-stockholder issues. With economist Gardner Means he coauthored *The Modern Corporation and Private Property* (1932), a chilling account of how the large corporation became an entity subject to little or no state administrative supervision, whose control resided overwhelmingly in the hands of its managers and directors rather than its stockholder "owners."[14]

For all these changes in the character and power of corporations, no commensurate adaptation of corporation law occurred until the 1930s. Instead, the liberalization of state corporation law, evident from the turn of the century, continued. The trend, thought one expert, represented the "acceptance . . . of the notion that incorporation is a kind of modern 'natural right' rather than a special privilege." In no instance between 1915 and 1930 did the courts allow a state to exclude a foreign corporation.[15]

In 1927 and 1929 leading New York corporation lawyers revised Delaware's statutes (already hospitable enough to make it the home state of 70,000 firms) so as to further strengthen the hand of management against stockholders. There and in a number of other states (including New York) the process of incorporation was further liberalized, as were restrictions on the capital backing for stock issues. The result was a deluge of no-par stock, which freed shareholders from corporate liability but further divorced stockholding from meaningful ownership. Unlike their British counterparts, American judges and legislators did little to protect shareholders' dividend rights.[16]

It took the Great Depression and the New Deal to change the climate of corporation law. The Securities Act of 1933 and the Securities Exchange Act of 1934 imposed rules on stock issues and securities trading at least as rigorous as those of European countries. New state corporation laws imposed tighter controls. Yet in retrospect the legacy of the 1930s was the enactment of gradually developing reforms and a response to immediate, major abuses rather than a basic policy change. Stockholders were better protected but were still regarded as investors more than as owners of their companies. The "faith in publicity" that animated Progressive remedies for corporate ills remained "the predominant characteristic" of corporation law reform.[17]

Trade and professional licensing was second only to incorporation in legislative and legal oversight of forms of economic organization. Government used licensing to set standards ostensibly to protect the public; practitioners used it to control entry into and performance within their occupation. These objectives were often in conflict; but both were vital factors in shaping licensing policy and practice.

The nineteenth century saw much opposition to licensing as a grant of privilege and monopoly. But organized groups ranging from craft unions and employers' associations to professionals, tradesmen, and skilled workers busily and with growing success secured protective legislation. Licensing laws generally allowed them to define their own terms—a form of "law making by private groups" that came into its own in the early twentieth century.[18]

Medicine was the most substantial realm of occupational licensing. A unanimous Supreme Court in 1888 allowed the states to require certification for medical practice. State boards of health and local medical societies restricted medical practice to those they deemed qualified. But they did so in the face of the fact that (to put it mildly) medicine still was an eclectic field. Many state medical licensing acts specified no particular method of practice for certification. Michigan in 1899 established a Board of Regulation that included one physiomedic, two homeopathic, and five allopathic practitioners. A 1900 South Carolina law allowed homeopaths to have their own examining board. The North Carolina court upheld an osteopath's petition to prevent the state board of health from interfering with his practice—but added a good-humored caveat: "Rubbing is well enough if the patient is not rubbed the wrong way."[19]

Some states defined medical practice as "the application and use of medicine and drugs." In this view Christian Scientists, faith healers, and osteopaths were not medical practitioners and might practice without certification. New York osteopaths, seeking respectability, fought that state's exclusionary definition.[20]

But traditional practitioners wielded increasing authority. The American Medical Association was reorganized in 1901 and aggressively sought to define legitimate medicine. Not surprisingly, the AMA fell subject to the antitrust feeling of the time. Independent medical journals, spokesmen for patent or proprietary medicines (a prime object of AMA criticism), "irregular" medical colleges and practitioners attacked the association as a conspiracy in restraint of trade. The *Central Law Journal* accused the AMA of fostering "a state establishment of medicine." But when a group of Iowa doctors was charged with violating the state's antitrust law by conspiring to fix medical fees, the state court held that, like members of a union, they had the right to agree on what they charged for their labor.[21]

The modern structure of medical licensing was pretty much in place before World War I and changed little thereafter. Legislatures and courts ever more readily accepted the authority of mainstream, professional medicine—and the authority of government licensing and regulation. In 1927 the Supreme Court upheld the right of a state to forbid the practice of osteopathy in its hospitals.[22]

The licensing of other trades and professions steadily expanded after 1900. Licensing laws tended to be "friendly"—that is, designed more to restrict entry than to protect the public. But for all its limits, licensing like antitrust was a response to the problem of bringing a complex and increasingly consumer-oriented economy under some sort of regulatory oversight.

The courts continued to have trouble with the licensing of trades whose public as distinct from their commercial purpose was not self-evident. But this attitude steadily diminished. Thus while in 1901 the Illinois supreme court struck down a state law licensing horseshoers, extensive licensing of barbers came early and spread widely, in part because of the belief that haircutting and shaving were potential hazards to public health, in part because licensing served as a form of unionization, and in part because it was a useful way to drive black barbers out of the trade.[23]

The Supreme Court often judged whether or not new categories of occupational licensing were constitutional under the public interest doctrine. In 1917 the Court refused to uphold an Ohio law licensing securities salesmen; and in the late 1920s it rejected state attempts to do the same for theater ticket brokers, employment agencies, gasoline dealers, and ice sellers. But more often it accepted the fact that the service industries of a modern economy had a public importance not readily denied. And of course as trades and occupations became better organized, their capacity to press for protective licensing increased.[24]

Beginning with California in 1917, states began to license agents and brokers engaged in the booming real estate business. By 1931, twenty-six of them, accounting for 65 percent of the nation's population, had such laws on their books. Almost all were drafted by that hardly disinterested source the National Association of Real Estate Boards (NAREB) and its state affiliates. Clearly, they were "enacted in deference to the demands of the interest affected and not in response to any public demand."[25]

In 1922 the Supreme Court reviewed Tennessee's real estate license law. The old American belief in free entry into occupations still existed; one justice querulously asked: "If a man under a cloud or down and out cannot go into the real estate business, where in God's name can he go?" Nevertheless the Court let the law stand, responding perhaps to the refreshingly frank argument of Nathan McChesney, NAREB general counsel and author of the model law, that this was a business "peculiarly susceptible to acts which are generally considered anti-social conduct."[26]

Another extension of licensing-as-regulation came in response to the rise of short-term credit agencies. These served (or, more accurately, preyed upon) the ever-growing number of wage and salary earners in American cities. Most state usury laws set maximum interest rates below the market level for small lenders. Yet civil servants, clerks, office workers, and the like were under increasing pressure to borrow the funds necessary to sustain a rising standard of living. In the early 1900s an estimated 125 loan offices in Chicago had about 70,000 customers with average loans of fifty dollars. Interest rates of 10–20 percent a month were common. The loan business was extensive—and abused—enough to produce a large-scale Russell Sage Foundation inquiry in 1905.

Devices such as wage assignments and the "purchase" of the borrower's salary evaded the usury laws. Often the consequence (and indeed the intent) of these loansharking operations was to entangle the borrower in never-ending debt repayment. Although the courts raised some objections to restrictions on wage assignments and other tricks of the trade, by 1933 twenty-seven states had small-loan acts. They used credit agency licensing to justify maximum interest rates and restrictions on the assignment or garnishment of wages.

But like gambling this was a marginal enterprise, not readily subject to the limited regulatory power of licensing. During the 1930s many criminals casting about for new work in the wake of prohibition repeal went into loansharking. Only with the return of better times in the 1940s and after did the small-loan business gain some measure of respectability.[27]

An observer in the early 1930s thought that licensing had become "one of the chief wedges used to break down the barriers to . . . regulation of the economic activities of the citizens of the state." A 1929 survey of eighteen states found 1,364 different types of licenses required in 219 occupations. But this was notably superficial oversight. Licensing acts substantially empowered occupational groups to determine the membership of certification boards and to set the terms of access to their ranks. Rarely did they provide for appeal to the courts of licensing board decisions. But judges were reluctant to intervene; they feared that to do so would unleash a flood of litigation.[28]

As we have seen, licensing became the basis for state regulation of new technologies: gas, electric, and telephone service; trucks and buses; radio and aviation. The national government, too, turned to this regulatory device with increasing frequency. Federal licensing undergirded many New Deal programs: the National Recovery Administration, the Agricultural Adjustment Administration, the Securities Exchange Commission. Over time the Supreme Court accepted the use of federal license taxes to regulate (or prohibit) oleomargarine, drugs, warehouses, water power development, livestock dealers and commission men, and grain futures trading.[29]

By the 1930s licensing was the regulatory device of choice for a substantial portion of America's trades and occupations. Surely this had something to do with the fact that it served the interests of licensees at least as well as it served the public. This flexibility had obvious utility in a varied and rapidly changing economy—and in a polity so open to special interests, so ambivalent in its attitudes toward public authority and power.

Commerce, Contracts, and Torts

Regulating a national business economy of necessity went beyond the structure of companies and occupations and into the vortex of business practices and transactions: the realm of commercial, contract, and tort law.

As in the case of the law of corporations, the reality of American federalism—the fact that most of the power to regulate business resided not in the central government but in the states—deeply affected the development of commercial law. States had been adequate regulatory units for a local, atomized economy. But conflicting state laws and their limited jurisdiction became major problems as economic activity spread beyond state boundaries.

A movement for uniform state (and, if possible, national) commercial law took form in the late nineteenth century. The American Bar Association and a continuing National Conference of Commissioners on Uniform State Laws took on the laborious task of bill drafting and legislative lobbying. The first success was a model negotiable instruments law in 1896, based in large part on Britain's 1882 Bills of Exchange Act, which every state adopted by 1916. Other model acts—bills of lading (1905), warehouse receipts (1906), sales (1907), stock transfers (1909)—followed. The National Civic Federation, more ambitious than the Commissioners on Uniform State Laws, wanted a federal commercial law.[30]

But as with so many other attempts to expand national authority, constitutional problems and the diversity of state and economic interests were powerful counterforces. By the mid-1920s the National Conference had drafted twenty-nine uniform acts, ranging from marriage, child labor, and workmen's compensation to a variety of business and commercial transactions. But state adoption remained spotty; only the negotiable instruments law won universal acceptance.

The reasons were evident. Resistance to uniform economic and social policy had a well-established place in both the theory and practice of American public life. Justice Oliver Wendell Homes accurately observed that the uniform acts were not merely offshoots of local law, but an attempt to establish a new, national commercial law. And that was the problem. As legal scholar Ernst Freund noted, "The enactment of a trade code for the United States would find as determined resistance as the enactment of a national marriage and divorce law."[31]

Examples abound of the clash of interests working against a uniform commercial law. Only seventeen states had laws punishing commercial bribery by 1932. But jurisdictional and other difficulties blocked attempts to pass a federal law, even though most European nations had such a statute. Another instance: banks wanted documents of title to be negotiable instruments, so as to enlarge the range of their credit facilities. But railroads did not want bills of lading—

essentially contracts between carriers and shippers—to have negotiable status.[32]

Even the negotiable instruments act, the jewel in the crown of the uniform commercial law movement, ran into trouble. Advocates of the law held that unrestricted circulation of commercial paper best served society. This meant that the holder of the moment had to be protected, regardless of previous defects in the document. But critics argued that too free a flow of this negotiable paper fed speculation and usury, which was best checked by state laws and judicial inquiry into the instrument's origins.[33]

Meanwhile, the federal courts frequently ignored the negotiable instruments act on the ground that it was merely declaratory of general commercial law. Studies of thousands of negotiable instruments cases showed that the act was not cited in about one-third of them. The Supreme Court itself found it increasingly difficult to develop a national common law within the framework established by Justice Joseph Story's *Swift v. Tyson* decision of 1842. That unease led finally in 1938 to the reversal of *Swift*.[34]

The diversity of interests and diffusion of authority that worked against a national commercial law also left its mark on the movement for commercial arbitration. The nonlegal resolution of business disputes had colonial antecedents: New York's Chamber of Commerce had an arbitration committee in 1768. But arbitration fell into disuse during the nineteenth century. The American business environment was too diverse, competitive, and individualistic to develop established nonlegal forms of conflict resolution. There was no pre-1900 counterpart to Britain's Arbitration Act of 1889, which created a system of separate arbitration tribunals.[35]

But the costs and delays of the overtaxed American legal system, along with the general turn-of-the-century quest for more efficient instruments of governance, gave new life to commercial arbitration after 1900. By one count, 12,000 to 13,000 disputes were so handled in 1910 alone. A federal judge sympathetically observed in 1915: "It is surely a singular view of juridical sanctity which reasons that, because the Legislature had made a court, therefore everybody must go to the court."[36]

Still, this essentially private form of dispute resolution had an uncertain relationship to the law. Arbitration settlements generally could not be enforced in the courts. A much-noticed 1915 decision of the federal circuit court in New York refused to compel compliance with a business contract that required the submission of disputes to arbitration. This state of affairs led to calls for national and uniform state arbitration laws. A federal law in 1917 set up a system for arbitrating maritime and interstate commerce disputes and New York's pioneering 1920 act made agreements to arbitrate judicially enforceable and legally binding. Several other states adopted arbitration laws in the 1920s, and the Chicago Association of Commerce created a Trade Court in 1921.[37]

But as in other areas of commercial law, state-by-state variations limited arbitration's utility as a national instrument of dispute resolution. New York gave legal standing to an arbitration decision; Massachusetts refused to do so. And the federal courts remained hostile to remedies that appeared to stray from established paths of legal procedure and review.

By 1930, arbitration had a secure place in commercial practice. But it did so by becoming a variation of rather than an alternative to the existing legal system. Lawyers, not businessmen, controlled the American Arbitration Association of 1926. And the courts continued to have the last word on the scope, method, and enforcement or arbitration.[38]

The same tension, between the desire for a national commercial law and the growing diversity of interests in a modern economy, affected the evolution of early twentieth-century American bankruptcy law. The federal Bankruptcy Act of 1898 came in response to the wave of insolvencies produced by the depression of the 1890s. That statute made it more difficult for a few creditors to block a settlement. But it also tried to meet business protests that the states' bankruptcy laws favored their own creditors and varied too much in their terms of discharge from debt. And it codified the legal doctrine that the assets of an insolvent firm were a "trust fund" to be equitably distributed among a large number of creditors—an ever-more-common situation in a corporate economy. Still, there was nothing like a national bankruptcy system. Most proceedings were handled by state not federal courts. And a well-established network of sheriffs, constables, lawyers, and judges had a substantial stake in existing arrangements.[39]

Widespread uncertainty about its proper economic role also impeded the rise of a uniform system of bankruptcy. British bankruptcy had a well-defined purpose: the equitable, economical, and rapid distribution of the bankrupt's assets to his creditors. But the American version had more ambivalent goals: to safeguard commercial morality, certainly, but also to walk a fine line between preserving creditors' rights and not allowing failure to weigh too heavily on the entrepreneurial spirit.[40]

Tinkering with bankruptcy law continued through the early twentieth century—not in any clear-cut policy direction, but rather as part of the continuing tug-of-war between debtors and creditors, mediated (usually to its own advantage) by the system's lawyer-referee-trustee infrastructure. Thus amendments in 1926 to the 1898 act were designed to foster "the equal and economical distribution of the debtor's property among his creditors." These changes owed most to the pressure of organizations—the National Association of Credit Men, the Commercial Law League of America—with a stake in reducing fraud. Business interests also looked for ways to wind up a bankrupt's affairs without recourse to the expensive and time-consuming bankruptcy courts. The Association of Credit Men worked with boards of trade in the late 1920s to develop a chain of "adjustment bureaus" in commercial centers, designed to settle a "vast number of merchant insolvencies in its own commercial forum."[41]

All in all, there appears to have been little change in the character and administration of bankruptcy in the early twentieth century. The appointment of referees and receivers remained intensely political—and readily subject to abuse, as a 1929 New York City Bar Association investigation of bankruptcy practices made clear. Studies in Connecticut, New Jersey, and Massachusetts showed that almost all receiverships in bankruptcy were voluntary; that the attorney for the (usually "friendly") complainant often became the receiver; that high fees and inexperienced receivers were the rule; and that creditors generally had little say in the election of trustees of examinations of the bankrupt's assets. The traditional American view of bankruptcy—that it was as much to enable failed businessmen to start over again as to punish business failure and compensate creditors equitably—prevailed.[42]

But the social character of bankruptcy was changing. The rise of a consumer economy made personal bankruptcy an ever-more-important problem. The ways of handling this varied from place to place: wage assignments were rare in Boston and New Jersey but common in Chicago. The same economic change that increased the pressure for uniform national policy fostered a growing diversity of conditions.[43]

The Depression greatly increased both personal and corporate bankruptcy and kindled demands for reform of the system. Amendments to the national act in 1933, seeking to make it easier to avoid bankruptcy, were passed "by a Congress which wanted to do something, but . . . did not know what to do, how to do it, or what it had done." And the Corporate Bankruptcy Reorganization Act of 1934 gave companies the same kind of relief previously granted to farmers and railroads, by encouraging alternatives to the expensive and cumbersome process of an equity receivership.[44]

While economic conditions gave a new gloss to bankruptcy in the early 1930s, the conflicting policy goals of the past remained—and remain—very much alive. Bankruptcy law continues to be a battleground between fair treatment for creditors and a fresh start for people and businesses burdened with debt.

It was in the realms of contracts and torts that the law most often mediated economic disputes. These legal categories had their origins in the direct, one-on-one confrontations of a relatively simple, premodern world: between the two parties to a contract; between the person who suffered harm and the person who was responsible for it. The emergence of a national, industrial economy, and the conditions of life associated with new technology and an urban-consumer lifestyle, greatly expanded both the pervasiveness and the complexity of these fields of law.

By the early twentieth century, contract and tort law were open to two modes of interpretation. One was the traditional model of roughly coequal parties contesting a contract or a tortious harm. The other sought to adapt contracts and torts to a new world of numerous parties with varying degrees of standing: manufacturers and middlemen, contractors and subcontractors, corporations and consumers, victims and bystanders.

What Roscoe Pound called the social relation of parties to one another occupied an ever more important place in contract and torts theory. As one of Pound's disciples put it, "Today in urban and industrial communities, groups as well as individuals must be reckoned with." But established legal beliefs—in the sanctity of contract, in no tort liability without fault—persisted. The idea of a social responsibility that overrode strict contract and tort doctrine coexisted with the view that it was necessary to maintain the values of individual obligation in a mass society. Once again, old views persisted while new ones rose: modernity fostered diversity of thought and action.[45]

During the nineteenth century, contract law became a vast edifice of precedents, rules, and theory. The increasingly elaborate production, marketing, and sales arrangements of a modern economy fed this development: "New varieties of transactions are constantly emerging for which new types of contracts are required." Just as contract had a central place in the production economy of the nineteenth century, so did it in the consumer economy of the twentieth.[46]

As in other areas of commercial law, attempts were made in the early twentieth century to bring uniformity and order to the law of contracts. Legal scholars worked out elaborate taxonomies of rules and practices; the American Law Institute sponsored an elaborate restatement of contracts law during the 1920s. But no uniform contracts act emerged: the modern usages of this legal instrument were too complex, varied, and ever-changing.[47]

Contract took on new importance in the realm of public law. During the early 1900s, liberty of contract appeared to be joining substantive due process as a major instrument in the corporate (and judicial) assault on social and economic regulation. But as in the case of due process, a variety of political and legal counterpressures—not least, the police power of the states—imposed constraints. A 1914 overview concluded: "The law . . . seems everywhere to be that the legislature may, to some extent, at least, restrict liberty of contract in the supposed interest of the persons restrained . . . Complete freedom of contract is inconsistent with the necessity in a highly organized community for legislation to safeguard the public health morals, safety, and general welfare."[48]

Change in contract law was subtle, glacial. But its general direction was clear enough: the gradual expansion of acceptable breach of contract, in response to the clear imbalance of parties in a modern economy. Judges granted stays of execution; courts and legislatures voided or prohibited contracts that limited the time in which a suit might be brought, included an agreement not to go to court, or paid employees in other than lawful money.[49]

The process by which the sanctity of contract was modified to accord with changing economic realities may be seen in the case of life insurance policies. Traditionally, the rule of warranty—that any false statement by the insured voided the policy—governed insurance contracts. But by the end of the nineteenth century, millions of people bought life and industrial insurance from tens of thousands of agents working for large national companies. Strict application of the warranty rule would have wrought havoc with these policyholders' equities—indeed, would have crippled the life insurance business itself.

By holding that contested contract declarations were not warranties but only representations or stipulations, and by liberally admitting parol (verbal) waivers as evidence, the courts substantially reduced the importance of the warranty rule. Meanwhile, state legislatures passed a growing body of laws protecting the contractual interests of policyholders. And the large life insurance companies gradually came to the conclusion that it was not good business (and was a bad legal bet) to be litigious toward their policyholders. But the facts that an insurance policy was, after all, a contract, and that a public interest did lie in preventing policyholder fraud, limited the degree to which the courts favored policyholders. The result: as elsewhere, specificity overrode theory.[50]

Still, it is important to recognize how powerful, how persistent was the traditional nineteenth-century view of contract. A 1929 review of recent legal developments in Britain concluded: "The law is still in a large degree clinging to the strict interpretation method of the past which holds a man to the actual words of his bargain." But beneath the veneer of received theory, judicial practice of necessity was far more varied and ambiguous. Over the ensuing decades this trend continued, to such an extent that an eminent scholar could speak in the 1970s of "the death of contract"—or, more accurately, of the death of a coherent theory of contract law.[51]

Just as nineteenth-century contract law rested on the assumption that the courts would not interfere with an agreement unless there was clear evidence of fraud, the law of torts rested on the assumption that liability existed only if there was clear evidence of fault. In both cases the underlying policy assumption was clear: allowing people to deal with one another with a minimum of interference by the state was the surest spur to material progress.

But in torts as in contracts, it became more and more difficult to subscribe to so constrained a view of social and economic relationships. The new technologies and compacted human relations of an urban-industrial society greatly expanded the prospect of injury or loss stemming from the contact of person with person, machine, or product. In consequence, torts became the area of the law that dealt most often with the harms suffered by individuals in modern life.

Courts, legal theorists, and legislatures responded ever more frequently to the fact that injured parties might have an exceedingly remote link (spatial or relational) to the source of their harm, yet have a socially compelling claim for compensation. Similarly, fault and liability came increasingly to be seen as concepts that needed to be altered to reflect the realities of a corporate-consumer economy.

As in so many other realms of American public policy, old and new views of tort coexisted in a complex relationship. For all the sweep of technological and social change, the tension between individual and social responsibility—what Roscoe Pound called "a constant quest of practical adjustment between the two principles, on the one hand the principle of responsibility for culpable conduct, and on the other hand the principle of responsibility as a means of maintaining the general security"—remained.[52]

In 1903 a federal circuit court reviewed a long line of nineteenth-century liability decisions. The pattern: manufacturers and others in the chain of production not directly in contact with the injured plaintiff were free from liability—except in cases that involved a gradually expanding list of inherently dangerous products. Extension of this principle to defective products in general came, appropriately enough, in a case involving the automobile, the great torts producer of the new century. *MacPherson v. Buick* (1916) addressed the responsibility of the Buick Motor Company for a defective wheel provided by one of its subcontractors. New York Circuit Court of Appeals judge Benjamin Cardozo's opinion was a milestone in the trend to hold manufacturers liable for harms suffered from their products, despite the lack of a direct contractual relationship with the consumer. Although Cardozo claimed "chiefly to clarify principles and not to create new interests," his governing principle—"If the nature of the thing is such that it is reasonably certain to place life and limb in peril when negligently made, it is then a thing of danger"—had broad implications for an advanced industrial-consumer economy.[53]

In our time the courts have moved decisively to the concept of a general duty of care. A view of liability prevails today that would have seemed unconscionably limitless during the earlier years of this century. Nevertheless, concern over the social consequences of no-fault automobile liability and the reaction to huge awards for plaintiffs in products and medical liability cases suggests that tort law, like contract law, remains replete with ambiguity.

Prices, Products, and Sales

The regulatory system most directly confronted the new consumer economy in the realms of prices, products, and sales. Here basic yet conflicting policy goals—to stimulate innovation and growth yet guard against overproduction and harmful price cutting—came to a head. But these intensely modern regulatory problems arose within a structure of law and government designed to deal more with the problems of production and competition than with the problems of consumption and distribution; to make war on scarcity rather than to come to terms with abundance.

A case in point is that innocuous appliance the electric refrigerator. By the 1930s about seventy manufacturers faced classic problems of overproduction and cutthroat competition. And their marketing techniques raised a host of legal issues. Devices such as conditional sales and time payments dated from the nineteenth century. But now they functioned in a larger and more complex economic and social setting, with commensurately more complex legal consequences.

Apartment house builders, and retailers such as meat markets and florists, were the first major customers for refrigerators. Often they failed before they paid for these appliances. As a result the manufacturers were enmeshed in sticky legal controversies involving foreclosures and creditors' claims, possession and repossession. Time payments and other personal finance plans were necessary to create a mass market for refrigerators. Manufacturers made arrangements with finance companies to buy installment paper from retail dealers, but this led to difficulties with state usury laws. Litigation stretching from conflicts over sales contracts with dealers to personal injury claims by consumers completed this Hobbesian scene. One observer understandably concluded: "the list of legal problems in national merchandizing might be multiplied without limit."[54]

Price regulation was rare in the market economy of the nineteenth century. But two new issues became important in the early 1900s: resale price maintenance by manufacturers, and the threat to independent retailers posed by department and especially chain stores.

At first few doubted that producers could make enforceable resale price maintenance contracts with their distributors and retailers. True, the Department of Justice challenged one such contract soon after the passage of the Sherman Antitrust Act. But a federal circuit court sustained the agreement in 1892, and the government did not challenge resale price maintenance again for twenty-three years.[55]

During the early twentieth century increasing numbers of consumer brands came to be marketed nationally, usually with contracts tying wholesalers, distributors, and retailers to a price structure determined by the manufacturer. "Price maintenance," said an observer in 1918, "has developed in part as a concomitant of national advertising." It became a matter of substantial political and legal concern—distinct from trust control, yet, like the concentration of corporate ownership, raising old fears of unfair competition in a new form.[56]

A number of lawsuits challenged the right of firms holding patents on new products to make price maintenance a stipulation in their licensing contracts. The courts consistently upheld the validity of these contracts. A circuit court of appeals decision affirmed the right of the Cream of Wheat Company to refuse to let the price-cutting A&P stores sell its product: "We have not yet reached the stage where the selection of a trader's customers is made for him by the government."[57]

Similar policies prevailed abroad, where cartel practices were much more widely accepted. A leading British case in 1901 held that price maintenance agreements did not restrain trade, and thus could be enforced in the courts. Decisions in the 1920s involving Dunlop tires and Palmolive soap came to a similar conclusion. French law went further: it held that to cut prices in itself might be a form of unfair trade.[58]

But as large-scale consumer marketing spread, policy considerations similar to those that fueled antitrust began to take hold. The first Supreme Court caveat came in *Miles v. Park* (1911). This case had to do with patent medicines, one of the oldest (and shadiest) of mass consumer products. Justice Charles Evans Hughes's majority opinion concluded that in this instance resale price maintenance was contrary to public policy. These were commodities in the "channels of trade," and under the Sherman Act the manufacturer could not interfere with the "traffic." Holmes dissented. A fair price, he thought, would emerge from "the competition of conflicting desires" and "the equilibrium of social desires." In any event, "the most enlightened judicial policy is to let people manage their own business in their own way." Louis D. Brandeis, too, favored resale price maintenance, but for his own, familiar reasons: it would help small manufacturers compete against large integrated firms and protect them from the coercion of big mail order and chain distributors.[59]

The issue of resale price maintenance grew in intensity as manufacturers and retailers competed for profits and consumer goodwill. The American Fair Trade League appeared in 1913 to support price maintenance, the National Trade Association in 1915 to resist it. Department, chain, and cut-rate stores—growing powers in retailing—led the opposition. Manufacturers and jobbers with a stake in the market value of brand-name products, and lesser retailers and wholesalers suffering from the competition of the large retail outlets sparked the defense. By 1916, Massachusetts, North Carolina, and South Dakota had laws outlawing resale price maintenance as an illegal restraint of trade. And about thirty "fair trade" laws enforcing price maintenance came before Congress from 1913 to 1932, though none passed.[60]

The Supreme Court responded cautiously to this complex new issue. Justice James McReynolds held in 1919 that a manufacturer could set the price at which his product might be resold and might refuse to sell to noncooperative dealers, as long as there was no monopolistic intent. But in 1922—Holmes and Brandeis dissenting—the Court upheld the contention of the Federal Trade Commission that the Beech-Nut Packing Company's resale price schedule violated the antitrust laws. This encouraged the FTC to issue complaints against a number of manufacturers and distributors. In the traditional pattern of regulator's thrust and regulatee's parry, large producers began to develop their own sales networks, with retailers acting as the manufacturer's agents and the firm holding title to its product: a practice upheld in *U.S. v. General Electric* (1926).[61]

Closely related to resale price maintenance was the growing demand of independent storekeepers (weak singly, politically potent in aggregate) for checks on large-scale retailing. Several states around the turn of the century tried to impose punitive taxes and otherwise restrict department stores, but the courts blocked these efforts on due process grounds.

Chain stores—"foreign-owned, community-wrecking"—posed a greater threat. Local retailers could not match their purchasing and competitive power. Pressure for regulation to preserve the independent storekeeper came to a head with the Depression: "The feeling aroused by the sight of the rapid expropriation of the field of merchandising by the chain store is of the same type, psychologically, as the fear of the growing power of the corporation and the consequent discouragement of individual initiative, so common fifty or seventy-five years ago."[62]

From 1929 to 1931 about 80 anti-chain-store laws were introduced in state legislatures. Six passed: in Georgia, Indiana, Kentucky, Mississippi, North Carolina, and South Carolina. They either imposed a license tax on each unit of a chain above a certain number or limited outright the quantity of retail units under central control. But like antitrust, the anti-chain-store movement faced substantial legal, political, and economic obstacles. Advocates of chain stores argued that these restrictions violated the due process and equal protection clauses of the Fourteenth Amendment; and there was an obvious consumer interest in the efficiencies and economies of large-scale retailing.[63]

Some state courts frowned on the anti-chain-store laws as violations of equal protection. The Supreme Court upheld Indiana's chain-store-license tax act in 1931. But in 1933 it struck down a Florida law outlawing chains with stores in more than one county: this, the Court said, was an unacceptable classification. Brandeis in dissent reviewed the history of the American corporation—"the Frankenstein monster which States have created by their corporation laws"—and warned that the decision unduly limited the power of the commonwealth to control that fearsome economic force.[64]

As the Depression went on, ever more deeply eroding the economic position of small retailers, pressure grew for state and national action against chain-store price-cutting. The Supreme Court accepted price-fixing by a trade association of coal producers in 1933, and a New York milk price-fixing law in 1934. But it did so on the ground that the Depression constituted a national emergency. The more ambitious attempts of the NRA and the first AAA to put a floor under industrial and agricultural prices ran into constitutional roadblocks. And in 1936 the Court upheld a government effort to dissolve the Sugar Institute for price-fixing.[65]

Meanwhile, state legislatures—about half of them by 1935—passed "fair trade" laws imposing controls on retail pricing. An extensive FTC report on the adverse impact of chain stores, together with political pressure from retailers, induced Congress to pass the Robinson-Patman Act of 1936. This law extended the constraints of the Clayton Act to chain and other multiple-outlet retailers and empowered the FTC to act against quantity discounting, advertising allowances, and other practices that made things difficult for independent retailers. A further attempt to buttress the position of small retailers came with the Miller-Tydings Act of 1937, which exempted state resale price maintenance laws from federal antitrust provisions.[66]

By the late 1930s an impressive regulatory dike had been erected to stem the erosive power of large-scale retailing. But in the long run it was not possible so to contain economic change. As the economy recovered, the courts looked less favorably on pricing regulation. The chains, labor unions, and consumer groups maintained a continuing pressure to secure the pricing and other advantages of mass marketing. And in the decades since World War II these restraints have all but disappeared.

The control of products, like the control of prices, attracted ever more regulatory attention during the early twentieth century. Patents and copyrights—traditional ways of signifying product ownership—had to respond to new issues and interests. So too did trademarks and advertising, the major modes of product identification.

Patent and copyright laws, based on the constitutional provision empowering Congress "to promote the Progress of Science and useful Arts, by securing for limited Times to Authors and Inventors the exclusive Right to their respective Writings and Discoveries," were among the earliest federal regulatory acts. The patent system was much admired for the protection accorded inventors (few countries matched its coverage of seventeen years) and for the efficiency of its examiners.

But by the beginning of the twentieth century, Anglo-American patent law seemed less than adequate to the conditions of modern economic life. The spur of German and American industrial competition led to a turn-of-the-century British movement "to restore the integrity of a corrupted theory and deteriorated practice of the law." Britain's new patent law of 1907 was supposed to increase the protection extended to its inventive citizens. But dissatisfaction persisted with a system that did not appear to be attuned to the needs of modern industry.[67]

The American patent system also came in for criticism. Well-founded complaints mounted that large corporations used patents to stifle competition and to assure their control of distribution and sales. But firms, too, complained that patenting was time-consuming, out of sync with the character and complexity of new technologies. Pressure rose for structural reform, along familiar Progressive lines of centralization and uniformity. Proposals were made for a separate patent court, and for a court of patent appeals in Washington. A 1906 congressional act (supported by the American Bar Association) sought to extend the period of patent protection, primarily to give inventors a longer period in which to protect themselves from infringement suits.[68]

The most heated issue was the degree to which the use of patents by large corporations conflicted with antitrust. From one point of view a patent granted "a true monopoly," bringing corporate patentees in interstate commerce within the purview of the Sherman Act. But a patent was also a privilege granted by law. Thus it could be—and was—argued that it escaped the sanctions of antitrust, which aimed at restraints of trade emerging from the play of the market.[69]

The Supreme Court accepted that distinction: patent protection, after all, was enshrined in the Constitution. The Court held in 1902 that fixing the price of a patented article did not violate the Sherman Act. A decade later it passed on the right of a patentee (the A. B. Dick Company, maker of the mimeograph) to require purchasers to use its own ink, paper, and other accessories. Traditionally, the Court said, the law of sales "permits one who by purchase becomes owner of a machine to use it in any way not forbidden by that law. But such right of user is in conflict with the right of the patentee to exclude others from all use of the invention. Which right shall yield?" By a four-to-three vote the justices upheld the mimeograph company.[70]

A bill before Congress sought to bring patent holders under the Sherman Act by compelling them to grant licenses after three instead of seventeen years. Manufacturers, patent attorneys, inventors, and representatives of commercial and scientific organizations testified in opposition, arguing that this would stifle inventiveness. President Taft, typically, proposed to appoint a patent commission to study the situation, and the bill failed to become law.[71]

By 1914 General Electric held an estimated 10,000 to 15,000 patents and International Harvester 17,000, stirring fears that they posed serious threats to industrial progress. After America entered the war, the number of German-held patents in the chemical and other industries reinforced the view that limits should be placed on the degree to which possessors of patents could control their use. The Supreme Court reflected this attitude in a pair of 1917 decisions. One struck down the requirement that users of a patented film projector restrict themselves to specified (but unpatented) films. The other rejected an attempt by the owners of a phonograph to fix the price at which the machine reached the "ultimate user." A changing Court appeared to be more aware of the danger implicit in unified control over the manufacture and sale of goods.[72]

These conflicts over patent policy continued—indeed, intensified—during the 1920s. The major function of many trade associations was to establish and enforce patent pools for their members. Providers of new products and services such as the telephone, radio broadcasting, motion pictures, cameras, electric appliances, and automobiles relied heavily on these pools to exclude the entry of competitors and enjoy the profits of invention and innovation. But in so doing they constantly ran the risk of prosecution under the Sherman Act. In 1926 the Supreme Court allowed General Electric to fix the price of patented products but struck down the company's attempts to control their resale. Soon afterward the Court refused to review a federal court finding that the Radio Corporation of America had substantially reduced competition by entering into licensing agreements with other radio tube manufacturers. In 1931 the Court for the first time passed on an extensive intercorporate system of patent pooling and cross-licensing—in this instance, the gasoline cracking process. But since the agreement affected only one-fourth of total gas output, it found no violation of the Sherman Act.[73]

As in other areas of business practice, the advent of the Depression toughened judicial attitudes. From 1901 to 1931 the Supreme Court heard an average of two patent cases a year; from December 1930 to December 1932 it decided eleven such cases, and all went against the patent holder. Still, the overall record of early twentieth-century patent law was not of a clear and distinct policy, but of an increasingly complex, continuously uncertain response.[74]

Copyright, like patents, protected property—but property with distinctive social and cultural overtones. The tendency in the law to equate literary or artistic creation with product invention was strong. Nevertheless, copyrighted works had their own special character.

Thus—in contrast to the policy for patents—nineteenth-century American copyright policy placed greater value on access to the product than on protecting its creator. Americans could freely pirate British and other foreign writing. And for all its length—twenty-eight years plus a fourteen-year renewal—the extent of American protection was less than that of other nations, whose copyright laws extended for the life of the author and beyond.[75]

But the exploding commercialization of words and pictures around the turn of the century brought pressures for change in copyright law similar to those at work in the realm of patents. A 1903 review of "Our Archaic Copyright Laws" observed that "the reproduction of the varying things which are the subject of copyright has enormously increased. The wealth and business of the country and the method and means of duplication have increased immeasurably. The law requires adaptation to these modern conditions. It is no longer possible to summarize it in a few sections covering everything copyrightable."[76]

The courts soon confronted a new world of words and images. A federal court in 1901 extended copyright protection to *The Black Crook*, widely regarded as a pornographic work; a Boston Sunday paper was sued for $150,000 for printing the text of a current Tin Pan Alley favorite, "Daddy Wouldn't Buy Me a Bow Wow"; a federal court in 1903 and statute law in 1912 brought moving pictures within the purview of copyright. Holmes in the Supreme Court set out a broad view of what might be copyrighted. Even circus scenes used for advertisements, he held, qualified as a "personal reaction . . . upon nature."[77]

The copyright law of 1909 reflected the play of new interests and ideas. The nation's leading publishers, seeking to control a chaotic market, created the American Booksellers' Association in 1901. The association set (higher) standard prices for books, blacklisted dealers who discounted, and lobbied for a new copyright law. A draft bill emerged from two Library of Congress conferences attended by representatives of authors and artists, lawyers, playwrights, librarians, book, newspaper, and music publishers, theater managers, and typographers—the community of word and picture makers.

The statute enacted by Congress codified existing copyright law. But it also served the interests of copyright holders (authors or publishers): it doubled the renewal period to twenty-eight years and extended copyright protection to lectures, sermons, speeches, sheet music, drama and art, compilations and abridgments, and works of a scientific or technical character. Though vague in its general principles, this was "a peculiarly busy piece of legislation, crammed with details," an open invitation to continuing judicial interpretation.[78]

One thing it did not do: give publishers permanent control over the prices charged for their books. Publishers, like other producers catering to a mass market, wanted to control the retail prices of their products. They argued that copyright like patenting implied the power of resale price maintenance. Librarians and Macy's department store, a leading book discounter, took issue. In the course of a decade of litigation, the Supreme Court held that copyright did not entitle holders to fix retail prices, nor did it exempt them from state and national antitrust law.[79]

But changing technology, not antitrust, shaped copyright law in the 1920s. The sudden rise of radio posed distinctive new problems. Early radio performers often were unpaid, and of course no direct charges were levied on listeners. Could broadcasters claim exclusive performance rights "publicly for profit" under the 1909 copyright act? A few judges initially thought not. But from the mid-1920s on the courts agreed that what went out on radio was unquestionably a public performance, and that profit was indeed the name of the broadcasting game. Another issue: did the unauthorized broadcasting of a musical production infringe its copyright? Brandeis, speaking for the Supreme Court, settled the matter in 1931: "Reproduction . . . amounts to a performance." [80]

In the same year the Vestal Copyright Act strengthened the claim of authors and composers to their work in radio and the movies. It also authorized the government to become a signatory to the Bern Copyright Convention. The increasing popularity overseas of American books, plays, and movies finally overrode the traditional view that Americans gained more than they lost by staying out of the International Copyright Union.

Only a few Democrats opposed the bill: advocates of the old belief that copyright infringed on the people's right to free access to ideas and information. But facts and thoughts increasingly were products disseminated in commercial contexts, and copyright was the only practical way to connect "the Progress of Science and useful Arts" to the world of the big media and massive consumer audiences. [81]

The appearance of a rich body of law and legislation dealing with trademarks was an even more vivid demonstration that the rise of a consumer economy gave new meaning to the concept of property. Common law doctrine held that the property right in a trademark derived from priority of use. An 1870 congressional act tried to add a federal registration requirement. But in 1879 the Supreme Court severely limited the impact of the law. [82]

As in patent and copyright law, constitutional limitations, jurisdictional infighting, the clash of interests, and economic change made it difficult to provide the protection that trademarks in theory afforded. Congress passed a law in 1905 (the same year as a new British trademarks act) that tried to clarify matters by declaring that an infringement existed if a similar trademark was used for merchandise with "substantially the same descriptive properties as those set forth in the registration." But this was a "slovenly piece of legislation." And courts added to the confusion by accepting any trademark "actively and exclusively used." The result: "what Congress left uncertain the Courts have made incomprehensible."[83]

Meanwhile, the number of trademarked consumer products kept rising. By 1912, 62,500 trademark applications had been filed in the Patent Office under the 1905 law. One captain of industry declared, "I would rather have a celebrated trade-mark than a million dollar plant." The American Tobacco Company's trademarks were valued at $45 million, one-fifth of its total assets. Like patents, trademarks had become a major instrument in the creation and marketing of the consumer products that fueled the modern American economy. The commissioner of patents and the District of Columbia Court of Appeals (which acted as the appellate tribunal for the commissioner's decisions) heard an ever-larger number of trademark disputes.[84]

The states now got into the act. The California and New York legislatures passed laws providing for state trademark registration. But the United States Trade-Mark Association opposed this challenge to a national system of registration and got the California law repealed on the ground that Congress's interstate commerce power enabled it to exercise exclusive control over trademarks.[85]

As the commercial importance of trademarks grew, so did their entanglement in the law of antitrust. In 1916 the Supreme Court defined trademarks not as a form of property, but as a business practice: "The common law of trade marks is but a part of the broader law of unfair competition."[86] By the 1920s, courts generally assumed that the purpose of a trademark was not to define prior claim to a product, but to foster consumer brand loyalty. A mark of ownership had become an instrument of sales. The chief policy concern now was to protect trademarks from exploitation by competitors, while not allowing them to stultify competition and innovation.

This changing view did not produce greater legal or regulatory clarity. If anything, trademarks became more difficult to define. Some product names—Kodak, Victrola—became part of the language; others—Blue Ribbon, Gold Medal—had doubtful claims to originality or exclusiveness. Nor did their sheer number help. By 1934 some 300,000 trademarks were registered with the Patent Office, and this was thought to be only about one-fifth of the total in use.

The courts paid increasing attention to the degree to which a trademark stood for some unique aspect of the product that it represented. As such it had real commercial value and needed to be protected in a mass consumer economy. Judge Learned Hand wryly took note of a growing "consciousness of the need for breadth and liberality in coping with the progressive ingenuity of commercial depravity." The Supreme Court in 1936 upheld an Illinois ban on the sale of trademarked items at a cut-rate price. But this was far from the last word on the subject. The legal future of this instrument of product differentiation would be no less complex and uncertain than its past.[87]

As trademarks were to patents, so advertising was to copyright: an application of ideas and images to the marketing demands of a consumer economy. It was in the early twentieth century that advertising assumed a place in American economic life substantial and distinctive enough to evoke a regulatory response. And as elsewhere, that regulation had a dual character: it dealt with the way in which the advertising business was conducted and with its impact on the society at large.

Advertising grew in pace with the consumer economy that it did so much to foster. The major advertisers were the companies whose products dominated the mass consumer market: packaged food, automobiles, tobacco, drugs. By 1929 advertising costs amounted to almost 3 percent of the gross national product, twice the pre-1914 level. But influence had its price. A federal law in 1872 forbade the use of patent medicines. In 1916 the Supreme Court held that a Florida real estate company's fanciful claims did not gain legitimacy from the fact that the land turned out to be worth its price: the mails could not be used for false representation.[88]

As the advertising business grew, it turned to the preemptive self-regulation favored by other major industries. Leading admen backed a model act that held advertisers responsible for falsity even in the absence of foreknowledge or of direct harm to an individual. Fourteen states passed versions of the model law in 1913, another fourteen by 1919. The Maine and Georgia legislatures rejected it because rural newspapers feared its effect on patent medicine revenue.

Like most general prohibitory legislation, these statutes were too broad-gauged to be enforceable. During the 1920s an increasing number of state laws dealt with common, specific practices of deception. Most required that labels accurately describe the products to which they were attached. But the variety and extent of advertising, the industry's political influence, and a reluctance to clamp down too tightly on a form of expression put severe constraints on regulation.[89]

After 1914 the Federal Trade Commission made false and deceptive advertising one of its concerns at the behest of, among others, the Associated Advertising Clubs, which like other spokesmen for large enterprises saw advantages in uniform, federal regulation. By 1920, 67 percent of the FTC's workload dealt with false and misleading advertising; by 1929, 85 percent; by 1932 (despite the Depression), 92 percent. Critics charged that the FTC went beyond its mandate to maintain competition, and entered the realm of censorship.[90]

The federal courts were divided between their distaste for commercial immorality and their disinclination to allow the FTC to encroach on what they saw as their jurisdiction. Thus the Supreme Court in 1920 weakened federal regulation of the advertising business by holding that, like insurance, it was not interstate commerce per se. When the FTC issued a cease-and-desist order against the Winsted Hosiery Company for advertising cotton goods as wool, a federal court set it aside, observing that the commission was "not a censor of commercial morals generally." But the Supreme Court reinstated the order on the ground that false advertising was a form of unfair competition.[91]

Judges, legislators, and regulators appear to have been uncertain whether the primary purpose in restricting fraudulent advertising was to protect competing producers or the consuming public—objectives that were by no means always compatible. Not surprisingly, their response was halting and ambiguous. Congress's authority rested primarily on its power over the mails—tempered by fear of censorship. The FTC intervened to check unfair or improper business practices—tempered by the courts' concern lest the commission overreach its mandate. The courts wavered between their commitment to an open market economy and their distaste for commercial fraud. Here as in so many other areas of business regulation, it was evident that the rise of a consumer economy did not clarify or concentrate but, instead, complicated and diffused the regulatory role of the state.

6 · Regulating Unions

Most writing on early twentieth-century American labor history echoes British historian Norman Stone's dictum: "After 1890, class-war made the basis of politics in Europe." Thus David Montgomery declares that it is "imperative to analyze the American experience of the late nineteenth and early twentieth centuries in terms of conflicting social classes ... class consciousness permeated social intercourse outside the workplace as well as within it." The turn-of-the-century European labor movement was the great carrier of socialism, syndicalism, and other ideologies of class conflict. So too, it is assumed, the American class struggle found its natural habitat in the realm of the work force—powerfully so, in the triumph of a corporate-managerial elite over organized labor and socialism; pathetically so, in the stillborn effort to create a viable American left; ambiguously so, in a middle class torn by conflicting fears of corporate power and worker radicalism.[1]

But this perspective obscures as much as it illuminates. To reify "labor," "capital," "the middle class," and "the state"—especially in the early twentieth century, when a revolution in technology, economic transactions, and the world of work comparable to the industrial revolution was under way—is to impose a structural coherence on the social and political order that simply did not exist. This is not to deny that class, as well as ethnicity, race, and gender, powerfully affected the experience of working men and women, and their relationship with those who employed them, during the early twentieth century. But it is important to recognize that persistence and pluralism—factors that weighed so heavily in the regulation of business—had a conspicuous place in public policy toward labor as well.

New Unionism and New Management

The prevailing view is much influenced by the fact that a more radical, politically conscious "new unionism" appeared in turn-of-the-century Europe: in British craft unions and their Labour party, in the pre–World War I flowering of the German Social Democrats (SDP), in the rise of the French Confédération Générale du Travail (CGT).

There were American parallels to these developments. Much—indeed, overmuch—attention has been paid to the syndicalist Industrial Workers of the World (IWW), organized in Chicago in 1905 as an American counterpart to France's CGT. New York garment workers, boot and shoe workers in New England, German brewery workers in the upper Midwest, and the International Association of Machinists shared in a "new unionism" imbued with turn-of-the-century socialist and other radical ideology. The United Mine Workers (UMW) in 1912 endorsed the principle of government ownership of all industries.[2]

At least as significant was the tendency of unions—like the ever-larger companies with which they dealt—to organize on an industry-wide basis. "What has been witnessed in the case of industrial trusts or combinations will be witnessed in the case of labor organizations," one observer predicted. Thus the miners began to admit all who worked in the coal industry. By 1912, 631 city labor federations were affiliated with the American Federation of Labor (AFL); only two independent local trades councils were left.[3]

But even in relation to the apparently analogous case of Great Britain, decisive differences prevailed in America. British labor found political expression in an ever-closer identification with socialist ideology, the Labour party, and a policy agenda of social welfare causes such as unemployment insurance and sickness benefits. The politics of American labor developed in a very different milieu, determined by the flood of new immigrants, the explosive growth of the economy, and the distinctive character of the polity. Unlike the British Trades Union Congress, the AFL committed itself to "educate, agitate, organize" outside politics and the state. American unions had opportunities in local politics, and problems with the courts, far beyond those of their British counterparts. And their relation to the burgeoning consumer economy mattered more to them: there was no British equivalent to the American union label movement.

The early twentieth-century American work force became not

more proletarian but more diverse. This was evident in the new statistical interest in the manifold employments of Americans. A 1908 Census Bureau report on women's occupations detailed the rise not only of a female industrial work force but also of stenographers, bookkeepers, nurses, and the like. The 1910 Census of Occupations concluded that the working class as a percentage of the labor force had if anything shrunk slightly over the past forty years, from 63 percent in 1870 to 61 percent in 1910. Economist John R. Commons estimated in 1908 that class conflict as such was limited to a potential of about 6 million wage earners and 1.5 million employers and investors. The remaining two-thirds of the population—"the public," consumers— were in effect a third class of interested, and ambivalent, spectators.[4]

But even these are overlarge, unrevealing categories. Organized workers were concentrated in small industries and the building trades; on the railroads, where skill and responsibility had not yet been displaced by the division of labor; and on the docks and in the mines, where strikebreakers could not easily be brought in. The potential for class solidarity was further reduced by the fact that the great majority of unions were based on trade and occupation; by spatial and social mobility, real or expected; and by the vitiating effects of immigration and rising female and child labor.

The "New Unionism" appeared not at the cost of but in pace with expanding craft unions. The "labor aristocracy" of skilled workers maintained its 12–14 percent share of the work force; its share of wages increased; the expansion of railroads, engineering, and urban trades and public services created a mass of new jobs calling for real or ostensible skills. As in Europe, skilled workers were on the cutting edge of socialism and labor radicalism. But more often they were apolitical or supported narrowly protective, antiblack, or anti-immigrant policies.[5]

In pace with the expansion of jobs, the number of American union members rose sharply, from about 1.1 million in 1901 to 3 million in 1917. Of these, 74 percent in 1901 and 75–80 percent in 1917 belonged to the AFL. (The IWW at its peak had only about 10,000 members.) Despite its turn-of-the-century promise, industrial unionism did not take hold until the 1930s. An observer concluded in 1916: "there are in the United States today hundreds of union organizations, each practically independent or sovereign, and each with its own and often peculiar structural arrangements, aims, policies, demands, methods, attitudes and internal regulations. Nor is there any visible or tangible bond that unites all these organizations into a single whole, however tenuous."[6]

The predominant style of American organized labor was—an American term—"business unionism." As one labor expert commented, "The truth is that the outlook and ideals of this dominant type of unionism are those very largely of a business type. Its successful leaders are essentially businessmen and its unions are organized to do business with employers—to bargain for the sale of the product which it controls." Twenty-seven percent of labor actions from 1897 to 1901 involved union rules or union recognition; by 1904, the proportion had reached 40 percent.[7]

There were of course major industrial conflicts—in steel, coal, railroads—as in Britain and on the Continent. The steel strike of 1901 and the subsequent defeat of the iron and steel workers' union made it clear that the rise of big business hardly promised capital-labor amity. A similar development occurred in the meat-packing industry, where the ethnic differences between a relatively few skilled and a mass of unskilled workers made it all the easier for the companies to break a 1904 strike.[8]

But no one pattern, no single set of conditions, characterized either the American labor scene or the relationship between unions and the polity. This variety of experience emerges in three settings, each with its own distinctive interplay of unions, bosses, and politics: the anthracite strike of 1902, the bitter IWW-led conflicts in western mines and eastern textile mills, and the frequent urban labor disputes involving the garment and building trades and streetcar workers.

The explosive growth of energy needs by American cities and industries gave coal a new economic and political importance. In 1900 the United Mine Workers staged a walkout in the anthracite fields, and the employers refused to arbitrate. But with a national election looming, Republican leaders put pressure on the companies, and even the protrust *Gunton's Magazine* criticized them for refusing to deal with the union. The miners won a 10 percent wage increase and went out again in 1902. This time the intransigence of management threatened a national fuel shortage, and the federal government intervened.[9]

It is difficult today to imagine that George F. Baer, president of the Philadelphia & Reading Railroad and of the holding companies that controlled most of the anthracite mines, was not the invention of some inspired prolabor satirist. He is best known for his declaration that "the rights and interests of the laboring men will be looked after and cared for, not by the agitators, but by the Christian men to whom God in his infinite wisdom has given the control of the property interests of the country." But this was only the tip of an iceberg of arrogance and insensitivity. He once observed: "Strikes began with Genesis. They originated at the beginning of the world. Cain was the first striker, and he killed Abel because Abel was the more prosperous fellow." As the threat of a fuel shortage in the nation's large cities inevitably made the strike a public issue, Baer stood his ground: "The duty of the hour is not to waste time negotiating with the fomenters of this anarchy, but to do as was done in the war of the rebellion—restore the majesty of the law." He warned off New York's Republican governor, Benjamin Odell, from involving himself in the strike: "I do say, and I reiterate it, that we will not accept political advice or allow the interference of politicians in this, our affair." [10]

The process of settlement turned out to be different from Baer's atavistic scheme of things. The miners' leader, John Mitchell, was widely regarded as a reasonable man; investment bankers J. P. Morgan, George W. Perkins, and George F. Baker pressed for a compromise; Secretary of War Elihu Root saw to it that the National Guard was not called in; and President Theodore Roosevelt took a public hand in bringing about a settlement through an arbitration board that granted some of labor's wage demands—but did not give the union the recognition it sought. The *New York Tribune* expressed the general view: "The old doctrine that a man may do what he will with his own worked well enough when the life of the community was not dependent on what he did own, but some way or other it does not fit the case when a whole community is under one control." [11]

Gunton's worried that "the first fruits of the coal strike have been to give political respectability to socialism, and make public ownership of industry a political issue in the United States." But this missed the mark. Neither Baer-faced capital nor the miners' union called the turn. Rather, the presence of a large urban-consumer stake in the outcome compelled political intervention, which (for the time) was relatively even-handed. [12]

IWW-led strikes evoked a very different set of responses. The syndicalist Western Federation of Miners (WFM) faced intransigent management in bitter conflict infused with both the rhetoric and the reality of class war. In the Cripple Creek, Colorado, strike of 1903–04 martial law was declared; the governor called out the militia, which acted with notable brutality; an explosion killed fifteen nonunion workers. WFM organizer Harry Orchard confessed to more than twenty-five murders for the union; and onetime Idaho governor Frank Steunenberg, who prosecuted Coeur d'Alene strikers, was killed by a bomb.

IWW leaders then, and labor historians since, have tried to place these events in a larger setting of revolutionary syndicalism. And indeed IWW leader Bill Haywood met with French syndicalist and CGT leaders in 1908. But the particularities of place and people weighed as much as ideology. A contemporary observed of the savage, tragic mining conflicts in the mountain states: "The men and the descendants of men who but recently were on the far-flung frontier lines are suddenly confronted by the most complex problems of modern industrialism." The public and political response was comparably passionate—strong and at times heroic support by those closely identified with the miners, hostility reflecting both class and general law-and-order sentiment by those more remote in space or interest.[13]

No less distinctive in context and locale were the IWW-led textile strikes of 1912 in Lawrence, Massachusetts, and Paterson, New Jersey. The grievances and struggles of a heavily immigrant work force with a substantial female component, effectively publicized by the IWW, evoked the sympathy and support of intellectuals and liberal-minded members of the middle class in Boston and New York—the first of a series of twentieth-century causes to galvanize these influential groups. But IWW leader Haywood's calls for "direct action" and differences over turf, personality, and ideology that set the AFL and the Socialists against the IWW weakened the base of popular support.[14]

Yet another distinct setting for labor-capital conflict was the large modern city, where "the public" was not a vague and remotely concerned presence but an intimately involved one. Strikes by garment workers, teamsters, members of the building trades, and streetcar employees occurred not in relatively remote factories or mining towns but in the midst of the flow of urban life.

The forms that these struggles took were as distinctive as their milieus. Thus the fact that most workers and employers in the garment trades were new Jewish immigrants gave a special cast to their conflict. It allowed leaders such as Socialist Meyer London for the union, attorney Julius Henry Cohen for the manufacturers, and prominent American Jews Louis Brandeis and Louis Marshall to produce the 1910 Protocol of Peace, which provided better wages and working conditions and union recognition.[15]

Teamsters, members of the building trades, and other city workers belonged to unions that joined together to form building trades councils or central labor unions. They dealt with small or middle-scale bosses organized into employers' associations. The character of their interaction varied from city to city, but everywhere these unions had a relationship to public authority very different from that of factory workers and miners.[16]

Turn-of-the-century San Francisco was the most thoroughly unionized city in America. A wave of strikes by teamsters, machinists, restaurant workers, and others, coordinated by a City Front Federation of fourteen unions, erupted in the summer of 1901. Most were broken by the opposing Employers' Association, with the support of Mayor James Phelan. In reaction a Union Labor Party emerged, and with the assistance of the Building Trades Council Eugene Schmitz won the mayoralty: the first labor candidate to do so in a major American city. For the next decade and more the Union Labor Party was a major presence in San Francisco politics, culminating in the election of Trades Council head Patrick H. McCarthy to the mayoralty in 1909.[17]

The police in big cities such as New York and Chicago often manhandled strikers. But large local crafts unions had enough political power to secure at times what by early twentieth-century standards was a relatively level playing field. New York City's Central Labor Union was less inclined than its San Francisco counterpart to participate directly in local politics, following instead Samuel Gompers' doctrine of rewarding friends and punishing enemies. Major 1905 strikes by the city's building trades pitted the merged Central Labor Union and United Board of Building Trades against a Building Trades' Employers' Association. The consequence was an arbitration agreement endorsed by the National Civic Federation.[18]

Chicago's building trades did not fare as well. A large-scale conflict erupted in 1900 between the Building Trades Council, seeking to speak for the work force, and the Building Contractors' Council, which preferred to deal with individual unions. The weakened economic state of the industry gave the contractors the upper hand. They brought in members of the Colored Federation of Labor as strikebreakers, and after a brief struggle punctuated by violence the Trades Council was defeated.[19]

But the city's teamsters had greater success. One source of their strength was the fact that they dealt with a multitude of small team owners rather than with large firms. The owners welcomed the union because it eased the pressures of competition among them and helped them against manufacturers and wholesale merchants who did their own hauling. Teamsters and owners entered into mutually beneficial arrangements, establishing a pattern in the industry that persists to this day. Employers and union business agents created an arbitration board. The employers' chief representative settled more than 400 strikes by bribing union leaders—and taking "fees" of from $100 to $1,000. Out of this came relative labor peace and a marked improvement in teamster hours and wages—but at the price of higher cartage costs and reduced milk deliveries. Muckraking journalist Ray Stannard Baker commented on the result from the consuming public's perspective: "We have been sighing for labor and capital to get together; we have been telling them that they are brothers, that the interest of one is the interest of the other. Here they are together; are we any better off?"[20]

Streetcar strikes had the most immediate and widespread impact on urban life, and hence were most likely to evoke a public—and political—response. During San Francisco's 1902 transit strike Mayor Schmitz used armed detectives to keep the companies from manning their cars. When Houston's streetcar company tried to entice black riders, its employees went out, with much public support—though without success. Popular hostility to a transit monopoly in St. Louis helped strikers there in 1900: more than 700 retail merchants supported their demand for the right to unionize.[21]

But as the century progressed, streetcar strikes became more violent, and public support was not so readily secured. A 1910 walkout in Columbus, Ohio, saw cars dynamited, several shootings, and the calling in of the National Guard. Although the police and the mayor showed some sympathy for the strikers, the company successfully refused to accept a closed shop or to submit to arbitration. Transit strikes in Philadelphia (1910) and New York (1916) had similar characteristics and similar results.[22]

The view of American labor that stresses the importance of its syndicalist/socialist element dwells also on the rise of a new, sophisticated corporate capitalism in the early 1900s. This "new management" talked of labor-capital amity and welfare capitalism. Along with the turn-of-the-century consolidation of large enterprise there appeared a rhetoric of labor-capital harmony, based not on the iron law of the market but on the rationale of managerial capitalism. As business-man-turned-Republican-politico Mark Hanna put it, "The trusts have come to stay. Organized labor and organized capital are but forward steps in the great industrial evolution that is taking place." Samuel Gompers of the AFL had a similar—though more adversarial—view: "Labor tends to specialize under the trusts, and thus its productive power may be increased . . . In this era of trusts it may be said that labor represents *organized numbers* opposed to *concerted power.*"[23]

The National Civic Federation was the most conspicuous exponent of this new view of labor-capital relations. Its Industrial Department encouraged representatives of organized capital and labor to work out their differences through collective bargaining: the first—though private—attempt at an approach to labor relations that ultimately took public form with the Wagner Act's National Labor Relations Board. Civic Federation leaders supported organized labor and collective bargaining as an alternative to state socialism—a view shared by Gompers and the mine workers' John Mitchell. By one estimate, twenty-six national or district collective bargaining agreements were forged or renewed between 1898 and 1905.[24]

But it soon became evident that the rise of big business did not bode well for unions or for more sophisticated labor-management relations. After the relatively broadminded Mark Hanna passed from the scene in 1904, the National Civic Federation came to be dominated by the more viscerally antiunion Ralph M. Easley. As was so often the case in early twentieth-century America, rapid social and economic change did not necessarily lead to a comparable shift in *mentalité*.

United States Steel may have been the model of a modern corporation, but its labor policy belonged to an earlier day: "we are unalterably opposed to any extension of union labor." Far from entering into an understanding with the Amalgamated, the leading steel union, Big Steel set out to—and did—break it. The union's membership plummeted from 14,635 in 1900 to 4,318 in 1912. A number of other large companies—National Biscuit, General Chemical, Pressed Steel Car, new combines in cordage, rubber, whiskey, salt—also refused to recognize union labor. Labor's experience with American Tobacco led to the conclusion that "a strong union of unskilled labor is almost impossible." Western Union broke a 1907 strike by the Commercial and Telegraphers' Union in part by introducing mechanical telegraphic equipment.[25]

Atavistic antiunionism coexisted quite readily with the precepts of scientific management. As the movement's leader Frederick W. Taylor put it, "Scientific management rests upon the fundamental assumption that a harmony of interests exists between employers and workmen. It is therefore organized for peace, while trade unionism is organized for war . . . Scientific management rests upon the assumption that the welfare of all demands ever increased efficiency and output; trade unionism is committed to the limitation of output." The *New Republic*, though attracted to scientific management, conceded that efficiency engineers tended not to see workers as citizens or even as persons. But only twenty-nine firms formally instituted Taylorism from 1910 to 1917. And another new approach to labor relations, the mix of company unions and benefits that came to be known as "welfare capitalism," fared little better. No more than a handful of firms attempted this form of suasion before World War I.[26]

Instead, a more traditional resistance to unionization and the closed shop remained the characteristic employer approach to labor relations. Initially, firms of middling size were the most forceful advocates: they induced the National Association of Manufacturers in 1903 to shift its emphasis from encouraging foreign trade to lobbying for the open shop. NAM president David M. Parry declared in 1904: "The key-note of the open-shop plea is 'liberty.' The term has an American ring. It savors of freedom for the employee as well as the employer." In 1909 his successor, John Kirby, Jr., accused the American labor movement of being "in rebellion against constitutional government."[27]

Employers' associations, initially designed to work out agreements with unions, turned increasingly to legal and political activity. The American Anti-Boycott Association emerged as an active pressure group, and a number of collective bargaining agreements were ended in 1907–1909. The National Founders' Association was a typical employers' organization made up of about 500 manufacturers of cast iron specialties. In 1904 it abrogated an 1898 arbitration agreement with the industry's union in a clash over workshop rules, the hiring of non-union help, and apprentice training. The association issued certificates of loyalty to "those men who had been faithful to their employers in time of labor troubles," thereby creating a "somewhat permanent force of strikebreakers." After 1904 it concentrated on developing a more permanent nonunion work force and joined with other employers' groups to oppose anti-injunction laws, wages and hours legislation, and workmen's compensation.[28]

For all the turn-of-the-century transformation in the structure of the American economy, neither a more diverse work force nor a more consolidated management underwent significant change in the way in which they dealt with each other. Neither the socialist nor the corporatist models attained more than a marginal place in American labor-capital relations. The same was true of the polity. The issues raised by a rapidly changing economy were handled in traditional ways by the traditional instruments of the American state: its courts and its parties.

Labor, Law, and Politics: The Progressive Years

Organized labor's most important contact with the American polity came not in the legislative, administrative, or even political realms, but in the courts. That experience was a deeply unsatisfying one, in good part because of the inborn hostility of the judiciary. But there was more to it than that. Post-1900 American labor law was a complex mix of class bias and the application of common and constitutional law.

Judging unions as associations—weighing their rights and responsibilities toward their members, their opponents, and the public—raised legal problems not unlike those posed by the trusts. As we have seen, antitrust cases obliged the courts to confront old issues of monopoly and restraint of trade in new economic and social contexts. Similarly, when the courts had to pass on the legitimacy of strikes, picketing, boycotts, the closed shop, and unions themselves, the antiunion predilections of most judges intermixed with the tension between old values and new realities that characterized the public life of the Progressive era.

Unions might reasonably have expected to find more congenial ground in the political system; and so—to some degree—they did. But here too inherited characteristics of American public life—federalism, weak government, the individualist creed, the dominance and diversity of the major parties—worked with the power of organized capital against their interests. By the time of the Great Depression, organized labor was a less significant presence in American public life than in the major European nations—not because it faced greater class hostility, but because it had to make its way in a polity whose persistence and pluralism posed powerful obstacles to the representation of labor's group interest.

Other nations, too, had to reconsider the place of unions in the social order after 1900. But only in Britain did the courts play a significant role; and in that country politics and legislation intervened much earlier and more substantially than in the United States. Unions had little standing in British law until the Trades Disputes Act of 1871 backhandedly defined them as "such a combination . . . as would, if this Act had not been passed, have been deemed to have been an unlawful combination by reason of some one or more of its purposes being in restraint of trade." The courts then determined which union acts were acceptable and which were not. The judges' social leanings led them to impose harsh constraints on British unions. And as in the United States, labor decisions became a substantial political issue.

British and American courts often judged the activities of labor organizations and large companies alike by the measuring rod of restraint of trade. In both cases, thought one commentator, "persuasion by business pressure is a new form of coercion from which the law must protect all classes of society." The Liberal historian A. V. Dicey saw in British labor cases a tension between freedom of association and individual liberty similar to those in the conflict over church and state in France, and over the trusts in the United States.[29]

British courts permitted companies to engage in restrictive cartel practices as long as these were sanctified by contract. In *Allen v. Flood* (1898) they even allowed a union to pressure an employer to fire nonunion men doing piecework: without a contract, the dismissed workers had no grounds for damages. But the decision left open just how freely unions could engage in strikes and picketing under other conditions.[30]

The *Taff Vale* decision of 1901 made it clear how narrow was that opening. Here the union, in support of a Welsh railroad strike, sent an agent to persuade men not to work. The court found this to be an illegal act: the union bore responsibility for what its agent did. What was more, it banned picketing that consisted in "watching and besetting" the property of a struck company, and thus threatened to make an effective strike almost impossible. Two weeks later *Quinn v. Leathem* struck at a union boycott. The members of a Belfast butchers' union refused to prepare meat for a nonunion shop. The court held this to be an unlawful interference with other employees' contractual relations.[31]

These cases had substantial consequences: "effective picketing was denied organized labor; effective use of the strike as a weapon in strengthening the union and in securing advanced working conditions as to wages and hours or labor was rendered uncertain and precarious ... activities of trade unions were seriously crippled by the drain on their treasuries in combating civil actions arising out of strikes and in paying damages to employers and discharged non-unionists." *Taff Vale* alone cost the union an estimated £50,000. In response to the ensuing outcry and to the growing political voice of labor, the Liberals in 1906 enacted a new Trade Disputes Act. It legalized peaceful picketing and inducing workers under contract to strike, and freed unions from liability for the acts of their agents.[32]

Labor conflicts worsened in pre–World War I Britain, fed by a rising cost of living that outstripped wage increases and by growing working-class consciousness and organization. Major railway, mining, and dock strikes led to fear that syndicalism was taking hold, and to proposals for nationalization to ensure decent wages and avoid strikes in key industries.

But the courts marched to a different drummer. The *Osborne* judgment of 1910 led to a storm of protest even larger than the response to *Taff Vale*. Equating unions with joint-stock and other incorporated associations, the *Osborne* judges held that compulsory levies on union members for political purposes were illegal. A class-bound legal system, dedicated to protecting individual liberty and property, was reluctant to accept unions as full-fledged participants in the economy. And the fact that unions had many of the attributes of incorporated bodies, yet in legal terms were closest to being unregistered voluntary associations, made it difficult to deal with them in a common law context without explicit legislative guidance.[33]

For a season the *Osborne* judgment became a touchstone issue in British politics. A cabinet memorandum rhetorically asked:

> Are we to admit the demand of Trade Unions, in regard to religion, foreign affairs, treaty rights, Naval and Military services, the character of national recreations, the State control of children, the distribution of wealth, the obligation of private property, the nationalisation of the means of production, etc., that all their members should be compelled to contribute to a fund to elect Members of Parliament who shall on these issues record votes according to the decision of the bare majority of the members of their Unions?

To do so, it warned, would "sap all civil and political liberty among the organised labour classes." The Trade Union Congress by a vote of

1,717,000 to 13,000 called on Parliament to reverse the decision. Ramsay MacDonald of the young Labour party saw in it evidence of an unholy alliance of capital, a procapital state, and unresponsive parties. Post Office head Sydney Buxton warned the cabinet: "It is generally recognized now that industrial disputes are not merely the concern of the parties who are immediately involved, and the question is not whether the state should interfere more in trade disputes, but what form their interference should take."[34]

The Liberal majority, intensely aware of the need to try to stem the flow of working-class votes to the Labour party, resolved the debate in 1913. That year's Trades Union Act allowed unions to maintain separate political funds. Once again the exigencies of politics and British parliamentary supremacy moved labor issues from the courts to the legislature.

The powers and responsibilities of unions, the extent of their capacity to strike, picket, and boycott, also figured prominently in early twentieth-century American labor law. As in Britain, union-management agreements were regarded not as social compacts but as contracts between parties—with legal consequences generally unfavorable to the union. The Sherman Antitrust Act, with its legislative sanction against conspiracies in restraint of trade, added a potent weapon to the judges' antiunion arsenal.

The growing assertiveness of unions and the flowering of judicial contractualism after 1900 made the courts a major forum for labor-capital conflict—one weighted heavily against the unions. Judges equated "abuse of process" with "interference with contract." A typical pronouncement was that "every one is perfectly free to bring his capital, or his labor, into the market on such terms as he may deem best." A New York decision struck down a law penalizing employers who forced their employees to enter into yellow-dog contracts, on the ground that this did not affect public health, safety, or morals and thus was beyond the state's police power. Opinions were peppered with near-caricatures of judicial union-bashing: "There is and can be no such thing as peaceful picketing, any more than there can be chaste vulgarity, or peaceful mobbing, or lawful lynching."[35]

Still, a growing diversity of issues and legal philosophy made American labor law more than an antiunion orgy. Thus the closed or union shop—a matter of great concern to American as to British unions—attained some measure of legal recognition. Most state courts, wedded to the principle that workers could freely dispose of their labor, initially thought otherwise. With the conspicuous exceptions of New York, Indiana, and New Jersey, they denied the authority of *Allen v. Flood,* the British decision that upheld the right of union workers to strike rather than work with nonunion men. Illinois and Wisconsin judges in 1904 banned all closed-shop agreements. And when the Massachusetts legislature in 1912 considered a law giving legal rights to unions similar to those of the 1906 British Trade Disputes Act, that state's Supreme Judicial Court unanimously advised that this would violate the Massachusetts constitution and the equal protection clause of the Fourteenth Amendment.[36]

But as the Industrial Commission of 1900–01 observed, there was "beyond question, much force in the argument of the union men in defense of their attempt to exclude others from employment." During the early years of the century the courts interpreted such labor agreements in a variety of ways: as nonbinding memoranda on current practices; as implying moral obligations; as a special form of legal compact; and as contracts. By the early 1920s, refusal to work with nonunion labor had won widespread judicial acceptance.[37]

Nineteenth-century American law, committed to individual rights and inclined to view the doctrine of conspiracy as a suspect statist concept, had more readily accepted the right to strike than its British counterpart. But by the early 1900s the techniques employed by unions—picketing, boycotting (the AFL called for 408 boycotts in twelve years)—came to be more at issue than the right to strike itself. The lack of state and national legislation along the lines of Britain's 1906 Trades Disputes Act, and the growing resort to litigation by organized employers, fed federal judicial intervention.[38]

That intervention usually took the form of responding to an employer's appeal for an injunction, aimed not at a strike per se but at picketing and boycotting. Developed by late nineteenth-century American courts as a way of blocking strikes, the labor injunction by the early twentieth century had become an essentially administrative device through which the courts regulated labor-capital conflict. It "enabled judges to punish by criminal process such concerted conduct as seemed to them socially oppressive or undesirable, even though the actual deeds committed constituted themselves no crime." Social conservatism and judicial amour-propre thus nicely conjoined. Supreme Court Justice David Brewer observed: "To restrict the power of injunction would be to return in the direction of barbarism."[39]

Every once in a while a union got an injunction vacated; and in the course of a bitter Omaha strike in 1903 a group of unions sought a sweeping counterinjunction against the local businessmen's association. But almost always injunctions were aimed at union strike activity; and almost always they were granted.[40]

The courts' abuse of the injunction evoked widespread criticism. *Gunton's Magazine,* noting that a West Virginia federal judge sent six union men to jail merely for speaking to striking miners, warned that enjoining free speech "is really converting the court into an enemy of labor . . . We can afford to take many chances with an indiscreet use of freedom rather than risk the danger of arbitrary restriction." Conservative legal scholar Frederick J. Stimson feared that the courts were turning the injunction into an instrument of "equity government" and warned that the judiciary was not competent to take on executive functions.[41]

Opposition to labor injunctions had pride of place on the AFL's political agenda from the 1890s on. The Federation formally brought the issue to Congress with a call in 1906 for a federal anti-injunction bill. Its passage became the chief legislative goal of the AFL. Gompers warned: "Association is the very essence of our modern existence and progress"; the courts now posed the greatest threat to labor's capacity to organize. The Federal Judicial Code of 1910 restricted the injunctive power of judges sitting alone. State anti-injunction laws spread, helped along by union campaigns such as those in Kansas (1913) and Massachusetts (1914). But the Bay State's Supreme Judicial Court found the law unconstitutional in 1916.[42]

The fact that the legal status of unions and the regulation of their behavior lay primarily within the purview of the states made national labor policy in the British mode a legal and political impossibility. Instead, a patchwork of legislative and legal practices prevailed. Thus the complexities of federalism led to a decade-long struggle between courts and legislatures over whether a state could determine the wages and hours of its private contractors. New York's Court of Appeals in 1901 denied the state that power; the Pennsylvania and Missouri courts followed suit; but judges in Kansas found otherwise. Finally, a constitutional amendment and enabling legislation induced the New York court to reverse itself.[43]

Whether or not unions might be incorporated was an important issue. Unions sometimes assumed that with incorporation they might be less vulnerable to injunctions. But employers—and courts—saw in that legal status a greater liability for breaches of contract or tort. By

1904 ten states (including Michigan, Ohio, and Pennsylvania) had extended the right of free incorporation to unions; New York and New Jersey allowed it for specific purposes; elsewhere its status was unclear. In addition, seven states exempted unions from trust and price control prohibitions; eight exempted them from the law of conspiracy. At the same time, a growing number of commonwealths restricted specific union practices such as the expulsion of members and boycotting. And the common law of contract and property—categories into which most labor issues fell—continued to be the province of the courts.[44]

Supreme Court decisions heightened the conflict between labor and law. *Adair v. U.S.* (1908) voided the portion of the 1898 Erdman (Railway Labor) Act that prohibited railroads from firing employees for joining a union. *Loewe v. Lawlor* (1908), the Danbury Hatters case, held that a secondary boycott was an illegal restraint of trade, for which the union was liable under the Sherman Act. *Gompers v. Bucks Stove* (1911) found the head of the AFL subject to criminal contempt for ignoring an antiboycott injunction. *Coppage v. Kansas* (1915) invalidated a state law forbidding yellow-dog contracts, as Adair had done with a federal statute. And *Hitchman Coal and Coke v. Mitchell* (1917) upheld an injunction forbidding the UMW from trying to induce miners who had signed such contracts to join the union.[45]

These cases added up to a powerful judicial assault on the legal standing and the most potent weapons of the American labor movement. They stirred a political furor comparable to that raised by their British counterparts. But the American legislative branch proved to be far less responsive to labor's demands for relief—in part because the political power of American labor was more diffuse, and in part because these decisions rested on a much more tenacious and deeply-rooted base of reservations as to the power of the state.

Adair was the work not of one of the Court's Bourbons but of John Marshall Harlan, its most liberal member. His position rested less on antiunion predilections than on a principled discomfort with the threat that national authority posed to personal rights. At the same time Richard Olney, who as Cleveland's attorney general in the 1890s had broken a major railway union strike, criticized the decision, not out of a newly discovered sympathy for unions, but because he thought that strong unions and strong corporations were needed in a national economy.[46]

The Danbury Hatters case involved a national campaign for a closed shop, which included a secondary boycott of firms dealing with non-union hatmakers. This, said the Court, constituted an illegal restraint of interstate commerce as defined—and outlawed—by the Sherman Antitrust Act. The decision opened the door to suits for triple damages against individual members of the union. As late as 1917, a federal district court ordered the sale of the homes of 140 Danbury Hatters employees to satisfy a $250,000 judgment.[47]

Bucks Stove dealt with a similar situation and had an even more political cast. James W. Van Cleave, the company's president, headed the National Association of Manufacturers, and Gompers himself was the chief AFL defendant. Van Cleave fired union men in the course of a labor dispute, and the AFL called for a boycott of his firm's products. In the ensuing litigation, 1904 Democratic presidential candidate Alton B. Parker represented the AFL. He argued that the federal district court's antiboycott injunction interfered with freedom of speech and press. But only the flagrant bias and technical errors of the federal district judge handling the case (who announced that the issue was "between the supremacy of law over the rabble or its prostration under the feet of the disordered thing" and enjoined distribution of *The Federalist* along with "We Don't Patronize" and "Unfair" lists) ultimately kept Gompers and his associates from going to jail.[48]

Organized labor looked on *Danbury Hatters* as "the American Taff Vale decision" and sought relief from the legislature. Even the National Civic Federation supported a bill exempting unions from the Sherman Act. In theory the Clayton Antitrust Act of 1914 did this. But the courts held that the Clayton Act only defined existing union rights; it did not create new ones. Undeterred, the Supreme Court applied the antitrust law to unions eighty-three times by 1928—18 percent of all Sherman Act cases to that date. The Clayton Act also confirmed the broad injunctive power of the equity courts, and private injury suits by employers against unions flourished.[49]

There is a doctrinal rigidity in the courts' labor decisions that is not apparent in other categories such as business regulation or even social welfare. In part, of course, this stemmed from a pervasive hostility to unions in the social air that most judges, and indeed most middle- and upper-class Americans, breathed. But unions also suffered because they were at heart collective associations making their way in a legal system suffused with a formalist commitment to the precepts of contractual individualism. Thomas Reed Powell observed, "We are not

likely to get a satisfactory solution of the problem of collective bargaining through the jurisprudence of abstract conceptions."[50]

The British response—legislation that legitimated the unions' legal
and corporate persona—was not readily accessible in a polity without
a labor party and with a strong tradition of judicial autonomy. The
same forces of persistence and pluralism that fended off an American
corporatism worked against the politics of social democracy.

Labor or socialist parties had an increasingly important place in the
politics of prewar Britain, France, and Germany. But a national labor
party in the United States remained as remote as ever. One reason was
the winner-take-all constitutional ground rules for national politics
and the broad appeal of the major parties. And American labor itself
was too diverse—in work, locale, social setting, religion, and ethnicity—to coalesce politically. Socialist William E. Walling concluded:
"The labor movement in this country has taken the shape of a business organization instead of a political machine, not because labor
fears to go into politics, but because the game does not seem worth
the candle."[51]

This is not to say that organized labor had no place in American
politics. But—like the unions themselves—the politics of labor focused on specific goals and grievances, and not on the broad programs
favored by socialists. Interest-based labor politics took form during
the late nineteenth century, when union labor sought, with substantial success, the restriction of prison-made goods, contract labor, and
Oriental immigration. This was a protective, preservationist agenda
very much like that of the dairy farmers who secured antioleomargar-
ine legislation in a number of states.[52]

A rising labor political consciousness was evident in state and local
politics around the turn of the century. In 1902 Eugene Schmitz of the
San Francisco musicians' union, the teamsters' union leader in Des
Moines, a switchman in Ashtabula, Ohio, and printers in Sioux City
and Yonkers won their cities' mayoral elections. The Connecticut
towns of Hartford, Bridgeport, Ansonia, and Derby elected union leaders as Democratic mayors; in 1906 Knights of Labor chief Terence
Powderly became mayor of Scranton, and Milwaukee and New York
sent union men to Congress.[53]

But the pressures working against a sustained and significant "labor
vote" could be seen in Philadelphia's November 1905 municipal election. This was a prototypically Progressive contest, in which a Fusion

good government ticket defeated the Republican machine by a large majority. The reformers got much labor support. But more important was the lack of political cohesion among workingmen. The Central Labor Union backed "its friends" in the GOP machine; and public service workers feared the loss of their jobs if the organization fell. Estimates of worker support for the Fusion ticket ranged downward from four-fifths of the textile workers to two-thirds of the iron and printing trades, half of the socialists, one-third of the railroad men and building trades, a minority of garment workers, longshoremen, and teamsters, and one-third of black workers. Occupational, religious, and ethnic interests overwhelmed class identity.[54]

In the United States as elsewhere, the conditions of modern industrial life fostered greater labor interest in national policy and politics. But its form reflected the peculiar conditions of American public life. Workers substantially divided in their party identifications, the product of a complex mix of culture and economics. Thus the Railroad Brotherhoods, caught up in the national economy, and workers in tariff-protected industries such as glass and woolens tended to be Republican; but so too might they be on grounds of ethnicity and region. Teamsters and others in urban trades, especially in Democratic cities such as New York and Boston, were largely Democratic; they also were largely Irish. It has been proposed that on a more general level the Democrats attracted AFL-style business unionists, the Republicans unskilled, immigrant industrial workers. This pattern suggests how blurred was the correlation between class consciousness and party ideology.[55]

Nevertheless, organized labor did make a mark on national party politics. The AFL Executive Council recommended in 1906 that local and federated unions secure the nomination of sympathetic candidates for Congress. It drew a lesson from the election that year of fifty-four trade unionists to Parliament: "If the British workmen with their limited franchise accomplished so much by their united action, what may we in the United States not do, with universal suffrage?" In the fall election, the AFL circulated a list of blacklisted congressmen and claimed (on shaky evidence) that this helped to reduce the GOP's House majority.[56]

In March 1906 the AFL's Executive Council sent "Labor's Bill of Grievances" to the president and Congress. It included violations of the federal eight-hour law in the construction of the Panama Canal, failure to exclude undesirable immigrants, ineffective enforcement of the Chinese exclusion law, inadequate protection of American seamen, judicial abuse of the injunction, the composition of the House Labor Committee, and denial of the right of petition to government employees. Of the 123 congressmen who replied, 81 approved wholly or partially; only 3 rejected the list.[57]

The AFL's alliance with the Democrats steadily grew. The party's 1908 platform had an anti-injunction plank; and Republican candidate William Howard Taft drew fire for the labor injunctions he had issued while a federal judge. William Jennings Bryan won the AFL's endorsement—its first of a presidential candidate—in that year. So did Woodrow Wilson in 1912, despite Progressive party candidate Theodore Roosevelt's strong appeal to workingmen. But major unions such as the typographers refused to go along with the AFL position, and Eugene Debs's Socialist candidacy attracted many union members. The AFL's 1912 membership of 1.8 million amounted to 12 percent of the popular vote—divided as it was, not enough to influence either major party profoundly. A "labor group" in Congress did become more visible after the Democrats took control of the House in 1910 and Wilson won the presidency in 1912. Legislative victories followed: the Clayton Act's (apparent) exemption of unions from the Sherman Antitrust Act; eight-hour laws for government and railroad employees; a national employment bureau; a literacy test provision for immigrants.[58]

The alliance between the AFL and the Democrats is supposed to have had even larger policy consequences, turning the party away from social democracy and a welfare state (to say nothing of socialism) and toward the protectionist broker state approach of the New Deal. Samuel Gompers, head of the AFL and the major American labor leader of his time, is the central figure in this story. While his British counterpart Keir Hardie identified himself with the fortunes of the Labour party and embarked on a parliamentary career, Gompers followed a very different path. He disdained a separatist, Socialist labor politics; and for this, critics of the left then and since have dismissed him as little better than a running dog of American capitalism, the Booker T. Washington of American labor. And it is true that Gompers had less faith than did many of his Socialist opponents that the American state might be weaned from capitalist control. He believed (not without reason) that labor's best hope lay in its ability to act as an organized pressure group. He had his share of racist and anti–new immigrant prejudices; and in this he reflected the views of his AFL unions.[59]

But although the character of early twentieth-century American life heightened workers' political consciousness, it did not necessarily raise their class consciousness. Rather, the increasing variety of forms and conditions of work, and the spread of a national culture, fed the affective power of other forms of identification. The flood of new immigrants eroded class solidarity: "Ethnic heterogeneity enormously complicates the situation for all parties concerned, but especially for the working classes themselves." Jane Addams and prolabor priest John A. Ryan worried about boycotts, the closed shop, and other restrictive union causes, when access to work was the primary need of the newcomers.[60]

Most organized labor, like most organized capital, resisted state intervention in labor disputes. Thus after pioneering French (1892) and British (1986) laws provided for public arbitration boards, the United States followed with the Erdman Act of 1898, which set up arbitration machinery for controversies involving railroad labor and management. But by 1913 its record was thin: sixty-one interventions and forty settlements, thirty-six of them by mediation. Aside from a few highly publicized instances (most notably, Theodore Roosevelt's role in the 1902 anthracite strike), government-sponsored (or any other) arbitration made little headway in American labor relations.[61]

Revealing also was the contrast between the close conjunction of Britain's frequent royal commissions and major parliamentary labor legislation, and the lack of anything comparable in the United States. True, two major inquiries—the United States Industrial Commission of 1899–1902, and the 1912 Commission on Industrial Relations— did probe deeply into American labor relations. But the major recommendation of the Industrial Commission—a broad system of arbitration—got nowhere. And while some of the Commission on Industrial Relations' proposals bore fruit in the Wilsonian labor legislation of 1915–16, its more sweeping recommendations fell on stony ground until the New Deal.[62]

The coming of World War I, and then America's entry, brought jobs and relative prosperity. Union membership climbed sharply, from 2.7 million in 1914 to 5.1 million in 1920. The eight-hour day suddenly became an acceptable policy. Only 11.8 percent of industrial workers enjoyed a forty-eight-hour work week in 1914; 48.7 percent did so in 1919. The abrupt cessation of immigrants (815,000 in 1913, 19,000 in 1916) and the rising demand for labor made these golden years of collective bargaining—and strikes: 1,420 in 1915, 4,450 in 1917.[63]

When the United States entered the war, organized labor participated in government as never before. Gompers served on the Advisory Commission of the Council of National Defense, the forerunner of the War Industries Board. The War Labor Board was supposed to provide "a comprehensive national labor program." But as in so many areas of public policy, this wartime corporatism proved to be evanescent. The unions' experience in the decade to come would make it clear how powerful and persistent was the traditional relationship between labor and the state.[64]

Labor, Law, and Politics: Prosperity and Depression Years

Everywhere in the West, the end of World War I unleashed forces of change—and of containment—given new shape and substance by the conflict. Nowhere was this more evident than in the realm of labor relations. The raised expectations of workingmen, the unsettling effects of postwar economic turmoil, and the upsurge of radicalism triggered by the Bolshevik revolution fueled an explosion of strikes and radical politics in the immediate postwar years. But in contexts determined by the wartime experience and the particularities of national culture, this potentially revolutionary impulse ran into both organized resistance from employers and a more general public opposition.

The theme of "a land fit for heroes" had a prominent place in the sustaining rhetoric of wartime Britain; and postwar expectations were correspondingly high. The Ministry of Reconstruction had more than thirty committees seeking ways to improve the condition of British labor; the air was thick with talk of social welfare, industrial councils, guild socialism. In 1924 Ramsay MacDonald became the first socialist head of a Western state.[65]

True, the record of British labor during the 1920s could hardly be called a progress from triumph to triumph. Membership declined, from 215 unions with 6.8 million members in 1920 to 203 with 4.3 million in 1925. Attempts to establish trade boards with the power to set minimum wages ran afoul of employer and public hostility. And the General Strike of 1926 produced the 1927 Trades Disputes Act, which tightened the existing law on picketing and the use of union funds for political purposes. Nevertheless the place of unions in British political and legal life still was substantially more secure than in the United States. The courts remained less inclined to interfere in labor disputes. Labour replaced the Liberals as one of the two major parties; MacDonald regained the prime ministership in 1929. And the 1927 law did not seriously impede labor's right to strike.[66]

Postwar American labor unrest and the response of employers and the state bore some resemblance to the British situation. The *New Statesman* thought that the American labor movement increasingly resembled its British counterpart: "Everywhere, the revolt against private capitalism is taking shape in the demand for one form or another of socialisation and workers' control."[67] But the class and ideological polarization that occurred in postwar Europe hardly had the same salience in the United States. True, the wartime experience with enforced conformity and the postwar fear of radicalism gave new authority to antiunion policy. This appeared on the national level in the injunctions secured against the railroad strikers of 1921 by Harding's attorney general, Harry Daugherty. It cropped up, too, in a series of antiunion decisions by the Supreme Court and in the greater readiness of state and local authorities to turn the instruments of state against unions in labor-capital disputes. But in a larger view, the situation of American unions during the 1920s was more notable for its continuity with the past.

The brief American involvement in the war brought markedly higher wages (however vitiated in fact by inflation), employment, and labor representation in councils of state. The sudden contraction of these conditions after November 1918 set off a wave of strikes, of a scale and intensity that led to talk of "American Industry in a State of War." They came in basic industries—coal, steel, railroads—and in unsettling new forms such as a police walkout in Boston and a general strike in Seattle. The reaction was correspondingly severe. The attack on radicalism during the Red Scare of 1919 and afterward readily extended to organized labor; Seattle mayor Ole Hanson and Massachusetts governor Calvin Coolidge won much public acclaim for their roles as staunch strikebreakers.[68]

Not so visible nationally, but no less violent, were numerous other local walkouts. A wave of streetcar strikes followed 1919 wage reductions in New Orleans, Chicago, Denver, and Brooklyn. Tennessee's governor broke a Knoxville streetcar strike by ordering in two infantry companies—2,000 troops in all. Federal judge Kenesaw Mountain Landis, arbitrating a Chicago building trades dispute, found for an open shop. A Citizens' Committee to Enforce the Landis Award, made up of bankers, lawyers, and merchants, pressured contractors not to deal with workers who refused to accept the decision. The Chicago Carpenters' Union fruitlessly sought an injunction against the Citizens' Committee's boycott against its members; nonunion shops were bombed; the police raided the union's headquarters.[69]

If the scale and intensity of postwar American labor unrest echoed European conditions, so too did the range of policy responses. As in other areas of public life, they reflected the expanded definition of government's role inherited from Progressivism and war. By the same token, the failure of these efforts to alter substantially the relationship of organized labor with capital and the state testifies to the strength of the fibers of continuity linking the American past to the present.

Postwar social reconstruction figured prominently in American as in British labor circles. An Independent Labor party, organized in Chicago in November 1918, issued a manifesto—"Labor's 14 Points"— that echoed the program of Britain's Labour party. The Plumb Plan to continue the government's wartime ownership and operation of the railroads closely resembled the British Miners' Federation nationalization proposal. The AFL supported the scheme; Gompers was president of the Plumb Plan League. But less ambitious labor goals had a stronger, more persistent claim. One was the need to strengthen the legal position of unions and to pass laws dealing with national, state, and local government as employers. The AFL's primary political objective during the 1920s, as before the war, was a federal anti-injunction act.[70]

The administration responded to postwar industrial strife with the methods of wartime corporatism. Wilson convened industrial conferences in 1919 and 1920 to devise new machinery for the resolution of capital-labor differences. But both the Socialist party and the AFL opposed a scheme to establish a national industrial tribunal with full judicial powers. And conservatives rejected a proposal to establish regional boards of industry and adjustment modeled on the Federal Reserve system: these, they held, too closely resembled the dreaded soviets of the Bolsheviks.[71]

As secretary of commerce in the new Harding administration, Herbert Hoover turned his formidable energies to government-fostered collective bargaining as an alternative to laissez-faire or socialism. He put pressure on Elbert Gary of United States Steel to end the twelve-hour day; and in the wake of the 1922 coal strike he established a Coal Commission charged with rationalizing the industry and reducing labor-capital conflict. But like other attempts to perpetuate wartime corporatism, these efforts bore little fruit. The Coal Commission foundered on the refusal of the operators (and its own reluctance) to accept the closed shop.[72]

The Railroad Labor Board, established by the 1920 Transportation Act, suffered a similar fate. Its decisions were supposed to establish fair wages reflecting the cost of living, work hazards, and training. But when it reduced the wage of railroad shop workers in 1922, the men walked out. The board handed down more than 2,500 decisions by 1925. But publicity was its only sanction; and that was not enough. President Harding observed in December 1922 that the work of the board seemed only to heighten labor-management conflict, and the Railroad Labor Act of 1926 restored the prewar system of mediation.[73]

A polity so deeply hostile to corporatist solutions made the going heavy even for more modest attempts to create machinery for the resolution of labor disputes. Contractor organizations in the building industry and the AFL Building Trades Department set up a National Board for Jurisdictional Awards in 1919. The secretaries of labor and commerce approved. But when New York City canceled a contract with a builder who refused to abide by a decision of the board, the federal circuit court upheld an injunction on the ground that the city's action constituted restraint of trade.[74]

Company unions also attracted employers: the railroads set up 25 of them in the wake of the 1922 shopmen's strike. But only one in five of the 100 or so company unions of the postwar years lasted for more than three years. Company-dominated works councils were more successful. In 1919, 225 represented almost 400,000 workers; by 1925, over 800 affected more than a million employees.[75]

The most substantial new approach to labor relations was the unpublic one of welfare capitalism. Owen D. Young and Gerard Swope of General Electric proclaimed a "New Capitalism" based on cooperation with the AFL, works councils, and life insurance, pensions, and stock option plans. Other big firms instituted pensions and other benefits. But their number was limited, and welfare capitalism never escaped the (well-merited) suspicion of organized labor that its major purpose was to avoid unionization of the work force. And indeed, yellow-dog contracts binding workers not to join unions flourished. The NAM's James Emery estimated in 1932 that more employees worked under these contracts than belonged to labor unions.[76]

The identification of Americanism and antiradicalism with the open shop became a major tenet of employer associations such as the

League for Industrial Rights. It was fair to say in 1920 that "the basic American industries are to-day, in fact, union-free," and to predict that "the labor world will be made up of unsteady folk-groups, separated by race and religion." Strikes and labor turnover declined as the decade progressed, and so did union membership: by 30 percent from 1920 to 1926. By the late 1920s about 90 percent of German and British industrial workers were unionized, compared with only about 10 percent of the American industrial work force.[77] Postwar Europe's class-laden corporatist past ironically made unionization (like social democracy) more viable. No less ironically, an individualistic, antistatist, pluralist culture hobbled the growth—and the legal status—of organized labor in America.

The Kansas Court of Industrial Relations was the most flamboyant, and in its fate the most revealing, of postwar attempts by government to shape the course of labor relations.

The court emerged in the wake of the bitter Kansas coal strike of 1919. The radical-led state UMW closed the mines, stirring widespread fears of a fuelless winter and social upheaval. The state responded by taking the mines into receivership and trying to work them with a jerry-built labor force made up of the National Guard, the American Legion, and volunteers. Governor Henry J. Allen, the court's chief advocate, argued that it would serve the interests of the public—that is, the nine out of ten Kansans who belonged neither to capital nor to labor.

But there was more than postwar antiradicalism to the Court of Industrial Relations. The Kansas legislature had not been hostile to unions; it empowered them to select the state commissioner of labor and chief mine inspector. William L. Huggins, the tribunal's originator and first chief judge, defended it as a humanitarian way of resolving labor conflict. It drew on precedents such as the labor arbitration laws of Canada and Australia and the British Industrial Courts Act of 1919.

Enacted in January 1920 by an overwhelming legislative majority, the three-member court (more an administrative board than a judicial tribunal) could pass on industrial conflicts brought to it by the contesting parties, by ten or more citizens, or by the state's attorney general. It was unlawful to strike or picket against its decisions. Finally, the court could take over and operate industries affected with a public interest, including public utilities, common carriers, and firms engaged in the production or transportation of food, clothing, and fuel.[78]

Peculiarly American constitutional issues immediately arose. Was this a proper extension of the state's police power? Did it interfere with liberty of contract? Gompers of the AFL denounced the court for subjecting workers to involuntary servitude; the Associated Industries of Kansas was no less opposed. Conservative lawyer George W. Wickersham doubted both the constitutionality and the wisdom of trying to prohibit strikes and called the court "the largest step towards State socialism ever taken by an American commonwealth."[79]

William Allen White, editor of the *Emporia Gazette*, at first favored the experiment but soon had cause to change his mind. When the court had the railroad shopmen's strike of 1922 under review, White posted a sign in the window of the *Gazette* announcing that he was 49 percent in favor of the shopmen and would increase his support by 1 percent a day as long as there was no violence. The Allen administration brought White's action before the Industrial Court, which held it to be illegal intimidatory picketing. White took issue on free speech grounds, the affair became a national *cause célèbre*, and embarrassed state authorities soon dropped the suit.[80]

Of the fifty-two cases that came before the court in its less than three years of existence, thirty-six were brought by labor. Its decisions were by no means uniformly antiunion. Reviewing strikes against street railway and power companies—its major cases—the court supported an eight-hour day and a decent wage rate. And in most instances the contesting parties accepted its decisions. When the court called on the Wolff Packing Company to pay a higher wage to its employees, the firm refused to comply. The ensuing legal conflict went to the Kansas and then to the United States Supreme Court, which in a unanimous 1923 decision held that the Industrial Relations Court violated the Constitution's due process and contract provisions. In 1925 the Kansas legislature abolished this ill-fated venture—a result applauded by both organized labor and organized capital.[81]

The same inertial forces that blocked the development of new forms of corporatism or state intervention in labor relations assured that labor's political role during the 1920s followed prewar lines. One observer thought that the great majority of American union members opposed independent political action. And American labor leaders were much less responsive than their European counterparts to postwar radicalism. The mine workers' John L. Lewis said in ending the coal strike: "We are Americans. We cannot fight our own government"—a striking contrast with British miners' leader Robert Smillie, an advocate of direct action to upset the existing economic order and a friend of the Soviet Union. Most of the AFL leadership strongly repudiated Communists and the fellow-traveling left. Gompers proudly claimed that the American labor movement was "less fantastical but more practical" than its counterparts abroad.[82]

At first the postwar AFL rejected third-party politics or a separate labor party. Gompers and the Federation supported the Democrat James M. Cox in 1920, although major unions such as the carpenters and the longshoremen backed Harding. Labor's agenda (as before the war) took the form of bills of grievances, dwelling on familiar issues: immigration restriction, an eight-hour day for federal employees, restrictions on the use of convict labor, and an anti-injunction law.

Otherwise, the AFL continued to rely on collective bargaining: "The Federation will not trust itself to the uncertain beneficence of the law when it can see any gain by the group's efforts." Aside from the protection of particularly vulnerable workers (women, children, seamen), the Federation called for "an individualistic, laissez-faire policy." Old age pensions and health and unemployment insurance smacked of paternalism, of socialism. The labor movement must "maintain the fullest freedom of normal activities and [remain] free from supervision, censorship, direction and control of governmental agencies."[83]

Yet the Railroad Brotherhoods played a major role in the formation of the Conference for Progressive Political Action (CPPA), which led to the formation of the Progressive party of 1924 and Robert La Follette's third-party presidential candidacy. The spur here was the relative deprivation suffered by the railroad unions after they lost their wartime bonanza of a sympathetic federal employer. The AFL initially supported La Follette's candidacy. But as socialist and other dissident elements gained a greater voice its interest waned, and after 1924 the Federation returned to the "reward your friends and punish your enemies" politics of the past. Gompers reaffirmed "the principle of voluntarism" and warned: "Industry must solve its own problems or we face the alternative of state intrusion which must inevitably lead to bureaucracy and breakdown."[84]

The mine workers' William Green replaced Gompers as head of the AFL in 1925. Green was more "progressive" than his predecessor; he supported prohibition and the American Association of Labor Legislation (which Gompers opposed as dominated by intellectuals). But until the Great Depression the AFL did not significantly alter its positions on politics, radicalism, or the active state.

It is not hard to see why. The Harding, Coolidge, and Hoover administrations hardly made government a promising vehicle for labor's interests. Nor had those interests undergone any significant transformation in the new century. Immigration restriction was "regarded by American labor as its greatest political and legislative achievement." The AFL supported the severely restrictive Johnson immigration act of 1924; Gompers condemned the opposition of employers and of "racial groups" who had contributed little to the country. Unions joined with manufacturers in an incessant demand for legislation restricting the sale of convict-made goods. The courts in 1895 struck down a New York law requiring that these products be so identified; labor pressure led to its reenactment in 1928. Congress in 1929 passed the Hawes-Cooper bill, which subjected out-of-state convict-made goods to state laws affecting in-state products.[85]

The AFL had little or none of the commitment to social democratic (to say nothing of socialist) thought and action so common to European labor. William Green argued in 1930 that the Federation placed as much importance on political action as did the British labor movement, but that the nation (and American labor) was too large and diverse for a single labor party. Just as industry failed to secure the corporatist state sought by some of its more sophisticated spokesmen, so too did labor-in-politics prefer to keep its distance from the state.[86]

The issue of greatest concern to organized labor during the 1920s was a familiar one indeed: the antiunion decisions of the courts. With good reason, labor leaders saw the judiciary as the most hostile branch of government. As before, the courts found it difficult to recognize collective labor agreements. American judges generally adhered to their traditional view of employment as a contractual arrangement between boss and worker, in which unions were third parties of uncertain standing. (In sharp contrast, labor courts in Germany heard 125,000 to 150,000 cases a year in which unions were parties.) Judicial decisions were said to seek "industrial disarmament," to restrict the permissible weapons in industrial disputes. Insofar as the courts' labor decisions added up to a public policy, they sought to serve social peace, economic progress, and individual (under which they included corporate) rights.[87]

A few signs of change could be seen, however. New York's courts took the lead in upholding the validity of collective bargaining agreements; they began to hand down dicta that legal rights and obligations arose directly from them. Other states followed with the coming of the Depression. By 1931 "the American law, as it now stands, tends to develop these collective agreements into something more than a custom and yet something different from a contract." There was some growth, too, of extrajudicial means of resolving labor disputes: through arbitration, public commissions, impartial chairmen, and the like. But both unions and bosses had a strong distaste for these alternatives. When the New Deal forged a new national labor policy in the 1930s, it legitimated collective bargaining rather than a corporatist or statist approach.[88]

The major labor decisions of the Supreme Court during the 1920s were, if anything, more hostile to organized labor than those before the war. They showed little sympathy for a broad view of unions' right to strike or for nonadversarial solutions to labor strife. Even the liberal Brandeis declared: "Neither the common law, nor the Fourteenth Amendment, confers the absolute right to strike." And even the conservative Arthur Sutherland caustically observed: "After an examination of judicial opinions and decisions, one is apt to arrive at the conclusion that the activities of labor are lawful so long as they are confined to means which are ineffective for achieving perfectly legitimate purposes."[89]

A set of opinions by Chief Justice William Howard Taft set the tone of the decade. His *American Steel Foundries* and *Duplex* decisions put an end to any hope that the Clayton Act protected unions from antipicketing injunctions. In *Truax v. Corrigan* Taft struck down an Arizona law that limited the use of the labor injunction. The *Coronado Coal* decisions of 1925 honed the edge of the Sherman Antitrust Act as an antiunion weapon. Taft held that the UMW, seeking to organize coal mines in the South, was liable for triple damages under the Sherman Act if (as here) its actions constituted a conspiracy in restraint of interstate commerce.[90]

True, unions were defendants in only 10 percent of the more than 300 government-initiated proceedings brought under the Sherman Act from 1880 to 1928. But the threat gave employers an effective additional weapon. By the end of the decade almost all state courts had followed the lead of the Supreme Court by striking down laws prohibiting yellow-dog contracts; the *Coronado Coal* decision significantly impeded the unionization efforts of the UMW.[91]

The injunction continued to be the most widely used and most controversial instrument in labor disputes. A federal judge observed that injunctions "have steadily grown in length, complexity, and the vehemence of their rhetoric." Employers with increasing frequency established diversity of citizenship to get their disputes into the federal courts, and then sought injunctions through private suits. Often not the courts but counsel for the complainant drafted the injunctions; judges rapidly, readily granted them; proper judicial notice was rarely given to those to whom their provisions applied.[92]

About one-third of the 250 or so injunctions sought in New York City from 1910 to 1930 came in the needle trades. In the mid-1920s, when communists got control of the garment unions' Joint Board, increased labor militancy produced 34 injunction requests; 21 were granted. On four occasions in 1925 and 1926 state courts prohibited peaceful picketing in the absence of a strike. Labor backhandedly recognized the power of the injunction by seeking to bend it to its own interests. New York supreme court judge Robert Wagner, later the senatorial architect of New Deal labor policy, granted that state's first injunction to a union in 1922. So did the United States Supreme Court in 1930: the Texas & New Orleans Railroad formed a company union in violation of a federal statute, and at the request of the Brotherhood of Railway Clerks the courts enjoined the line. Less successful was an AFL attempt to stop New York's Interborough Transit Company from using yellow-dog contracts.[93]

But in general the AFL frowned upon its members' seeking injunctions. Often they became a weapon in intra- and interunion fights; even the IWW secured injunctive relief against rival AFL hod carriers in Massachusetts. The readiness of the courts to grant injunctions to unions as well as to management—of seventy-three such cases by 1930, twenty-four ended in union victories—suggests the judiciary's taste for this potent writ.[94]

Labor waged its war against the injunction on several fronts. Unions agitated for state anti–yellow dog laws immune to injunctive assault. These were long, hard struggles: Ohio's law of 1931 came after an eight-year effort by the AFL. But the major union cause was a federal law that banned the use of federal injunctions in labor disputes. This campaign had a place in the pre–New Deal politics of labor very much like the long and so often frustrated struggle of the National Association for the Advancement of Colored People for a federal antilynching law. In each case a sense of basic civil rights grievously violated found its voice. A survey of the labor injunction concluded in 1930 that after "three decades of legislative activity . . . the position of labor before the law has been altered, if at all, imperceptibly."[95]

The Great Depression brought exploding unemployment and declining union membership. Yet unions no less than the rest of the society were slow to change their traditional modes of thinking. One observer said of the industrial program enacted by the AFL's 1930 convention: "Except for occasional phrases, it might have been issued by the United States Chamber of Commerce."[96]

But the Depression also dramatically changed the political environment, producing both a new labor agenda and a polity ready to respond to it. The Norris-LaGuardia Anti-Injunction Act of 1932 was passed by overwhelming congressional margins (75–5 in the Senate, 363–15 in the House). A number of state laws further restricted the use of labor injunctions. A legal device used an estimated 2,400 times by state and federal courts since its origin in the late nineteenth century now came under substantial legislative constraint.[97]

The New Deal, of course, signaled a new era in labor's relation to government. Section 7a of the National Industrial Recovery Act inaugurated a federal policy of social welfare and support for collective bargaining, whose landmarks were the Social Security and National Labor Relations Acts of 1935 and the Fair Labor Standards Act of 1938. But the inertial force of prevailing assumptions and constraints was not so readily overborne. Initially the courts held that Section 7a did not override the rule limiting legal strikes to objects permissible at common law. A strike against a firm operating under an NRA code might be an unconstitutional impediment to the NRA itself. And lower state courts continued to enjoin strikes whose goal was unionization.[98]

Jurisdictional disputes over power, policy, and membership burgeoned among and between the old craft unions of the AFL and the new industrial unions of the Congress of Industrial Organizations (CIO), frequently ending up in the courts. Often they were reluctant to intervene. The old adversarial relationship between unions and judges was waning. A changing judiciary accepted NLRB-directed collective bargaining in the late 1930s.

Historians of the left have argued that the major change in labor policy during the 1930s was the legitimation of the collective bargaining approach to labor relations that had been the basic objective of the AFL since the late nineteenth century. Given the historical record, it is hard to imagine that a more corporatist—or socialist—outcome was within the realm of social possibility.[99]

7 · Regulating the Countryside

If Americans traditionally agreed on one thing, it was the primacy of the land—and of their mission to exploit it. Agriculture's special place in the national culture was as old as Jefferson; and nineteenth-century Americans rarely doubted that the land and its resources were there to be put to use as quickly and completely as possible.

But by the turn of the century these verities, like so much else of American life, were beset by ambiguity and doubt. The long slide in farm prices and the agrarian unrest culminating in the 1890s made pricing and marketing more important than productivity and the availability of land. As early as 1871 Charles Dudley Warner put into words the paradox that was to set the terms of twentieth-century agricultural policy: "Blessed be agriculture! if one does not have too much of it." [1]

Traumatic, too, was the end of the frontier as a continuous line of settlement, announced by the Census of 1890. That fact may or may not have had much substantive meaning. But there is no denying its impact on public opinion. The endless abundance of land was no longer an American truism; is it coincidence that the conservationist movement took form in its aftermath? Yet the problem of conservation—of land, of resources—rested on a perception quite the reverse of what afflicted the farmers; scarcity, not abundance, was its keynote.

Together, these problems—marketing agricultural products, conserving natural resources—gave a new and distinctive character to post-1900 public policy affecting the countryside. As in other realms of public life, the result was a growing diversity of issues and interests—another manifestation of the politics of pluralism.

Marketing Agriculture

"American Agriculture Comes of Age"; "From Pathos to Parity": this is how historians characterize the shift of agriculture's place in American life at the turn of the century. The first call on public policy now was not to open access to the land and reduce transportation costs to markets, but to provide credit, control pricing, handle surpluses. The old concerns continued, of course. But in addition politics and government were expected to bring the agricultural sector into "parity" (now that word had gained wide currency) with the burgeoning industrial, commercial, and consumer sectors of the economy. A "new agrarianism" no less than a new corporatism and a new unionism enriched the agenda of the early twentieth-century American polity.[2]

British agricultural policy faced very different social conditions. Its major objective was to preserve the status and rights of the tenants who farmed land held by a few large landholders. The Liberals' Small Holdings and Allotments Act of 1907 and Consolidation Act of 1908 sought to limit the degree to which fixtures and improvements remained the property of landlords, and to increase the number of small farmers. The 1908 law provided for the acquisition of land by county councils—by compulsory purchase if necessary—to be relet to tenants in smallholdings of up to fifty acres. The tenants could purchase the land (but rarely did so).

Liberals encouraged also the formation of cooperative smallholdings and allotment associations, cooperative trading societies, and credit banks. The Land Report of 1913 proposed a system of Wage Boards for agricultural laborers, a Land Court, and incentives to smallholdings. But the larger British agricultural reality, of heavily concentrated land ownership and widespread, rigid tenancy, continued to be the norm.[3]

American agricultural policy concentrated not on land ownership but on production and marketing. The same desire to master economic forces that fueled the National Civic Federation and scientific management gave new importance to the technical and other services of the Department of Agriculture. Agricultural research was far more important in the United States than in Britain: in 1902 the British agricultural research budget was £1,400, the American one more than $500,000 (equivalent to £100,000).[4]

The department tried to foster farmers' business and economic efficiency as well as increased crop yields. This was its golden age. With appointments such as Seaman Knapp, Gifford Pinchot, and Harvey Wiley and much-expanded scientific research and demonstration and extension work, Secretary James F. Wilson (1897–1913) and his Democratic successor, economist David F. Houston (1913–1921), brought the Department of Agriculture to a new level of political influence. This may well have been the most powerful and effective government department during the Progressive era. British conservationist Horace Plunkitt thought it "now the most popular and respected of the world's great administrative institutions."[5]

A flow of legislation testified to agriculture's political importance. The Newlands Reclamation Act of 1902 opened an era of federal subsidies to foster land development. The Forest Homestead Act (1906) and the Enlarged Homestead Act (1909) extended the original Homestead Act of 1862 to forest and cattle lands. In 1914 the Smith-Lever Act created what quickly became an extensive system of agricultural extension work; a year later the Smith-Hughes law provided federal aid for vocational education, most of it in agriculture; in 1916 the Farm Loan Act launched the government on its extensive commitment to a federal farm credit system. Woodrow Wilson summed up the new goals of farm policy in his First Inaugural:

> We have a body of agricultural activities never yet given the efficiency of great business undertakings or served as it should be through the instrumentality of science taken directly to the farm, or afforded the facilities of credit best suited to its practical needs . . . We have studied as perhaps no other nation has the most effective means of production, but we have not studied cost or economy as we should.[6]

Agriculture, like the other major sectors of the American economy, came under extensive—though brief—government direction during World War I. The Food and Fuel Control Act and the Federal Food Administration oversaw production, marketing, and distribution; state councils of defense set up marketing committees; state agricultural censuses gathered information.

Wartime prices and government controls gave the nation's farmers an intense experience with the benefits of a regulated, assured market. Neither the pressure of need nor the traditions of government led to anything like the price-fixing and rationing of Britain and other European nations. But even the limited wartime American corporatism failed to contain the pressures of a massive, diffuse agricultural economy. Herbert Hoover's Food Administration had to deal with producers organized into marketing cooperatives, large and powerful dealers, and increasingly vocal consumer spokesmen. Wartime attempts to mediate the resulting conflicts in the dairy industry through federal commissions and conferences failed to handle this explosive mix of interests—a warning signal for postwar attempts at a *dirigiste* agricultural policy.[7]

The problems of agriculture had an important place in postwar Britain. To stimulate wartime food production, the Corn Production Act of 1917 guaranteed minimum prices through the 1922 harvest. The 1920 Agricultural Act proposed to maintain those minimums for an indefinite period; but the collapse of cereal prices in the spring of 1921 led to its abrupt repeal even before it came into effect. The Labour party and (more obliquely) Lloyd George spoke grandly of land nationalization. But little came of this. Even marketing cooperatives met with strong opposition from cattle and corn dealers, manure and machinery interests, the Milk Combine, and other holders of farmer debts.[8]

Nevertheless Parliament passed some fifty agricultural acts from 1920 to 1926, and British agriculture became ever more cosseted by protective duties and subsidies. Land under cultivation shrank by about 1.5 million acres from 1913 to 1927, and by the late 1920s livestock accounted for 70 percent of agricultural output.

In sharp contrast to American farmers, those in Britain remained less organized than industrial workers. True, the National Farmers' Union (NFU) appeared in 1908 as a parliamentary pressure group, and there was a postwar attempt at an independent farmers' party. But the NFU became an adjunct of the Conservatives. And although there was much rhetoric about the need to preserve the farmer and the countryside, British agricultural politics was only a pale reflection of its far more intense counterpart in the United States.[9]

Agriculture figured prominently in American postwar policy debates. Proposals sought to secure easier access to land and capital, homesteads for veterans, agricultural insurance, and government-guaranteed price stabilization. The postwar drop in farm prices set off a number of attempts to improve the situation. A scheme to reduce cotton acreage at the 1919 Southern States Cotton Acreage Reduction Convention foreshadowed the Agricultural Adjustment Act of the New Deal years. Congress passed a bill authorizing the War Finance

Corporation to finance the export of farm surpluses; but Wilson vetoed it. A congressional Joint Committee of Agricultural Inquiry un-
dertook a comprehensive survey of agricultural conditions in 1921,
when the unprecedented fall in farm prices reawakened a host of old
agrarian concerns: falling farm purchasing power, high freight rates,
inadequate credit facilities, growing tenancy.[10]

The prewar effort to expand farmers' access to credit persisted. The
Agricultural Credits Act of 1923 added government-chartered loan
companies, a system of intermediate credit banks similar to the Federal Reserve, and other instrumentalities to the Federal Farm Loan
system. But the most substantial postwar government response was
to begin to regulate the futures market.

The grain futures market came under nominal government supervision in 1922. As the president of the Chicago Board of Trade smugly
put it, "American grain exchanges have now been given the stamp of
government approval." The 1921 Packers and Stockyards Act dealt
similarly with cattle stockyards and packing houses. A bill proposed
in 1918 called for government ownership and operation of stockyards,
refrigerator cars, and storage facilities, with a licensing system for
packers and commission men. But what emerged three years later was
an altogether more moderate system of oversight, reflecting packer
rather than consumer interests. The secretary of agriculture, not the
Federal Trade Commission, oversaw the business. The packers welcomed the greater uniformity of federal as against state regulation.
And the Supreme Court, though ever on the alert for too intrusive a
government presence, accepted these modest measures as appropriate
exercises of the commerce power.[11]

The American Farm Bureau Federation was the chief agricultural
lobbying agency during the 1920s. It emerged from the county and
state farm bureaus that rose in tandem with the county and agricultural extension agents mandated by the 1914 Smith-Lever Act. By November 1919 there were more than 1,000 of these bureaus, and in that
month their representatives met in Chicago to form the Farm Bureau
Federation.

"Largely American and English speaking, made up of intelligent entrepreneurs," the federation set out to mobilize the nation's farmers
as a political force. Claiming 1.5 million members in forty-two states
by 1921, it developed a program designed to recast agricultural marketing. It held that farmers, like the trusts, should control the distribution of their products, and backed the "California Marketing Plan"

of cooperatives based on commodities, not on localities—in effect, trade associations.[12]

Gray Silver, the Washington representative of the Farm Bureau Federation, played a major part in the development of a farm bloc of senators, not unlike the role of the Anti-Saloon League's Wayne Wheeler in fostering congressional support for prohibition. The bloc's agricultural policy came to center on the McNary-Haugen scheme to sell farm surpluses abroad at competitive prices, with government underwriting to assure farmers their "fair exchange value." As industry benefited from the protective tariff, so would farmers from subsidized exports.

But for all its political clout, agribusiness could not escape the debilitating constraints of old values and conflicting interests. Congress passed McNary-Haugen Acts in 1924 and again in 1928. Both were vetoed by Coolidge, who questioned the constitutionality and economic viability of the scheme. Its price-fixing provision weighed against it. And Treasury Secretary Andrew W. Mellon opposed McNary-Haugen because it would lower food prices and hence industrial costs abroad, thereby strengthening competition with American manufacturing.[13]

The saga of agricultural cooperatives vividly demonstrates the difficulty of collective action in American agriculture. Cooperatives figure prominently in the argument that the Populists were primitive socialists, and in the agendas of twentieth-century socialism and social democracy. But in fact American farmer cooperatives were more like cartels and trade associations than precursors of democratic socialism.[14]

Cooperative buying and marketing associations had a small but significant place in late nineteenth-century American agriculture. After 1900 they took on added importance, as did concentration and consolidation in other sectors of the economy. And some of them had social and political as well as economic motives. Such was the Farmers' Educational and Cooperative Union of America, formed in Texas in 1902, which peaked in 1907 and at one point sought to limit cotton production by plowing up 10 percent of the crop. The American Society of Equity, also established in 1902, consisted of separate local, state, and national "unions" for each major crop. Its chief objective was to secure uniform, profitable prices by apportioning crop yields and timing distribution to take advantage of favorable market conditions. Half-union, half-cartel, it was "a very ambitious attempt at creating a national produce Trust." But as with so many similar efforts before and after, the Society could not cope with the scale and diversity of agricultural production and marketing.[15]

Agricultural cooperatives spread in pace with the dramatic concentration in other sectors of the economy. Tobacco growers forced to deal with one major buyer, the American Tobacco Company, sought "to meet Trust methods in buying with Trust methods in selling." The Burley Society and the Planters' Protective Association secured a Kentucky law allowing cooperative pooling in the sale of tobacco. But the difficulty of getting 40,000 Kentucky and Tennessee growers to sign contracts and then to abide by them led to a revival of an all too common local custom: an epidemic of "night riding," in which recalcitrants were threatened, beaten, and had their barns burned.[16]

Their distance from eastern markets and dependence on the Central Pacific Railroad posed special difficulties for California's fruit growers. Frequent attempts at pooling foundered when members (encouraged by large packers and distributors) broke their contract terms and the pools were unable to enforce their writ in the courts. A 1910 survey concluded: "Viewed in the most favorable light, the achievements of co-operation in the marketing of California fruit are still largely prospective."[17]

The Clayton Act's exemption of nonstock agricultural associations from antitrust law spurred new efforts to add legislative and legal force to marketing co-op contracts. The California legislature created a state Marketing Commission in 1915, charged with encouraging the formation of cooperative marketing associations. Harris Weinstock, the commission's first director, had served on American commissions studying cooperatives and rural credit in Europe. Along with his half brother and business partner David Lubin, this typical Progressive nurtured marketing co-ops in the major California fruit crops.[18]

Aaron Sapiro, legal counsel to the Marketing Commission and related by marriage to Lubin and Weinstock, persuaded the legislature to pass a Cooperative Marketing Act exempting these co-ops from antitrust and making their contracts enforceable in the courts. Sapiro wanted farmers to benefit from the same efficiency and pooled effort evident in big business. For a while he was successful beyond his wildest hopes. By 1917 the California Fruit Growers' Exchange had over 8,000 members, two-thirds of the state's orange and lemon growers. Major California marketing cooperatives made Sunkist oranges, Sun-Maid raisins, and Diamond walnuts familiar national brand names.[19]

When farm prices collapsed after World War I the California approach was widely copied. By the mid-1920s more than forty states had variants of the statute, and about 12,000 marketing co-ops did an annual business of $2.5 billion. Sapiro grandly announced that "a new national policy has been proclaimed and has been universally followed . . . The State has become the encourager of cooperation." Farmers, he argued, need not turn to radical political movements such as the Non-Partisan League.[20]

Texas cotton prices reached abysmal depths in 1921, igniting a major campaign to bring the state's cotton farmers into a marketing cooperative. In its fervor the effort evoked memories of the Granger, Alliance, and People's Party crusades of the previous century; in its style and substance it was pure Babbitt boosterism. The Texas economic establishment—the Farm Bureau Federation, the Bankers' Association, the Federal Reserve branch, local chambers of commerce, retail associations, Rotary and Kiwanis clubs, "practically every organized force which could be counted upon to influence the opinions and actions of the farmer"—supported the campaign. Publicity methods forged in wartime Liberty Loan and Red Cross drives—signs, posters, auto stickers, buttons, barbecues, rallies—were put to use. And as a final touch, Aaron Sapiro came in:

> At Abilene nearly twenty-five hundred farmers walked nearly a mile through the streets following Sapiro from place to place in their endeavor to find a meeting place large enough to hold the crowd . . . and when they finally decided to try the First Baptist Church, with a seating capacity of 2500, the big crowd broke into a run several blocks before the church was reached, every man anxious to get a seat so that he could hear Sapiro talk. After he got the crowd in the church, Sapiro held them for three hours while he talked cooperative marketing. At times the crowd was so quiet you could hear a whisper; again Sapiro would evoke thunders of applause and wild cheers when he pictured the plight of the farmer and the solution. It was the same all over Texas. Sapiro "delivered the goods."[21]

By 1925, 300,000 farmers had signed "ironclad" contracts guaranteeing to deliver more than $100 million worth of cotton to their association. Tobacco farmers, encouraged by marketing laws modeled on the California act, followed suit. Sapiro helped to organize the Tri-State Tobacco Growers Cooperative Marketing Association in 1920–21, signing up about half the tobacco farmers of Virginia, North Carolina, and South Carolina in what was called "the most spectacular event in American agriculture since the days of Populism." The night riding of prewar days gave way to a legislatively and legally enforced cartel. By 1926 marketing co-ops accounted for almost half the tobacco crop. Economist Walton Hamilton thought that "'a new and different unit' for the doing of business has been in process of development"; another observer concluded that "the corporate entity, that useful legal mechanism, has served once more to effect a practical adjustment between the interests of a group and the habits and customs of society."[22]

Federal legislation and court decisions fostered the process. A 1921 law authorized the War Finance Corporation to make loans to marketing cooperatives. The Agricultural Credit Act of 1923 established federal credit banks empowered to discount, purchase, or lend on the co-ops' paper. The 1922 Capper-Volstead Act—called the Magna Carta of cooperative marketing—extended the Clayton antitrust exemption to stock as well as nonstock cooperatives. The Cooperative Marketing Act of 1926 exempted co-ops from paying income taxes and authorized the secretary of agriculture to establish a Bureau of Cooperative Marketing.[23]

The courts did their bit by holding that members of a marketing co-op entered into the equivalent of a contractual obligation. And they enforced the legal remedies, provided by the state marketing acts, that co-ops used against errant members: damages for breach of contract, injunctive constraints, the obligation of specific performance. In 1928 the Supreme Court upheld the constitutionality of the provision in Kentucky's marketing act that made it a crime for third parties to interfere with contracts between a cooperative and its members.[24]

But severe practical and legal limits kept most marketing co-ops from becoming effective cartels. American farmers were too numerous and individualistic, wholesalers too assertive, marketing outlets too varied for the co-ops to get secure control of most crops. Many were mismanaged, and failures mounted. By 1926 co-ops marketed only 8 percent of the cotton and 10 percent of the wheat crops, and Sapiro's Tobacco Association was in receivership. The same economic vulnerability of farmers that led legislatures and courts to give legal muscle to the marketing cooperatives prevented them from having more than a minor impact on American agriculture. There was even a problem with Sapiro's ethnicity. In 1927 he brought suit over a series of articles in Henry Ford's *Dearborn Independent* that accused him of being the agent of a band of "International Jews" bent on controlling American agriculture. Sapiro held the *Independent* responsible in part for the sharp decline in co-ops.[25]

Nor did the cooperatives' legal position remain unchallenged. The Supreme Court in 1929 struck down an Oklahoma law that allowed them to enter into the cotton-ginning business on terms more favorable than those accorded individuals. This decision weakened the position of the marketing cooperative as an agency entitled to special classification, and thus to favored legal status. More important, no state thereafter dared to empower co-ops to set pricing and production standards, for it was obvious that the courts would not enforce them. In sum, agricultural marketing cooperatives, like other market-controlling devices of the early twentieth century, were constrained by a regulatory culture more committed to a competitive-individualistic past than to a cooperative—or corporatist—future.[26]

The Great Depression deeply compounded the structural and marketing problems of American agriculture. The ills of decades—tenancy, foreclosure, low crop prices, overproduction—spread now on a previously unmatched scale.

Various credit agencies—the Federal Farm Loan boards and intermediate credit banks, joint-stock land banks, rediscount corporations, national agricultural credit associations, life insurance companies—tempered (and prolonged) the farm problem by providing about $2.5 billion in new first mortgage money from 1917 to 1931. The Reconstruction Finance Corporation and the Farm Act of 1932 (with an additional authorization of $2 billion in credit) added to the debt burden—and thereby increased the productivity that fed the farm problem. The Depression made it evident that the great need was not easy credit but higher prices.

Early efforts to restrict output ran into the roadblock of the courts' refusal to regard the Depression as an emergency sufficient to justify abandoning their traditional aversion to government regulation of production and price. The Supreme Court proclaimed in 1932: "this court has definitely said that the production or sale of food or clothing cannot be subjected to legislative regulation on the basis of a public use."[27]

The New Deal's Agricultural Adjustment Administration sought to restrict production by subsidies and marketing agreements. The chief beneficiaries were landlords, mortgagees, and family farmers; tenants, sharecroppers, and poorer farmers were, if anything, hurt. And even this socially circumscribed program ran into legal difficulties. It took years, and considerable constitutional legerdemain, before the Court accepted the principle that government might directly constrain output.[28]

Even more subject to deeply ingrained policy (or, rather, antipolicy) predispositions were attempts to deal with the social dimension of agriculture in the Great Depression: rural poverty, and in particular the displacement brought about by mortgage foreclosure and the uprooting of tenants, sharecroppers, and farm laborers. Tenants—most often blacks or younger farmers—cultivated half of the nation's farm acreage in the early 1930s. And despite decades of criticism of rent and crop liens as favoring landlords, that system still accounted for 40 percent of American agricultural output in 1932. The predisposition against contractual default, together with a substantial body of southern criminal and racial provisions regulating the landlord-tenant relationship, gave the courts sufficient grounds for strict enforcement.[29]

By one estimate, foreclosure accounted for title changes in 44 of every 100 farms in the north central states in 1932. But manifest need began to erode deeply entrenched legal principles. Equity courts at times refused to grant a deficiency judgment for the unpaid balance of a mortgage when the farm had been sold below fair value. The Supreme Court held that a bank might delay foreclosure proceedings if the property's market value was unacceptably low. And Chief Justice Charles Evans Hughes in 1934 sustained Minnesota's foreclosure moratorium law on the basis of the emergency police power. But few such cases arose, and the courts generally were reluctant to interfere.[30]

Given this record, it is not surprising that World War II and the technological change and human outmigration that swept over the land in the decades since, would change the face of American agriculture far more than public policy.

Conserving Resources

Nineteenth-century American resources policy had a luminous singleness of purpose: develop them as rapidly as possible. Nothing in the post-1900 public agenda better displays the changing consciousness of modern times than the appearance of a concern with resource conservation. This was not a single, coherent policy postion, but rather one made up of two distinct and often conflicting strands: aesthetic conservation, seeking to preserve the natural environment for cultural, ethical, and psychological purposes; and conservation for use, whose goal was to maintain the abundance or slow the exhaustion of exploitable natural resources.

Theodore Roosevelt, that embodiment of the Progressive persuasion, thought his conservation program—most notably the Newlands Reclamation Act of 1902 to encourage irrigation projects in desert areas—was his most important achievement. Certainly no one identified more intensely with both wilderness and conservation for use. He saw in the aesthetic of nature an essential way of coping with the strains of modern life. At the same time his commitment to make the desert bloom through irrigation, and to preserve woodland from voracious cutting, stemmed from an equally heartfelt desire to preserve or enhance resources for the use of generations to come.[31]

The "country life" movement showed how intertwined were the themes of preservation and use. Roosevelt appointed a Commission on Country Life in 1908, charged to find ways to save that endangered species. Typically, its dominant figures were not sons of the soil but professional rural leaders and urban sympathizers. The commission's report led to much discussion, prominently featured in the media. Its chief legislative consequences were the Smith-Lever Act of 1914, which provided subsidies for agricultural and domestic science education; and the Farm Loan Act of 1916. In their impact on American country life, they turned out to be the legislative equivalent of emptying the sea with a slotted spoon.[32]

The restriction of outdoor advertising, which had an important place in a new urban aesthetic, became part of rural preservationism as well. As early as 1879 a Colorado law sought to protect the countryside from commercialism's encroachments: in Clear Creek County "every available rock was . . . plastered or painted over."[33]

An antibillboard campaign erupted in the cities during the early 1900s. But as automobiles penetrated the countryside in ever-larger numbers, this aesthetic concern moved with them. The National Committee for the Restriction of Outdoor Advertising worked against roadside advertisements in the 1920s. So did the National Association of Real Estate Boards, whose concern for property values led it onto unfamiliar ideological terrain: "The view from the highway does not belong to the individual who owns the property along the right of way. It is a community possession." A California study put it more succinctly: "beauty pays." But so did advertising, and as auto traffic on the highways increased, billboards kept pace. Regulation mounted in response: licensing and taxation, restrictions serving safety needs at railroad crossings, curves, and hills. Thirty national advertisers agreed in the mid-1920s to restrict the use of billboards in scenic areas; a number of beautification committees in Florida took the more direct course of tearing down offending signs.[34]

A conservationist ethic that responded to change by seeking to preserve the past was not a uniquely American phenomenon. British organizations dedicated to preserving the nation's natural and architectural heritage—the Commons, Open Spaces and Footpaths Preservation Society (1865), the Town and Country Planning Association (1899), the National Trust for Places of Historical Interest or Natural Beauty (1895)—appeared before the turn of the century. In early twentieth-century Britain, as in the United States, "a new and more intelligent public opinion has been created, is active in making itself felt, and is too powerful to be ignored." These British preservationists feared that expansion and growth threatened "visible records of the great past, and much of that natural beauty, which, equally with those great memories, is among the most precious parts of the inheritance of the British race."[35]

Octavia Hill, the central figure in the founding of the National Trust, participated also in housing, charity, and moral reform movements. A similar mix of conservation and social purification was part of the cultural baggage of many American conservationists. Thus the Save the Redwoods Association included among its directors those prominent advocates of immigration restriction and racial eugenics Madison Grant and Henry Fairfield Osborne. In this sense aesthetic conservation was part of a tradition of hostility to growth and diversity that stretched from Thoreau through John Muir and his Sierra Club (1892) to the ecologism of the present day.[36]

The primary conservationist impulse of the early twentieth century was not to escape from modernity, but to use its organization and technology to stop the waste of natural resources and assure their continuing contribution to a more abundant life. The Refuse Act of 1899, which in the 1960s became an important weapon in the fight for clean waters, was in fact designed to empower the Army Corps of Engineers to keep waterways free of obstructions to shipping.[37]

A National Conservation Congress sponsored by lumbermen in 1909 proposed "to act as a clearing-house for all allied social forces of our time, to seek to overcome waste in natural, human or moral forces." One participant called this "Our Nation's New Patriotism." Frederick Newell of the U.S. Reclamation Service embodied the dual Progressive desires to preserve traditional values and foster planning and efficiency. Wilson's secretary of the interior, Franklin K. Lane, testified to the continuing vitality of the utilitarian strand in 1913: "We have called a halt on methods of spoliation which existed, to the great benefit of many, but we have failed to substitute methods, sane, healthful, and progressive, by which the normal enterprise of an ambitious people can make full use of their own resources. We abruptly closed opportunities to the monopolist, but did not open them to the developer." [38]

The Ballinger-Pinchot controversy of 1910–11 showed how intense and emblematic the politics of conservation could be. Taft's secretary of the interior, Richard A. Ballinger, and Gifford Pinchot of the Forest Service clashed over whether or not Alaskan coal leases were properly let. The episode contributed substantially to the break between Taft and Theodore Roosevelt (to whom Pinchot was close). But it also became a symbolic encounter between the centralized, statist progressivism of Roosevelt's New Nationalism and more local and regional interests championed by Ballinger, who saw Pinchot as a spokesman for large over small coal companies and an eastern threat to the development of the West. [39]

In its larger aspects resource conservation reflected major new national concerns, and thus became part of an ever-more-complex public life. But at the grass roots (a not inapt metaphor) it was something else, something more traditional and familiar: a congeries of specific issues in which law, politics, and public policy intertwined. The politics and policymaking of particular resources—timber, water, fish and game, gas and oil—demonstrate this dual character. [40]

The turn of the century saw the rise (and fall) of what turned out to be the timber depletion myth. An observer in 1903 noted "the remarkable progress of the cult for the preservation of forests." The 1891 and 1897 Timber Acts set aside large-scale forest reserves; the Forest Service under Pinchot (with the help of the large lumber companies, who welcomed restraints on a timber-glutted market) became an influential exponent of the view that a shortage loomed; Roosevelt warned in 1905 of an imminent timber famine. Railroads in particular depended on a steady supply of timber for their ties and trestles. But the solution to their problem lay in technology, not in policy: the substitution of concrete and steel for wood, and the production of treated wood (by 14 factories in 1900, 102 in 1915), which largely expanded the variety of usable trees. The use of trucks similarly increased accessible logging areas. And the major lumber companies went heavily into scientific forestry. By World War I (and indeed ever since), timber depletion was among the least of the nation's conservationist concerns.[41]

America's water supply posed distinctive and increasingly complex policy problems. The major point of contention was not the danger of depletion, but the allocation of a mobile, readily accessible resource among an ever-larger number of claimants.

Nineteenth-century water law had dealt chiefly with priority of access to streams and rivers. The rise of industrial and urban users in the East and of mining and agrarian users in the West generated constant litigation and political controversy. In the East, the traditional Anglo-American common law of riparian rights—that priority rested on the user's contiguity to the stream—prevailed. In the West, prior appropriation—the rule that priority rested on the primacy of the user's claim—came to be the controlling legal principle. But after 1900, courts, legislatures, and public opinion began to adopt the view that access and use had public importance, and that there could be no absolute ownership of this essential, elusive substance.

Federal authority became an increasingly attractive option. Gifford Pinchot in 1913 got the National Conservation Congress to pass a resolution favoring control of water power, despite strong opposition from advocates of state authority. But decades passed before the national government took a significant part in hydroelectric regulation or generation.

More important was the role of the states. The Supreme Court upheld their right to protect water and other natural resources against the claims of riparian proprietors. Oliver Wendell Holmes sweepingly declared in 1908 that a state's police power enabled it "to protect the atmosphere, the water and the forests within its territory, irrespective of the assent or dissent of the private owners of the land most immediately concerned." By the end of the 1920s, public ownership and control by irrigation districts, state administrative systems, and interstate compacts had turned much of the nation's running water into a *res publica;* and state courts applied a "reasonable user" rule governing access to percolating (underground) waters.[42]

Water policy had special importance in California, where booming agriculture, a rapidly growing urban population, and a water supply difficult of access defined the terms of controversy. "Moisture Means Millions" was the slogan of the irrigationists; but advocates of flood control and of urban water needs had very different agendas. California's courts upheld the duty of compulsory service by water suppliers, and of consumers' rights to the flow and use of water. By 1910 a substantial body of case law rested on a public utilities model of equal, prompt, and reasonable water service. A statewide referendum in 1913 approved a new water code with a "beneficial use" provision that limited the traditional claim to full use under either riparian or prior appropriation law. But the courts continued to enforce fixed terms of service and contracts that made water charges a lien on the land.[43]

Conflict between conservation and use spectacularly erupted over a project to add to San Francisco's water supply by turning the scenic Hetch Hetchy Valley, near Yosemite, into a reservoir. The city's political, business, and labor leaders, as well as Gifford Pinchot, supported the project. John Muir and the Sierra Club (and the Spring Valley Water Works, a private company that sold San Francisco its water) opposed it. Labor leader James D. Phelan held that the fight for the reservoir was a battle to save the city from "monopoly and microbes"; the Taft administration—including Pinchot's enemy Ballinger—fought to save the valley. A similarly intense political struggle between Los Angeles and inland agricultural interests (the inspiration for the movie *Chinatown*) raged over the Los Angeles aqueduct plan to bring water from the Sierras to the city. In both cases urban water needs won—triumphs not so much of development ideology as of inescapable necessity.[44]

The development of hydroelectric power created another new realm of water resource law, politics, and regulation. Publicly owned hydroelectricity came as a matter of course in Europe. But federalism, private interests, and hostility to the active state produced a more complex situation in the United States. Hydroelectric power in the East, like irrigation needs in the west, strained the traditional private-rights basis of water law. State hydroelectric acts bore some resemblance to the mill acts of the nineteenth century, in that they justified takings under the power of eminent domain. But they went beyond earlier practice by providing for regulation of hydroelectricity as a public utility.[45]

This power source became an object of concern for conservationists and antimonopolists. It was estimated in 1909 that ten leading combines, led by General Electric and Westinghouse, controlled one-third of the nation's commercial hydroelectric power. Conservationist protests induced the federal government to refuse to grant additional power sites from 1907 to 1914. But counterpressure mounted to add the hydroelectric potential to the extensive electrical grids then taking form.[46]

During the 1920s hydroelectric, irrigation, conservation, and other water interests converged on a finite number of major water sources. The Federal Power Act of 1920 established a Federal Power Commission (FPC) to foster hydroelectric development, improve navigation, and provide water for irrigation. The commission's members—the secretaries of interior, war, and agriculture—reflected this congeries of interests. It could give fifty-year leases—in effect, revocable licenses—to private companies: a not inconsiderable commitment, given the fact that the federal government still controlled about one-fourth of the nation's potential hydroelectric sites. But a troika of cabinet members could not oversee so technically complex and politically sensitive an activity, and the Water Power Act of 1930 transformed the FPC into an independent commission.[47]

The increasing water demands of agricultural, industrial, and domestic users fed political conflict among the states. Modernity enriched not only the national policy agenda but also the politics of federalism. Thus the explosive economic and population growth of southern California made the use of the Colorado River—for irrigation, for electric power, for urban water needs—a major regional issue. Commerce Secretary Herbert Hoover, ever alert to expand his department's role in fostering cooperative ventures, oversaw in 1922 the drafting of a seven-state compact for the use of the Colorado's waters. But ratification by the states proved to be difficult. The conflict over the Colorado raised the oldest of water law questions: is there a legal right to equitable apportionment—in this case to each state—of the benefits from a stream that flows through their territories? Or do water rights vest according to prior appropriation, regardless of state lines or public policy?

The compact in effect favored equitable apportionment over prior appropriation. But just what that meant varied with the interests of the affected commonwealths. The upper basin (and sparsely populated) states of Arizona, Utah, and Colorado wanted limits on the allocation of the Colorado's waters. California of course wanted water to suit its needs. It had a special interest in a high dam to supply power and water for Los Angeles and protect the Imperial Valley from flood and silt. The result was stalemate. Arizona never accepted the 1922 compact; Utah withdrew in 1927; California refused to enter in 1926, stressing instead the construction of what came to be Boulder (later Hoover) Dam in Nevada.[48]

After the federal Boulder Dam Project Act passed in 1928, the controversy entered the courts. In 1930 Arizona filed for an injunction against California and five other states, to prevent diversion of the Colorado's waters. But the Supreme Court in 1931 granted the other states' motion to dismiss, citing the authority of the government over irrigation and water power.[49]

An interstate conflict of comparable character and scope arose over the Chicago Sanitary District, which diverted the flow of the Mississippi, Illinois, and Calumet rivers in order to flush the city's sewage downstream. One of the longest and most complicated lawsuits in American history began at the end of the nineteenth century, when Missouri brought suit against Illinois to stop the flow of this unwelcome Chicago export. After six years of litigation and some 300 witnesses, Holmes in a 1903 decision dismissed Missouri's suit. He appears to have been influenced by the fact that no complaint had been raised while the Sanitary District spent over $30 million on its sewage disposal project.[50]

As downstream objections multiplied, the federal government entered the controversy. In 1925 Hughes upheld an injunction blocking Chicago's wholesale diversion of water, on the ground that the transportation function of the affected rivers took precedence over that city's sanitary requirements. But the decision gave the Sanitary District until 1938 to build a sewage disposal plant designed to end the need for diversion, and meanwhile the secretary of war fixed the amount of water allowed.[51]

Interstate conflicts over water use also occurred in the East. Connecticut sued Massachusetts over its diversion of water from the Connecticut River to met Boston's needs; the Supreme Court upheld Massachusetts on the ground that drinking and other domestic uses of water had highest priority. New York and New Jersey engaged in a similar struggle—similarly resolved—over the diversion of Delaware River water to New York City.[52]

All of this added up to reshaping the common law of water rights to serve the general welfare. Equitable apportionment became the key determinant, overriding those shibboleths of the past, prior appropriation and riparian rights. The Supreme Court, rather than a federal administrative body, had become the primary arbitrator of water disputes.[53]

Why? Surely in part because these controversies deeply engaged the states as political entities. Judicial review, and not administrative fiat, was the only viable way of handling an issue so close to the wellsprings of federalism. And in part too (to persist in aquametaphor) because the regulatory issues were as fluid and elusive as the substance that produced them.

Water was not the only natural resource whose growing, ever-more-varied uses dictated new forms of regulatory thought and action. The law traditionally regarded fish and game as no one's property unless and until they were captured (although the states had a trusteelike sovereignty over them as wild animals, *ferae naturae*). But at the end of the nineteenth century the question arose of the states' interest in the export of fish and game across their borders. The Supreme Court in 1896 decided that they had a proprietary interest in the preservation of their wildlife, and consequently a police power right to limit its transportation across state lines—just as Holmes held for water in 1908.[54]

Wildlife conservationists turned the use of game birds for women's hats into a matter of public concern. The Lacey law of 1900 made it illegal to bring game into a state that forbade its importation. The analogy here (on not dissimilar grounds of social morality and public policy) was with constraints on interstate commerce in liquor. In 1913 the Weeks-McLean Migratory Bird Act, enforcing a game preservation treaty with Canada, put all wild game under the protection of the federal government and regulated the killing of migratory birds. State and lesser federal courts questioned its constitutionality; sportsmen in Missouri and elsewhere sought exemption from the law. But in *Missouri v. Holland* (1920) the Court upheld the federal government: an important extension of national over state power.[55]

Even here the relationship of self-interest to conservationist policy was not a simple one. Sportsmen's associations supported the first state legislation against stream pollution in the 1920s—attempts that industrial interests usually defeated. Once again the increasing richness and diversity of conservation issues is more striking than their ideological clarity or the polity's response.[56]

Far more important were the politics and policymaking engendered by the emergence of oil and gas as essential resources. State court decisions in the late nineteenth century equated them with *ferae naturae* such as fish and game. Unlike coal and other minerals they were fluid and mercurial; hence a landowner had no proprietary claim to the oil and gas below unless he could "capture" them. By the same token, almost every state accepted the landowner's right to extract these resources with little or no regard for the claims of his neighbors.[57]

The twofold intent of this policy was to encourage rapid extraction and to prevent large companies from reserving oil-rich lands for future use. West Virginia's highest court in 1902 favored a rule of construction "which discourages tying up and rendering unproductive vast fields of mineral wealth, construes every contract and lease . . . so as to best promote production, development and progress, and frowns upon every attempt to evade it as being in contravention of both good morals and public policy."[58]

But after the turn of the century, oil took off as a source of heating, diesel, and gasoline fuel. The prevailing legal status of this resource stimulated pell-mell, often wasteful extraction; expensive storage above ground, before one's neighbor tapped a shared pool; and a widespread reliance on leases rather than on land ownership. Courts and legislatures began to craft a new policy of oil (and soon gas) conservation. In 1900 the Supreme Court upheld an Indiana law forbidding oil extraction unless proper storage facilities were available, on the ground that although the state could not prohibit the taking of oil, under its police power it could prevent waste. In 1911 the Court applied this principle to natural gas.[59]

Judicial thinking moved toward a doctrine of reasonable use, which took account of the rights of adjacent owners and a public interest in conservation. But it made way slowly in the face of a powerful, deeply entrenched commitment to development: "Waste may be prohibited, the method of disposal regulated, but the right to commercially exploit what lies above or beneath the surface of one's own property can be taken away—never."[60]

Oil invoked not only state regulation but also national defense and strategic considerations. As the Navy shifted from coal- to oil-fired warships, an executive order by Taft in 1909 created a reserve of 3 million oil-rich acres in California and Wyoming. Private oil developers challenged the legality of the act, but the Supreme Court upheld it in 1915.[61]

Thus the stage was set for the Teapot Dome scandal. In 1922 Harding's secretary of the interior, Albert Fall, leased portions of the naval reserve to favored oil men in return for "loans." A Senate committee unearthed these dealings in 1924. The ensuing brouhaha echoed the prewar Ballinger-Pinchot affair. It raised a multitude of policy and political issues: extraction versus conservation; bureaucratic infighting (Interior, Navy, and Justice departmental rivalries over the impact of the oil reserves on water power and national park and forest interests); and the corruption that attended the growing value of natural resources.[62]

An oil-shortage scare much like the earlier concern over timber depletion rose and fell in the wake of World War I. The increasingly auto-laden United States consumed 70 million barrels more than it produced in 1919. The nation used three-quarters of the world's oil but extracted a far smaller proportion. Crude oil imports, 14 percent of domestic production in 1914, rose to 27 percent in 1921. The Senate wanted to know what restrictions foreign governments (Great Britain in particular) imposed on American companies in the Middle East and Asia. Henry Cabot Lodge and others warned that the British bid fair to control the world's oil supply; there was talk of a federal oil corporation to stimulate American oil development overseas.[63]

President Coolidge's Oil Conservation Board (the secretaries of Commerce, Interior, War, and Navy) somberly predicted in 1926: "On the present basis of production and consumption, with no new discoveries of oil lands, and without considering foreign fields, the United States has just *six years* of joy-riding left. Other estimates vary from ten to twenty-five years—none of which reckonings leave much hope for our gasoline civilization." New finds might be expected, but "certainly we are much nearer the end of new discoveries that we were a generation ago." One observer thought that a serious shortage would lead to price rises, increased oil imports from Mexico and elsewhere, and if necessary the large-scale development of oil from shale and fuel alcohol. But (not for the last time) the crystal ball of oil prediction turned out to be cloudy. New finds soon undercut the fear of oil depletion.[64]

Barrel value at the wells went from $30.70 in 1920 at the height of the postwar oil "crisis" to $1.34 in 1923, as annual production rose from 442 to 732 million barrels. A gasoline price war swept through the Midwest in 1923; and in 1927 oil company heads complained of an unparalleled "orgy of overproduction." By 1928, known reserves had climbed to 70 billion gallons: 100 years' supply at current consumption rates. Oil stocks lost half a billion dollars in value from

1925 to 1927; Commerce Secretary Hoover wanted the Sherman Act amended to allow pooling to avoid overproduction; the large companies called for temporary suspension of drilling. But direct federal regulation of oil production was of doubtful constitutionality. And the industry was too diversified and anarchic for self-regulation.[65]

The Depression sharply worsened these conditions, increasing the pressure to transform the regulatory structure into one designed to spur rather than to impede production. Proration (fixed quotas for individual firms) and unit operation (the consolidation of all properties in a field into a single operating unit) were the devices of choice. But they faced substantial obstacles of law, politics, and self-interest.

A structure of restraint gradually grew, corallike, on the base of the states' resource conservation power. Oil-and-gas-rich Oklahoma used this rationale to limit the output of major pools as early as 1915. In the same year a Texas statute empowered that state's Corporation Commission to close down production on the ground that overproduction led to waste. As former Interior secretary Hubert Work delicately put it in 1927: "Conservation in recent years has lost much of its theoretical flavor and is now understood as having to do with everyday life."[66]

It was on this basis that California in 1929 created a Department of Natural Resources to supervise oil drilling and extraction. The Supreme Court unanimously upheld that state's law setting an optimum oil-gas extraction ratio. But proration was defeated in a 1931 referendum: low gas prices had their charms in car-laden California.[67]

Texas had more oil and fewer cars. The state's Railroad Commission was empowered in 1931 to reduce production in order to prevent waste—with the stern proviso that "this shall not be construed to mean economic waste." And as the Depression worsened, proration came with a rush. By the end of 1931 Oklahoma, Kansas, and even California had enacted such laws; and the courts state and federal raised no objection.[68]

In what an ironist called "one of the most spectacular conservation gestures of all time," Oklahoma's governor "Alfalfa Bill" Murray declared martial law and called out the National Guard in the summer of 1931 to close flush wells, on the ground that they violated the states' oil and gas conservation law. More than 3,000 wells were shut down to force up a price that had sunk to 20 cents a barrel. The official rationale was the need to protect the value of the state's school oil lands and hence its tax revenue, and to uphold the Fourteenth

Amendment rights of independent producers against monopolistic corporations. In fact, political pressure came in good part from oil landowners, who complained that the extraction and sale of oil at giveaway prices reduced their royalties. Martial law was imposed in East Texas as well, where 1,600 wells were closed. In principle, the purpose was to conserve oil and avoid the danger of mob action; in practice, to stop the headlong rush to get as much oil as possible out of the state before the Railroad Commission's proration rules came into effect. The Oklahoma and Texas actions cut off a million barrels a day, 40 percent of U.S. production.[69]

This was too much for the judiciary. The Supreme Court in 1932 upheld an injunction blocking a proration order by Texas's governor that limited wells to an output of 100 barrels a day. Although the courts accepted a broad interpretation of the states' conservation power, they were not ready to define the oil business as one affected with a public interest. At the same time, there were powerful constitutional obstacles to national control of oil production.[70]

Once again, the structure of the polity made it difficult for regulation to keep pace with rapid change in the quantity and use of a major natural resource. The roller coaster of oil glut and scarcity continued in later decades, but the awkward fit of policy and practice remained.

8 · Regulating the City

We have seen how modernity, imposing as it did new conditions of agricultural marketing and resource use, involved the American countryside in an ever-larger range of policy issues during the early twentieth century. Urban housing and land use underwent a strikingly similar development. In neither case did a broad national policy emerge. Instead, interests, issues, and outcomes proliferated—the whole encased in the traditional framework of interest-group politics and continuing judicial scrutiny. Zoning became the preferred form of determining urban land use. As in the case of the conservation of natural resources, it had both utilitarian and aesthetic motives, and once again the utilitarian impulse was the determining one. More imaginative work in urban land use and tenement design went on outside the realm of government, in organizations such as the Regional Planning Association.

Housing

American urban land, like its rural counterpart, differed most from Europe in its relatively diffuse ownership. True, urban landholding in Britain was not as concentrated as in the countryside. But great London estates such as those of the dukes of Bedford and Westminster, complex freehold and leasehold tenure systems, and heavily encrusted land transfer procedures made urban land ownership and use a far more portentous matter than in America.[1]

One issue that transcended national differences was the quest for a permanent land title registration system to make the transfer of property simpler and faster and to reduce the need for expensive title searches. Parliament passed a law in 1897 providing for official title registration in London. But solicitors faced with a threat to an important source of their revenue, courts reluctant to upset traditional conveyancing practices, and the high costs and low efficiency of the Land Registry Office made permanent registration a reform that grew slowly and was never fully achieved.[2]

Heavy death duties and other forms of taxation, and the increasing importance of urban/commercial as distinct from rural/agricultural land, raised the pressure to modernize (or at least to codify) the dense, confusing, centuries-old body of British property law after World War I. The result was the 1925 Law of Property Act, a consolidation of the law of real property designed to make real estate as readily transferable as personal property.[3]

Americans might have been expected to establish permanent land registration much more readily. Land was more widely held, more frequently bought and sold: "Settled property is the rule in England. It is the exception in the United States." And indeed states began to try title registry in the late nineteenth century. The Supreme Court in 1900 upheld the constitutionality of the Torrens registration system, which allowed title to pass by entry in an official register. By 1917 nearly twenty states, including Illinois, New York, California, and Ohio, had Torrens laws. But then the movement stopped; and from then on it led "a somewhat anaemic and precarious existence." Torrens registration scored its biggest success in Chicago; but even there it accounted only for about 15 percent of property transfers.[4]

Title insurance and mortgage loan companies, and lawyers with a stake in the existing system, effectively opposed the Torrens reform. The cost, cumbersomeness, and continuing legal uncertainty of permanent registration militated against it. And the courts were reluctant to vest what they saw as a judicial function—determining land ownership—in the registrars administering the Torrens system. Every Torrens state allowed an appeal to the courts to quiet title disputes; none allowed its legislature to make the registrar a judicial officer. As so often was the case, powerful interests impeded the implementation of administrative oversight.[5]

In any event, not ease of land transfer but the character and availability of housing for a burgeoning population became a major urban issue in the early twentieth century. British housing policy had an intimate relationship to the more general problem of improving the lot of the lower classes. A Royal Commission on the Housing of the Working

Classes issued an influential report in 1885, and Charles Booth's scarifying descriptions of the living conditions of London's poor intensified public (or, more accurately, official) awareness.

The Housing of the Working Classes Act (1890) gave local authorities the power to condemn land, take down unsanitary buildings, and construct housing for sale or rent. This was Britain's major housing law until after the war, when the 1919 Housing Act set off a great and sustained expansion of subsidized council-house building. The 1925 Housing Act added national subsidies, and yet another law in 1930 substantially extended the land clearance and other powers of local authorities. The courts put constraints on the administrative powers granted by these laws, and landlords fought (often successfully) for increased compensation. Nevertheless, from 1919 to 1934 1,250,000 dwelling units were built, more than half of them with government assistance.[6]

In America, too, concern mounted over the living conditions of workers and the poor. But the scale of the immigrant inflow, the rapid growth of tenements, and deeply entrenched resistance to public or assisted housing led to a different policy stress: less on the size of the housing stock and more on regulating the structures (in particular, the tenements) erected by private builders.

The state of housing became a conspicuous part of the turn-of-the-century American social agenda. Voluntarism played a part; for example, civic associations and socially prominent citizens in the nation's capital formed the Washington Sanitary Improvement Company in 1897 to buy lots and build houses for poor whites and blacks. But the major effort went into tougher regulation. And here the classic strengths and weaknesses of a pluralist polity came into play. Thus Wisconsin, the forcing house of state progressivism, enacted a model housing law in 1907—model, that is, from the perspective of reformers seeking stricter safety and sanitary requirements. Its opponents—builders and the building trades fearful that it would stifle the industry, Progressives and social democrats resentful that it did not go further—thought otherwise.[7]

New York City's experience vividly displays the potential—and the limits—of housing regulation. Its tenements, and the problems that came with them, embodied for many the social dangers of modern life. An 1894 commission headed by *Century* editor Richard Watson Gilder dwelt on the moral as well as the public health consequences of tenements and slums. So did the publications and photographs of

Jacob Riis and others, which vividly conveyed a sense of those evils to the public.

There ensued a spate of public activity classically Progressive in character. The Greater New York charter of 1898 provided for a commission to revise the city's building code. Housing reformer Lawrence Veiller was chiefly responsible for the Tenement House Act of 1901, which broke new ground by imposing specific building requirements. From now on every tenement room must have a window, every apartment a toilet. Enforcement was entrusted to a new, independent Tenement House Department.[8]

This "new law" code of 1901 served as the model for a multitude of other state and local housing laws over the next couple of decades. Machine politicians generally supported these acts. The votes of the immigrant masses counted for more than the blandishments of tenement owners; and the Chicago city council appears to have adopted its 1902 code in part because of the greater prospects for graft that lay in higher standards.[9]

Nearly 2 million people were housed in "new law" tenements erected from 1902 to 1923—and in that period no lives were lost in them because of fire.[10] But site clearing for municipal improvements (such as the new East River bridges, which led to the razing of hundreds of tenements), the constant replacement of old and small by new and larger tenements, and above all the sheer size of the immigrant flood pouring into New York—by 1910 over 40 percent of the city's population of 5 million was foreign-born—made New York City's housing market uniquely tight and volatile.

These conditions, along with the intensely speculative character of the housing market, created powerful rent-raising pressures. One observer thought that from 1903 to 1905 almost every Manhattan tenement was sold at least once, at ever-increasing prices. The great majority of landlords were small real estate entrepreneurs, often leasing to middlemen ("leasters") or tenants who in turn sublet to boarders: a process guaranteed to push rents up. Lower East Side rents increased an estimated 25–30 percent in 1903–04 alone; in some locations rents rose as much as 60 percent in six years. The threat (far less often the actuality) of evictions grew: 1,300 petitions to evict were filed in three municipal courts during the first ten days of April 1904. One consequence was a rash of rent strikes: in 1904, and again in 1908 during the hard times following the panic of 1907. Tenants' associations blossomed, as did Socialist organizers such as Bertha Leibson, the "Joan of Arc of the East Side." Rent levels joined housing conditions as a staple of local housing politics.[11]

At the same time, the growth of a lower-middle-class clientele fostered a shift in residential construction from tenements to apartment houses—a change first evident in the 1905–1907 building boom. Another spur was the availability of cheap new land, as new bridges, subways, and tunnels made Brooklyn and the Bronx accessible to large segments of New York's population. The existence of empty apartment houses in the Bronx by 1908 indicated that construction had at least caught up with lower-middle-class needs. This fact also affected the Lower East Side. Tenement landlords signed rent-reduction agreements with rent strike leaders, and high rents and the housing shortage subsided as an issue until World War I. A striking aspect of this drama of housing crisis and response was the minimal role of the state. Here was an area of modern American life in which public policymaking had a particularly marginal place.[12]

How difficult it was for law and regulation to keep pace with a rapidly changing housing market was apparent in the *Grimmer* case, which came before the New York Court of Appeals in 1912. A building had been erected as an "apartment hotel." Then the owner (as he intended all along) converted it to a tenement. The Tenement House Department moved to block him; the court decided that a structure with marble floors, elevators, and a kitchen and bath for each apartment was not a tenement under the law, and ordered the building vacated. This decision had substantial implications. According to the court's definition, an estimated 85% of the "new law" buildings, housing 1.5 million people, were not in fact tenements because they provided separate kitchens and bathrooms for each family. By implication, they no longer came under the regulations of the 1901 Tenement Act. Within twenty-four hours, the legislature reaffirmed the definition of a tenement (dating from 1867) as a building in which three or more families did their own cooking, regardless of the rent they paid.[13]

For all the regulation-copying that went on among states and cities, housing law remained an intensely local affair, reflecting a variety of needs, conditions, and interests. Outside New York the value of land was not so overriding a factor, and multifamily working-class housing usually had three or fewer stories. Indeed, two-thirds of the housing units built in America from 1900 to 1920 were for one family, one-fifth for three or more. Single-family units were a substantial majority of the housing built in American cities from 1900 to 1930.

Chicago's 1902 housing ordinance encouraged building out rather than up by requiring fire-resistant walls for tenements more than three stories high. More than a million Philadelphians lived in small row houses in the early years of the century: a pattern sustained by low land costs, eased building requirements for houses less than sixteen feet wide, and an 1895 building code that made tenement houses too costly.[14]

The Massachusetts housing law of 1892 also discouraged the construction of multiunit tenements: only nineteen were built in Boston in 1903. Instead it fostered the proliferation of that distinctive habitat the Boston wooden three-decker. Its great appeal lay in the fact that it did not come under the law's fire safeguards, which applied to units housing more than three families. A Boston commission in 1903 and state commissions in 1904 and 1906 sought to tighten the housing laws, and in 1912 a new tenement act set down requirements that had the effect of substantially increasing the construction cost of three-deckers.[15]

More positive state intervention in the housing market ran into legal and other difficulties. When the legislature in 1909 created a Massachusetts Homestead Commission and proposed to offer state aid for workingmen to build houses in the suburbs and the country, the Supreme Judicial Court intervened. It advised the legislature that the commonwealth could not "engage in real estate operations," even of a philanthropic nature: it could not tax homeowners in order to aid people whose "temperament, environment or habits" kept them from owning homes.[16]

A strong popular belief in the social virtue of homeowning led an overwhelming majority of Massachusetts voters to approve a referendum proposition that would allow use of the state's credit and capital to help people obtain homes. Labor unions in particular supported the measure, which allowed cities and towns to develop, build, and sell houses—though not at less than cost. But in ten years the state Homestead Commission erected a grand total of twelve frame houses on one seven-acre tract. Regulation might affect the character of mass housing, but there appeared to be little prospect of a more direct government role in what remained an overwhelmingly private, small-unit mode of production.[17]

Then America entered World War I, and housing needs unparalleled in their scale and immediacy erupted around army camps, shipyards, and factories. The response to this emergency included the first significant venture in government-built and operated housing.

About a dozen wooden communities for from 1,500 to 30,000 people went up for munitions and shipyard workers, primarily in New England and the middle Atlantic states. Some $150–175 million was spent—a modest sum compared with Great Britain's $700 million wartime expenditure on workers' housing—most of it during the six months from mid-May to mid-November 1918. A number of agencies joined in this effort: the United States Housing Corporation (established in July 1918), the Department of Labor's Bureau of Housing and Transportation, the Emergency Fleet Corporation's Division of Passenger Transportation and Housing, the War and Navy departments. But its ephemerality turned out to be the most notable aspect of this venture in public housing. By the end of the war almost no Housing Corporation projects were operating; and practically all government-built housing was emptied, dismantled, or sold off after the Armistice.[18]

The protection of tenants was a much more significant issue during and after the war. The need to attract and hold labor and the public sentiment against wartime profiteering gave a powerful impetus to the efforts of arsenal and navy yard officers, corporation presidents, unions, and local councils of defense to do something about escalating housing costs. That something turned out to be voluntary, not public. The middle-class Tenants' Protective Association of Pennsylvania claimed 30,000 members in Philadelphia alone. It publicized evictions and fought them in the courts. A wartime Philadelphia ordinance obliged landlords to maintain a temperature of at least sixty degrees, provided for six-month instead of monthly leases and new standard lease forms, and eliminated the right of landlords to require tenants to waive their right to appeal magistrates' decisions in lease disputes. But this was untypical. Though more than eighty city committees on rent profiteering sprang up, most promoted by the Emergency Fleet Corporation, they could do little more than publicize the issue and mediate disputes. And they soon discovered how difficult it was to determine fair rent.[19]

The skyrocketing cost of living, the return of veterans, and the tightness of housing in most major cities made rent regulation a major postwar issue. New York City housing once again became an important subject of public concern. The Ottinger Law of 1918 set the stage for trouble when it substituted month-by-month tenure for the prevailing unwritten one-year tenancy. Much speculative buying and selling of buildings went on in 1919 and 1920; and an estimated 100,000 dispossession notices were served on tenants for the traditional end-of-lease day of October 1, 1920. At the same time the state legislature's Lockwood Committee, led by its flamboyant counsel Samuel J. Untermyer, told an unsavory tale of collusion among contractors, materials dealers, and union leaders to keep building costs high.[20]

In April and September the legislature passed more than twenty housing laws. These provided for state and New York City rent controls; strengthened the power of the judiciary to grant stays on and limit the ground for eviction; put the burden of proof for lease noncompliance on the landlord; restored yearlong oral leases; made failure to provide water, heat, and light a misdemeanor—and, to stimulate new building, offered the lure of a twelve-year exemption from the property tax. During the summer of 1920, New York City's Municipal Court stayed thousands of eviction notices.[21]

More ambitious reformers thought that the situation demanded bolder action, on the scale of Britain's Housing and Town Planning Act of 1919. Proposals—and enactments—designed to ease the housing shortage abounded. Commerce Secretary Herbert Hoover called for increased housing investment by banks and the postal savings system. Massachusetts and Illinois joined New York to pass laws blocking evictions by empowering the courts to set temporary reasonable rents. An Illinois Housing and Building Commission was established in 1919, charged with reporting to the legislature in 1921. Wisconsin, the bellwether Progressive state, authorized homebuilding cooperatives in whose stock local authorities could invest. And it created a Milwaukee administrative board, like a public utilities commission, which could regulate rents (subject to judicial review). The Housing Committee of the New York Reconstruction Commission proposed a comprehensive program of local housing boards, low-interest state credit for moderately priced homes, tax-exempt State Land Bank bonds, and a law enabling cities to annex adjoining land and build housing on it. Most notably, Congress in October 1919 enacted a rent-control law for the District of Columbia.[22]

The New York Court of Appeals sustained that state's rent control laws as a proper application of the police power. One legal commentator approved: "Why should contract rights be more sacred, where public welfare is involved, than other property rights?" But Wisconsin and District of Columbia courts struck down their communities' rent laws.[23]

Then the Supreme Court reviewed—and a Holmes majority opinion upheld—rent control in Washington and New York. It did so on the ground that the conditions of the war and postwar period made housing a business affected with a public interest. Rent control was justified as an application of the state's emergency police power. Justice Joseph McKenna dissented, acidly inquiring if "Socialism, or some form of Socialism, is the only permanent corrective or accommodation," if the Constitution "had become an anachronism." But when the Washington rent-control law expired in 1925, President Calvin Coolidge, fearing that high rents fed government workers' demands for larger salaries, supported an act of Congress granting the District's Rent Commission the power to determine fair and reasonable rents.[24]

The housing shortage in New York (as elsewhere) rapidly eased after 1921. Wage increases and immigration restriction reduced the strain on the Lower East Side. New York City granted tax exemptions to builders, stimulating a building boom fed by more general economic and demographic factors. The rate of construction in 1922 was four times that of the previous year, and housing for 38,000 families (more than half of it one- or two-family units) went up in seven months. But most of this boom involved middle-class homes and apartment houses. The supply of low-income housing remained tight, and the tenements inexorably deteriorated. In 1926 Governor Alfred E. Smith put forward a grandiose plan to get rid of the slums. He proposed a state Housing Board empowered to offer a variety of incentives to builders of low-cost housing, such as tax-exempt bonds and use of the city's condemnation power to put together large parcels. But a Republican-dominated legislature rejected state financing and created a Housing Board limited to private sources of funds.[25]

Only a handful of Housing Board–sponsored projects got under way before the Depression. Instead, New York housing policy continued to rely on fine-tuning existing law and the private housing market. The Multiple Dwelling Law of 1928 ended once and for all the distinction between tenements and apartment houses. Henceforth all multifamily houses would be built to the same (more stringent) light, air, and safety standards. Meanwhile the courts gradually expanded the scope of landlord responsibility for building repairs and restricting noise and disorder—in good part, presumably, because multiunit dwellings were more and more a part of the middle-class way of life.[26]

With the advent of the Depression, the focus of housing policy shifted once again; from availability, rent, and quality to foreclosure and blight. The change of emphasis appeared in Minnesota's mortgage moratorium law of 1933. This measure, which empowered the courts to refuse confirmation of foreclosure sales if the price was "unreasonably and unfairly inadequate" and to extend mortgage redemption periods on "just and equitable" terms, copied New York's Emergency Housing Act of 1920. The Supreme Court upheld the Minnesota law on the familiar basis of the emergency police power. "In the last analysis, the only legal question before the Court was whether what was done in a New York housing shortage in 1920 could be done in Minnesota in 1933," one expert observed.[27]

Other states sought to put legal obstacles in the way of foreclosure. And lower courts in New York, Illinois, and elsewhere found ingenious justifications for refusing to confirm deficiency judgments. While foreclosures sharply rose—from 135,000 in 1929 to a peak of 252,000 in 1933—many lenders (in particular, banks and insurance companies) were reluctant to be saddled with marginal property. Compromise arrangements were far more common than outright seizure.[28]

Even in this parlous time and in this socially sensitive area, public housing policy remained marginal and attenuated. In 1932 Herbert Hoover convened the President's Conference on Home Building and Home Ownership—typical of his response to the Depression. Old-time Progressive housing reformer Lawrence Veiller played a prominent role at the meeting, which called on the government to aid in clearing slum housing sites but for private enterprise to do the actual rebuilding.[29]

The Emergency Relief and Construction Act of 1932 authorized the Reconstruction Finance Corporation to lend money to housing firms engaged in slum reconstruction or putting up low-income housing. This was the first peacetime housing subsidy. But real estate interests imposed severe limits on the size and terms of these loans. Nor was there any real commitment on the part of the RFC: by the end of 1933 fourteen states had housing corporations eligible for this program, but the RFC agreed to only one tentative loan and never disbursed any funds.[30]

With the coming of the New Deal, national housing policy entered a new phase. In 1933 the Home Owners' Loan Corporation brought the advantages of government underwriting to existing home mortgages, and a year later the Federal Housing Administration extended that benefit to new housing, with massive future consequences for American homeowning.

Slum clearance and public housing proved to be more difficult policy areas. The Public Works Authority (PWA) included slum clearing among its projects. The cautious leadership of Harold Ickes and strict equity requirements at first severely limited its impact. But then a Public Works Emergency Housing Corporation, based on the same rationale as the post–World War I housing laws, was created with a $100 million fund to build low-cost housing. A federal circuit court held that the corporation's power of eminent domain unduly extended federal authority within a state. Nevertheless, additional infusions of funds and a more aggressive policy of encouraging localities enabled the PWA to play an active part in slum clearance and rebuilding.[31]

Pressure for a more direct and substantial government role burgeoned in the hothouse environment of the New Deal years. New York, Ohio, and New Jersey created state housing authorities in 1933 and 1934; and a 1934 New York law opened the way to publicly financed slum clearance and construction. In 1936 the New York Court of Appeals broke new ground when it held that because housing was a "public use," the state could use its power of eminent domain to acquire land. And in 1937, in the wake of Roosevelt's grim Inaugural picture of "one-third of a nation ill-housed, ill-clad, ill-nourished," Congress established the United States Housing Authority: the federal government's first nonemergency commitment to the construction of public housing.[32]

But the counterforces of interest and ideology were not readily overridden. Federal district courts continued to deny the constitutionality of eminent domain for slum clearance. The sorry story of public housing over the next half-century made clear how dense and tenacious were the constraints—political, legal, sociocultural—on a large and direct housing role by the American state.[33]

Planning and Zoning

As technology and the inflow of people altered the American urban landscape around the turn of the century, the sense of what government and law might do to shape that environment became richer and more varied. The agenda expanded from the traditional concerns of nuisance law—light, air, noise—to include a new stress on the aesthetics of urban space, city planning, and (most notably) citywide zoning.

It is as common today to ascribe this development to real estate interests and social control as it once was to ascribe it to the reform impulse. Certainly self-interest both economic and social was an important factor. But as in so many other realms of early twentieth-century public life, the more meaningful perspective is the widening range of urban policy. "The interests" of the American city were richer, more powerful than before. But so too were "interests": the multitudinous wants of an ever-larger and more-diverse population, the complex requirements of an ever-more-intricate technological and social setting. And as elsewhere, this drama of new needs and new demands was played out within the bounds of a tenaciously persistent traditional polity.

The City Beautiful movement around the turn of the century embodied the Progressive spirit in city planning. The ideal of a great urban civic center, in which commerce, the arts, and government came together in functional and architectural unity, expressed in material terms the dominant element in the Progressive consciousness: a social unity transcending region, class, and ethnicity. Its most direct source was Daniel Burnham's White City, the Chicago World's Fair of 1893. Grandiose schemes based on that architectural vision of classic order and unity appeared for a number of cities, including the District of Columbia's plan of 1902, Burnham's 1909 Chicago Lakefront Plan, the San Francisco Civic Center, Philadelphia's Parkway complex, new centers for New York and Cleveland—some forty-four cities in all by 1908.

More than the physical well-being of America's cities was at stake here. A 1909 National Congress on City Planning commingled urban aesthetics, cheap transportation, factory zoning, tenement laws assuring adequate heat and light, and land taxes designed to discourage speculation. "American cities," said one commentator, "have in the main capitulated to the real estate interests. They are now summoned to conserve the health, well-being, and morals of the community to which the city plan is essential."[34]

A few civic centers were in fact (and in part) built. But neither the

City Beautiful nor comprehensive urban planning made much of a mark in the early years of the century. Historian Charles Beard asked in 1927 why two decades of city planning added up to little more than some civic plazas and boulevards that made it easier for businessmen to drive to work. His answer: a congeries of special interests—real estate, utility, manufacturing, commercial, transportation, banking, labor, political—on a scale and of a variety that segmented the citizenry and made unified planning impossible.[35]

The interests of individual property holders had deep roots in law and social custom. Anglo-American law at the turn of the century still held that an owner had an absolute right to use his property as he desired, a right limited only by the uncertain restraints of nuisance law and by what the legislature chose to do (and could do) under the state's police power. Thus the Supreme Court in 1899 reaffirmed that special assessments for street improvements could not be greater than the benefits derived by the abutting property owners. The belief that the free use of property was the primary engine of economic growth reinforced this inclination. Turn-of-the-century American courts (more retrograde than their British counterparts) did not recognize a neighboring property owner's right to an easement of light, because this would impede new building construction.[36]

The first significant modification of this mind-set came in the unlikely context of urban aesthetics. The same reaction to the chaos and disorder of modern city life that fueled the City Beautiful movement led to more modest goals: beautified parks and parkways, and a substantial assault on that particularly obtrusive object the billboard. But the story of the antibillboard campaign makes clear how strong was the courts' disinclination to include so nonmaterial a consideration as aesthetics in the calculus of damage and recovery, or even to bring it within the public interest as defined by the police power.

A new distaste for unsightly advertising was not a peculiarly American phenomenon. British judges for centuries had frowned on aesthetic regulation: "for prospect which is a matter only for delight and not of necessity, no action lies for stopping thereof" (1587); "It cannot be said of a hoarding [billboard] that it will offend against any sense: the utmost that can be said against it is that it is a blot on the landscape" (1907). But around the turn of the century an antibillboard crusade began. The British Society for Checking the Abuses of Public Advertising (SCAPA) broadcast its views in its journal *A Beautiful World* and sought parliamentary action that would "mark the

turning-point in the contest between the forces which make for rest-
fulness and order . . . and the forces which make for vexatious confusion." The London Sky Signs Act of 1891 took aim at overambitious
billboards in the metropolis; the Advertisements Regulation Bill of
1907 (justified on the ground that the eye is as entitled to protection
as the ear) gave local authorities the power to regulate. hoardings.
SCAPA secretary Richard Evans declared: "for the first time scenery
is treated as a national asset." Nations on the Continent took similar
steps: billboards were prohibited on public buildings and the approaches to Paris; a 1902 Prussian law forbade advertisements that
disfigured the landscape; Italian officials were empowered to prevent
"antiestitico" commercialism.[37]

Intimations in American courts that aesthetics had legal standing
begin to appear after 1900. In 1905 the Massachusetts Supreme Judicial Court observed of beautified parks and boulevards: "the promotion of the pleasure of the people is a public purpose, for which public
money may be used and taxes laid, even if the pleasure is secured
merely by delighting one of the senses." But this did not mean that it
countenanced a proposed regulation limiting the size of billboards visible from the Metropolitan Park Commission's parkways. To erect a
billboard on contiguous property was "as natural a use of such lands
as is the use of store fronts and show windows for display of goods . . .
or other modes of advertising. It resembles the placing of advertising
pages on each side of the literary portion of a periodical."[38]

A 1911 review of the legal standing of municipal aesthetics concluded: "The courts of this country have, with great unanimity, held
that the police power cannot interfere with private property rights for
purely aesthetic purposes." New Jersey's high court declared: "Aesthetic considerations are a matter of luxury and indulgence rather
than of necessity, and it is necessity alone which justifies the exercise
of the police power to take private property without compensation."
But the growing tension between the conditions of modern urban life
and the free use of property could not be forever denied. The regulation of billboards rested on a mechanism of judicial indirection by
which aesthetic regulation was made acceptable—an urban analogue
to the legitimation of state restrictions on the exploitation of natural
resources.[39]

In tone and spirit the movement to regulate or abolish billboards
closely resembled the concurrent campaigns against liquor and pros-

titution. A Chautauqua lecture series dwelt on the billboard evil in 1908; the American Civic Association and other citizens' groups joined in the assault. Billboard interests fought back. The Associated Bill-Posters of the United States argued that their business had great commercial value; and in a burst of self-interested public spirit they offered space for a million antituberculosis posters.[40]

Given the shakiness of the legal argument from aesthetics, it was necessary to demonstrate that billboards endangered the health, safety, morals, or welfare of the community, and thus came under the states' police power. A 1911 Missouri decision set out the rationale for billboard regulation:

> In cases of fire they often cause their spread and constitute barriers against their extinction; and in cases of high wind, their temporary character, frail structure, and broad surface, render them liable to be blown down and to fall upon and injure those who may happen to be in their vicinity . . . common observation teaches us that the ground in the rear thereof is being constantly used as privies and dumping ground for all kinds of waste and deleterious matters, thereby creating public nuisances and jeopardizing public health; the evidence also shows that behind these obstructions the lowest form of prostitution and other acts of immorality are frequently carried on, almost under public gaze; they offer shelter and concealment for the criminal while lying in wait for his victim; and last, but not least, they obstruct the light, sunshine, and air, which are so conducive to health and comfort.

Even this *catalogue raisonée* of horrors was incomplete. It left out one argument advanced by the advocates of a similar ordinance in Kansas City: billboards "intensified the heat by reflecting the sun's rays in the streets."[41]

On this basis billboard regulation became an accepted part of the urban scene. In the mid-1920s a group of Massachusetts billboard companies sought to enjoin the accumulating restrictions on their business. A decade later the Supreme Judicial Court got around to dismissing their complaint, thereby recognizing, said one commentator, that this regulation "tended to the enlargement of the total liberty of the citizen rather than to the multiplication of restraints."[42]

Noble words; but the hard fact of the matter was that judicial opposition persisted to takings without compensation for purely aesthetic purposes. The decline of billboards had much more to do with economic and technological change (rising land values, higher buildings, faster cars) than with the decades-long effort to regulate them.

Zoning was the major American policy response to the rise of the modern city. There were European antecedents: Frankfurt in particular. French law first classified urban buildings according to their aesthetic and historic value in 1887; the regulations were codified in 1913 in the Law with Regard to Historic Monuments—the same year as the passage of Britain's Ancient Monuments Consolidated Amendment Act.

But these restrictions dwelt either on large and comprehensive city planning as in Frankfurt, or on the height, use, or historical importance of individual buildings. Americans, typically, sought more to regulate the present and the future than to preserve the past. The idea that a city should be divided by law into zones of distinctive character and use emerged from the dominant economic, legal-political, and cultural values of the early twentieth-century United States.[43]

Large-scale planning may have been politically unfeasible; yet piecemeal ordinance-by-ordinance (or case-by-case) responses to the problems of the modern city hardly met its needs. This inutility was evident in two Supreme Court decisions: *Welch v. Swasey* (1909) upheld a Boston restriction on building heights; *Eubank v. Richmond* (1912) struck down a similar law in Richmond. Ordinances aimed at particular problems such as noxious factories often allowed local property owners to waive their restrictions. Nor did private covenants limiting the use of property serve: they were too piecemeal; if perpetual, too restrictive; if limited in time, too uncertain.[44]

There was no need to look to European precedents for constraints on urban land use. California communities excluded Chinese-run laundries during the 1870s and 1880s, and by 1915 almost all of Los Angeles had been zoned for residential or industrial use. In 1913 alone, Minnesota, Illinois, New York, and Wisconsin laws empowered their cities to enact zoning ordinances. Citywide zoning found ready nourishment in the prevailing mind-set of the Progressive years: "The day of the palliatives and the patent medicine is passing—in city-growth as in the fight on disease. We must do all that is necessary to combat the forces of congestion at their source. For in that direction lie . . . a beautiful environment, a home for children, an opportunity to enjoy the day's leisure and the ability to ride on the Juggernaut of industry, instead of being prostrated under its wheels."[45]

But New York's Building Zone Plan of 1916, the first comprehensive zoning law and the most influential one of the time, did not stem from these elevated social goals. Its immediate source was Fifth Avenue merchants who feared the encroachment of garmentmaking lofts into the street's lower reaches: land values on Fifth between 23rd and 24th streets had been halved. Their pressure led to the enactment of a general zoning law based on a 1914–15 survey of Manhattan that elaborately mapped the use, density, and value of the island. Five use districts were established, their legality based on the comprehensiveness of the plan and on the police power.[46]

The movement for comprehensive zoning reached flash point in the mid-1920s. On January 1, 1922, 55 municipalities had such ordinances; four years later the total was 425, covering more than half the nation's urban population. As with all new regulatory systems, zoning raised fresh administrative, political, and above all legal issues.

The politics of zoning rested not on power elites but on coalitions of interested elements. As the head of the District of Columbia Zoning Commission explained to a British visitor: "The real city is a federation of neighborhoods. To recognize this is the function of zoning." Pittsburgh's 1923 ordinance was the product of a six-year campaign by the city's Civic Club and a number of other business and reform groups. The opposition was even more diverse: a mix of building and trust companies, realtors and real estate speculators, savings and loan associations, local boards of trade, unions, small businessmen, and lower- and lower-middle-class spokesmen. In Portland, Oregon, where workers tended to live in detached houses, organized labor and small homeowners were zoning's most vocal supporters, real estate speculators its chief opponents. Indeed, outside the larger industrial cities this was the prevailing pattern. No less politicized were the administrative boards that oversaw the implementation of zoning and reviewed appeals. Boston's zoning board included representatives of the Associated Industries of Massachusetts, the Central Labor Union, and the Boston Chamber of Commerce.[47]

Comprehensive, citywide zoning did not win immediate or easy judicial acceptance. One observer noted: "A new mode of property regulation is not likely to sustain itself in the courts, unless it can be shown to bear some analogy to recognized and sanctioned traditional methods of regulation." But how to square so novel and intrusive (in the sense that it limited the free use and disposal of property) a policy as zoning? One way was to treat it as a sweeping modern application of the old nuisance law rule that one man shall not use his property so as to injure another. But the most promising approach for the courts was to accept zoning as a legitimate extension of the states' police power. This was by no means automatic. Constitutional law expert Thomas Reed Powell wrote in 1919, "It will not be surprising if [zoning] legislation is condemned as an attempt to restrict the profitable use of one man's land for the benefit of his neighbors." [48]

Zoning advocates took a leaf from earlier billboard cases and identified their cause with the public's health, safety, and morals. The Department of Commerce prepared a Standard State Zoning Enabling Act, which closely linked density and use with the general welfare. By the mid-1920s almost every state had passed an enabling act; and state courts, which often rejected zoning ordinances adopted without express legislative consent, accepted this form of urban regulation. [49]

Progress occurred incrementally as well. Courts had a problem with the exclusion of retail stores from residential districts. Into the 1920s the weight of authority held this to be an unconstitutional infringement of property rights. As one decision put it: "There is nothing inherently dangerous to the health or safety of the public in conducting a retail store." And the argument that retail establishments detracted from the ambience of a neighborhood bore little weight with courts reluctant to give legal standing to aesthetic values. The high court in Kansas broke new ground in 1923 when it accepted the exclusion of retail stores from residential areas: "there is an aesthetic and cultural side of municipal development which may be fostered within reasonable limits. Such legislation is merely a liberalized application of the general welfare purposes of the State and Federal Constitutions." [50]

The restriction of apartment houses posed a similar problem. Ohio's supreme court rejected an ordinance excluding apartment houses from residential districts: "It is commendable and desirable, but not essential to the public need, that our aesthetic desires be gratified . . . Certain legislatures might consider that it was more important to cultivate a taste for jazz than for Beethoven, or for posters than for Rembrandt, and for limericks than for Keats." Opinions still varied in a 1920 Minnesota case: one judge thought that apartments were no less safe or aesthetic than shabby single-family homes; others that they threatened to replace private dwellings and tended to segregate classes. [51]

But soon there emerged a bestiary for apartment houses similar to that developed earlier for billboards. Courts came to accept the view that the apartment house was a fire hazard; a breeder of immorality, crime, and disease; "a deadly menace to life, health and morals" and thus fitly subject to zoning restrictions. The California supreme court upheld the exclusion of multiunit buildings from a residential district in terms of the broadest conceivable public policy:

> justification for residential zoning may, in the last analysis, be rested upon the protection of the civic and social values of the American home ... It is axiomatic that the welfare, and indeed the very existence, of a nation depends upon the character and caliber of its citizenry. The character and quality of manhood and womanhood are in a large measure the result of home environment ... The establishment of a single family residence district offers inducement not only to the wealthy but to those of moderate means to own their own homes. With ownership comes stability, the welding together of family ties and better attention to the rearing of children. With ownership comes increased interest in the promotion of public agencies, such as church and school, which have for their purpose a desired development of the moral and mental make-up of the citizenry of the country.

One commentator was more specific: "there is little doubt in any one's mind that the freedom of arrival and departure which the apartment offers to its single residents has been no small contributing factor in the violation of the moral laws."[52]

Similar boiler-plate rhetoric justified the utility of zoning itself. It lessened the risk of fire and disease; it would "stabilize the use and value of property and promote the peace, tranquility, and good order of the city." This was "a concession to the orthodox ratiocination invoked by conservative jurists to explain the constitutionality of new types of regulatory legislation."[53]

"A generation ago," said an observer in 1925, "modern zoning under the police power would have been difficult, if not impossible." By 1926 a number of states' courts, among them New York, Massachusetts, California, and Ohio, had upheld comprehensive zoning ordinances. But they had been rejected or were in doubt in about ten others, including Maryland, New Jersey, Michigan, Texas, and Missouri. Each decision reflected "the environment and whole social attitude of the judge and the court in which he sits."[54]

The Supreme Court finally passed on comprehensive zoning in *Euclid v. Ambler* (1926), "the 'open sesame' of land use planning in this country." A 1922 zoning ordinance in the Cleveland suburb of Euclid established six classes of use, four of area, three of height. The Ambler

Realty Company owned sixty-eight acres of vacant land slated for industrial use, worth an estimated $10,000 an acre. The zoning ordinance restricted the tract to residential use, thereby reducing its value to $2,500 an acre.[55]

The rhetoric enfolding the case as it made its way through the courts suggests how large in scale were the policy issues at stake. A defense of the ordinance argued:

> Undoubtedly there are some groups in the community whose economic interests are furthered by stable values; but there are those whose advantage lies in rapidly fluctuating values. Which group is more deserving of protection? . . . Stabilization of expectations of future events and conduct is being recognized increasingly as a desirable end of economic policies, both public and private . . . A public policy designed to minimize such wastes as are incurred [by forced adaptation to rapid changes] would seem to be in the public interest, even though it cut down some individual rights.

Wilsonian progressive Newton D. Baker, representing the realty company, saw a different principle at stake: "That our cities should be made beautiful and orderly is, of course, in the highest degree desirable, but it is even more important that our people should remain free."[56]

A federal district judge conceded: "The blighting of property values and the congestion of population, whenever the colored or certain foreign races invade a residential section, are so well known as to be within the judicial cognizance." Nevertheless he struck down the ordinance as a taking without compensation that violated Fourteenth Amendment due process. But the Supreme Court's Justice Arthur Sutherland upheld zoning on broad public policy grounds as an appropriate application of the police power. The segregation of residential, business, and industrial areas, he argued, "will increase the safety and security of home life . . . decrease noise and other conditions which produce or intensify nervous disorders; preserve a more favorable environment in which to rear children."[57]

The *Euclid* decision gave full legitimacy to comprehensive zoning and thereby assured its place as the primary policy determinant of modern American urban (and suburban) development. It gave birth as well to no less long-lived critiques: that zoning was open to abuse by real estate or business interests; that the automobile, new methods of merchandising, and new ways of living raised problems of land use requiring less static, more socially responsive planning.[58]

New York's Regional Plan of 1929–1931, the product of a Russell Sage Foundation–sponsored survey under way since 1922, was the most ambitious alternative scheme of the period. It superseded the Progressive search for the City Beautiful with a quest for the City Efficient: "Where the early plan was once content to be a noble design, the modern plan aspires to qualify as a productive piece of economic machinery." As befitted a product of the 1920s, the Regional Plan was socially conservative, business-minded, technocratic, short-term, and pragmatic. Like zoning it sought to "prevent the parasitic encroachments of lower functions upon the facilities of the higher functions." [59]

More radical planners sought an urban environment that fostered social change. The Regional Planning Association of America (RPAA), founded in 1923, offered in counterpoint to the New York Regional Plan (which it dismissed as a scheme to perpetuate "dinosaur cities") an approach that mixed socialist classlessness, high technology, and the values of antimodern, small-town community.[60]

The New York Regional Plan led to Robert Moses's New York infrastructure of highways and bridges and to postwar suburbia; the RPAA approach prefigured Rexford Tugwell's Resettlement Administration, Greenbelt, and the New Towns of recent times. But the American city itself remained what it had always been—apart from zoning an unplanned environment, shaped by demography, the market, and technology; a vivid instance of the more general truth that a messy (and vital) pluralism, rather than the precepts of planning, defined the relationship between the public and the private spheres in modern America.

9 · Regulating Trade, Capital, and Revenue

The oldest, most familiar forms of American economic policy dealt with trade and capital, the fundaments of a market economy, and with the fiscal and revenue needs of the state. The tariff and the currency dominated economic policymaking throughout the nineteenth century; banking, investment, and taxation took on increasing importance in the twentieth. Here if anywhere the autonomous, administrative state might have been expected to assert itself, for these were activities whose public character was both well established and uncontroverted. Yet the same controlling forces of persistence and pluralism that so emphatically defined other realms of economic policy prevailed in these areas as well.

The Tariff

An ever-more-integrated world economy, increasingly organized and self-conscious domestic interest groups, and the growth of popular party politics made the tariff a major public issue in the late nineteenth-century Western world. On the Continent as in the United States, farmers suffering from prolonged agricultural depression demanded increased protection; and each nation responded in its distinctive way. France's mildly protectionist Méline tariff of 1892 consolidated rural support for the still shaky Third Republic. Germany's comparable tariff of 1902 emerged from government-led consultations with representatives of agricultural and other interest groups.[1]

The nineteenth-century British consensus on free trade faced its first serious challenge in the early 1900s. "Tariff reform," espoused by Joseph Chamberlain and other Conservative-Unionists, consisted of higher duties aimed at American and German products and preferential status for imports from the empire. This had a political as well as an economic base: additional revenue was needed for military and social reform spending. And Unionists expected a more secure home market to increase their working-class and industrialist support, much as did Republican protectionists in the United States.

Yet for all its appeal, tariff reform did not succeed in early twentieth-century British politics. The threat that tariffs posed to cheap staples, and the lure of more emotive issues such as rearmament, home rule, and labor unrest, sustained the free trade tradition; and not only in the Liberal party. A 1903 Unionist cabinet memorandum conceded: "We are no longer the workshop of the world, without a rival; we have formidable competitors." But it argued that the dangers of dumping were exaggerated, and pinned its hopes on increased productivity and the earning power of invisibles, not on tariff protection.[2]

The tariff was the most prominent and persistent category of nineteenth-century American economic policymaking. This was so in part because of its importance to an economy devoted at first to the export of raw materials and then to nurturing infant industries. Tariff-making mattered, too, because it so well served the American party system. Republican protectionism reinforced that party's nationalist ideology and attracted manufacturers and workingmen fearful of competition from abroad. The Democrats' free trade rhetoric similarly reflected their general antigovernment stance and appealed to the party's diverse constituency of southern cotton farmers, northern merchants, and Irish voters happy to see a challenge to Britain's trading supremacy.[3]

To what degree did the new conditions of American life after 1900 transform the politics of tariff policy? Can we find here support for the view that corporate power and an administrative state gave new form and substance to American public policy? Certainly the characteristically progressive emphasis on making the tariff more efficient and apolitical, less subject to the vagaries of party politics, took a more conspicuous place. But by 1930 the traditional American style of tariff-setting, in which a mass of interest groups worked within the party system to get their own, still prevailed.

Other issues—antitrust in particular—took center stage in American public life during the first decade of the century. But around 1909 the tariff suddenly became a matter of some political weight once again—not only in the United States, but in France, Germany, Britain, and other nations as well. Tariff politics in prewar Europe was fueled by the pressures of economic competition, rising military and social welfare costs, and intensifying popular nationalism. French manufacturers sought increased protection, and in 1906 the Chamber of Deputies appointed a Customs Commission to look into the tariff needs of new and changing industries. The commission, led by its secretary, Jean Morel, issued a protectionist report; but powerful exporters of luxury goods successfully resisted. In Germany the issue entered into the bitter politics of right and left: the government wanted to rely on indirect customs and excise duties, the Social Democrats favored an income tax.[4]

Post-1900 American tariff politics centered on two major enactments: the protectionist Payne-Aldrich Act of 1909 and the low-tariff Underwood Act of 1913. They were the products not of heightened ideological conflict, growing corporate power, or a more assertive national state, but of the politics of pluralism: the quantum leap in the number and character of interests and ideas feeding into the public sector. The old tariff politics of special interests and party ideology continued to flourish. Now it was joined (but not replaced) by the calculations of sophisticated corporate interests and progressive reform, and by a new-fashioned belief in government expertise.

Arguments for tariff reduction after 1900 ranged widely over the ideological spectrum. William Jennings Bryan and Senator Albert B. Cummins (whose "Iowa idea" it was to end protection for trust-made products) identified lower industrial tariffs with hostility to big business. Some reform-minded advocates of a low tariff argued that by giving employment to new immigrants, protected industries added to the nation's social problems. But the National Association of Manufacturers saw a more symbiotic relationship between lower duties and the new economy: "it is as important now to protect the manufacturers by open doors as it was to build them up by a tariff which has . . . begun to be hurtful."[5]

Tariff reform appealed also to the newly fashionable desire to rely on bureaucracy and expertise instead of policy-by-politics. The tariffs of 1890, 1894, and 1897 had vast numbers of schedules, each the product of a political deal between politicos and particular economic interest groups. They raised the art of political wheeling and dealing to new heights. In procedure and result, this highly politicized tariff-making was a standing rebuke to the progressive ideal of rational, efficient policymaking.[6]

Old and new approaches to tariffmaking clashed head-on in the 1908 revival of the issue, after a decade of relative quiescence. Public concern over the rising cost of living, and the appeal of a nonpolitical approach to rate-setting, gave a fresh cast to the old rite of tariff revision. The fight, thought the *Edinburgh Review*, was primarily between the promoters of the turn-of-the-century merger movement, who wanted high duties to protect the prices charged by their watered combines, and manufacturers who still directly controlled their own plants. Pressure for revision came from "the revolt of manufacturers who found themselves seriously hampered in buying their raw materials." Their major spokesman was Herbert E. Miles, a Racine, Wisconsin, farm implements manufacturer who headed the NAM's Tariff Commission. Miles condemned the 1897 Dingley tariff as a tool of the trusts. He called for an ICC-like tariff commission similar to those in Britain, France, and especially Germany, which would gather relevant data and present it to Congress.[7]

But once tariff revision entered the congressional maw, a familiar drama played itself out. Each of numerous special interests secured its own rate schedule, thereby raising the general level of customs duties. House Ways and Means Committee chairman Sereno Payne, a Republican politico of the old school, believed in "frying the fat" out of manufacturers in return for protection. And Senate Finance Committee chairman Nelson Aldrich, close to the trusts, conducted hearings along traditional lines: in private, with full deference to special interests. The resulting Payne-Aldrich bill altered 847 tariff rates, the great majority of them upward.[8]

President William Howard Taft was sufficiently sensitive to the winds of political change to call for explicit consumer representation at the Ways and Means Committee's hearings. He tried—too late—to secure some rate reductions when he realized what was happening in Congress. But the general—and correct—impression was that the Payne-Aldrich tariff spectacularly violated both the spirit and the letter of Taft's 1908 campaign rate-reduction promises. He tried to meet this political problem by urging the creation of a permanent Tariff Commission—hardly evidence of the triumph of the organizational over the political state.[9]

It is not surprising that Woodrow Wilson made tariff reduction an important part of his 1912 campaign. It had long enjoyed a secure place in Democratic party ideology, and now it took on additional appeal as a weapon in the war against the trusts. After their electoral victory, he and the Democrats put through the rate-cutting Underwood tariff of 1913 with relative dispatch. In many ways it echoed the last Democratic tariff, the Wilson-Gorman Act of 1894. As in the earlier case, an income tax provision was added to the tariff bill to offset the expected decline in revenue from lower rates.

But the general political atmosphere and the character and alignment of interests had changed. Consumer concern over the cost of living now joined agricultural low tariff sentiment. And many large manufacturers did not even bother to voice their concerns at the tariff hearings: they already dominated the domestic market and owned plants abroad to service overseas markets.[10]

Raw materials producers had more complex tariff interests than in the past. Take sugar, for example. In the early 1890s the American Sugar Refining Company controlled more than 90 percent of refinery output, and thus was able to live with high sugar duties. But by 1913 its share of refinery output had shrunk to less than 40 percent. Major figures in the industry such as Claus Spreckels (who had extensive interests in Cuban sugar) advocated lower sugar rates; and a number of canners—a rapidly growing industry in a consumer economy—favored lower rates.[11]

The Underwood tariff appeared to signify a sea change in tariffmaking. The *New York Evening Post* spoke of the end of a protectionism dominant in industrial nations (except Britain) since the 1870s. After half a century of steadily increasing protection, American tariff policy now moved in the direction of a pure revenue system, reflecting the fact that the nation had a surplus of manufactured goods to export and a vastly expanded urban population to consume its farm products. For the first time since the Civil War, American manufacturers could not hide behind a strong protectionist shield. But they had access to duty-free raw materials, and the result, it was thought, would be an increase in the efficiency of American industry.[12]

Underwood supposedly marked the advent of a new style as well as substance in tariff policymaking. Leadership had passed from Congress to the president, even though Wilson's insistence on free wool and sugar duties was his only specific recommendation in a tariff bill of 4,000 items. Portentous, too, was his call for an independent Tariff Commission. The tariff, announced one observer, was no longer a political or party issue. In 1916 Congress established this analogue to the ICC, the FTC, and the Federal Reserve Board. Independent from the existing bureaucracy, bipartisan in composition, the Tariff Commission was charged with helping Congress enact scientific, objectively constructed schedules.[13]

The desire of large industries for government assistance in the export of manufactured products seemed to be another sign of a new era in government trade policy. Traditionally the major American exports were agricultural products and raw materials. But by 1914 manufactured goods made up almost half of American exports, and large firms such as United States Steel, International Harvester, Standard Oil, Westinghouse, and Armour accounted for about 90 percent of the total. (On the other hand, the value of exports from 1869 to 1914 stayed within the range of 6–8 percent of the gross national product. And firms whose foreign sales made up a substantial proportion of their business were concentrated in specialized areas such as machine tools.)[14]

Overseas sales of manufactured goods required more specific and intensive market-seeking than did wheat or cotton. Private institutions such as the NAM and the United States Chamber of Commerce, as well as the State and Commerce departments, were called on for aid. The American International Corporation, chartered in 1915 with a capital of $50 million by a group of leading financiers, was to foster foreign trade. As exports sharply rose during World War I, closer cooperation developed between large manufacturers and the government's National Foreign Trade Council and War Trade Board. The Webb-Pomerene Act of 1918 exempted export trade associations from the cartel and trust restrictions of the Sherman and Clayton Acts.[15]

So by 1920 it appeared that a less political approach to tariffmaking and a sophisticated cooperation between government and big business in fostering overseas trade had come into being; that the old days of tariffmaking by deals between politicos and economic interests were past. A forward look in 1914 concluded that the tariff "has become . . . a force of third-rate importance in our industrial development" and predicted that after the war the United States might well be a leading exponent of free trade, much as Britain had in the nineteenth century.[16]

But it quickly became clear that there was to be no postwar New Era of depoliticized tariffmaking, no close business-government partnership fostering export growth and free trade. Rapidly expanding American consumer purchasing power, managerial rigidities such as Henry Ford's refusal to adapt the Model T to foreign markets, and European economic constraints reduced the American trade potential abroad. True, a few industries saw possibilities in overseas trade. The Copper Institute, the industry's trade association, argued for lower tariffs on that metal and entered into a cartel with foreign copper producers. But the government agencies most concerned with trade—the War Trade Board, the departments of Commerce and State—fell to bureaucratic quarreling, and firms doing business abroad relied increasingly on their own arrangements. For all the talk by Commerce Secretary Hoover and others of partnership between the public and the private sectors, government trade policy was just that: more talk than reality.[17]

The Fordney-McCumber Act of 1922 and the Smoot-Hawley Act of 1931, the major tariff laws of the postwar years, bore witness to the power and persistence of traditional tariff politics. Tariff debates during the 1920s, as in earlier decades, dwelt on the disposal of surpluses and the maintenance of American wages, not on the pros and cons of foreign trade or a new business-government relationship. Wartime and postwar nationalism invigorated protectionism's popular appeal. The National Tariff Institute spoke of "America First" and linked a high tariff with the exclusion of undesirable immigrants. Republican senators and congressmen representing western farmers hard hit by the postwar drop in agricultural prices added to the political strength of protectionist sentiment.

The Fordney-McCumber tariff substantially raised existing rates. The Tariff Commission tried to influence the result by proposing a cost-of-production standard in rate-setting—very like the concurrent search for a valuation basis for public utility rates. But Fordney-McCumber's final schedules emerged instead from the traditional, intensely political process of give-and-take between legislators and particular economic interests. William Starr Myers, close to Herbert Hoover, later said of the result: "It is one of the most ill-drawn legislative acts of recent political history." No new corporatism here; only old politics. Insofar as the bill had a larger context, it was the traditional confrontation of Republican protectionism and Democratic free trade.[18]

Fordney-McCumber did have a flexible tariff provision authorizing the president to change specific rates on the recommendation of the Tariff Commission. But in practice, neither the commission nor the flexible tariff provision led to a more rapid or "scientific" adjustment of tariff rates. The commission stayed firmly in the hands of Republican protectionists. It spent four years investigating the cotton hosiery business; the report went to the president in 1927; half a year later no action had yet been taken. Only three schedules were reduced from

1922 to 1927, and these could hardly be said to be of major economic importance: live bobwhite quail, paintbrush handles, and millfeed.[19]

Protectionism flourished through the 1920s, fed by postwar nationalism, the fears of farmers and workers, and the fact that exports remained a small proportion of American output. Similar pressures worked on the tariff policies of European nations, even Great Britain. Prime Minister Stanley Baldwin resurrected the prewar Conservative flirtation with higher duties in the 1924 election. British trade unionists and younger Socialists also were drawn increasingly to a protectionist position.[20]

For all his internationalism and his commitment to scientific policymaking and the associative state, Herbert Hoover signed the Smoot-Hawley tariff of 1931. What began as an attempt at "limited revision" in 1929 degenerated under the impact of the Depression into an orgy of special-interest protectionism equal to anything produced in the bad old days before the Tariff Commission and the flexible tariff provision. Informed opinion was appalled by what had happened: the American Bankers' Association, leading newspapers, and most economists objected to Smoot-Hawley; 343 newspapers in 43 states opposed the bill by a three-to-one margin; Wall Street reacted unfavorably. It was clear that the major consequence of the new economy was not more "scientific" tariffmaking, but the inflation of special interests. This is what gives Smoot-Hawley its place of honor in the pantheon of rampant protectionism.[21]

Reed Smoot, the bill's Senate sponsor, took care of Utah's beet sugar interests; David Reed of Pennsylvania headed the hoary eastern manufacturers' bloc; Hiram Bingham of Connecticut added to the glossary of protectionism when he spoke feelingly of "aged industries" in need of protection. Northwestern and mountain state representatives sought protection for their regions; William Borah of Idaho wanted tariff increases limited to agricultural products. Southern Democrats sacrificed their low-tariff ideology to serve hard-pressed agricultural constituents. California's Imperial Valley was a strong new voice for cotton protection; Matthew Woll of the AFL wanted higher duties on books to protect the printing trades; fruit packers wanted higher duties to weaken the preference of Italian Americans for Italian tomatoes. The Ways and Means hearings, stretching through 1929 and into 1930, produced 7,000 pages of testimony from more than 1,100 tariff advocates—a monument of sorts to the ability of pluralist particularism to override the forces of corporative order.[22]

Events in the decades following—the grinding effect of the Great Depression, the post-1945 rise of American exports and of liberalized world trade agreements—would substantially erode the old politics of tariffmaking. But its reappearance in recent years suggests that it is far from past.

Banking and Investment

Just as the tariff was the major battleground of nineteenth-century American agricultural and industrial policy, so was financial policy fought out over the currency—in particular, the relative worth of gold, silver, and paper. No less than protectionism and free trade, gold, bimetallism, and free silver were evocative political symbols, embodying complex sets of social, economic, and moral attitudes.[23]

The emotive force of the tariff as a political issue diminished after 1900; and so too did that of the currency. Historians explain this change by noting the decisive defeat of free silver in the election of 1896 and the sharp expansion of the world's gold supply around the turn of the century. Although the Gold Standard Act of 1900 settled the question of convertibility in favor of a gold-based currency, the rising stock of gold allowed coinage and certificates of that metal to increase from $497 million in 1896 to $1.1 billion in 1905.

Significant too was the growth of local and state banking networks, which expanded access to credit. From 1896 to 1905, the number of nationally chartered banks increased from 3,689 to 5,664, of state banks from 7,785 to 12,488; their combined assets jumped from $6.5 billion to $14.5 billion. As important was their growing integration with major money market institutions, which weakened interregional interest rate differentials and barriers to capital mobility.[24]

While the politics of the currency ebbed, the politics of banking and investment swelled. This was a different sort of issue, resting not on two camps—goldbugs and silverites—but on complex and varied issues, interests, and ideas: a representative expression of the politics of pluralism.

The early twentieth-century American banking system was a richly diverse institution. Despite the spur to federal chartering provided by the National Banking Act of 1864, the incentives (and weaknesses) of state regulation meant that most banks continued to be state banks.

To ease the political impact of adopting the gold standard, the Gold Standard Act of 1900 allowed national banks to establish branches in towns with a population of less than 3,000. State banking authorities accordingly reduced the capital requirements for state banks. A vigorous rivalry between state and national banks ensued, with politically potent local banks often calling the regulatory tune.[25]

As a result of decentralized chartering, geographic spread, and the sheer number and variety of enterprises, the great majority of American banks continued to be single-office (unit) institutions. The larger metropolitan banks, culminating in the major New York establishments, entered into elaborate correspondent relationships with these local banks. Nevertheless, the American banking system remained a highly localized and decentralized one, particularly in comparison with the central bank–dominated structures of the major European states. The inevitable tension between localism and concentration was fertile ground for politics and policy.

While both state and national banks rapidly grew in number, so too did new instrumentalities of national (and international) capital and credit accumulation. The vastly increased capital demands of an expanding economy and of the corporate consolidation movement fed the growth of investment bankers such as Morgan and Kuhn Loeb, major insurance companies such as New York Life and the Equitable, New York banks such as Chase and National City, and trust companies (which did not have the credit expansion and cash reserve restrictions of deposit banks). This new, potent force in American finance generated fresh issues and concerns—and political responses.[26]

These facts of financial life led to a new politics of banking and investment. More and more state legislation dealt with banks, insurance companies, and other financial and credit intermediaries. Courts, too, faced an ever-widening range of issues related to capital and credit. But formidable constraints impeded effective banking legislation.[27]

Laws guaranteeing deposits were the most conspicuous state banking reform of the time. Smaller rural banks in the South and West, hit hard by the panic of 1907, pushed for these measures against the opposition of state banking associations and larger urban banks. Oklahoma enacted the first deposit guaranty act; Kansas, South and North Dakota, Nebraska, Texas, Mississippi, and Washington followed. *Noble State Bank v. Haskell* (1911) challenged the constitutionality of the Oklahoma and Nebraska laws; and a unanimous Supreme Court sustained them under the states' police power. But this hardly guaranteed their success. Continuing hard times in Oklahoma led to the failure of twenty-seven banks with deposits of $7 million by 1913. Charges of political influence and fraud dogged the system, and deposit guaranty did not spread beyond its original core.[28]

The increasing political influence of the saving public led to the creation of the United States Postal Savings Bank. After the 1907 panic and the revelation of major financial scandals weakened public confidence in banks, President Taft among others took up the idea. Against the opposition of the American Bankers' Association (and warnings that it would drain capital to Washington), Congress established the postal savings system in 1910. But it took a form guaranteed to cripple its effectiveness: accounts were limited to $500; the system had to have a much higher cash reserve than its private competitors; and it could offer interest of no more than 2 percent, lower than the market rate. By 1917 the bulk of deposits came from immigrants in large cities; New York City alone had about one-fourth of the total.[29]

The Federal Reserve Act of 1913 was the major legislative monument to the shift in focus of national financial policy from the currency to banking. Calls for changes in the American banking system dated from the 1890s. But different interests wanted different things. Southern and western spokesmen attacked the concentration of capital and credit in the northeast and particularly in the New York banks. They sought a regional system of government banks designed to equalize access to capital and credit. Major banks and their political representatives wanted a central banking system (or at least one that they controlled) and greater elasticity in the supply of money and credit.

Pressure for reform rose in the wake of the 1907 panic, which dramatically revealed the inability of the banking system and of gold-secured Treasury note issues to meet changing business needs. In particular, it strengthened the demand of financial and corporate leaders for a central bank: the United States was the only major Western nation without one. True, from 1897 to 1907 the volume of money expanded at a rate equal to the silverites' expectations. But the chief beneficiaries were promoters of industrial consolidation, not the public at large. Currency expansion, touted in 1896 as an instrument to stop the concentration of wealth, instead fostered it.[30]

As with so many reforms of the Progressive period, the movement for national banking reform had significant European sources. Senator Nelson Aldrich led members of the National Monetary Commission to Europe in 1909, where German bankers converted him to the need to base the currency on commercial paper as well as on gold.

The commission's report acquainted lawmakers with the extensive controls exercised by European nations over their banking, fiscal, and monetary systems.[31]

The Aldrich-Vreeland Act of 1908 was a hasty and confused bill, "an amazing lesson on the folly of politics in banking." There followed a long, convoluted effort to establish a new system of national banking regulation, in which banking interests (some favoring a more sophisticated system of regulation, others opposed to any change), business and agricultural interests, professional economists, and political partisans jousted with one another.

The Democrats' Owen-Glass Act of 1913 created a Federal Reserve system of a dozen regional districts under a new administrative agency, the Federal Reserve Board. This structure sought to secure the advantages of a central bank and yet show due regard for local and regional banking interests, agrarian needs, and popular fear of overmuch concentration of banking resources and power. The result was not so much a central bank in the European sense as a system of regional clearinghouses, "neither publicly owned nor privately controlled." In that sense the Federal Reserve Act signifies not the political triumph of corporate capitalism or state corporatism, but the receptivity to multiple interests and ideas that lay at the heart of the pluralist polity.[32]

The ensuing experience of the Federal Reserve resembled that of the Interstate Commerce Commission and the Federal Trade Commission: repeated lessons in the difficulty of creating an administrative state in a diffuse and decentralized polity. Woodrow Wilson's secretary of the Treasury, William G. McAdoo, engaged in constant bureaucratic warfare with investment banker Paul Warburg, the key figure on the Federal Reserve Board. And politically powerful regional banking interests along with the well-entrenched system of state regulation kept the Federal Reserve from central-bank-like muscle-flexing.[33]

Smaller state banks were reluctant to enter the new system. By 1922 only about 1,500 of 20,000 had done so, and the old correspondent structure continued. Agrarian supporters of the Federal Reserve failed to get the interregional redistribution of banking assets they had hoped for. Although southern banks by 1922 had increased their share of national bank resources from 7.5 to 15 percent (primarily because of wartime cotton profits), New York's share declined only from 26 to 24 percent; during the early 1920s the New York Federal Reserve branch held about one-third of the system's assets.[34]

The explosive growth of the American economy during the 1920s affected banking policy and practice far more than did law or legislation. The economic roller coaster of 1919–1923—sharp inflation, sharp deflation—reflected the availability of goods and consumer decisions rather than government fiscal or credit policies. Other factors weakened the authority and effectiveness of the Federal Reserve. Depositors were an ever-more-vocal and important factor in the politics of banking. Their number rose from 12.6 in 1912 to 38.9 million in 1925. Bank loans fed new investment outlets—urban real estate, overseas bonds, Wall Street speculation—that escaped the oversight of the Federal Reserve. Presidents Harding and Coolidge appointed political hacks to the Board, who countenanced a low rediscount rate that encouraged stock speculation.[35]

As before, almost all banking regulation lay in the hands of the states. Often the practical result was the protection of local bank and depositor interests from the pressures of a national economy. A 1921 Wisconsin law expanded the state banking commissioner's power to approve or disapprove of commercial banks—part of a tendency to increase supervision on behalf of depositors. A wave of bad-check laws sought to protect local banks against fraud. A number of southern states resisted Federal Reserve Board efforts to end the banks' practice of charging for check clearances. The major achievement of this localistic impulse was the McFadden Act of 1927, in which Congress confined most branch banking to the home state of the mother bank. But effective state banking regulation had severe limits in the face of the powerful national (and international) financial currents of the 1920s. Bank failures, ranging from 50 to 150 a year before the war, now averaged well over 600 annually, most of them in the South, the Great Plains, and the Northwest.[36]

The prewar movement for deposit guaranty laws sputtered out in the face of these figures. Oklahoma's pioneering law was repealed in 1923. The collapse of wheat, corn, and cotton prices led to a sharp rise in bank closures, a guaranty fund deficit of more than $8 million and the flight of still-solvent state banks to the national banking system (and hence out of the fund's obligations). The Kansas supreme court allowed banks to withdraw from the state's guaranty fund, thus ending a system burdened by a deficit of more than $4 million.[37]

The numerous deficiencies of the banking system came home to roost in the Great Depression. Failures peaked at more than 4,000 in 1933; the system spiraled downward to its nadir with the national bank "holiday" after FDR's inauguration in March 1933. There followed the most important national banking legislation since the creation of the Federal Reserve: the Glass-Steagall Banking Acts of 1933 and 1935. These laws created a system of national deposit insurance run by a new federal agency, the Federal Deposit Insurance Corporation. They tightened the Federal Reserve's control over the capital requirements and investment policies of banks, an effective step because so many small banks outside the Federal Reserve system had failed. And they dictated a separation of deposit from investment banking not substantially changed until our own time.

These New Deal banking laws were not a revolution in banking policy, but a successful effort to shore up the existing system. Most bankers vigorously opposed deposit insurance and what they took to be undue Federal Reserve authority over their practices. Their ideological astigmatism kept them from seeing the possibilities of a cosier relationship with the state. It is perhaps sufficient comment on the inertial power of American banking policy that the New Deal's most conspicuous attainment, its national system of deposit insurance, was an early twentieth-century state reform writ large.[38]

Early in the century, stock and bond trading did not have even the modicum of national regulation accorded banking. Resistance to securities market regulation was not unique to America: an 1896 German law registering traders was repealed as a failure in 1908. Still, no country (certainly not Britain, whose late nineteenth- and early twentieth-century Companies Acts began to put constraints on stock offerings) matched the United States in its reluctance to interfere with capital accumulation.[39]

Commodity futures trading was the first major object of regulatory attention. As the market took form in the late nineteenth century, centering on the Chicago Board of Trade, it came under frequent legislative and legal scrutiny. In part this stemmed from the manifest importance of the wheat and other crops on which futures contracts were traded. And gambling in the price of staples had for many a special obloquy, tapping moral wellsprings similar to those that fed the prohibition movement.[40]

State courts and legislatures wrestled with the question of the validity of futures contracts that did not envisage actual delivery. Despite widespread judicial acceptance of many of the fictions by which traders fudged the issue, by 1931 twenty states had laws forbidding such contracts. But futures trading was too important a part of the national—indeed the international—agricultural market system to be abolished. In 1905 the Supreme Court decided that by self-regulation the Chicago Board of Trade met its public responsibilities, in effect accepting the legitimacy of commodities futures trading.[41]

After the price dislocations in staples during World War I, the federal government began to take a hand. The Grain Futures Trading Act of 1921 imposed a prohibitory tax on contracts that did not meet certain procedural conditions. The Supreme Court found this to be an unconstitutional use of the tax power. But it accepted a hastily redrawn Grain Futures Act based on Congress's authority to regulate interstate commerce. This hardly amounted to close regulation. A Grain Futures Administration collected and analyzed information, and the secretary of agriculture had limited supervisory powers. The courts occasionally voided fraudulently secured contracts. Essentially, though, futures trading remained a self-regulating investment realm.[42]

Regulation of securities investment came more slowly—as did securities investment itself. The volume of annual sales on the prewar New York Stock Exchange ranged from 48 million shares in 1914 to 282 million in 1906.[43] The stock market came under inquiry in Congress's Pujo investigation of 1912–13, but this led to no serious attempt at federal or state regulation.

"Bucket shops"—fly-by-night establishments for betting on the rise and fall of securities prices without the pretense of actual purchase and sale—did, however, come in for substantial regulatory attention. By 1931 three-quarters of the states had "blue sky" laws aimed at bucket shops—in many cases at the behest of the established securities exchanges. The movement began in Kansas, where the state banking commissioner launched an effective campaign against shady securities merchants, who, he said, would sell shares "in the blue sky itself."[44] Presumably his sense of outrage was heightened by his awareness that these investments absorbed savings that otherwise might have gone into bank deposits. The Kansas law passed in 1911, and fourteen other states quickly followed.

Effective enforcement was difficult. During the first eighteen months under the Kansas statute more than 1,500 securities companies applied to enter the state, the great majority of them hawking fraudulent stock schemes. A 1915 amendment obligated state officials to determine the soundness of securities issues before allowing them to be sold. But a number of federal court decisions held the Kansas, Ohio, and other "blue sky" laws unconstitutional as a burden on interstate commerce. Finally in 1917 the Supreme Court decided that securities issues and dealing could come under state licensing and control.[45]

By the late 1920s almost every state had empowered its securities commissioners to look into the condition of stock-issuing corporations. But these laws had limited effect. Securities regulation in Indiana, Ohio, Pennsylvania, and other states suffered from supervisory laxness and political corruption; New York, New Jersey, and Maryland did not restrict sales until fraud was discovered. Sixteen states exempted securities listed on an exchange from their "blue sky" laws, which along with the lack of federal oversight helped the Great Bull Market to roar on unchecked.[46]

As early as 1919 a congressional bill, modeled on the British Companies Acts and supported by the Investment Bankers Association, called for securities offerings to be filed in Washington. It failed to pass. The vast increase in the number of securities issues and consumers intensified the problem. An estimate in 1927 held that stock swindles—more than three-quarters of them issuing from New York—amounted to $1.7 billion a year. Most fraudulent securities were marketed through the mails, and demands arose for enforcement of the Federal Postal Frauds Act and a federal "blue sky" law. The Denison bill of 1922 sought to bar the use of the mails to transport or sell securities that were illegal in any state. Even though the Post Office, the Investment Bankers' Association, and the National Association of Securities Commissioners endorsed the bill, it got nowhere. As was so often the case in the 1920s, the existing structure of state regulation, a complex of interests resistant to more stringent oversight, and public complacency, indifference, or both, reinforced the stasis of federal government. During the decade the Investment Bankers Association dropped its support of federal regulation, another instance of the erosion of the corporatist impulse of the Progressive and war years.[47]

As in so many other areas of public policy, the Great Depression and the New Deal opened the way to federal securities regulation. The Securities Act of 1933, providing closer government oversight of stock issues, had many elements in common with the British Companies Act of 1928–29. But it went beyond that law in its disclosure, registration, and enforcement provisions. Indeed, its requirements were more substantial and comprehensive than those of any European nation.

No other country had a permanent supervisory body comparable to the Securities Exchange Commission (SEC).[48]

Financial law expert William O. Douglas had doubts about the act's effectiveness. It would not, he thought, have contained the bull market of the 1920s, the pyramiding of holding companies, or the behavior of irresponsible management. As a staff member and an SEC Commissioner from 1934 until he joined the Supreme Court in 1939, Douglas helped to make it a relatively effective regulatory tool. But as in the case of the New Deal's banking legislation, this was regulation at a remove, hardly a statist intervention in the process of capital formation. Benjamin Cohen, Thomas Corcoran, James Landis, Douglas—key figures in the drafting and implementation of the SEC—were professional bureaucrats and neither servants of big business nor progenitors of a corporatist state. Their inspiration lay rather in the minimalist, anti-big-business tradition of the Sherman Antitrust Act and Louis D. Brandeis.[49]

Taxation: The Progressive Years

Taxation is the most widely and persistently experienced relationship between Americans and their government. And of all forms of regulation—in the sense of obligations and constraints imposed on the citizenry—except military conscription, it most readily feeds the archetypal American tension between freedom and responsibility.

Social norms and constitutional constraints kept nineteenth-century taxation low and indirect. Federal levies (primarily customs and excises) took only 2.4 percent of the gross national product in 1902; state and local taxes (primarily on real property), 4 percent. But the salaries, fees, and equity investments of modern society created new forms of wealth not readily tapped by prevailing modes of taxation. The accumulations of large corporations and great capitalists gave new, politically potent form to old American public concerns over equity and equality. And inexorably the needs of government grew: of a federal authority dabbling (however gingerly) in war and imperialism, of state and local governments beginning to face up to the infrastructure, service, and welfare demands of modern life.[50]

It was against this background that early twentieth-century American tax policy took shape. But considerations central to the experience of other Western nations—the pre–World War I arms buildup, the rise of welfare expenditure, continuing traditions of central government authority and activism—had little or no relevance to the American case (see Table 2).

But the rise of a modern urban-industrial economy did affect post-1900 American taxation. New exactions came into being, aimed at transactions and at equitable rather than real property: stock transfer, inheritance, and corporate and personal income taxes. And long-held ideas of tax reform—greater uniformity and efficiency, more centralized administration, tax commissions and boards of equalization—now came into their own.

But here the pluralist character of the polity emerged with special clarity. A welter of conflicting goals and interests determined tax policy and practice: antistate economizing and expanding government; the antipathetic attractions of centralization and diversity, efficiency and equity. The distinguishing feature of early twentieth-century American tax policy was a marked increase in the range and variety of interests, issues, and ideas.[51]

Cities in particular felt the pressure to adapt their tax base to a changing economy and growing fiscal demands. But here the weight of traditional limits on government hung heavy. The established legal doctrine that taxes could not be levied for private purposes constrained municipal authorities. So too did the Supreme Court's *Norwood v. Baker* decision in 1900, which held that a special assessment on real estate to help meet the costs of street improvement violated the Fourteenth Amendment. One response was constitutional amendments in Massachusetts (1911), Ohio (1912), and New York (1913) empowering cities to condemn property beyond what was needed for specific public improvements. But these measures hardly came to grips with rapidly escalating urban expenditures.[52]

Another alternative was to streamline and cleanse the often archaic, and almost always corrupt, tax assessing and collecting ma-

Table 2. Taxation as a percentage of national income, 1900–1914

Country	1900–01	1913–14
United States	7.76	6.68
United Kingdom	9.99	11.29
France	14.96	12.44
Germany	7.99	10.51

Source: Edwin R. A. Seligman, "Comparative Tax Burdens in the Twentieth Century," *Political Science Quarterly*, 39 (1924), 143.

chinery of the big cities. The assessor's office in the Chicago business district was worth an estimated $500,000 a year in payoffs to the incumbent and his political party. Complaints led to its abolition in 1895. In its stead a board of review received assessment ratings from 200 citizens' committees, each representing a line of business. This procedural change raised the valuation of personal property in Chicago from $21 to $88 million—still a sliver of its true value.

New York's mayor (and, behind him, Tammany Hall) appointed and removed tax commissioners in the late nineteenth century. Assessments ranged from 7.5 to 130 percent of full value. The city's debt in 1900 came close to the legal maximum of 10 percent of the assessed value of real estate, and in 1902 the mayor ordered the reappraisal of all property at full value. As a result assessments went up by nearly $1.5 billion, while real estate tax rates were reduced. But when the state relinquished the personal property tax to local governments a few years later, the city's tax base came to rest almost entirely on real estate. Personal property all but disappeared from the tax rolls. Landlords and tenants petitioned for relief; single-taxers wanted levies to rest on land, not on buildings. A solution of sorts came with the passage of state corporation and personal state income taxes in 1917 and 1919, their yield to be divided among New York's cities and towns.[53]

Pittsburgh had tax problems of comparably Byzantine complexity. Until 1912 the city labored under a nineteenth-century classification of "agricultural," "rural," and "full city" real estate, paying respectively 50, 67, and 100 percent of the tax rate. As late as 1910, 28 percent of the city's land was still classified as "rural." Among the resulting anomalies were suburban homes with large plots taxed at the lower "rural" rate, and working-class housing and small workshops taxed at the "full city" rate. In 1907 the number of Pittsburgh wards was reduced from fifty-nine to twenty-seven, but sixty-three school tax districts still cut across ward lines, adding to the welter of tax disparities. School-district tax rates affected the general tax rate of a particular piece of land; as a result, the downtown business triangle had the lowest levies. Railroads and utilities benefited further from large-scale tax exemptions. Finally, 1911 legislation abolished the old real estate tax classification, and a new school code ended the separate subdistrict school tax levies.[54]

The general property tax remained the largest source of state tax revenue at the turn of the century: 53 percent of the total in 1902. But the ever-more-spectacular late nineteenth-century imbalance between the assessment and taxation of realty (land, buildings, and animals that could not readily be hidden) and of personalty (cash, securities, profit and income, far more readily concealed) fed growing discontent with the existing system.[55]

The states' most common solution was to reduce their dependence on the property tax by leaving it to localities and to rely on a variety of new sources such as sales and excise, corporate, and income taxes. These and motor vehicle levies took up the slack: an evolution of tax policy neither corporatist nor redistributionist, but rather the modification of traditional categories (and the persistence of traditional parsimony) in response to the rise of a modern society (see Table 3).

The courts raised no serious obstacles to these changes. They accepted the increasingly significant state levies on out-of-state corporations as long as domestically chartered firms had no favored position. The Supreme Court, upholding New York's 1899 public utilities franchise tax (which added an estimated $200 million to the tax rolls), observed: "In the complex civilization of to-day a large portion of the wealth of a community consists in intangible property." The New York Court of Appeals accepted a stock transfer tax on the ground that the legislature had the power to tax any class of property or contract.[56]

Some thirty states had inheritance taxes by the early 1900s. But only in New York and Pennsylvania did they yield more than $1 mil

Table 3. State tax revenues, 1902–1932 ($ million; % in parentheses)

Year	General property	Sales and excise	Individual income	Corporate income	Auto registration and driver's license	Other	Total
1902	82	28	—	—	—	46	156
	(53)	(18)				(29)	
1913	140	55	—	—	5	101	301
	(47)	(18)			(1)	(34)	
1922	348	134	43	58	152	212	947
	(37)	(14)	(5)	(6)	(16)	(22)	
1927	370	445	70	92	301	330	1,608
	(23)	(28)	(4)	(6)	(19)	(21)	
1932	328	726	74	79	335	348	1,890
	(17)	(38)	(4)	(4)	(18)	(18)	

Source: U.S. Bureau of the Census, *Historical Statistics of the United States, Colonial Times to 1970* (Washington, D.C., 1975), pp. 1129–30.

lion in revenue. A levy that Andrew Carnegie and others thought to be *echt*-American, assuring a fresh start for each generation, in practice ran into constitutional limitations and a general public desire to perpetuate family wealth. Many states excluded real estate from inheritance levies; about half taxed only collateral and exempted direct heirs; very few imposed graduated rates. Britain, France, Austria, and Canada derived a much larger share of revenue—per capita, and by wealth—from inheritance taxes.[57]

Henry George's panacea of a single tax on unimproved lands had wide appeal in the turn-of-the-century Western world; but it fell on fallow ground in its land of origin. It had its greatest appeal in Oregon, where large idle tracts of government land grants were held by corporations and railroads. Even so, single-tax referenda lost badly there in 1908 and 1912. Missouri voters, too, rejected a single-tax amendment in 1912. Farmers strongly opposed it, as did the Kansas City Democratic machine.[58]

Wisconsin in 1911 enacted the first significant state income tax, aimed primarily at manufacturing companies. From then until 1929 the income tax generated about two-thirds of the state's tax revenue. But this was no product of populist egalitarianism; its chief supporters were bankers and farmers seeking to reduce the impact of rising property valuation. Banks, trust companies, railroads, and insurance companies paying license fees and *ad valorem* taxes were exempt. Until the mid-1920s, progressive and conservative state administrations alike, more responsive to banking and agricultural than to manufacturing interests, vigorously enforced it.[59]

A number of states had (usually marginal) income levies by the 1920s. Corporate and individual returns together amounted to 11 percent of state tax revenues by 1922, compensating almost precisely for the decline in general property revenues. It took a state constitutional amendment in 1915 to open the way to a proportional income tax in Massachusetts. The law went into effect in 1917, accompanied by a large-scale publicity campaign to spur participation. But more than 180,000 returns yielded only $12.1 million in revenue.[60]

State tax systems were richly varied and complex. New York, with the nation's largest and most diverse economy, had a notable range of revenue sources, the result of a unique convergence of interests: upstate Republicans who wanted to restrict the general property tax to localities, and advocates of the public services required by a growing urban-industrial society. The property tax was localized in the early

1900s, the revenue lost to the state to be recovered through a liquor license tax. But this measure did not achieve its purpose, and New York relied increasingly on other revenue sources such as levies on inheritances, mortgages, stock transfers, corporations, and public utilities franchises. By 1907 its liquor tax yielded $20 million a year, its mortgage tax $4–5 million, its stock transfer tax more than $6 million. By 1912 the inheritance tax was the largest revenue source, providing more than $12 million. One expert noted that New York had gone furthest in taxing the material or functional sources of wealth rather than the individual wealth-holder.[61]

Expanded tax sources inevitably led to a larger and more active politics of tax policy. New York's inheritance tax was amended more than eighty times from its enactment in 1885 to 1912. Graduated rates were added in 1910. Bankers estimated that as a result more than $400 million disappeared from state accounts; the expected increase in revenue failed to materialize; and in 1911 inheritance rates were lowered.

New York's 1899 public service franchise levy was no less enmeshed in politics. The original proposal was to tax public utility franchises as though they were a form of property. Commercial and manufacturing interests welcomed this alleviation of their tax burdens. The utilities and the Republican machine objected, preferring the existing method of taxing only gross receipts. GOP boss Tom Platt warned that the requirement for local assessments of the value of utility franchises would give the Democrats a strong claim on campaign contributions from the companies. Governor Theodore Roosevelt duly called a special session of the legislature, which changed the bill to assure that assessment remained in statewide (that is, Republican) hands.[62]

Elsewhere, new forms of taxation shared pride of place with efforts to centralize, equalize, and increase the efficiency of property assessment. Thus Massachusetts relied increasingly on private agencies to collect information on corporate stock ownership. And in 1908 the commonwealth empowered its tax commissioners to supervise local assessors more closely. The result was a big jump in personal property assessments: from $767 million in 1907 to $1.2 billion in 1915.[63]

Indiana took the lead in reforming the machinery of state taxation. An 1891 law sustained by the Supreme Court set up a state board of tax commissioners and a new system of county assessors. (They replaced some 1,300 elected, low-paid township and ward assessors, infinitely susceptible to local pressures.) The board had broad power to assess railroad and other public utility property, and in its first year raised the roads' valuations from $60 to $160 million. But this effort at more efficient valuation and collection soon ran into difficulties. A 1901 amendment restricted the investigative authority of local assessors. The state's banks had more than $100 million on deposit, but only about $1 million was assessed for tax purposes. The tax commission ordered the banks to open their books. They refused, and the Indiana supreme court held that the commission had gone beyond its legal powers.[64]

Michigan in 1899 created an even more powerful state tax commission, empowered to review the assessments of townships, cities, corporations, or citizens. Newspaper announcements citing hundreds of delinquent taxpayers soon became common. Valuations rose sharply—those of copper mines from $28 to $108 million—while tax rates remained unchanged. But here, too, localism remained a potent force. The state court struck down a Committee on Appeal empowered to review the assessment-equalizing decisions of local supervisors, on the ground that it deprived counties of their inherent right to self-government.[65]

Growing public needs strained Ohio's tax base: from 1897 to 1911 local expenditures increased by 97 percent, state expenditures by 90 percent. Yet between 1871 and 1910 the assessed value of Ohio land, subject only to decennial appraisals, rose by a risible $21 million. In response the legislature increased the frequency of tax appraisals; created a permanent state tax commission with the power to assess and not merely to equalize tax rates; and made provision for state-appointed county assessors, in principle free from local political pressures. Spectacular changes resulted. The 1911 reassessment raised the state's land valuation to $1.7 billion—an increase of 154 percent. Personalty and personal property valuation leapt from $2.5 billion to $6.2 billion. The share of the state's taxes paid by public utilities increased from 9.1 percent in 1910 to 15.7 percent in 1913.

But as Ohio taxation grew in scale and complexity, so did its politicization. Proposals for a more uniform, equitable tax system had a prominent place in the state's 1912 constitutional convention but ran into popular and special interest hostility to more efficient tax collecting. The legislature wanted to exempt state and local bonds from taxation, but this proposal lost narrowly in a popular referendum. Republicans in 1915 denounced the state-appointed assessors of the incumbent Democratic administration as products of political machine patronage and pledged in effect to return to the past by making county assessors elective.[66]

By 1914 the machinery of state taxation differed substantially from that of a generation before. Revenues came much more from income, sales, and intangible property than from the real property base of the nineteenth century; classification widely replaced uniform taxation; specific taxes replaced *ad valorem* levies; state tax commissions prevailed; state and local assessment was much improved; the courts substantially expanded legislative freedom from constitutional constraints on the taxing power. Yet no profound change had occurred in underlying tax philosophy: taxation remained a minimalist instrument of minimal government, not a means of populist redistributionism or a tool of the active state.

On the national level, however, something more portentous took place: the appearance of the federal income tax. The Sixteenth Amendment, legitimating such a levy, became law in 1913: the first alteration of the Constitution since Reconstruction. It coincided with Britain's adoption of an income tax in 1907 and graduation of its rates in 1910 to help pay for Lloyd George's welfare budget; and with the French income tax laws of 1909 and 1914, enacted at a time of heavy military expenditure over the fierce opposition of the upper classes, shopkeepers, and peasants. The American tax might reasonably be thought to have some relationship to a new era of active government. Theodore Roosevelt called in December 1906 for a heavily progressive inheritance tax and spoke of the social desirability of a graduated income tax; two weeks later British prime minister Herbert Asquith told the House of Commons that it was time to consider a graduated tax on income.[67]

But neither proponents of social welfare programs nor advocates of increased military spending figured prominently in the movement for an American income tax. Rather, it emerged from a typically complex public policy crucible: party politicians enmeshed in the traditional issues of tariff protection, corporate powers, and party advantage; public opinion increasingly sensitive to great wealth and attracted to the idea of progressive taxation as a moderate leveler; economists and other newly influential experts; a society in which salaried and professional income had come to be a conspicuous fact of life.

The Spanish-American War set off a search for new federal revenue sources. The 1898 War Revenue Act included a graduated inheritance tax; and pension and other war costs significantly added to post-1900 federal expenditure. So too (on a lesser scale) did new federal activities: rural free delivery, land reclamation, the Panama Canal. But the pressure for an income tax did not reach flash point until 1909. In that year several factors—an imminent $90–100 million federal deficit, the largest since the Civil War; widespread belief that new taxes were one way to deal with growing inequities of personal and corporate wealth; the Democrats' search for revenue alternatives to the tariff—coincided with the politics of the Payne-Aldrich tariff.[68]

Democratic leaders tried to strengthen the case for low tariff rates by adding an income tax provision to the tariff bill, as they had done with the Wilson-Gorman Act of 1894. To ease the political pressure mounting against Payne-Aldrich, President Taft proposed an income tax amendment to the Constitution, and inheritance and corporation taxes as part of the tariff bill. The administration apparently did not expect the amendment to be enacted; after all, none had been since 1870.

But then the explosive possibilities of a pluralist politics made themselves felt. "I shall vote for a corporation tax," said Senate Finance Committee chairman Nelson Aldrich, "as a means to defeat the income tax." Democrats and progressive Republicans of course also supported it—in part for its revenue potential, in part because they saw it as a step toward federal control of corporations. The corporation tax became law as an amendment to the Payne-Aldrich tariff. Within a year of its passage a treatise on the federal corporation tax offered companies "practical assistance in what may not inappropriately be described as an emergency." But the Supreme Court in 1911 held it to be an excise not an income tax, and hence constitutional, even though it was pegged to corporate profits.[69]

So many congressmen found it politic to support an income tax amendment, and so many thought its enactment all but impossible—Aldrich himself introduced it in the Senate—that no senator and only fourteen members of the House voted against it. Why? The most comprehensive (and necessarily the most general) explanation is that Progressive ideas and rhetoric were at their height in periodicals and the press, in academic discussion, and among reform-sensitized politicos. An income tax made eminent good sense to them. Even the *Wall Street Journal* thought it "a mark of economic progress" to change from indirect to direct taxation. *Bankers' Magazine* expected the tax to modernize the fiscal system, strengthen freer trade, and be the best and fairest way of taxing the rich. The most conspicuous dissents came from corporation lawyers and from progressive governor Charles Evans Hughes of New York, who opposed the amendment because he feared it would lead to federal taxation of state and municipal bonds.[70]

By February 1913 the requisite number of state legislatures had ratified the amendment by overwhelming majorities: New York's 65 percent was among the closer protax votes. Southerners and westerners expected the urban-capitalist East to bear the brunt of the income tax; and strong support came from urban, immigrant-based Democratic machines in the large industrial states.[71]

The first implementation of this new tax came in a most traditional way: as a revenue-enhancing amendment to the Democrats' Underwood Tariff of 1914. Its terms were modest: 1 percent on incomes from $4,000 to $20,000 (a far higher starting point than in other countries); a surtax rising to a maximum of 3 percent on incomes over $200,000; state and municipal bonds, life insurance proceeds, and business expenses exempt. Edwin R. A. Seligman, the leading expert on the subject, observed that this was a tax based on a conception of income as a regular and periodic return.[72] In this sense it was yet another government response to an economy increasingly characterized by the flow of recurrent transactions rather than by the pulse of contractual agreements.

Never before was so precise and elaborate a set of obligations imposed on so many citizens by the government in peacetime. (The first Form 1040 in 1914—"so complicated in its operation," complained the secretary of the Treasury—was three pages long.) Cordell Hull of Tennessee, the levy's principal draftsman, predicted that it "will mark the beginning of a new era in the fiscal affairs of the country, which will most probably prove of long duration."[73]

At first the tax affected only 2 percent of the work force. But the war soon changed that. In 1916 about one-third of a million people paid income taxes of $68 million (65 percent more than the year before). Two-thirds of that sum came from the surtax levied on incomes over $20,000. This was only 9 percent of the government's revenue, almost all of which still derived from customs and excise receipts. Rising defense (and soon war) costs and declining customs receipts quickly made the income tax a primary source of additional government revenue. The Revenue Act of 1916 doubled the base rate of 2 percent, sharply raised the surtax, and increased corporation and inheritance taxes; the 1917 act added a significant excess profits levy. One-third of the huge cost of the American war effort was met by taxation: a higher share than that of the other warring powers.[74]

Just how much of a landmark was the income tax in the rise of the modern American state? Wilson and Treasury Secretary William G. McAdoo intended to make it a permanent part of the tax system; and during the 1920s corporate and individual income levies accounted for 55–60 percent of federal tax revenues. But this shift in the revenue base hardly fostered a more interventionist state during the postwar decade. Nor did the redistributionist sentiment evident at the time of the initial passage of the income tax play much of a role in the politics of the 1920s. As in the case of the states and localities, the form of federal taxation altered in response to the economic transformation of the early twentieth century. But its purposes were far more resistant to the winds of change.[75]

Taxation: Prosperity and Depression Years

The financial burden imposed by World War I dominated postwar tax policies. Debt management and reductions in revenue and expenditure everywhere became the most compelling government goals. Thus despite their staggering burden of debt the British cut their income tax at the war's end, and higher local taxes stemming from rising labor and materials costs met with strong popular protest. British Liberal economist J. A. Hobson's voice was lonely and largely unheard when he proposed a single levy on all forms of capital.[76]

The United States had a much smaller postwar public debt burden than the European powers. Still, its growth was dramatic enough: from $1.25 billion in 1916 to $25.5 billion in 1919. And the political pressure for tax reduction was great. Traditional American attitudes toward a balanced budget and a weak state were if anything strengthened by the postwar passion for "normalcy." For the next decade government spending on all levels, measured as a percentage of GNP, remained substantially lower in the United States than in Europe (see Table 4).

Treasury Secretary Andrew Mellon's assault on the income tax figures prominently in historical accounts of the 1920s. But American taxation during the postwar decade had a more complex reality. The government continued to depend far more on the income tax for its revenue than did other countries: 63.8 percent came from this source in 1926–27, compared with 46.5 percent in Britain, 35.2 percent in Germany, and 29.7 percent in France (Table 5).

As before, the states and localities bore the brunt of building and maintaining the schools, roads, hospitals, and utilities of a modern urban society. Their expenditure, debt, and taxation mounted rapidly during the 1920s (Table 6).

By 1927 these commitments pushed the total of federal, state, and local taxes above their wartime level. And in striking contrast with other countries—though quite in keeping with American federal-

Table 4. Government spending as a percentage of GNP, 1920–1929

Year	United States	France	Britain	Germany
1920	5.5	25.5	19.3	—
1925	3.1	15.1	15.9	8.1
1929	3.2	14.3	16.6	9.3

Source: Carolyn Webber and Aaron Wildavsky, *A History of Taxation and Expenditure in the Western World* (New York, 1986), p. 451.

Table 5. Federal tax revenues, 1922–1932 ($million; % in parentheses)

Year	Individual income	Corporate income	Customs	Alcohol and tobacco	Death and inheritance	Other	Total
1922		1,939[a] (58)	318 (9)	314 (9)	139 (4)	662 (20)	3,372
1927	879 (26)	1,259 (37)	585 (17)	396 (12)	90 (3)	154 (5)	3,364
1932	405 (22)	598 (33)	311 (17)	406 (22)	41 (2)	42 (2)	1,813

Source: U.S. Bureau of the Census, *Historical Statistics of the United States, Colonial Times to 1970* (Washington, D.C., 1975), p. 1122.
a. Information combined in reporting.

Table 6. State and local expenditure, debt, and taxation, 1913–1927 ($ billion)

Year	Expenditure	Debt	Taxation
1913	2.26	4.41	1.61
1922	5.65	10.11	4.02
1927	7.81	14.88	6.09

Source: U.S. Bureau of the Census, *Historical Statistics of the United States, Colonial Times to 1970* (Washington, D.C., 1975), p. 1104.

ism—gasoline and sales taxes, the major tax innovations of the 1920s, were state not federal instruments.[77]

Federal tax policy in the 1920s had two compelling (and contradictory) goals: to reduce the incidence of taxation and to reduce the war debt and restore a balanced budget. The excess profits tax law of 1918, which applied to all businesses, was by far the most substantial federal tax measure to that time. By 1920, income and excess profits taxes produced 69 percent of federal revenue, and business criticism mounted. Wilson recommended repeal of the excess profits levy in his 1919 State of the Union message, and the 1921 Revenue Act abandoned it.[78]

Criticism of unnecessary government spending pervaded postwar public discourse, even though 93 percent of the 1920 federal budget dealt with war-related costs. The liberal *Nation* commended Harding's 1922 budget for reducing federal expenditures, though it took him to task for seeking cuts from scientific research and social services rather than from the military and by increased government efficiency and honesty. At the same time, pressures for debt reduction led to a decline in the national debt from $25 billion in 1919 to under $16 billion in 1930.[79]

These conflicting impulses found their voice in Treasury Secretary Mellon. Throughout the decade he campaigned for lower personal income tax rates (to sustain initiative, he said) and for economy in government. But his deep commitment to debt reduction and a balanced budget led him to support higher corporate than individual tax rates, a higher tax on unearned (investment) than on earned (wages and salary) income, and taxation of state and local bonds. Much like Herbert Hoover, Mellon turns out to have been an updated American individualist rather than an advocate of corporatism.[80]

A rapid succession of Revenue Acts—in 1924, 1926, 1927, and 1928—resembled nothing so much as tariff bills: recurrent *rondes* enacted by organized interests and their congressional spokesmen. The usual outcome was lowered income surtax, estate, and corporation levies. Congressional leaders from both parties and the advisers of Presidents Wilson, Harding, and Coolidge agreed on the desirability of tax reduction. After all, the states bore the brunt of social spending, and there was little public demand for a substantial increase in national welfare, or defense, or any other expenditure. Besides, business prosperity produced federal revenue increases despite the tax cuts of 1924, 1926, and 1927. So the tax cutters had their way.[81]

In other areas of taxation, change was nominal. With prohibition, liquor excise taxes faded away—from $223 million in 1913 to $8 million in 1932. But as cigarettes took hold, tobacco excise revenues went from $77 million in 1913 to $398 million in 1932.[82] The bottom line: excises produced a slowly expanding portion of federal tax revenue during the 1920s.

There was much talk of a national sales tax to replace excess profit and income surtax levies. A number of European countries (including France and Germany) adopted it after the war. Farmers supposedly favored the tax; support came from several industries that felt they had paid more than their share of special war taxes. Utah's Senator Reed Smoot attached a sales tax proposal to the 1921 Revenue Act, and it was narrowly defeated. Organized labor opposed it; so did retailers and businessmen closely tied to marketing and sales. Critics of the tax, including Mellon, warned that it discriminated in favor of large, vertically integrated, self-contained enterprises as against smaller businesses. The sales tax remained an instrument of state and local, not national, taxation. Why? Perhaps the best explanation is the quid pro quo inherent in federalism. Once the federal commitment to an income tax was made, the sales tax became the appropriate trade-off to the states. By the same token, progressive state income taxation has been only slightly less difficult to achieve than a national sales tax.[83]

Throughout the 1920s, sustaining the existing revenue system took precedence over structural innovation. One sign of this was a growing legal-judicial voice in tax matters. The Supreme Court held that Congress could not tax dividends as income. The 1921 Revenue Act created a Board of Tax Appeals, which rapidly became in effect a special tax court. The Treasury came under criticism for taxing income not yet received under the legal concept of "constructive receipt," an example of "the extent to which a doctrine, sound in its origin, may be stretched to cover a great variety of doubtful cases by guardians of the revenue who are assiduous to prevent the minimizing of taxes."[84]

Some thought that tax-exempt state and municipal bonds for the massive road and school building going on in the 1920s threatened the progressive income tax. There was talk of a constitutional amendment to prohibit tax-exempts; defenders of these bonds proposed to give the states the power to tax federal securities if the national government could tax state bonds.[85]

Finally, the government's tax-collecting machinery did not seem adequate to the scale of its task (a modest one indeed by later standards). By one estimate 50,000 lawyers, tax consultants, accountants, and the like eroded the system. Evasion might decline if rates were lowered; but in the estimation of one observer, for all its reductions "the Revenue Act of 1928 cannot be said to have simplified income tax procedure." *Plus ça change* . . . [86]

In contrast to stagnation on the federal level, state and especially local tax revenues grew substantially during the 1920s. These were the branches of government that dealt most directly with the demands of a modern urban society. But they did so in a distinctively American manner. Expanded local expenditure in postwar Europe went primarily for social welfare; in the United States, primarily for roads, schools, hospitals, and urban infrastructure.

Property taxes transferred by the state or collected in localities were the mainstay of local revenue during the decade. As this source of state income declined, corporation and excise taxes, automobile and other license fees, and, by the end of the decade, sales and gasoline levies took up the slack. State debt grew rapidly—from $380 million in 1913 to almost $2 billion in 1927—helping to finance new roads and schools much as federal bonds did the war effort.[87]

The increasing worth of urban property, and the tax revenues generated by business expansion and the mushroom growth of the automobile, provided added sustenance for state and local spending. Special tax districts—for flood prevention, for bridges and tunnels, for drainage and irrigation—multiplied. A 1928 Massachusetts legislative commission concluded that popular demands for state spending on roads, schools, and the like outweighed protests against the tax level, even though the average rate had risen by 66 percent from 1916 to 1926.[88]

As the transactions and forms of wealth of the American economy became more complex, so did taxation. The traditional view—"one man, one thing, one tax"—gave way to multiple state levies: on land, income, inheritance, sales, tobacco, gasoline, automobiles. But these new revenue sources were suspended in a web of political, legal, and cultural constraints.[89]

Twenty states had some form of personal income tax by 1930, but this yielded only 4 percent of total revenue. A 1924 Florida constitutional amendment prohibited a state income tax; Oregon voters repealed it after a year's trial. State courts struck down attempts to tax unearned income at a different rate from earned income; Alabama's tribunal ruled against a progressive income tax on the ground that it was a discriminatory property tax. By 1931 the extent of a state's jurisdiction over income for tax purposes was still uncertain.[90]

Oregon imposed the first gasoline tax in 1919, a move that of course led to litigation. But the Supreme Court in 1921 held that the state could tax particular commodities: the uniformity requirement in its constitution applied only to property taxes. Nor—the Court added in 1924—did it violate due process to require gasoline companies to collect the tax from consumers without compensation.[91]

The gasoline tax had its own problems. Farmers and gas dealers frequently evaded it; state legislatures diverted gas revenues to nonhighway uses. But its utility and importance sustained it even though it was a sales levy on an essential, frequent transaction by large numbers of citizens. By 1927 the gasoline tax produced $259 million, 12 percent of state revenue; during the Depression the yield rose to 16–17 percent.[92]

A movement by independent retailers to get the states to levy punitive taxes on chain stores testifies to the diversity of tax policy. This was in the tradition of the successful late nineteenth-century effort by dairy farmers to use the tax power against oleomargarine. From 1928 to 1930 more than eighty chain-store tax bills came before twenty-nine state legislatures; six became law. State courts struck down most of them on the ground that chain stores were not sufficiently distinct to justify separate classification for tax purposes. But in 1931 the Supreme Court approved Indiana's graduated chain-store tax law. And the spur of hard times induced fifteen southern and western states to impose special taxes on chain stores in 1933 and 1934.[93]

Burgeoning state taxation gave new life to an old problem: the place of federalism in an increasingly nationalized economy. Maintaining an independent system of state taxation in the face of transactions and wealth accumulation that had little or nothing to do with state lines dominated tax law in the 1920s. The courts wrestled with issues such as whether or not taxation discriminated between residents and nonresidents, or between incomes derived inside or outside the state. There was a special need to sort out in-state and out-of-state corporate income for tax purposes. Intricate methods of calculation—subject to court review—contributed to the complexity and litigiousness of tax policy.[94]

Wisconsin judges declared that a state should tax only income derived from sources within its borders; their New York counterparts held that residents should be taxed on their entire income regardless of source. For the most part the courts let nondiscriminatory state taxes stand; and from 1911 to 1925 the Supreme Court found for the taxpayer in only eight of fifty-one Fourteenth Amendment challenges to state taxation. But in 1925 the Court found Pennsylvania's 1919 inheritance levy unconstitutional to the extent that it taxed property outside the state. This reversed the longtime judicial tendency to endorse a broad inheritance tax power. For the rest of the decade the Court tended to find for taxpayers in conflicts involving the multiple taxation of intangibles.[95]

For all the impact of modernity, local taxation rested heavily on an older—indeed, a preindustrial, preurban—base. The levy on property accounted for an ever-larger proportion of local tax revenue: 87 percent in 1902, 91 percent in 1913, 97 percent in 1922, 98 percent in 1927.[96] A tax dating from a time when property was concrete and manifest, and rates were low, continued to flourish when property was complex and untraceable, and revenue needs were high.

The old problem of relative overtaxation of realty because of its visibility was now compounded by rising rates. A survey of Kansas real estate taxation from 1910 to 1923 found that while the market value of farmland went up 39 percent, taxes rose by 168 percent, mainly because of higher expenditures for schools and roads. A similar situation prevailed in Kansas cities: taxes increased 261 percent, real estate values 68 percent.[97]

The cities' responses to the growth of nonrealty wealth varied greatly. New York's 1931 tax base was 98 percent realty, 2 percent personalty; San Francisco's ratio was 58 percent to 42 percent; Baltimore's, 50–50. But underassessed realty and hidden, untaxed personalty were universal problems. The Illinois Tax Commission ordered a reassessment of the state's real estate in 1928, for all-too-familiar reasons: it found valuation to be grossly inequitable, politicized, corrupt. In the well-off community of Hyde Park only 6,000 of 38,000 people paid a personal property tax; 93 percent of Jefferson township's taxpayers were delinquent in their tax payments. While the nature and forms of personal property grew exponentially, undervaluation and tax evasion remained the rule. In 1900, thirty-eight items appeared on Illinois's personal property tax schedule; by 1927 the list had grown to only forty items. Fewer clocks and watches were assessed in 1927 than in 1867. Cook County (Chicago) had issued 474,146 automobile licenses by 1925; but only 19,175 autos were assessed for taxation.[98]

Efforts at assessment equalization in Chicago during the early 1920s reduced the average deviation from uniformity from 40 percent to 38 percent: hardly a breakthrough. Decentralized and overlapping jurisdictions, the strength of friends-and-neighbors politics, corruption, and vested interests—familiar standbys in the politics of taxation—worked against significant reform. The old ways also persisted in Pennsylvania. Local tax collectors, nearly all of whom worked on a fee or commission basis, were as numerous, and as political, as ever. Hazleton County's tax collectors gave the county commissioners a list of 6,000 residents permanently freed of poll or occupational taxes, apparently a payoff for party work.[99]

So in tax policy as in other areas, the polity of the 1920s responded to the demands of modernity, but in ways deeply conditioned, and constrained, by the existing political and governmental culture. Perhaps stasis in its physiological sense—"a slackening of the blood current, as in passive congestion"—best describes the prevailing state of affairs.

One of the earliest uses of what would be the accepted designation of the economic disaster of the 1930s—"this depression for a great many years to come may warrant the title 'The Great Depression'"—came appropriately enough in a 1932 survey of recent tax legislation. The impact of the slump on taxation was immediate and devastating. Income tax receipts during the first quarter of 1931 fell 40 percent below the previous year's level. At the same time government expenditures surpassed estimates by $300 million. By 1932 the government faced a deficit of $2.7 billion, far larger than any previous peacetime shortfall.[100]

Pressure rapidly mounted for aid to the depressed economy and its victims. The Revenue Acts of 1932 and 1934 (the first under Hoover, the second under FDR) raised taxes by increasing excise levies on items such as alcohol, furs, cosmetics, automobiles, and gasoline. The *New Republic* approved of the 1932 excise taxes; Democratic congressional leaders had no objection to a national sales tax. For all the strains imposed by the Depression and the political change presaged by the New Deal, traditional commitments to a balanced budget and the existing tax structure continued.

The 1935 Revenue Act, with substantially heavier levies on wealthy individuals and corporations, was the high water mark of New Deal tax reform. This, plus an improving economy, raised income tax receipts to 36 percent of total revenues in 1936 and to 49 percent in 1938 (after having fallen from 63 percent in 1927 to 27 percent in 1934). But borrowing rose from 25 percent of the tax total in 1934 to 47 percent in 1938, and the income tax continued to affect no more than 5 percent of the population. And major new levies during the New Deal—on liquor, on agricultural commodities under the first AAA—were regressive rather than redistributive. Not until World War II did the present configuration of federal taxation—withholding and a substantial broadening of the income tax base—take form.[101]

The most striking feature of state and local taxation during the Depression was the rise of tax delinquency, as incomes fell faster than tax rates. By the end of 1931, 40 million acres of farmland in five agricultural states were tax delinquent. Cities, swamped by mounting relief and unemployment costs, faced the same problem: 41 percent of Chicago's real estate and 48 percent of its personal property tax payments fell into arrears by the writer of 1931–32; elsewhere delinquency rates of 25 percent to 30 percent were common. Sixty-three percent of Cleveland's levies were unpaid in 1932. Courts that had once concerned themselves with the scope of local taxation now had to deal with a mounting wave of government bankruptcies and receiverships. An Illinois Tax Receivership Act authorized the courts to make Cook County's collector of taxes the receiver of delinquent properties, with the power to apply their income to the payment of taxes.[102]

The politics of taxation also changed. Pressure rose for reduced government spending. Taxpayer rebellions in the cities became as frequent as farmers' refusal to sell crops at giveaway prices and resistance to foreclosure sales. Thousands demonstrated in Philadelphia, where 51,000 homes had been sold for taxes in 1930 and 1931, forcing the city to abandon its plans for a substantial tax increase and higher assessments. New York City's situation was so desperate that the state legislature in 1933 empowered it to levy any taxes that the state could legally impose.[103]

Property taxes in general underwent their greatest reduction in American history. But mounting welfare costs compelled the states to find new revenue sources. Thirteen raised their gas taxes in 1931; the same number adopted income and inheritance levies from 1931 to 1934. Special taxes were imposed on intangibles such as stocks and bonds. States turned increasingly to the sales tax. About twenty had adopted it by 1933, though almost all specified that it lapse in two or three years. Agricultural interests welcomed the tax as an alternative to the property levy; more generally, it was regarded—and accepted— as a tax on business. The courts, most of whom held that all occupations were taxable privileges, raised no significant opposition. The sales tax rose from .3 percent of state tax revenues in 1932 to 15 percent in 1940.[104]

By 1940, sales and excise levies provided 56 percent of state tax revenues, testimony to what turned out to be the Depression's greatest fiscal legacy: the adaptation of the revenue system to a modern consumer economy.[105] But the general property tax to this day is by far the major source of local revenue. And newer levies—on income, inheritance, sales—cannot be said to have escaped the old, nagging problems of regressivity, concealment, constitutional limitations, and the ambiguities and complexities of federalism.

Afterword

This book ends with the coming of the New Deal. Then, it is commonly agreed, began a new era in American politics, government, and law: an era in which we still live, and which in terms of public policy (and much else besides) is sharply distinct from the period that preceded it. And yet a great deal of the history of early twentieth-century economic policymaking turns out to have been not antipodal to but a precedent for the decades since.

The concerns—and—ambiguities—of antitrust still are very much alive. Debate over the perils and payoffs of bigness and over the proper stance of the state toward large enterprise is as evident today as in the early 1900s. Who can escape a sense of *déjà vu* when comparing the context and consequences surrounding the breakup of Standard Oil in the 1910s and the breakup of American Telephone & Telegraph in the 1970s?

Recent public policy toward declining industries such as steel and metal-bashing has been no more surefooted than it was toward the railroads seventy years ago. Our public utilities are almost as likely to be private today as in the early 1900s; and they operate under the regulatory system and legal conditions created during the decades before 1930. The same is true of new technology. Television and the computer may be transforming instruments of our time, in the sense that the telephone, the automobile, movies, and radio were in the early twentieth century. But the regulatory and legal response has not deviated significantly from the earlier experience; indeed, much of that response relies on agencies and policies adopted then.

Have there been significant changes in the tone and texture of business regulation in general? In many particulars, yes; in the relationship of the state to business, not necessarily. Manufacturers' and product liability law is far more extensive than it was. Yet we are, if anything, less likely today than in the early years of the century to try to control prices: fair trade and resale price maintenance are things of the past. And the legal and regulatory treatment of patenting, copyright, trademarks, and advertising, to understate the matter, has not been clarified in the age of photocopying, computers, and television. At the end of the century as at its beginning, it appears that factors relatively detached from the polity—new technology, foreign competition—still do far more than public policy to shape the course of the American economy.

Is this as true for the traditional factors of production: labor, agriculture and natural resources, urban land use, capital, trade, and taxation? Of course very great changes of public policy have occurred in these areas since 1930. But now, as we approach the end of the century, we may properly ask how fundamental a transformation there has been.

The New Deal and the wartime boom did much to foster industrial unionization, and organized labor attained a significant place in the Democratic party. But a labor-driven social democratic politics did not come into being. And unionization of the labor force turned out to be more a phenomenon of the 1930s and 1940s than an ongoing change in American labor relations: 11.6 percent of the nonagricultural work force was unionized in 1930; 26.9 percent in 1940; 31.5 percent in 1950; 25.2 percent in 1980.

Land and resource conservation, like product liability, has a much larger place in public policy today than in the first three decades of the century. But the one like the other has occurred in pace with an expansion of use that reduces its relative impact: we try to conserve more, but we use more. Our urban record is even more dramatic testimony to our distinctive public policy mix of persistence and pluralism. The people who occupy our cities and suburbs, and the ways in which we use them, are ever more varied. Yet zoning, not planning, remains the primary policy determinant of urban land use.

Recent developments in the politics of the tariff, in banking and securities regulation, and in tax policy, would be all too familiar to an early twentieth-century observer. Tariffmaking, which for a few decades appeared to lose much of its earlier political salience, is back in politics with a vengeance. Banking and investment continue to strain at—and to break away from—their loose regulatory reins. And the popular ambivalence toward taxation as a form of redistribution is as lively now as it was before 1930, although (or perhaps because) the scale of taxation has greatly expanded.

The persistence of old values and an ever-more-dense, pluralistic interplay of diverse, conflicting interests characterized economic policymaking during the first three decades of the twentieth century. Some—or even much—of the same may be said of the six decades since. Ours remains a polity deeply skeptical toward government management of economic affairs, yet full of strong and growing demands upon the state; fearful of corporate size and power, yet hungry for its material fruits; ambiguity itself in its view of the roles of politicians, legislators, lawyers, judges, and administrators. The response of the early twentieth-century American polity to the coming of a new economy left a legacy that is very much alive today.

Abbreviations

ABA	American Bar Association
Am LR	*American Law Review*
Annals	*Annals of the American Academy of Political and Social Science*
Atl	*Atlantic Monthly*
Bus Hist R	*Business History Review*
Cal LR	*California Law Review*
Cent LJ	*Central Law Journal*
Col LR	*Columbia Law Review*
Cornell LQ	*Cornell Law Quarterly*
GB	Great Britain
Harv Bus R	*Harvard Business Review*
Harv LR	*Harvard Law Review*
HS	U.S. Bureau of the Census, *Historical Statistics of the United States, Colonial Times to 1970* (Washington, D.C., 1975)
Ind	*Independent*
J Comp Leg	*Journal of the Society of Comparative Legislation*
J Land PU Ec	*Journal of Land and Public Utility Economics*
J Pol Ec	*Journal of Political Economy*
Lit Dig	*Literary Digest*
Mich LR	*Michigan Law Review*
NICB	National Industrial Conference Board
NAR	*North American Review*
PRO, *Cab 37*	Public Record Office, Cabinet Papers, 1880–1916 (Microfilm)
Pol Sci Q	*Political Science Quarterly*
Q J Ec	*Quarterly Journal of Economics*
Sci Am	*Scientific American*
U Pa LR	*University of Pennsylvania Law Review*
Yale LJ	*Yale Law Journal*

Notes

Introduction

1. E. J. Hobsbawm, *The Age of Empire, 1875–1914* (New York, 1987), p. 7; Norman Stone, *Europe Transformed, 1878–1919* (Cambridge, 1984), p. 15; Mark Sullivan, *Our Times: The United States, 1900–1925* (New York, 1926), I, 24–26.

2. John Chamberlain, *Farewell to Reform: Being a History of the Rise, Life, and Decay of the Progressive Mind in America* (New York, 1932); Matthew Josephson, *The President Makers: The Culture of Politics and Leadership in an Age of Enlightenment, 1896–1919* (1940; reprint, New York, 1964).

3. Eric F. Goldman, *Rendezvous with Destiny: A History of Modern American Reform* (New York, 1952); Arthur S. Link, *Woodrow Wilson and the Progressive Era, 1910–1917* (New York, 1954); George E. Mowry, *The Era of Theodore Roosevelt, 1900–1912* (New York, 1958); Richard Hofstadter, *The Age of Reform: From Bryan to F.D.R.* (New York, 1955).

4. Gabriel Kolko, *The Triumph of Conservatism: A Reinterpretation of American History, 1900–1916* (Glencoe, Ill., 1963).

5. Stuart Ewen, *Captains of Consciousness: Advertising and the Social Roots of the Consumer Culture* (New York, 1976); David F. Noble, *America by Design: Science, Technology, and the Rise of Corporate Capitalism* (New York, 1977), p. 75.

6. James Weinstein, *The Corporate Ideal in the Liberal State, 1900–1918* (Boston, 1968); Martin J. Sklar, *The Corporate Reconstruction of American Capitalism, 1890–1916: The Market, Law, and Politics* (Cambridge, 1988). See also Jeffrey Lustig, *Corporate Liberalism* (Berkeley, 1982).

7. Hofstadter, *Age of Reform*, p. 214; Robert H. Wiebe, *The Search for Order, 1877–1920* (New York, 1967), esp. pp. xiii–xiv. See also Samuel P. Hays, "The New Organizational Society," *Building the Organizational Society: Essays on Associational Activities in Modern America*, ed. Jerry Israel (New York, 1972), pp. 1–15; Louis Galambos, "The Emerging Organizational Synthesis in Modern American History," *Bus Hist R*, 44 (1970), 279–290; and Stephen Skowronek, *Building a New American State: The*

Expansion of National Administrative Capacities 1877–1920 (Cambridge, 1982), for other examples of the organizational approach.

8. Sklar, *Corporate Reconstruction*, p. 46n.

9. L. P. Hartley, *The Go-Between* (New York, 1967), p. 3.

10. Beard quoted in Goldman, *Rendezvous*, p. x.

1. A New Economy

1. Richard Hofstadter, *The Age of Reform: From Bryan to F.D.R.* (New York, 1955), p. 94.

2. Alexander D. Noyes, "The Recent Economic History of the United States," *Q J Ec*, 19 (1904–05), 181–182; W. T. Stead, *The Americanization of the World* (London, 1901); Vicomte G. d'Avenal, "Aux Etats-Unis," *Revue des deux mondes*, 3d ser., 41 (1907), 518–553; Frank A. Vanderlip, *The American "Commercial Invasion" of Europe* (New York, 1902); Louis J. Magee, *The American and the German "Peril"* (New York, 1906), p. 11.

3. "Politics and Business Prosperity," *Gunton's Magazine*, 23 (1902), 207; Brooks Adams, *America's Economic Supremacy* (New York, 1900), pp. 44–49; Noyes, "Recent Economic History," pp. 178–179. See also Carroll D. Wright, "The Commercial Ascendancy of the United States," *Century Magazine*, 60 (1900), 422–427.

4. William C. Redfield, *The New Industrial Day* (New York, 1912), pp. 16–17; Laurence Gronlund, *The New Economy* (New York, 1907), pp. 6, 11; Arthur J. Eddy, *The New Competition* (New York, 1912), p. 347. See also John B. C. Kershaw, "The Promotion of Industrial Efficiency and National Prosperity," *Engineering Magazine*, 25 (1903), 329–431.

5. Dooley quoted in Carl J. Friedrich, *The Pathology of Politics* (New York, 1972), p. 171. On Kruttschmitt, see Charles D. Hine, *Modern Organization* (New York, 1912), pp. 14–15; Charles P. Steinmetz, *America and the New Epoch* (New York, 1916), p. 218; on Steinmetz, James Gilbert, *Designing the Industrial State: The Intellectual Pursuit of Collectivism in America, 1880–1940* (Chicago, 1972), chap. 7.

6. Harrington Emerson, *Efficiency as a Basis for Operation and Wages* (New York, 1909), pp. iv, vii; C. Bertrand Thompson, "The Literature of Scientific Management," *Q J Ec*, 28 (1913–14), 553–557. See also Arthur Shadwell, *Industrial Efficiency: A Comparative Study of Industrial Life in England, Germany, and America* (London, 1909); David Nelson, *Frederick W. Taylor and the Rise of Scientific Management* (Madison, Wis., 1980).

7. Arno Mayer, *The Persistence of the Old Regime* (New York, 1981), pp. 35–44. There is a growing literature on American consumerism. See Daniel M. Fox, *The Discovery of Abundance: Simon N. Patten and the Transformation of Social Theory* (Ithaca, 1967); Daniel Horowitz, *The Morality of Spending: Attitudes toward the Consumer Society in America, 1875–1940* (Baltimore, 1985); and the more tendentious Richard W. Fox and T. J. Jackson Lears, eds., *The Culture of Consumption: Critical Essays in American History, 1880–1980* (New York, 1983).

8. Walter Lippmann, *Drift and Mastery* (New York, 1914), pp. 54–55; Richmond Mayo-Smith, "Price Movements and Individual Welfare," *Pol Sci Q*, 15 (1900), 14–36; "The Cost of Living," *World To-Day*, 18 (1910), 319; Albert S. Bolles, "Rising Prices: Their Causes, Consequences and Remedies," *NAR*, 191 (1910), 795–804; Daniel Pope, "American Economists and the High Cost of Living: The Progressive Era," *Journal of the History of Behavioral Science*, 17 (1981), 75–87. See also James MacKaye, *The Economy of Happiness* (Boston, 1906).

9. Allyn A. Young, "Do the Statistics of the Concentration of Wealth in the United States Mean What They Are Commonly Assumed to Mean?" *Journal of the American Statistical Association*, n.s., 15 (1916–17), 475; Willford J. King, *The Wealth and Income of the People of the United States* (New York, 1915), pp. 130, 231, 254–255.

10. Joseph Schumpeter, "On the Concept of Social Value," *Q J Ec*, 23 (1908–09), 218, 222; Wesley C. Mitchell, "Human Behavior and Economics: A Survey of Recent Literature," *Q J Ec*, 29 (1914–15), 12.

11. Arthur J. Penty, *Post-Industrialism* (London, 1922); "'Fordism,'" *New Statesman*, 27 (1926), 729–730; Sydney Webb, *Decay of Capitalist Civilization*, 3d ed. (Westminster, 1923), chap. 6.

12. "The New Industrial Gospel," *Spectator*, 136 (1926), 260; Philip Kerr, "Can We Learn from America?" *Nation* (GB), 40 (1926–27), 76–77; Ernest J. P. Benn, *The Return to Laisser-Faire* (London, 1928), pp. 12, 32–33; Sisley Hudleston, "America's New Industrial Doctrines," *New Statesman*, 34 (1929), 395–396.

13. Harrington Emerson, *The Twelve Principles of Efficiency*, 6th ed. (New York, 1924), p. xii.

14. Stuart Chase, *The Tragedy of Waste* (New York, 1925), p. 10; Z. Clark Dickinson, "Chase's Tragedy of Waste," *Q J Ec*, 41 (1926–27), 174–180.

15. Edward A. Filene, "The New Capitalism," *Annals*, 149 (1930), 6. See also Vanderveer Curtis, *The Foundation of National Efficiency* (New York, 1923).

16. William McClellan, "Halting American Development," *NAR*, 213 (1921), 184, 187.

17. Walter R. Ingalls, *Wealth and Income of the American People*, 2d ed. (York, Pa., 1923), pp. v, 321–324; Franklin W. Fort, "The Decline in the Purchasing Power of American Farmers since 1900," *Proceedings of the Academy of Political Science*, 12 (1927), 689–693.

18. Edward S. Cowdrick, "The New Economic Gospel of Consumption," *Industrial Management*, 74 (1927), 209–211; Woodlief Thomas, "The Growth of Production and the Rising Standard of Living," *Proceedings of the Academy of Political Science*, 12 (1927), 651–661; Paul H. Douglas, "The Modern Technique of Mass Production and Its Relation to Wages," ibid., pp. 663–664; Robert M. Davis, "Long-Time Guarantees of Prosperity," *Journal of the American Statistical Association*, n.s., 23 (1928), 138–139. See also Walter Meakin, *The New Industrial Revolution* (New York, 1928).

19. Lawrence B. Mann, "The Importance of Retail Trade in the United States,"

American Economic Review, 13 (1923), 609–617; idem, "Occupational Shifts since 1920," *Journal of the American Statistical Association*, n.s., 24 (1929), 42–47; Davis, "Long-Time Guarantees," pp. 139–142.

20. Committee on Recent Economic Changes, *Recent Economic Changes in the United States* (New York, 1929), I, ix, x, xv; Donald W. McConnell, *Economic Virtues in the United States: A History and an Interpretation* (New York, 1930), p. 149; Ralph Borsodi, *The Distribution Age* (New York, 1927); Robert J. McFall, "The Census of Distribution," *Journal of the American Statistical Association*, n.s., 28 (1933), 159–164.

21. Massachusetts Commission on the Necessaries of Life, *Report* (Boston, 1923); NICB, *The Cost of Living, 1914–27* (New York, 1928); John J. Raskob, "The Development of Installment Purchasing," *Proceedings of the Academy of Political Science*, 12 (1927), 619–639; Edwin R. A. Seligman, "Economic Problems Involved in Installment Selling," ibid., pp. 583–594; idem, *Economics of Installment Selling* (New York, 1927).

22. Irving Fisher, "To Abolish Business Crises," *Industrial Management*, 73 (1927), 9.

23. John R. Dunlap, "Why Panics Now End Quickly," ibid., p. 5; National City Bank quoted in Gustav Cassel, *Recent Monopolistic Tendencies in Industry and Trade* (Geneva, 1927), p. 13; Committee, *Recent Economic Changes*, I, x.

24. "Wall Street's 'Prosperity Panic,'" *Lit Dig*, 103 (Nov. 9, 1929), 5–6; *New Statesman*, 34 (1929), 110.

25. "Can Business Be Stabilized?" *New Republic*, 61 (1929), 4–6; *World* quoted in "The Outlook for Prosperity in 1930," *Lit Dig*, 104 (Jan. 18, 1930), 5–7.

26. *Wall Street Journal* quoted in *Lit Dig*, 104 (Jan. 18, 1930); "Adults Idle as Children Labor," ibid., p. 14.

27. Alfred L. Bernheim, "Prosperity by Proclamation," *Nation*, 129 (1929), 772–774; Chase in ibid., p. 624.

28. *Washington Post* quoted in *Lit Digest*, 107 (Oct. 11, 1930), 7–9; Felix Somary, "The American and European Economic Depressions and their Political Consequences," *Journal of the Royal Institute of International Affairs*, 10 (1931), 169.

29. John M. Keynes, "The Great Slump of 1930," *Nation* (GB), 48 (1930–31), 402; idem, "The World's Economic Outlook," *Atl*, 149 (1932), 525; idem, Causes of World Depression," *Forum*, 85 (1931), 24; idem, "National Self-Sufficiency," *New Statesman and Nation*, n.s., 6 (1933), 36–37, 65–67. See also J. M. Bonn, "Some Problems of the Present Crisis," *Bankers' Magazine*, 123 (1931), 569–576.

30. Keynes, "National Self-Sufficiency," p. 66.

31. Lawrence K. Frank, "The Principle of Disorder and Incongruity in Economic Affairs," *Pol Sci Q*, 47 (1932), 521, 524–525.

32. On Scott and Technocracy, Arthur M. Schlesinger, Jr., *The Crisis of the Old Order, 1919–1933* (Cambridge, Mass., 1957), pp. 461–464; Magnus Bjorndal, "Banks and Engineers Can Restore Our Former Prosperity,"

Bankers' Magazine, 125 (1932), 575–578; on Hoover, Albert U. Romasco, *The Poverty of Abundance: Hoover, the Nation, the Depression* (New York, 1965); William E. Leuchtenberg, "The New Deal and the Analogue of War," in *Change and Continuity in 20th Century America*, ed. John Braeman (New York, 1966), pp. 81–143.
33. Elmer Davis, "Economists and the World Crisis," *American Scholar*, 2 (1933), 94.
34. Theodore Dreiser, *Tragic America* (New York, 1931), p. 412.

2. Regulating Trusts

1. Jeremiah W. Jenks, "The Trusts: Facts Established and Problems Solved," *Q J Ec*, 15 (1900–01), 73; Henry W. Macrosty, *Trusts and the State: A Sketch of Competition* (London, 1901), p. 12. See also Morton Keller, "Regulation of Large Enterprise: The United States Experience in Comparative Perspective," in *Managerial Hierarchies*, ed. Alfred D. Chandler, Jr., and Herman Daems (Cambridge, Mass., 1980), pp. 161–181; Jan Romein, *The Watershed of Two Eras: Europe in 1900* (Middletown, Conn., 1978), chap. 12. The authoritative work on the rise of big business is Alfred D. Chandler, Jr., *The Visible Hand: The Managerial Revolution in American Business* (Cambridge, Mass., 1977).
2. Leslie Hannah, *The Rise of the Corporate Economy: The British Experience* (Baltimore, 1976), pp. 23–24; Robert Donald, "Trusts in England: Recent Developments of Industrial Concentration," *Review of Reviews*, 22 (1900), 578–584; J. W. Grove, *Government and Industry in Britain* (London, 1962), p. 27; P. L. Payne, "The Emergence of the Large-Scale Company in Great Britain, 1870–1914," *Economic History Review*, 2d ser., 20 (1967), 519–520, 527.
3. NICB, *Mergers and the Law* (New York, 1929), p. 15; F. D. Simpson, "How Far Does the Law of England Forbid Monopoly?" *London Quarterly Review*, 41 (1925), 393. See also William Letwin, "The English Common Law concerning Monopoly," *University of Chicago Law Review*, 21 (1954), 385.
4. Mogul v. McGregor [1891] A.C. 25; Maxim v. Nordenfelt [1894] A.C. 535; judge quoted in Samuel P. Orth, "Germany and England's Attitude toward Trusts," *World's Work*, 25 (1912–13), 683.
5. Talcott Williams, "No Combinations without Regulation," *Annals*, 32 (1908), 248.
6. G. R. Searle, "The Edwardian Liberal Party and Business," *English Historical Review*, 98 (1983), 28–60; Payne, "Emergence," pp. 520–521. See also Gilbert H. Montague, "German and British Experience with Trusts," *Atl*, 107 (1911), 162.
7. White quoted in Heinrich Kronstein, "The Dynamics of German Cartels and Patents," *University of Chicago Law Review*, 9 (1941–42), 646; Keller, "Regulation of Large Enterprise," pp. 163–164; Rudolf Roesler, "Attitude of German People and Government towards Trusts," *Annals*, 42 (1912),

173–174; Montague, "German and British Experience," pp. 158–59. See also Francis Walker, "The Law concerning Monopolistic Combinations in Continental Europe," *Pol Sci Q*, 20 (1905), 13–21.

8. Thyssen quoted in Gerald D. Feldman, *Iron and Steel in the German Inflation* (Princeton, 1977), p. 37.

9. Gilbert H. Montague, "Business and Politics at Home and Abroad," *Annals*, 42 (1912), 161.

10. Ballin cited in U.S. Congress, Committee on Interstate Commerce, *Trusts in Foreign Countries* (Washington, D.C., 1912), p. 115. See also Francis Walker, "Policies of Germany, England, Canada and the United States towards Combinations," *Annals*, 42 (1912), 185, 187, 201; D. H. Macgregor, "The Development and Control of German Syndicates," *Economics Journal*, 24 (1914), 29–30; Elmer Roberts, "German Good-Will towards Trusts," *Scribner's Magazine*, 49 (1911), 298; Orth, "Attitude toward Trusts," pp. 679–681.

11. James Bryce, "America Revisited: The Changes of a Quarter-Century," *Outlook*, 79 (1905), 847.

12. Gabriel Kolko, *The Triumph of Conservatism: A Reinterpretation of American History, 1900–1916* (New York, 1963); Martin J. Sklar, *The Corporate Reconstruction of American Capitalism, 1890–1916* (Cambridge, 1988), p. 426.

13. Thomas K. McCraw, "Regulation in America: A Review Article," *Bus Hist R*, 49 (1975), 159–183. See also James May, "Antitrust in the Formative Era: Political and Economic Theory in Constitutional and Antitrust Analysis," *Ohio State Law Journal*, 50 (1989), 258–395.

14. Richard C. Maclaurin, "Presidential Candidates and the Trust Problem in America," *Contemporary Review*, 102 (1912), 651.

15. William Z. Ripley, "Industrial Concentration as Shown by the Census," *Q J Ec*, 21 (1906–07), 651–658; Naomi R. Lamoureaux, *The Great Merger Movement in American Business, 1895–1904* (Cambridge, Mass., 1985), pp. 1–2, 11–12.

16. Mary O. Furner, "The Republican Tradition and the New Liberalism," in *The State and Social Investigation in England and America*, ed. Michael J. Lacey and Mary O. Furner (Cambridge, forthcoming); Jeremiah W. Jenks, *Trusts and Industrial Combinations*, U.S. Department of Labor Bulletin no. 29 (Washington, D.C., 1900), pp. 661–831. See also Arthur McEwen, "The Trust as a Step in the March of Civilization," *Munsey's Magazine*, 22 (1899–1900), 571–574; Charles J. Bullock, "Trusts and Public Policy," *Atl*, 87 (1901), 745; Sklar, *Corporate Reconstruction*, pp. 185–186.

17. Chandler in "The Trust Question," *Munsey's Magazine*, 22 (1899–1900), 569–570.

18. J. A. Hobson, "The American Trust," *Economic Review*, 14 (1904), 1–22. See also Sklar, *Corporate Reconstruction*, chap. 2.

19. Thomas C. Spelling, *Bossism and Monopoly* (New York, 1906), p. 345; Frank Parsons, "Public Ownership," *Arena*, 29 (1903), 124.

20. "National Incorporation and Control of Corporations," *Am LR*, 37 (1903), 237–254; James B. Dill, "National Incorporation Laws for Trusts," *Yale LJ*,

11 (1901–02), 273–295; Bruce Wyman, "The Law of the Public Callings as a Solution of the Trust Problem," *Harv LR*, 17 (1903–04), 156–173, 217–247. See also Sydney D. M. Hudson, "Federal Incorporation: The Power of Congress over Combinations Affecting Interstate Commerce," ibid., pp. 83–103; Melvin I. Urofsky, "Proposed Federal Incorporation in the Progressive Era," *American Journal of Legal History*, 26 (1982), 160–183.

21. Charles W. McCurdy, "The *Knight* Sugar Decision of 1895 and the Modernization of American Corporation Law, 1869–1903," *Bus Hist R*, 53 (1979), 304–342.

22. *Pol Sci Q*, 23 (1908), 364–367; *Outlook*, 65 (1900), 328–329, 376; Morton Keller, *The Life Insurance Enterprise, 1885–1910* (Cambridge, Mass., 1963), chaps. 12, 13.

23. Bruce Bringhurst, *Antitrust and the Oil Monopoly: The Standard Oil Cases, 1890–1911* (Westport, Conn., 1979); Herbert N. Casson, "The Anti-Trust Crusade in Texas," *Ind*, 65 (1908), 1057–59; Isaac F. Marcosson, "The Kansas Oil Fight," *World's Work*, 10 (1905), 6155–56; Steven L. Piott, *The Anti-Monopoly Persuasion: Popular Resistance to the Rise of Big Business in the Midwest* (Westport, Conn., 1985), chap. 6.

24. Oswald W. Knauth, *The Policy of the United States towards Industrial Monopoly* (New York, 1914), pp. 86, 92, 78–79n.

25. Theodore Roosevelt, "The Standard Oil Decision and After," *Outlook*, 98 (1911), 240; Sklar, *Corporate Reconstruction*, pp. 203–285, 334–364. See also Morton Keller, "The Pluralist State: American Economic Regulation in Comparative Perspective, 1900–1930," in *Regulation in Perspective*, ed. Thomas K. McCraw (Boston, 1981), pp. 68–74.

26. Edward G. Lowry, "The Supreme Court Speaks," *Harper's Weekly*, 55 (June 3, 1911), 8; James C. Geman, Jr., "The Taft Administration and the Sherman Antitrust Act," *Mid-America*, 54 (1972), 172–186; Sklar, *Corporate Reconstruction*, pp. 364–382.

27. Robert R. Reed, "American Democracy and Corporate Reform: The Democratic Anti-Trust Plank," *Atl*, 113 (1914), 261; Melvin I. Urofsky, "Wilson, Brandeis, and the Trust Issue, 1912–1914," *Mid-America*, 49 (1967), 3–28.

28. Sklar, *Corporate Reconstruction*, chap. 6.

29. British companies: Payne, "Emergence," p. 526. American companies: Chandler, *Visible Hand*, app. A. Case figures: *All England Law Reports Annotated Index and Table of Cases 1895–1935* (London, 1936) and *American Digest System, First Decennial Digest, 1896–1906* (St. Paul, 1908).

30. Northern Securities Co. v. United States, 193 U.S. 197 (1904).

31. Robert I. Cutting, "The Northern Securities Company and the Sherman Anti-Trust Law," *NAR*, 174 (1902), 528–535; on federal courts and holding companies, Carlton D. Adams, "Legal Monopoly," *Pol Sci Q*, 19 (1904), 177; Northern Securities Co. v. United States, 193 U.S. 197, 405–406 (1904).

32. Victor Morawetz, "The Supreme Court and the Anti-Trust Act," *Col LR*, 10 (1910), 687, 698. See also Sklar, *Corporate Reconstruction*, chap. 3.

33. Standard Oil Co. v. United States, 221 U.S. 1 (1911); United States v. American Tobacco Co., 221 U.S. 106 (1911); Gilbert H. Montague, "German and British Experience with Trusts," *Atl*, 107 (1911), 155.
34. Robert L. Raymond, "The Standard Oil and Tobacco Cases," *Harv LR*, 25 (1911–12), 31. See also Sklar, *Corporate Reconstruction*, chap. 3.
35. Henry R. Seager, "The Recent Trust Decisions," *Pol Sci Q*, 26 (1911), 596.
36. Albert C. Muhse, "The Disintegration of the Tobacco Combination," *Pol Sci Q*, 28 (1913), 254, 276; "The Trust Problem and the Railways," *Pol Sci Q*, 23 (1908), 364.
37. Untermyer quoted in "The Supreme Court Decisions," *NAR*, 194 (1911), 87; Edgar Watkins, "Anti-Trust Laws a Protection to Monopoly," *Cent LJ*, 96 (1923), 189.
38. William Z. Ripley, *Trusts, Pools and Corporations*, rev. ed. (Boston, 1915), chap. 18; James T. Young, "The New Government Regulation of Business," *Annals*, 59 (1915), 214; Albert Fink, "Trust Regulation," *NAR*, 197 (1913), 62–77; "The Tobacco Decision," *Nation*, 92 (1911), 570–571; "Price-Regulation by Government," ibid., 94 (1912), 51–52.
39. Joseph E. Davies, "The Federal Trade Commission and Business—Big and Little," *World's Work*, 30 (1915), 110–14.
40. Wilson quoted in Henry Veeder, "The Federal Trade Commission and the Packers," *Illinois Law Review*, 15 (1921), 451; Woodrow Wilson, "Address on the Relation of the United States to the Business of the World," in *The Messages and Papers of Woodrow Wilson*, ed. Albert Shaw (New York, 1917), I, 31.
41. Davies, "Federal Trade Commission," p. 110; Douglas W. Jaenicke, "Herbert Croly, Progressive Ideology, and the FTC Act," *Pol Sci Q*, 93 (1978), 471–493. See also William D. Foulke, "An Interstate Trade Commission," *J Pol Ec*, 20 (1912), 406–415; *American Economic Review*, 3 (suppl.) (1912), 114–142; George C. Lay, "The Federal Trade Commission—Its Origin, Operation, and Effect," *Am LR*, 60 (1926), 340–342.
42. Gerard C. Henderson, *The Federal Trade Commission: A Study in Administrative Law and Procedure* (New Haven, 1925), p. 339; Myron W. Watkins, "The Federal Trade Commission: A Critical Survey," *Q J Ec*, 40 (1925–26), 565.
43. Root in *Current Opinion*, 58 (1915), 320–323.
44. C. S. Duncan, "Legalizing Combinations for Export Trade," *J Pol Ec*, 25 (1917), 313–318; William Notz, "Cartels during the War," *J Pol Ec*, 27 (1919), 1–38. See also Melvin I. Urofsky, *Big Steel and the Wilson Administration: A Study in Business-Government Relations* (Columbus, 1969).
45. "Capitalism after the War," *New Statesman*, 8 (1916–17), 413–414; Arthur Greenwood, "The Nationalization Movement in Great Britain," *Atl*, 125 (1920), 406–416.
46. J. W. Grove, *Government and Industry in Britain* (London, 1962), pp. 39–41; Greenwood, "Nationalization Movement," p. 408; Leslie Hannah, *The Rise of the Corporate Economy: The British Experience* (Baltimore, 1976), pp. 47–50. See also Huntly Carter, *The Limits of State Industrial Control*

(London, 1919); and William Notz, "Recent Developments in Foreign Anti-Trust Legislation," *Yale LJ*, 34 (1924–25), 159–74.

47. "'Americanize' Industry," *Saturday Review*, 141 (1926), 439–440; "Rationalization in Great Britain," *Banker's Magazine*, 119 (1929), 259–266; Hannah, *Rise*, pp. 29, 58; Bishop C. Hunt, "Recent English Company Law Reform," *Harv Bus R*, 8 (1930), 183.

48. "The Anti-Trust Law of the British Commonwealth of Nations," *Col LR*, 32 (1932), 325–327; "Trusts and the State," *New Statesman*, 29 (1927), 528–529.

49. Gerald D. Feldman, *Iron and Steel in the German Inflation, 1916–1923* (Princeton, 1977), pp. 8–9, 65, 76, 113, 464; Robert Liefmann, *Cartels, Concerns, and Trusts* (New York, 1932), pp. 168–170; idem, "German Industrial Organization since the World War," *Q J Ec*, 40 (1925–26), 82–110.

50. NICB, *Rationalization of German Industry* (New York, 1931), pp. 32–45; William C. Kessler, "German Cartel Regulation under the Decree of 1923," *Q J Ec*, 50 (1935–36), 680–693.

51. Myron Watkins, "The Sherman Act: Its Design and Its Effects," *Q J Ec*, 43 (1928–29), 32, 37. See also Felix H. Levy, "A Contrast between the Anti-Trust Laws of Foreign Countries and of the United States," *Annals*, 147 (1930), 125–137.

52. United States v. United Shoe Machinery Co., 247 U.S. 32, 56 (1918); Dexter M. Keezer and Stacy May, *The Public Control of Business* (New York, 1930), p. 49; United States v. U.S. Steel Corp., 251 U.S. 417 (1920); United States v. International Harvester Co., 274. U.S. 693 (1927).

53. Milton Handler, "Industrial Mergers and the Anti-Trust Laws," *Col LR*, 32 (1932), 171, 181, 271; on Donovan, Robert F. Himmelberg, *The Origins of the National Recovery Administration* (New York, 1976), p. 55; Robert Choate, "Donovan Has Charge of That," *Ind*, 117 (1926), 8–10; William J. Donovan, "Consent Decrees in the Enforcement of Federal Anti-Trust Laws," *Harv LR*, 46 (1932–33), 885; on expenditures, Howard E. Wahrenbrock, "Federal Anti-Trust Law and the National Industrial Recovery Act," *Mich LR*, 31 (1932–33), 1014n.

54. George W. Alger, "The Letter Law and the Golden Rule," *Atl*, 130 (1922), 229; Paul T. Homan, "Industrial Combination as Surveyed in Recent Literature," *Q J Ec*, 44 (1929–30), 247.

55. On National Food Products, *Lit Dig*, 88 (March 6, 1926), 8–9; Keezer and May, *Public Control*, pp. 63–65.

56. G. O. Virtue, "The Meat-Packing Investigation," *Q J Ec*, 34 (1919–20), 638; "The Packer Consent Decree," *Yale LJ*, 42 (1932), 81–94; Robert M. Aduddell and Louis P. Cain, "Public Policy Toward 'The Greatest Trust in the World,'" *Bus Hist R*, 55 (1981), 217–242; idem, "The Consent Decree in the Meatpacking Industry, 1920–1956," ibid., pp. 359–378.

57. Charles S. Maier, *Recasting Bourgeois Europe* (Princeton, 1975), pt. 3; Ellis W. Hawley, "The Discovery and Study of a 'Corporate Liberalism,'" *Bus Hist R*, 52 (1978), 309–320, and works cited there; idem, "Herbert Hoover, the Commerce Secretariat, and the Vision of an 'Associative State,' 1921–1928," *Journal of American History*, 61 (1974), 116–140;

idem, "Three Facets of Hooverian Associationalism: Lumber, Aviation, and Movies, 1921–1930," in McCraw, *Regulation in Perspective*, pp. 95–123.

58. U.S. Dept. of Commerce, *Commercial and Industrial Organizations of the United States* (Washington, D.C., 1926); NICB, *Trade Associations* (New York, 1925); Franklin D. Jones, *Trade Association Activities and the Law* (New York, 1922); Herman Oliphant, "Trade Associations and the Law," *Col LR*, 26 (1926), 382–395.

59. Hoover quoted in David L. Podell and Benjamin S. Kirsch, "The Problem of Trade Association Law," *St. John's Law Review*, 2 (1927), 6n; Robert F. Himmelberg, "Business, Antitrust Policy, and the Industrial Board of the Department of Commerce, 1919," *Bus Hist R*, 42 (1968), 1–23.

60. American Column & Lumber Co. v. United States, 257 U.S. 377, 412–413, 415 (1921); William G. Robbins, "Voluntary Cooperation vs. Regulatory Paternalism: The Lumber Trade in the 1920s," *Bus Hist R*, 56 (1982), 358–379.

61. Maple Flooring Assn v. United States, 268 U.S. 563, 587 (1925); Cement Manufacturers' Protective Assn. v. United States, 268 U.S. 588 (1925); William J. Donovan, "The Legality of Trade Associations," *Proceedings of the Academy of Political Science*, 11 (1926), 571–578.

62. United States v. Trenton Potteries Co., 273 U.S. 392, 397 (1927); "Does the Sherman Act Prohibit the Adoption of Standard Contracts and Arbitration Agreements by Trade Conferences?" *Yale LJ*, 40 (1930–31), 640–666.

63. Myron Watkins, "The Federal Trade Commission: A Critical Survey," *Q J Ec*, 40 (1925–26), 568–569; E. Pendleton Herring, "Politics, Personalities, and the Federal Trade Commission," *American Political Science Review*, 28 (1934), 1021; F.T.C. v. Raladan, 283 U.S. 643 (1931).

64. Herring, "Politics," p. 1021; G. Cullom Davis, "The Transformation of the Federal Trade Commission, 1914–1929," *Mississippi Valley Historical Review*, 49 (1962), 437–455.

65. F.T.C. v. Gratz, 253 U.S. 421, 427, 435, 432, 428 (1920).

66. Davis, "Transformation," pp. 441–442. See also "Federal Trade Commission—Recent Trends in Interpretation of the Federal Trade Commission Act," *Mich LR*, 32 (1933–34), 1142–54; Carl McFarland, *Judicial Control of the Federal Trade Commission and the Interstate Commerce Commission, 1920–1930* (Cambridge, Mass., 1933).

67. Jonathan Mitchell, "Little People vs. Big Fellows," *Outlook*, 154 (1930), 403–406, 436–438; John K. Holbrooke, Jr., "Price Reporting as a Trade Association Activity, 1925 to 1935," *Col LR*, 35 (1935), 1059, 1061.

68. Appalachian Coals, Inc., v. United States, 288 U.S. 344 (1933), and *Virginia Law Review*, 19 (1932–33), 851–867; *Mich LR*, 31 (1932–33), 837–841.

69. Nebbia v. New York, 291 U.S. 502 (1934); "Legislative Regulation of the New York Dairy Industry," *Yale LJ*, 42 (1933), 1259–70.

70. Schechter Poultry Corp. v. United States, 295 U.S. 495 (1935).

71. Ellis W. Hawley, *The New Deal and the Problem of Monopoly: A Study in*

Economic Ambivalence (Princeton, 1966); Donald R. Brand, *Corporatism and the Rule of Law: A Study of the National Recovery Administration* (Ithaca, 1988).

3. Regulating Utilities

1. Munn v. Illinois, 94 U.S. 113 (1877).
2. PRO, *Cab 37*, 116 (1913), no. 51; Philip Williams, "Public Opinion and the Railway Rates Question in 1886," *English Historical Review,* 67 (1952), 37–73; S. J. McLean, "The English Railway and Canal Commission of 1888," *Q J Ec,* 20 (1905–06), 1–58; P. J. Cain, "The British Railway Rates Problem, 1894–1913," *Bus Hist R,* 20 (1978), 876–899; Cain, "Railway Combination and Government, 1900–14," *Economic History Review,* 2d ser., 25 (1972), 623–641; on 1911 law, A. M. Sakolski, "The New British Law on Railroad Reports," *Q J Ec,* 26 (1911–12), 536–537.
3. Kimon A. Doukas, *The French Railroads and the State* (New York, 1945); Yves Guyot, *La crise des transports* (Paris, 1908); Harvey J. Bresler, "The French Railway Problem," *Pol Sci Q,* 37 (1922), 211–226. See also W. M. Acworth, "The Relation of Railways to the State," *Economics Journal,* 18 (1908), 501–519; Royal Economic Society, *The State in Relation to Railways* (London, 1912).
4. Alfred D. Chandler, *The Visible Hand: The Managerial Revolution in American Business* (Cambridge, Mass., 1977), pt. 2.
5. Frank Parsons, *The Railways, the Trusts, and the People* (Philadelphia, 1905), I; U.S. Library of Congress, *Selected List of References on Government Ownership of Railroads* (Washington, D.C., 1903).
6. Morton Keller, *Affairs of State: Public Life in Late Nineteenth Century America* (Cambridge, Mass., 1977), p. 429; Ari Hoogenboom and Olive Hoogenboom, *A History of the ICC: From Panacea to Palliative* (New York, 1976), chap. 1; B. H. Meyer, "The Past and Future of the Interstate Commerce Commission," *Pol Sci Q,* 17 (1902), 394–437.
7. United States v. Trans-Missouri Freight Association, 166 U.S. 290 (1897); United States v. Joint Traffic Association, 171 U.S. 505 (1898); Minnesota Rate Cases, 134 U.S. 362 (1894); Smyth v. Ames, 169 U.S. 466 (1898); David Willcox, "Government Rate-Making Is Unnecessary and Would Be Very Dangerous," *NAR,* 180 (1905), 423. Another estimate was that by January 1, 1906, the courts had refused to enforce twenty-eight of forty-four ICC decisions that came before them; Albert N. Merrit, *Federal Regulation of Railway Rates* (Chicago, 1906), pp. 160–61.
8. Elkins quoted in Hoogenboom and Hoogenboom, *History of ICC,* p. 44; Andrew Carnegie, "My Experience with Railway Rates and Rebates," *Century Magazine,* 75 (1907–08), 722–728.
9. Ray S. Baker, "The Railroads on Trial," *McClure's Magazine,* 26 (1905–06); Morton in *Outlook,* 79 (1905), 110–111, 119–121.
10. Baer in *Harper's Weekly,* 49 (1905), 718, 720.
11. Earling in ibid., p. 731; Henry S. Haines, *Railway Corporations as Public Servants* (New York, 1907), pp. 139, 126. Gabriel Kolko's attempt to attrib-

ute the federal regulation movement primarily to the major railroads in *Railroads and Regulation, 1877–1916* (Princeton, 1965) has been effectively refuted by Edward A. Purcell, Jr., "Ideas and Interests: Businessmen and the Interstate Commerce Act," *Journal of American History,* 54 (1967), 561–578; Robert W. Harbeson, "Railroads and Regulation, 1877 and 1916: Conspiracy or Public Interest?" *Journal of Economic History,* 27 (1967), 230–242; and Albro Martin, "The Troubled Subject of Railroad Regulation in the Gilded Age—A Reappraisal," *Journal of American History,* 61 (1974), 339–371.

12. Grover G. Huebner, "Five Years of Railroad Regulation by the States," *Annals,* 32 (1908), 138–156; Maxwell Ferguson, *State Regulation of Railroads in the South* (New York, 1916), p. 22; Stanley P. Caine, *The Myth of a Progressive Reform: Railroad Regulation in Wisconsin 1903–1910* (Madison, 1970).

13. Baer quoted in William H. Glasson, "The Crusade against the Railroads," *South Atlantic Quarterly,* (1907), 168; Robert E. Ireton, "The Legislatures and the Railroads," *American Monthly Review of Reviews,* 36 (1907), 217–220; on North Carolina, *Current Literature,* 43 (1907), 241–246.

14. Hoogenboom and Hoogenboom, *History of ICC,* pp. 44–45; William Z. Ripley, *Railroads: Rates and Regulation* (New York, 1912), pp. 206–207.

15. Ray Morris, "Federal Rate Regulation," *Atl,* 95 (1905), 738; Richard H. K. Vietor, "Businessmen and the Political Economy: The Railroad Rate Controversy of 1905," *Journal of American History,* 64 (1977): 47–66.

16. Martin A. Knapp, "National Regulation of Railroads," *Annals,* 26 (1905), 613–628; Frank H. Dixon, *Railroads and Government: Their Relations in the United States, 1910–1921* (New York, 1922), chap. 5. See also Hoogenboom and Hoogenboom, *History of ICC,* chap. 2.

17. Albro Martin, *Enterprise Denied: Origins of the Decline of American Railroads, 1897–1917* (New York, 1971).

18. Frank H. Dixon, "Railroads in their Corporate Relations," *Q J Ec,* 23 (1908–09), 34–65; William Z. Ripley, "Railway Speculation," *Q J Ec,* 25 (1910–11), 185–215; idem, "Railroad Over-Capitalization," *Q J Ec,* 28 (1913–14), 601–629; Thomas W. Mitchell, "The Collateral Trust Mortgage in Railway Finance," *Q J Ec,* 20 (1904–05), 443–467.

19. Stuart Daggett, "Recent Railroad Failures and Reorganization," *Q J Ec,* 32 (1917–18), pp. 446–486; Thomas A. Thacher, "Some Tendencies of Modern Receiverships," *Cal LR,* 4 (1915–16), 32. See also Ralph E. Clark, "English and American Theories of Receivers' Liabilities," *Col LR,* 27 (1927), 679–685, for a comparison with the much stricter English approach to receiverships.

20. William Z. Ripley, "Federal Railroad Regulation," *Atl,* 105 (1910), 414–427; E. P. Ripley, "The Railroads and the People," *Atl,* 107 (1911), 12–23; Morrell W. Gaines, "Reasonable Regulation of Railroad Rates," *Yale Review,* 1 (1911–12), 657–677; Carl S. Vrooman, "A 'Square Deal' for the Railroads," *Arena,* 40 (1908), 273–282; B. L. Winchell, "The Drift toward Government Ownership of Railways," *Atl,* 110 (1912), 746–758.

21. Frank H. Dixon, "The Mann-Elkins Act, Amending the Act to Regulate Commerce," *Q J Ec,* 24 (1909–10), 593–633.

22. Illinois v. Illinois Central R.R., 215 U.S. 452 (1910); James W. Bryan, "The Railroad Bill and the Court of Commerce," *American Political Science Review,* 4 (1910), 537–554. See also Hoogenboom and Hoogenboom, *History of ICC,* pp. 53–54, 66–67.

23. Hoogenboom and Hoogenboom, *History of ICC,* pp. 68–83; *Pol Sci Q,* 28 (1913), 364–367; Otto H. Kahn, *The Government and the Railroads* (New York, 1916), p. 10; Bruce Wyman, "Jurisdictional Limitations upon Commission Action," *Harv LR,* 27 (1913–14), 545–569.

24. William W. Cook, "The Legal Legislative and Economic Battle over Railroad Rates," *Harv LR,* 35 (1921–22), 39; Simpson v. Shepard, 230 U.S. 352 (1913); Houston E. & W. Texas Railway Co. v. United States, 234 U.S. 342 (1914).

25. Harold Kellock, "Fair Play for the Railroads," *Century Magazine,* 93 (1916–17), 578–583; Martin, *Enterprise Denied,* chaps. 9–11.

26. William W. Cook, "Legal Possibilities of Federal Railroad Incorporation," *Yale LJ,* 26 (1916–17), 212–213; idem, "A Plan for the Nationalization of Railroads," *Yale LJ,* 24 (1914–15), 379.

27. George Kennan, "War-Time Reflections on the Sherman Anti-Trust Law," *NAR,* 206 (1917), 878; Henry Hill, "Some Legal Aspects of the Federal Control of Railways," *Harv LR,* 31 (1917–18), 860–874; C. O. Ruggles, "Railway Service and Regulation," *Q J Ec,* 33 (1918–19), 129–179.

28. H. M. Hyndman, "The National Railways after the War," *Nineteenth Century,* 79 (1916), 461–477; Alfred W. Gattie, "National Railways after the War: A Reply," ibid., pp. 1328–42; Sydney Brooks, "British Railways during and after the War," *NAR,* 207 (1918), 196–208.

29. J. A. R. Marriott, "The State and the Railways," *Independent Review,* 115 (1921), 942–953, and 116 (1921), 28–40; W. M. Acworth, "Railway Nationalisation," *Quarterly Review,* 232 (1919), 153–176; idem, "Grouping under the Railways Acts, 1921," *Economics Journal,* 33 (1923), 19–38. See also Frank H. Dixon and Julius H. Parmalee, *War Administration of the Railways in the United States and Great Britain* (New York, 1918); and James A. Dunn, Jr., "Railroad Policies in Europe and the United States: The Impact of Ideology, Institutions, and Social Conditions," *Public Policy,* 25 (1977), 205–240.

30. Harvey J. Bresler, "The French Railway Problem," *Pol Sci Q,* 37 (1922), 211–226.

31. K. Austin Kerr, *American Railroad Politics, 1914–1920* (Pittsburgh, 1968), p. 163; "The Plumb Plan through British Eyes," *Living Age,* 303 (1919), 182–185.

32. Joseph B. Eastman, "The Advantages of National Operation," *Annals,* 86 (1919), 77–90; Frederic C. Howe, "The Necessity for Public Ownership of the Railways," *Annals,* 76 (1918), 158.

33. Kerr, *American Railroad Politics,* chaps. 6, 8; on the Senate bill, *New Republic,* 20 (1919), 251–52.

34. "The Waning Power of the States over Railroads," *Harv LR,* 37 (1923–24), 890; George G. Reynolds, *The Distribution of Power to Regulate Interstate Carriers between the Nation and the States* (New York, 1928); Frank T. Hypps, *Federal Regulation of Railroad Construction and Abandon-*

ment under the Transportation Act of 1920 (Philadelphia, 1929), p. 75. See also Kerr, *Railroad Politics*, chap. 9.

35. William Z. Ripley, "Railroads: Recent Books and Neglected Problems," *Q J Ec*, 40 (1925–26), 161; Emma C. Johnson, "The Interstate Commerce Commission: History, Functions, and Procedure," *National University Law Review*, 6 (1926), 48.

36. Cook, "Legal Legislative and Economic Battle," 30–46; A. M. Sakolski, "Practical Tests of the Transportation Act," *Pol Sci Q*, 36 (1921), 376–390.

37. Homer B. Vanderblue, "The Long and Short Haul Clause since 1910," *Harv LR*, 36 (1922–23), 428–430; "The Sherman Act as Applied to Railroads Regulated under the Interstate Commerce Act," ibid., pp. 456–460; Samuel P. Huntington, "The Marasmus of the ICC: The Commission, the Railroads, and the Public Interest," *Yale LJ*, 61 (1952), 467–509. See also "Our Changing Commerce Commission," *World's Work*, 55 (1928), 357–358.

38. E. Pendleton Herring, "Special Interests and the Interstate Commerce Commission," *American Political Science Review*, 27 (1933), 742; Gustavus H. Robinson, "The Hoch-Smith Resolution and the Future of the Interstate Commerce Commission," *Harv LR*, 42 (1928–29), 610–638; Harvey C. Mansfield, "The Hoch-Smith Resolution and the Consideration of Commercial Conditions in Rate-Fixing," *Cornell LQ*, 16 (1930–31), 339–358; "Consideration and Control of Commercial Conditions in Railroad Rate Regulation," *Yale LJ*, 40 (1930–31), 600–616.

39. Homer B. Vanderblue, "Railroad Valuation by the Interstate Commerce Commission," *Q J Ec*, 34 (1919–20), 299; Henry W. Edgerton, "Value of the Service as a Factor in Rate Making," *Harv LR*, 32 (1918–19), 516–556; on cost, Edwin C. Goddard, "Fair Value of Public Utilities," *Mich LR*, 22 (1923–24), 777–779.

40. Bryan quoted in Edwin C. Goddard, "The Evolution of Cost of Reproduction as the Base Rate," *Harv LR*, 41 (1927–28), 567n; William Z. Ripley, "The American Railroad Outlook," *NAR*, 215 (1922), 433–438.

41. James C. Bonbright, "The Economic Merits of Original Cost and Reproduction Cost," *Harv LR*, 40 (1926–27), 593–622; St. Louis & O'Fallon Railway Co. v. United States, 279 U.S. 461 (1929); William L. Ransom, "Undetermined Issues in Railroad Valuation under the O'Fallon Decision," *Pol Sci Q*, 44 (1929), 321–333.

42. Robert E. Cushman, *The Independent Regulatory Commission* (New York, 1941), pp. 130–141; Lloyd K. Garrison, "The National Railroad Adjustment Board: A Unique Administrative Agency," *Yale LJ*, 46 (1937), 567–598; I. L. Sharfman, "The Interstate Commerce Commission: An Appraisal," ibid., pp. 915–954. See also idem, *The Interstate Commerce Commission*, 5 vols. (New York, 1931–1937).

43. Edwin C. Goddard, "The Evolution and Devolution of Public Utility Law," *Mich LR*, 32 (1933–34), 578; Gustavus H. Robinson, "The Public Utility Concept in American Law," *Harv LR*, 41 (1927–28), 277–308; Irwin S. Rosenblum, "The Common Carrier–Public Utility Concept: A

Legal-Industrial View," *J Land PU Ec*, 7 (1931), 155–168; Marshall A. Dimock, "British and American Utilities: A Comparison," *University of Chicago Law Review*, 1 (1933–34), 265. See also Bruce Wyman, "Introduction," in *Cases on Public Service Companies, Public Carriers, Public Works, and Other Public Utilities*, 2d ed. (Cambridge, Mass., 1909).

44. R. Fulton Cutting, "Public Ownership and the Social Conscience," *Municipal Affairs*, 4 (1900), 5; Frederic C. Howe, *European Cities at Work* (New York, 1913); Christopher G. Tiedeman, "Government Ownership of Public Utilities," *Harv LR*, 16 (1903), 476–490; see also Malcolm Falkus, "The Development of Municipal Trading in the 19th Century," *Bus Hist R*, 19 (1977), 134–161.

45. "The Recent History of Municipal Ownership in the United States," *Municipal Affairs*, 6 (1902), 524–538; Carman F. Randolph, "Municipal Ownership of Public Utilities," *Yale LJ*, 22 (1913), 366–367; *HS*, p. 821. See also John P. McKay, *Tramways and Trolleys: The Rise of Urban Mass Transport in Europe* (Princeton, 1976).

46. Edison quoted in J. A. Fleming, "Official Obstruction of Electric Progress," *Nineteenth Century*, 49 (1901), 358; Ernest E. Williams, "How London Loses by Municipal Ownership," *NAR*, 183 (1906), 729–736; Robert P. Porter, "European and American Methods and Results Compared," *Municipal Affairs*, 6 (1902), 539–578; William B. Munro, "The Civic Federation Report on Public Ownership," *Q J Ec*, 23 (1908–09), 161–174. See also Carman F. Randolph, "Municipal Ownership of Public Utilities," *Yale LJ*, 22 (1913), 356–358; Allen R. Foote, *Public Ownership vs. Regulated Natural Monopolies* (Chicago, 1900); for a French critique, Yves Guyot, *Where and Why Public Ownership Has Failed* (New York, 1914).

47. Clyde L. King, *Regulation of Municipal Utilities* (New York, 1921), p. 42; Alton D. Adams, "The Holyoke Case," *Q J Ec*, 17 (1902), 643–668; Roland Phillips, "The Problem of Municipal Ownership," *Harper's Weekly*, 51 (1907), 1344, 1357.

48. United Railroads v. San Francisco, 249 U.S. 517 (1919); "Municipal Utilities: Jurisdiction of State Commissions," *Col LR*, 33 (1933), 343n, 353n; "The Trolley's Battle for Life," *Nation*, 117 (1923), 284–285; *Lit Dig*, 49 (Oct. 20, 1923), 16.

49. "Municipal Acquisition of Public Utilities," *Col LR*, 34 (1934), 324–332; "Municipal Operation of Public Utilities," *Yale LJ*, 40 (1931, 116–123.

50. Blackburn Easterline, "The Street Railway Litigation of Chicago," *Am LR*, 39 (1905), 244–253; John A. Fairlie, "The Street Railway Question in Chicago," *Q J Ec*, 21 (1906–07), 371–404; Edward W. Bemis, "The Street Railway Settlement in Cleveland," *Q J Ec*, 22 (1907–08), 543–575; idem, "The Cleveland Street Railway Settlement," *Q J Ec*, 24 (1909–10), 550–560; Delos F. Wilcox, "The Control of Public Service Corporations in Detroit," *Annals*, 31 (1908), 576–592; Paul Leake, "The Street Railway Situation in Detroit," *Conference for Good City Government* (Philadelphia, 1910), pp. 120–141; J. W. S. Peters, "Kansas City Franchise Fight," ibid., pp. 156–169; Frank D. McLain, "The Street Railways of Philadelphia," *Q J Ec*, 22 (1907–08), 233–260.

51. Stiles P. Jones, "The Minneapolis Gas Settlement," *Conference for Good City Government*, pp. 142–155.
52. Kensey v. Union Traction Co., 169 Ind. 561 (1907); Isaac C. Sutton, "The Interurban Electric Railway as an Additional Burden upon the Streets and Highways," *U Pa LR*, 59 (1911), 165–177; David Nord, "The Experts versus the Experts: Conflicting Philosophies of Municipal Utility Regulation in the Progressive Era," *Wisconsin Magazine of History*, 58 (1974–75), 219–236. Borden D. Whiting, "Street Railways and the Interstate Commerce Act," *Col LR*, 10 (1910), 451–457.
53. Randolph, "Municipal Ownership," p. 364.
54. William G. McAdoo, *Relations between Public Service Corporations and the Public* (New York, 1924), pp. 11, 26–31; John J. Broesamle, *William Gibbs McAdoo: A Passion for Change, 1863–1917* (Port Washington, N.Y., 1973), pp. 26–27.
55. I. Leo Sharfman, "Commission Regulation of Public Utilities: A Survey of Legislation," *Annals*, 53 (1914), 1–18; Dimock, "British and American Utilities," pp. 275–278.
56. Martin Glaeser, *Public Utilities in American Capitalism* (New York, 1957), pp. 113–114; Richard L. McCormick, *From Realignment to Reform: Political Change in New York State, 1893–1910* (Ithaca, 1981), pp. 235–238; Bruce W. Dearstyne, "Regulation in the Progressive Era: The New York Public Service Commission," *New York History*, 58 (1977), 331–347; Henry Bruère, "Public Utilities Regulation in New York," *National Municipal Review*, 6 (1917), 535–551.
57. Felix Frankfurter, "Public Services and the Public," *Yale Review*, 20 (1930–31), 5.
58. Delos F. Willcox, The Crisis in Public Service Regulation in New York," *National Municipal Review*, 4 (1915), 547–563; idem, "Experts, Ethics, and Public Policy in Public Utilities," *National Municipal Review*, 6 (1917), 472–485.
59. Stiles P. Jones, "State versus Local Regulation," *Annals*, 53 (1914), 97; on the National Civil Federation, W. K. Jones, "Origins of the Certificate of Public Convenience and Necessity: Developments in the States, 1870–1920," *Col LR*, 79 (1979), 451–454.
60. C. S. Duncan, "The Paternalism of Public Service Commissions," *Forum*, 53 (1915), 104; Dexter M. Keezer and Stacy May, *The Public Control of Business* (New York, 1930), pp. 245n–248n. See also Farley Gannett, "The Change in Attitude of the Public and Public Service Companies toward State Regulation," *American City*, 24 (1921), 280–281.
61. Dimock, "British and American Utilities," pp. 269–271; William A. Prendergast, *Public Utilities and the People* (New York, 1933), pp. 277–292.
62. Clyde O. Fisher, "Commission Regulation of Public Utility Service in Connecticut," *J Land PU Ec*, 8 (1932), 200–208, 313–322. See also Thomas R. Powell, "State Utilities and the Supreme Court, 1922–1930," *Mich LR*, 29 (1925–26), 811–838, 1001–30.
63. "Right of a Public Utility to Cease Operation and Dismantle Its Plant without Consent of the State," *Harv LR*, 32 (1918–19), 716–720; Oliver P.

Field, "The Withdrawal from Service of Public Utility Companies," *Yale LJ*, 25 (1925–26), 169–190.

64. Bruce Wyman, "The Inherent Limit of the Public Service Duty to Particular Classes," *Harv LR*, 23 (1909–10), 352; Roscoe Pound, *The Spirit of the Common Law* (Boston, 1921), p. 29; Guy A. Miller, "Some Questions in Connection with State Rate Regulation," *Mich LR*, 8 (1909–10), 116; "The Relational Duty of the Public Service Commission to the Public," *Harv LR*, 28 (1914–15), 620–622. See also Gustavus H. Robinson, "The Filed Rate in Public Utilities Law: A Study in Mechanical Jurisprudence," *U Pa LR*, 77 (1928–29), 213–254.

65. N. Matthews, Jr., and W. G. Thompson, "Public Service Company Rates and the Fourteenth Amendment," *Harv LR*, 15 (1901–02), 354–355.

66. Raymond T. Bye, "Social Welfare in Rate Making," *Pol Sci Q*, 32 (1917), 522–541; I.C.C. v. B&O R.R., 145 U.S. 263 (1892).

67. Bye, "Social Welfare," p. 541; Northern Pacific R.R. v. North Dakota, 266 U.S. 585 (1915); Consolidated Gas Co. v. N.Y.C., 212 U.S. 19 (1909).

68. Francis J. Swayze, "The Regulation of Railway Rates under the Fourteenth Amendment," *Q J Ec*, 26 (1911–12), 423; Richard J. Smith, "The Judicial Interpretation of Public Utility Franchises," *Yale LJ*, 39 (1929–30), 957–979. See also Goddard, "Fair Value," 777–797.

69. Ralph E. Heilman, "The Development by Commissions of the Principles of Public Utility Valuation," *Q J Ec*, 28 (1913–14), 269–291; Frankfurter, "Public Services and the Public," p. 15; Nathaniel Gold, "The New York Telephone Rate Decision," *National Municipal Review*, 19 (1930), 180–188; Goddard, "Fair Value," p. 601.

70. Godfrey Goldmark, "The Struggle for Higher Public Utility Rates because of War Time Costs," *Cornell LQ*, 5 (1920), 227–246; Brooklyn Borough Gas Co. v. Public Service Commission, P.U.R. 1919 Fed. 335 (1918); "Public Utility Valuation—Cost-of-Reproduction Theory and the World War," *Mich LR*, 18 (1919–20), 774–779.

71. Southwestern Bell Tel. Co. v. Public Service Commission, 262 U.S. 276 (1923); Bluefield Water Works v. Public Service Commission, 261 U.S. 79 (1923); Butler in McCardle v. Indianapolis Water Co., 272 U.S. 400, 420–421 (1926); *New Republic*, 49 (1926), 181–182; Thomas R. Powell, "Protecting Property and Liberty, 1922–1924," *Pol Sci Q*, 40 (1925), 406–407. See also Donald R. Richberg, "Value—By Judicial Fiat," *Harv LR*, 40 (1926–27), 567–582.

72. Brandeis quoted in Goddard, "Fair Value," p. 607; Morris L. Cooke, "Taking Stock of Regulation in the State of New York," *Yale LJ*, 40 (1930–31), 33.

73. David E. Lilienthal, "Regulation of Public Utilities during the Depression," *Harv LR*, 46 (1933), 775; Irston R. Barnes, "Federal Courts and State Regulation of Utility Rates," *Yale LJ*, 43 (1933–34), 417–443; Corporation v. Railroad Commission of Cal., 289 U.S. 287 (1933).

74. Louis Cox, "The Regulation of Public Utilities, Other than Railroads, by State Administrative Commissions," *Kentucky Law Journal*, 20 (1931–32), 135–140; D. L. Marlatt and Orba F. Taylor, "Public Utilities Legisla-

tion in the Depression," *J Land PU Econ*, 11 (1935), 173–186, 290–301, 390–399.

4. Regulating New Technologies

1. "'Jitney-Bus' Regulation," *Harv LR*, 29 (1915–16), 437–439; Barrett v. N.Y., 223 U.S. 70 (1912).
2. John J. George, "Establishing State Regulation of Motor Carriers," *Southwestern Political and Social Science Quarterly*, 10 (1929), 217–229; idem, *Motor Carrier Regulation in the United States* (Spartanburg, S.C., 1929), pp. 263–264. See also David E. Lilienthal and Irwin S. Rosenbaum, "Motor Carriers and the State: A Study in Contemporary Public Utilities Legislation," *J Land PU Ec*, 2 (1926), 257–260.
3. Henry R. Trumbower, "The Regulation of the Common Carrier Motor Vehicle with Respect to Its Competitive Aspects," *American Economic Review*, 19 (1929) (suppl.), 226–235.
4. Irwin S. Rosenbaum and David E. Lilienthal, "Motor Carrier Regulation: Federal, State and Municipal," *Col LR*, 26 (1926), 956; Mich. Public Utilities Comm'n. v. Duke, 266 U.S. 570 (1925), Frost v. R.R. Comm'n., 271 U.S. 583 (1926); Brandeis in Buck v. Kuykendall, 267 U.S. 307, 315 (1925).
5. Irwin S. Rosenbaum, "The Common Carrier-Public Utility Concept: A Legal-Industrial View," *J Land PU Econ*, 7 (1931), 154; Stephenson v. Binford, 287 U.S. 251 (1932).
6. Ari Hoogenboom and Olive Hoogenboom, *A History of the ICC* (New York, 1976), pp. 130–131. See also LaRue Brown and Stuart N. Scott, "Regulation of the Contract Motor Carrier under the Constitution," *Harv LR*, 44 (1930–31), 530–571; and Paul G. Kauper, "State Regulation of Interstate Motor Carriers," *Mich LR*, 31 (1932–33), 920–952, 1097–1111.
7. Ford P. Hall, "Certificates of Convenience and Necessity," *Mich LR*, 28 (1929), 111. See also David E. Lilienthal and Irwin S. Rosenbaum, "Motor Carrier Regulation by Certificates of Necessity and Convenience," *Yale LJ*, 36 (1927–28), 163–194; W. K. Jones, "Origins of the Certificate of Public Convenience and Necessity: Developments in the States, 1870–1920," *Col LR*, 79 (1979), 514.
8. H. B. Brown, "The Status of the Automobile," *Yale LJ*, 17 (1907–08), 227; *Survey*, 34 (1915), 316. See also James J. Flink, *America Adopts the Automobile* (Cambridge, Mass., 1970); idem, *The Car Culture* (Cambridge, Mass., 1975); and idem, *The Automobile Age* (Cambridge, Mass., 1980).
9. M.P. quoted in John Scott-Montagu, "Automobile Legislation: A Criticism and Review," *NAR*, 178 (1904), 168–169; Edward Manson, "The Regulation of Motor-Cars at Home and Abroad," *J Comp Leg*, n.s., 7 (1906), 333–355; PRO, *Cab 37*, 65 (1903), no. 37, and 89 (1907), no. 61.
10. "The Public and the Motor-Car," *Quarterly Review*, 210 (1909), 143; "The Motorist and the Law," *Justice of the Peace*, 69 (1905), 458–460, 469–471; Henry Norman, "The Public, the Motorist, and the Royal Commission," *Fortnightly Review*, 85 (1906), 683–695.
11. "Development of Standards in Speed Legislation," *Harv LR*, 46 (1933),

838; on California, Manson, "Regulation," pp. 341–342; "The Law of Automobiles," *Law Notes*, 9 (1905), 147–150; Sumner Kenner, "The Legal Rights of Automobile Drivers upon the Public Streets and Highways," *Cent LJ*, 61 (1905), 464–468.

12. Manson, "Regulation," p. 336; William P. Eno, "Street Traffic Legislation and Regulation in the United States of America," *J Comp Leg*, 3d ser., 7 (1925), 239–240.

13. David H. Morris, "The Legislative Needs of the Motorist," *Harper's Weekly*, 51 (1907), 380; Charles T. Terry, "Federal License for Automobiles," ibid., p. 532; H. P. Burchell, "Our Chaotic Automobile Laws," *Harper's Weekly*, 52 (May 16, 1908), 17.

14. On speed limits, *Lit Dig*, 75 (Nov. 18, 1922), 73–76; "Development of Standards," p. 839n; on New York law, *Harper's Weekly*, 54 (Sept. 13, 1910), 12–13; "A New Automobile Law," *Outlook*, 96 (1910), 147–148; Charles W. Tooke, "The Centralization of Highway Traffic," *Georgetown Law Journal*, 14 (1925–26), 257–269.

15. Terry, "Federal License," p. 532; Brown, "Status," pp. 231–233; *Scribner's Magazine*, 59 (1916), 181–190; ibid., 61 (1917), 360–367; *HS*, p. 1124.

16. Newton Fuessle, "Pulling Main Street out of the Mud," *Outlook*, 131 (1922), 640–643.

17. George L. Ellsworth, "The Automobile and the Law," *New England Magazine*, n.s., 42 ((1910), 49–51; Francis W. Laurent, *The Business of a Trial Court* (Madison, 1959), pp. 35–36, 49, 78–79; F. R. Aumann, "The Changing Relationship of the Judicial and Executive Branches," *Kentucky Law Journal*, 22 (1933–34), 254n. See also Anthony A. Ballantine, "Compensation for Automobile Accidents," *ABA Journal*, 18 (1932), 221–228, 282.

18. *HS*, p. 720.

19. Ellsworth, "The Automobile and the Law"; "Automobiles and Vicarious Liability," *Am LR*, 59 (1925), 451–461; Holmes in B&O R.R. v. Goodman, 275 U.S. 66, 69–70 (1927).

20. Cardozo in Pokora v. Wabash R.R., 292 U.S. 98, 104 (1934). The fullest discussion of these developments is Richard M. Nixon, "Changing Rules of Liability in Automobile Accident Litigation," *Law and Contemporary Problems*, 3 (1936), 476–490. See also Francis Déak, "Automobile Accidents: A Comparative Study of the Law of Liability in Europe," *U Pa LR*, 79 (1930–31), 281–292, which discusses the evolution in French automobile law from the view that the injured party had the burden of proving the fault of the defendant, to the view (by 1930) that the presumption of fault fell on the driver.

21. Herbert D. Laube, "The Social Vice of Accident Indemnity," *U Pa LR*, 80 (1931–32), 189–190; "The Massachusetts Compulsory Automobile Insurance Legislation," *Col LR*, 27 (1927), 314–319; Robert S. Marx, "Compulsory Compensation Insurance," *Col LR*, 25 (1925), 164–193; "Compensation for Automobile Accidents: A Symposium," *Col LR*, 32 (1932), 785–824. See also Edison L. Bowers, ed., *Selected Articles on Compulsory Automobile Insurance* (New York, 1929).

22. Walter E. Treanor, "The Family Automobile and the Family Purpose Doc-

trine," *Indiana Law Journal*, 1 (1925), 89–95; *Georgetown Law Journal*, 15 (1926–27), 471–474; Norman D. Lattin, "Vicarious Liability and the Family Automobile," *Mich LR*, 26 (1927–28), 846–879; Philip A. Maxeiner, "Missouri and the 'Family Automobile,'" *St. Louis Law Review*, 21 (1935–36), 218–234. See also "The Development of the Family Purpose Doctrine," *United States Law Review*, 65 (1931), 645–651.

23. William E. McCurdy, "Torts between Persons in Domestic Relation," *Harv LR*, 43 (1929–30), 1030–82.

24. "The Law of the Air," *Sci Am*, 104 (1911), 584; Wayne C. Williams, "The Law of the Air," *Outlook*, 126 (1920), 144–145; William R. McCracken, "Air Law," *Am LR*, 57 (1923), 102.

25. Rochester Gas & Electric Co. v. Dunlop, 266 N.Y. Supp. 469 (County Ct., 1933); Roger F. Williams, "The Existence of the Right of Flight," *U Pa LR*, 79 (1930–31), 729–741.

26. Francis H. Bohlen, "Aviation under the Common Law," *Harv LR*, 48 (1934), 217–218.

27. Hiram L. Jones, "Property in the Air as Affected by the Airplane and the Radio," *Am LR*, 62 (1929), 887–914; Smith v. New England Aircraft Co., 170 N.E. 385 (Mass., 1930); Swetland v. Curtiss Airports Corp., 55 Fed. 2d 201 (6th Cir., 1932).

28. Williams, "Right to Flight," p. 733; M. W. Royce, "An Air Law for America," *Nation*, 123 (1926), 659–660; Arthur L. Newman II, "Aviation Law and the Constitution," *Yale LJ*, 39 (1929–30), 1113–29; Chester W. Cuthell, "Development of Aviation Laws in the United States," *Air Law Review*, 1 (1930), 86–93.

29. Warren J. Davis, "State Regulation of Aircraft Common Carriers," *Air Law Review*, 1 (1930), 47; *American Political Science Review*, 25 (1931), 62; Robert E. Cushman, *The Independent Regulatory Commissions* (New York, 1941), pp. 389–393.

30. *HS*, pp. 821, 827–828.

31. "High Finance in the 'Twenties: the United Corporation," *Col LR*, 37 (1937), 785–816, 936–980; Forrest McDonald, *Insull* (Chicago, 1962). See also Irwin S. Rosenbaum and David E. Lilienthal, "Issuance of Securities by Public Service Corporations," *Yale LJ*, 37 (1927–28), 716–745, 908–934.

32. Judson King, *The Challenge of the Power Investigation to American Education* (Washington, D.C., 1929); Gifford Pinchot, *The Power Monopoly: Its Make-Up and Its Menace* (Milford, Pa., 1928); Drew Pearson, "Public Control of the Power Trust," *Nation*, 129 (1929), 300–301; "Power Supplement," *New Republic*, 47 (1926), 18–36.

33. Herbert Hoover, "Government and Power Development," *English Review*, 39 (1924), 786–796.

34. Cushman, *Regulatory Commissions*, pp. 275–297.

35. Russell L. Post, "A Proper Supervision of Electric and Gas Utilities," *Virginia Law Review*, 19 (1932–33), 27; Smith v. Illinois Bell Telephone Co., 282 U.S. 133 (1930). See also Ernest O. Eisenberg, "Recent Tendencies in the Regulation of Public Utility Holding Companies," *Marquette Law Re-*

view, 17 (1932–33), 283–291; David Lilienthal, "The Regulation of Public Utility Holding Companies," *Col LR*, 29 (1929), 404–440.

36. Arthur N. Holcombe, *Public Ownership of Telephones on the Continent of Europe* (Boston, 1911); idem, "The Telephone in Great Britain," *Q J Ec*, 21 (1906–07), 96–135; Hugo R. Meyer, *Public Ownership and the Telephone in Great Britain* (New York, 1907); "The State and the Telephone," *Edinburgh Review*, 217 (1913), 466–484; Gerald W. Brock, *The Telecommunications Industry* (Cambridge, Mass., 1981), pp. 174–176.

37. Hudson River Tel. Co. v. Watervliet Tpke. & Rway. Co., 135 N.Y. 393 (1892); Cincinnati Inclined Plane Rway. Co. v. Telegraph Assocn., 48 Ohio St. 390 (1891).

38. Helm Bruce, "The Law Applicable to the Use of Electricity in Modern Industrial Life," *American Lawyer*, 12 (1904), 337; McKinley Telephone Co. v. Cumberland Telephone Co., 152 Wis. 359 (1913); *American City*, 29 (1913), 317. See also "Municipal Regulation and Control of Telephone and Telegraph Companies," *Cent LJ*, 56 (1903), 125–127; Home Telephone Co. v. Los Angeles, 211 U.S. 265 (1908).

39. Theodore N. Vail, "Public Utilities and Public Policy," *Atl*, 111 (1913), 309; U.S. Post Office Department, *Government Ownership of Electrical Means of Communication*, 62nd Cong., 2d sess. (Washington, D.C., 1914). See also A. N. Holcombe, "Public Ownership of Telegraphs and Telephones," *Q J Ec*, 28 (1913–14), 581–586; Samuel O. Dunn, "Some Political Phases of Government Ownership," *Atl*, 115 (1915), 202–214.

40. *HS*, p. 783; "Telephone Consolidation under the Act of 1921," *J Land PU Ec*, 7 (1932), 22–35.

41. J. Bryan McCormick, "Some Legal Problems of the Motion Picture Industry," *ABA Journal*, 17 (1934), 316–322, 407–409; on RKO, "A Merger in Entertainment," *Lit Dig*, 99 (Nov. 3, 1928), 12.

42. Mutual Film Corp'n. v. Industrial Comm., 236 U.S. 230 (1915); U.S. v. Motion Picture Patent Co., 247 U.S. 524 (1917); FTC v. Paramount-Famous-Lasky, 57 F. 2d 152 (C.C.A. 2d, 1932); "The Motion Picture Industry and the Anti-Trust Laws," *Col LR*, 36 (1936), 635–652.

43. McReynolds in Paramount-Famous-Lasky Corp'n. v. U.S., 282 US 30, 43 (1930); "The Effect of the Sherman Act upon Monopolies in Amusement Enterprises," *U Pa LR*, 73 (1923–24), 293–296.

44. "Motion Picture Industry," p. 652.

45. Robert J. Williams, "The Politics of American Broadcasting: Public Purposes and Private Interests," *Journal of American Studies*, 10 (1976), 329–340.

46. *Nation* (GB), 38 (1925–26), 766–767, 799–800; J. C. W. Reith, "Broadcasting, the State, and the People," *Nineteenth Century*, 102 (1927), 667–674; R. Jardine Brown, "The Constitutional Law and History of Broadcasting in Great Britain," *Air Law Review*, 8 (1937), 177–200. See also Asa Briggs, *The Birth of Broadcasting* (London, 1961), chap. 3.

47. Morris Ernst, "Who Shall Control the Air?" *Nation*, 122 (1926), 443–444; Dane York, "The Radio Octopus," *American Mercury*, 23 (1931), 385–

400; on WCFL, *American Federationist*, 34 (1927), 449–452. See also Philip T. Rosen, *The Modern Stentors: Radio Broadcasters and the Federal Government, 1920–1934* (Westport, Conn., 1980); Susan J. Douglas, *Inventing American Broadcasting, 1899–1922* (Baltimore, 1977), chaps. 7–8.

48. John W. Van Allen, "State and Municipal Regulation of Radio," *Journal of Radio Law*, 1 (1931), 35–42; Great Lakes Broadcasting Co. v. FRC, 36 F. 2d 993 (1930).

49. Louis G. Caldwell, "Principles Governing the Licensing of Broadcasting Stations," *American Political Science Review*, 79 (1930–31), 113–157.

50. Mauritz A. Hallgren, "The Radio Trust Rolls On," *Nation*, 126 (1928), 41–43; *Lit Dig*, 105 (May 31, 1930), 12. See also Paul Hutchinson, "The Freedom of the Air," *Christian Century*, 48 (1931).

51. J. Warren Wright, "State and Federal Regulation of Radio Broadcasting," *George Washington Law Review*, 2 (1933–34), 13–34; "Administrative Control of Radio," *Harv LR*, 49 (1936), 1333–43.

5. Regulating Business

1. *HS*, p. 914; NICB, *Local Taxation of Business Corporations* (New York, 1931), p. 4.

2. FTC estimate in Hugh E. Willis, "Corporations and the United States Constitution," *University of Cincinnati Law Review* 8 (1934), 13; *HS*, p. 911.

3. G. H. B. Kenrick, "The New Commercial Code of Germany," *J Comp Leg*, n.s., 2 (1900), 342–347; N. W. Sibley, "Companies Act, 1900," *Westminster Review*, 155 (1901), 70–85; Edward Manson, "The Companies Act, 1900," *London Quarterly Review*, 16 (1900), 414–417; Harry Shapiro, "The Formation of Companies under the English Company Law: A Comparison with American Legislation," *U Pa LR*, 60 (1912), 419–442. See also Francis M. Burdick, "Limited Partnerships in America and England," *Mich LR*, 6 (1908), 525–532.

4. James W. Hurst, *The Legitimacy of the Business Corporation in the Law of the United States* (Charlottesville, Va., 1970); Morton Keller, *Affairs of State: Public Life in Late Nineteenth Century America* (Cambridge, Mass., 1977), pp. 173–176, 431–434, 437–438; Morton J. Horowitz, "Santa Clara Revisited: The Development of Corporate Theory," *West Virginia Law Review*, 88 (1985), 175–224.

5. James B. Dill, *The General Corporation Act of New Jersey* ([Trenton], 1899), p. xvii; Harold J. Laski, "The Personality of Associations," *Harv LR*, 29 (1915–16), 404–426; on Dill, Daniel Boorstin, *The Americans: The Democratic Experience* (New York, 1973), pp. 413–422; Edward Q. Keasbey, "New Jersey and the Great Corporations," *Harv LR*, 13 (1899), 210–211.

6. E. Merrick Dodd, "Statutory Developments in Business Corporation Law, 1886–1936," *Harv LR*, 50 (1936), 33–36; Maurice Robinson, "The Proposed New York Companies Act, 1900," *Yale Review*, 9 (1900), 79–85.

7. George W. Alger, *The Old Law and the New Order* (Boston, 1913), p. 231.

8. S. R. Wrightington, "Voluntary Associations in Massachusetts," *Yale LJ*, 21 (1911–12), 311–326; Alfred D. Chandler, *Express Trusts under the Common Law* (Boston, 1912); Robert C. Brown, "Common Law Trusts as Business Enterprises," *Indiana Law Journal*, 3 (1927–28), 595–626; Commonwealth of Massachusetts, Legislature, *Report of the Special Commission to Investigate Voluntary Associations* (Boston, 1913); R. J. Powell, "The Passing of the Corporation in Business," *Minnesota Law Review*, 2 (1918), 401–414.

9. Herbert M. Heath, *Comparative Advantages of All the Corporation Laws of All the States and Territories* (Augusta, Me., 1902), p. 3; Horace L. Wilgus, *Should There Be a Federal Incorporation Law for Commercial Companies?* (Ann Arbor, 1904); Frank Hendrick, *The Power to Regulate Corporations and Commerce* (New York, 1906); Frederick H. Cooke, "State and Federal Control of Corporations," *Harv LR*, 23 (1909–10), 456–464.

10. Myron Watkins, "Federal Incorporation," *Mich LR*, 17 (1918–19), 64–80, 145–164, 238–260; Edward Q. Keasbey, "The Power of Corporations Created by Acts of Congress," *Harv LR*, 32 (1918–19), 689–708; Morton Keller, *The Life Insurance Enterprise, 1885–1910* (Cambridge, Mass., 1963), pp. 235–242.

11. Allgeyer v. Louisiana, 165 U.S. 578 (1897); Western Union v. Kansas, 216 U.S. 1 (1910); Looney v. Crane, 245 U.S. 178 (1917). See also Harold M. Bowman, "The State's Power over Foreign Corporations," *Mich LR*, 9 (1911), 549–575; William C. Coleman, "Constitutional Limitations upon State Taxation of Foreign Corporations," *Col LR*, 11 (1911), 393–427.

12. Rathenau quoted in Adolph A. Berle and Gardiner C. Means, *The Modern Corporation and Private Property*, rev. ed. (New York, 1968), p. 309; Bishop C. Hunt, "Recent English Company Law Reform, 1930," *Harv Bus R*, 8 (1936), 170–183; Joseph L. Weiner, "The Reorganization of Corporations in Germany," *Yale LJ*, 37 (1927–28), 746–772; Richard Rosendorff, "The New German Company Law and the English Companies Act, 1929," *J Compar Leg*, 3d ser., 14 (1932), 94–100.

13. Henry R. Seager and Charles A. Gulick, Jr., *Trust and Corporation Problems* (New York, 1929), pp. 20, 22; H. T. Warshow, "The Distribution of Corporate Ownership in the United States," *Q J Ec*, 39 (1924–25), 15–38; Berle and Means, *Modern Corporation*, p. 56.

14. Adolf A. Berle, *Studies in the Law of Corporation Finance* (Chicago, 1928), pp. 190, 23–25.

15. Wiley B. Rutledge, Jr., "Significant Trends in Modern Incorporation Statutes," *Washington University Law Quarterly*, 22 (1937), 311; "The Adoption of the Liberal Theory of Foreign Corporations," *U Pa LR*, 79 (1930–31), 956–972, 1119–38.

16. Robert T. Swaine, "Reorganization of Corporations: Certain Developments of the Last Decade," *Col LR*, 28 (1928), 29–63; A. A. Berle, Jr., "Investors and the Revised Delaware Corporation Act," *Col LR*, 29 (1929), 563–581; James C. Bonbright, "No-Par Stock: Its Economic and Legal Aspects," *Q J Ec*, 38 (1923–24), 440–465; Joseph L. Weiner, "Theory of

Anglo-American Dividend Law," *Col LR*, 28 (1928), 1046–60; and 29 (1929), 461–482. See also Sveinbjorn Johnson, "Recent Judicial and Legislative Trends in Corporation Law," *ABA Journal*, 19 (1933), 631–634.

17. Chester Rohrlich, "The New Deal in Corporation Law," *Col LR*, 35 (1935), 1169; A. H. Feller, "The Movement for Corporate Reform: A World-Wide Phenomenon," *ABA Journal*, 20 (1934), 347–348. On the perception of investors, compare the American Max Lowenthal's *The Investor Pays* (New York, 1933) with the British Horace B. Samuel's *Shareholders' Money* (London, 1933).

18. Louis L. Jaffe, "Law Making by Private Groups," *Harv LR*, 51 (1937), 201–253; Keller, *Affairs of State*, pp. 411–412; Lawrence M. Friedman, "Freedom of Contract and Occupational Licensing, 1890–1910: A Legal and Social Study," *Cal LR*, 53 (1965), 487–534.

19. State v. McKnight, 42 S.E. 580, 582 (N.C., 1902); Dent v. West Virginia, 129 U.S. 114 (1888); Champe S. Andrews, "Medical Practice and the Law," *Forum*, 31 (1901), 542–551; H. B. Hutchins, "Characteristics and Constitutionality of Medical Legislation," *Mich LR*, 7 (1909), 301–310.

20. "The Requirement of a License to Practice Osteopathy," *Yale LJ*, 12 (1902–03), 446–448; Harold W. Holt, "The Need for Administrative Discretion in the Regulation of the Practice of Medicine," *Cornell LQ*, 16 (1930–31), 495–521; Paul Starr, *The Social Transformation of American Medicine* (New York, 1982), pp. 102–112.

21. "Is the American Medical Association an Unlawful Combination?" *Cent LJ*, 68 (1909), 190; Richard H. Shryock, *Medical Licensing in America, 1650–1965* (Baltimore, 1967), pp. 60, 64; Rohlf v. Kasemeier, 118 N.W. 276 (Iowa, 1908).

22. Hayman v. Galveston, 273 U.S. 414 (1927).

23. *Albany Law Journal*, 69 (1907), 280–282; O. H. Myrick, "Statutory Regulation of Trades and Professions," *Lawyer & Banker*, 3 (1910), 174–187; Bessette v. People, 62 N.E. 215 (Ill., 1901); Friedman, "Freedom of Contract," p. 517.

24. Hall v. Geiger-Jones, 242 U.S. 539 (1917); Tyson v. Banton, 273 U.S. 418 (1927); Ribnik v. McBride, 277 U.S. 350 (1928); New State Ice Co. v. Liebmann, 285 U.S. 262 (1932).

25. Nathan W. MacChesney, "Legal Regulation of the Personnel of Business," *Am LR*, 58 (1924), 5; A. D. Theobold, "Real Estate License Laws in Theory and Practice," *J Land PU Ec*, 7 (1931), 13–21, 138–154.

26. Unidentified Justice quoted in MacChesney, "Legal Regulation," p. 6; ibid., p. 18; Bratton v. Chandler, 260 U.S. 110 (1922).

27. Mark Haller and John V. Alviti, "Loansharking in American Cities: Historical Analysis of a Marginal Enterprise," *American Journal of Legal History*, 21 (1977), 125–156. See also *Charities*, 21 (1908–09), 407–409; *Survey*, 27 (1911–12), 920–921, 1572–73; "Efforts to Eliminate Some Evils of Unrestricted Credit for Wage Earners," *Harv LR*, 45 (1931–32), 1103–08.

28. Hugo Wall, "The Use of the License Law in the Regulation of Businesses and Professions," *Southwestern Political and Social Science Quarterly*, 12 (1931), 120–132; Lane W. Lancaster, "The Legal Status of 'Private' Corporations Exercising Governmental Powers," ibid., 15 (1934), 325–336.

29. Charles V. Koons, "Growth of Federal Licensing," *Georgetown Law Journal*, 24 (1936), 293–344.
30. James W. Hurst, *The Growth of American Law* (Boston, 1950), pp. 72, 363; Ernst Freund, "Unifying Tendencies in American Legislation," *Yale LJ*, 22 (1912–13), 104–107; William Schofield, "Uniformity of Law in the American States as an American Ideal," *Harv LR*, 21 (1907–08), 416–430, 510–526, 583–594; Amasa M. Eaton, "The Negotiable Instruments Law: Its History and Its Practical Operation," *Mich LR*, 2 (1903–04), 260–297; Nathan W. MacChesney, "Uniform State Laws: A Means to Efficiency Consistent with Democracy," *Chicago Legal News*, 48 (1916), 353.
31. Freund, "Unifying Tendencies," p. 112; on Holmes, Joseph H. Beale, "Studies in the Conflict of Laws—Conflicting Influences at Work Tending to Differentiate and to Make Uniform Laws of Different States," *Cent LJ*, 84 (1920), 107; Sumner Kenner, "The Function of Uniform State Laws," *Indiana Law Journal*, 1 (1925–26), 133; James M. Kerr, "Nature and Interpretation of Uniform State Laws," *Am LR*, 55 (1921), 111.
32. "Bribery in Commercial Relationships," *Harv LR*, 45 (1931–32), 1248–52; Freund, "Unifying Tendencies," pp. 100, 106.
33. H. W. Danforth, "Illegality under the Negotiable Instruments Law," *Cent LJ*, 92 (1928), 27–35.
34. On studies, Amasa M. Eaton, "The Attitude of the Bench and the Bar toward the Uniform Negotiable Instruments Law," *Cent LJ*, 77 (1913), 283–287; idem, "The Uniform Negotiable Instruments Law in the Courts of Missouri," *Cent LJ*, 79 (1915), 123–125; "Some Recent Implications of Swift v. Tyson," *Harv LR*, 48 (1935), 979–983; Erie R.R. Co. v. Tompkins, 304 U.S. 64 (1938). See also H. Parker Sharp and Joseph H. Brennan, "The Application of the Doctrine of Swift v. Tyson since 1900," *Indiana Law Journal*, 4 (1929), 370–372; Tony Freyer, *Forums of Order: The Federal Courts and Business in American History* (Greenwich, Conn., 1979).
35. Jerold S. Auerbach, *Justice without Law?* (New York, 1983), chap. 4; Charles L. Norton, "British Experience with Arbitration," *U Pa LR*, 83 (1934–35), 314–325.
36. Judge quoted in Martin Gant, "Commercial Arbitration in California," *Cal LR*, 15 (1927), 290; Auerbach, *Justice without Law?* pp. 102–114; Sabra A. Jones, "Historical Development of Commercial Arbitration in the United States," *Minnesota Law Review*, 12 (1927–28), 240–262.
37. U.S. Asphalt Refining Co. v. Petroleum Co., 222 Fed. 1006 (S.D.N.Y., 1915); Paul L. Sayre, "Development of Commercial Arbitration Law," *Yale LJ*, 37 (1927–28), 595–617; on Chicago Trade Court, *Lit Dig*, 70 (July 23, 1921), 51.
38. Richard C. Curtis, "A Comparison of the Recent Arbitration Statutes," *ABA Journal*, 13 (1927), 567–570; "Enforcement of State Arbitration Laws in Federal Courts," *Harv LR*, 42 (1928–29), 801–805.
39. Keller, *Affairs of State*, pp. 421–422; Charles Warren, *Bankruptcy in American History* (Cambridge, Mass., 1935), pp. 140–144; Henry G. Newton, "The United States Bankruptcy Law of 1898," *Yale LJ*, 9 (1900–01), 287–296; S. Whitney Dunscomb, "The Federal Bankruptcy Law," *Pol Sci Q*, 13 (1898), 606–616; Hyman Zettler, "The 'Trust Fund' Theory: A

Study in Psychology," *Washington Law Review,* 1 (1925), 81–100; Harold Remington, "Preferences and the Bankruptcy Law," *Forum,* 32 (1901–02), 360–365.

40. Richard Brown, "The Law of Bankruptcy in England and Scotland," *Law Times,* 104 (1897), 36–39, 63–64; George C. Holt, "Merits and Defects of the Bankrupt law," *Journal of Social Science,* 40 (1902), 96–109.

41. James J. Robinson, "The Scope and Effect of the 1926 Amendments to the Bankruptcy Act," *Cornell LQ,* 12 (1926–27), 49; Thomas C. Billig, "Extra-Judicial Administration of Insolvent Estates: A Study of Recent Cases," *U Pa LR,* 78 (1929–30), 317; Ralph L. Colin, "An Analysis of the 1926 Amendments to the Bankruptcy Act," *Col LR,* 26 (1926), 789–808.

42. William O. Douglas, "Some Functional Aspects of Bankruptcy," *Yale LJ,* 41 (1931–32), 329–364; William O. Douglas and John H. Weir, "Equity Receiverships in the United States District Court for Connecticut: 1920–1929," *Connecticut Bar Journal,* 4 (1930), 1–30; William O. Douglas and J. Howard Marshall, "A Factual Study of Bankruptcy Administration and Some Suggestions," *Col LR,* 32 (1932), 25–49; "Federal Receiverships in Massachusetts, 1929–1932," *Harv LR,* 47 (1934), 828–840.

43. William O. Douglas, "Wage Earner Bankruptcies—State vs. Federal Control," *Yale LJ,* 42 (1932–33), 591–642.

44. Reuben G. Hunt, "National Bankruptcy Legislation—Past, Present and Future," *Commercial Law Journal,* 38 (1933), 637; Saul Seidman, "Decade of Bankruptcy Legislation," *Connecticut Bar Journal,* 10 (1936), 24–33; Edwin S. Sunderland, "A Brief Sketch of the Historical Background and of the Events Leading up to the Enactment of the New Corporate Bankruptcy Reorganization Act," *Corporate Reorganizations,* 1 (1934–35), 4–15, 46–50.

45. Roscoe Pound, "The End of Law as Developed in Juristic Thought," *Harv LR,* 30 (1916–17, 211–225; E. F. Albertsworth, "From Contract to Status," *ABA Journal,* 18 (1922), 19.

46. Nathan Isaacs, "Business Postulates and the Law," *Harv LR,* 41 (1927–28), 1019.

47. Grant Gilmore, *The Death of Contract* (Columbus, 1974); George K. Gardner, "An Inquiry into the Principles of the Law of Contracts," *Harv LR,* 46 (1932–33), 1–43.

48. "Freedom of Contract under the Constitution," *Harv LR,* 28 (1914–15), 496; Roscoe Pound, "Liberty of Contract," *Yale LJ,* 18 (1909), 454–487; "Extent of the Legislative Power to Limit Freedom of Contract," *Harv LR,* 27 (1913–14), 374. See also P. S. Atiyah, *The Rise and Fall of Freedom of Contract* (Oxford, 1979), pt. 3, on the British experience.

49. Keller, *Affairs of State,* pp. 416–417. See also Lawrence M. Friedman, *Contract Law in America* (Madison, 1965), chap. 5.

50. Morton Keller, "The Judicial System and the Law of Life Insurance, 1888–1910," *Bus Hist R,* 35 (1961), 317–335; idem, *Life Insurance Enterprise,* pt. 5. See also Hugh J. Fegan, "Some Recent Tendencies in the "Law of Insurance,'" *Virginia Law Review,* 15 (1929), 415–436; Spencer L. Kimball, *Insurance and Public Policy* (Madison, 1960).

51. "Recent Tendencies in English Jurisprudence," *Law Times*, 168 (1929), 77; Gilmore, *Death of Contract*. See also Morris R. Cohen, "The Basis of Contract," *Harv LR*, 46 (1932–33), 553–592.

52. Roscoe Pound, "The Economic Interpretation of the Law of Torts," *Harv LR*, 53 (1939–40), 377. See also Francis H. Bohlen, "Fifty Years of Torts," *Harv LR*, 50 (1935–36), 725–748, 1225–48; G. Edward White, *Tort Law in America: An Intellectual History* (New York, 1980).

53. MacPherson v. Buick Motor Co., 111 N.E. 1050, 1053 (N.Y., 1916); Huset v. Case, 120 Fed 865 (8th Cir., 1903). See also Warren A. Seavey, "Mr. Justice Cardozo and the Law of Torts," *Harv LR*, 52 (1938–39), 372–373; Kenzo Takayanagi, "Liability without Fault in the Modern Civil and Common Law," *Illinois Law Review*, 16 (1921–22), 163–173, 268–303; and 17 (1922–23), 187–210, 417–439.

54. Richard Ford, "Legal Problems in National Merchandising," *Mich LR*, 32 (1913–14), 433–450.

55. E. R. A. Seligman and Robert A. Love, *Price Cutting and Price Maintenance: A Study in Economics* (New York, 1932), pp. 44–45.

56. H. R. Tosdal, "Price Maintenance," *American Economic Review*, 8 (1918), 31. See also Waldemar Kaempffert, "Price Maintenance and Modern Merchandising," *Sci Am*, 108 (1913), 566; *Sci Am*, 109 (1913), 7, 20; Myron W. Watkins, "The Change in Trust Policy," *Harv LR*, 38 (1921–22), 830.

57. A&P v. Cream of Wheat Co., 224 Fed. 566 (2nd Cir., 1915); Sumner H. Slichter, "The Cream of Wheat Case," *Pol Sci Q*, 31 (1916), 392–412.

58. Elliman v. Carrington [1901] 2 Ch. 275; "Price Maintenance Agreements in England," *Am LR*, 49 (1915), 271–274; "Price-Maintenance Agreements," *Law Times*, 164 (1927), 263–264; on France, Charles L. Miller, *Legal Status of Maintenance of Uniform Resale Prices* (New York, 1916), p. 22.

59. Hughes and Holmes in Miles v. Park, 220 U.S. 373, 408–409, 411–412 (1911); A. D. Neale, *The Antitrust Laws of the United States of America*, 2d ed. (Cambridge, 1970), chap. 10. See also "Price Cutting as a Tort," *Harv LR*, 27 (1913–14), 374–375; "On Maintaining Makers' Prices," *Harper's Weekly*, 57 (June 14, 1913), 6.

60. Tosdal, "Price Maintenance," pp. 33–35; "Fair Trade Legislation: The Constitutionality of a State Experiment in Resale Price Maintenance," *Harv LR*, 49 (1936), 811–821. See also "Price Maintenance at Common Law and under Proposed Legislation," *Harv LR*, 30 (1916–17), 68–75.

61. U.S. v. Colgate, 250 U.S. 300 (1919); F.T.C. v. Beech-Nut Packing Co., 257 U.S. 441 (1922); U.S. v. General Electric Co., 272 U.S. 476 (1926); Gilbert H. Montague, "Price Fixing, Lawful and Unlawful," *Am LR*, 62 (1928), 505–528; Seligman and Love, *Price Cutting*, p. 87.

62. *Nation*, 72 (1901), 125; on department stores, Chicago v. Netcher, 55 N.E. 707 (Ill., 1899); State v. Ashbrook, 55 S.W. 627 (Mo., 1900); Samuel Becker and Robert A. Hess, "The Chain Store License Tax and the Fourteenth Amendment," *North Carolina Law Review*, 7 (1928–29), 127. See also F. J. Harper, "'A New Battle in Evolution': The Anti–Chain Store Trade-at-Home Agitation of 1929–1930," *Journal of American Studies*, 16 (1982),

407–426; "Organizing Retail Trades," *New Republic*, 1 (1915), 19–20; John T. Flynn, "Chain Stores: Menace or Promise?" *New Republic*, 66 (1931), 270–273.

63. J. Ross Harrington, "The Chain Store Era and the Law," *Notre Dame Lawyer*, 4 (1929), 491–505; Edward Simms, "Chain Stores and the Courts," *Virginia Law Review*, 17 (1931), 313–324.

64. Brandeis in Liggett v. Lee, 288 U.S. 517, 567 (1933); Tax Commissioners v. Jackson, 283 U.S. 527 (1931). See also Juliet Blumenfeld, "Retail Trade Regulations and Their Constitutionality," *Cal LR*, 22 (1933–34), 86–105.

65. Appalachian Coals, Inc., v. U.S. 288 U.S. 344 (1933); Nebbia v. New York, 291 U.S. 502 (1934); Robert L. Hale, "The Constitution and the Price System: Some Reflections on Nebbia *v.* New York," *Col LR*, 34 (1934), 401–425; Sugar Institute, Inc., v. U.S., 297 U.S. 553 (1936); George J. Feldman, "Legal Aspects of Federal and State Price Control," *Boston University Law Review*, 16 (1936), 570–594.

66. Ewald T. Grether, "Experience in California with Fair Trade Legislation Restricting Price Cutting," *Cal LR*, 24 (1935–36), 640–700; Charles D. Evans, "The Anti–Price Discrimination Act of 1936," *Virginia Law Review*, 23 (1936–37), 140–177; Milo F. Hamilton and Lee Loevinger, "The Second Attack on Price Discrimination: The Robinson-Patman Act,"*Washington University Law Quarterly*, 22 (1937), 153–186. See also Karl G. Ryant, "The South and the Movement against Chain Stores," *Journal of Social History*, 39 (1973), 207–222; Ellis W. Hawley, *The New Deal and the Problem of Monopoly* (Princeton, 1966), pp. 249–254; Joseph C. Palamountain, Jr., *The Politics of Distribution* (Cambridge, Mass., 1955), chaps. 6, 7.

67. J. W. Gordon, "Reform of the Patent Law," *Law Magazine and Review*, 31 (1906), 31; R. W. Wallace, "The Working of the Patent Acts," ibid., pp. 257–272; "American vs. British Patent Protection," *Sci Am*, 119 (1918), 523, 526, 539; "Reform of the British Patent System," *Nature*, 122 (1928), 757–761. See also G. H. B. Kenrick, "The Development of Patent Law," *Law Magazine and Review*, 26 (1901), 5–19.

68. Frederick P. Fish, "The Patent System in Its Relation to Industrial Development," *Forum*, 42 (1909), 8–22; William Macomber, "Patents and Industrial Progress," *NAR*, 191 (1910), 805–813; "Proposed Bill for the Extension of Patents," *Sci Am*, 94 (1906), 267; H. Ward Leonard, "The Legal Monstrosity of Our Patent System," *Forum*, 41 (1909), 496–505; Isaac L. Rice, "Suggestions for Amendments to our Patent Laws," ibid., pp. 189–198. See also David F. Noble, *America by Design* (New York, 1977), chap. 6.

69. Edwin H. Abbot, Jr., "Patents and the Sherman Act," *Col LR*, 12 (1912), 709–723.

70. Henry v. A. B. Dick Co., 224 U.S. 12 (1912); Bement v. National Harrow Co., 186 U.S. 70 (1902); Thomas R. Powell, "The Nature of a Patent Right," *Col LR*, 17 (1917), 666. See also *Lit Dig*, 44 (1912), 573–574.

71. "The Sherman Anti-Trust Act and the Patentee," *Sci Am*, 107 (1912), 434; Gilbert H. Montague, "The Proposed Patent Law Revision," *Harv LR*, 26

(1912–13), 128–145; idem, "The Spirit of the American Patent System," *NAR*, 196 (1912), 682–693; *J Pol Ec*, 20 (1912), 633–635; Montague, "The Bogey of the 'Patent Monopoly,' *Annals*, 42 (1912), 251–262.

72. William Macomber, "The War and Our Patent Laws," *Yale LJ*, 25 (1915–16), 396–404; Straus v. Victor Talking Machine Co., 243 U.S. 490 (1917); Motion Picture Patents Co. v. Universal Film Mfg. Co., 243 U.S. 502 (1917).

73. Floyd L. Vaughan, "The Relation of Patents to Industrial Monopolies," *Annals*, 147 (1930), 40–50; U.S. v. General Electric Co., 272 U.S. 476 (1926); R.C.A. v. Lloyd, 278 U.S. 648 (1928); Carbice Corp. v. Amer. Patents Development Corp., 283 U.S. 27 (1931); Standard Oil Co. of Indiana v. U.S., 283 U.S. 163 (1931). See also "Patent Pools and the Sherman Act," *Yale LJ*, 40 (1931), 1297–1303; Horace R. Lamb, "The Relation of the Patent Law to the Federal Anti-Trust Laws," *Cornell LQ*, 12 (1927), 261–285; Alfred McCormack, "Restrictive Patent Licenses and Restraint of Trade," *Col LR*, 31 (1931), 743–777.

74. John Dickinson, "Some Recent Developments in Patent Law," *ABA Journal*, 20 (1934), 576.

75. George H. Putnam, "The Copyright Law of the United States and the Authors of the Continent," *Critic*, 44 (1904), 60–64; PRO, *Cab 37*, 103 (1910), no. 31.

76. Samuel J. Elder, "Our Archaic Copyright Laws," *Am LR*, 37 (1903), 225.

77. Holmes in Bleistein v. Donaldson Lithographing Co., 188 U.S. 239 (1903); Hegeman v. Springer, 110 Fed. 374 (1901); Edward S. Rogers, "Copyright and Morals," *Mich LR*, 18 (1919–20), 390–404; Edison v. Lubin, 122 Fed. 240 (1903); on song, Elder, "Archaic Copyright Laws," p. 223. See also George P. Brett, "The Need of a New Copyright Law," *Ind*, 56 (1904), 612–614; Benjamin Kaplan, *An Unhurried View of Copyright* (New York, 1967), p. 34–37.

78. Kaplan, *Unhurried View*, p. 38; W. P. Cutter, "The Book Trust and the Copyright Bill," *Ind*, 63 (1907), 1239–41; Thorvald Solberg, "Copyright Law Reform," *Yale LJ*, 35 (1925–26), 62–65; "The New Copyright Law," *Outlook*, 91 (1909), 755–756.

79. Bobbs-Merrill Co. v. Straus, 210 U.S. 339 (1908); R. H. Macy & Co. v. Amer. Publishers' Assn., 231 U.S. 222 (1913); H. R. Tosdal, "Price Maintenance in the Book Trade," *Q J Ec*, 30 (1915–16), 86–109.

80. Brandeis in Buck v. Jewell-LaSalle Realty Co., 283 U.S. 191 (1931); W. Jefferson Davis, "Copyrighted Radio," *Virginia Law Review*, 16 (1929–30), 49; Lawrence P. Simpson, "Broadcasting as Copyright Infringement," *Air Law Review*, 1 (1930), 134–139.

81. Thorvald Solberg, "The Present Copyright Situation," *Yale LJ*, 40 (1930–31), 184–214; on Vestal bill, *Publishers Weekly*, 119 (1931), 296–297, 826–827; Lawrence P. Simpson, "The Copyright Situation as Affecting Radio Broadcasting," *NYU Law Quarterly*, 9 (1931–32), 180–197. See also Charles B. Collins, "Some Obsolescent Doctrines of the Law of Copyright," *Southern California Law Review*, 1 (1927–28), 127–140.

82. Keller, *Affairs of State*, pp. 420–421; Baker v. Selden, 101 U.S. 99 (1879).

83. Edward S. Rogers, "The Expensive Futility of the United States Trade-Mark Statute," *Mich LR*, 2 (1913–14), 668, 665, 667; Arthur P. Greeley, "The Proposed New Trade-Mark Law," *Sci Am*, 92 (1905), 19.

84. "Trade-Mark Development during the Last Seven Years," *Sci Am*, 106 (1912), 569; Arthur W. Barber, "The Constitution and Trade-Marks," *Lawyer & Banker*, 5 (1912), 210–217.

85. "Trademarks: Relation of Trademark Infringement to the Law of Unfair Competition," *Cal LR*, 7 (1919), 201–204; Frank I. Schechter, "The Rational Basis of Trademark Protection," *Harv LR*, 40 (1926–27), 814–818.

86. Hanover v. Metcalf, 240 U.S. 403, 413 (1916).

87. Hand in Ely-Norris Safe Co. v. Mosler Safe Co., 7 Fed. 2d 603, 604 (2d Cir., 1925); Schechter, "Rational Basis," pp. 822–831; idem, "Fog and Fiction in Trade-Mark Protection," *Col LR*, 36 (1936), 69; Old Dearborn Distributing Co. v. Seagram Distillers Corp., 299 U.S. 183 (1936).

88. Roland Marchand, *Advertising and the American Dream* (Berkeley, 1985); on percentage of GNP, Daniel Pope, *The Making of Modern Advertising* (New York, 1983), p. 26; Tom E. Shearer, "The National Government and False Advertising," *Iowa Law Review*, 19 (1933–34), U.S. v. New South Farm and Home Co., 241 U.S. 64 (1916), James H. Young, "Legalized Morality in Advertising," *Outlook*, 111 (1916), 300–301.

89. "Untrue Advertising," *Yale LJ*, 36 (1926–27), 1155–62; "The Imitation of Advertising," *Harv LR*, 45 (1931–32), 542–548.

90. On FTC statistics, "Comments," *Mich LR*, 32 (1933–34), 1145; Milton Handler, "False and Misleading Advertising," *Yale LJ*, 39 (1929–30), 22; "Scope of the Jurisdiction of the Federal Trade Commission over False and Misleading Advertising," *Yale LJ*, 40 (1930–31), 617–631.

91. Winsted Hosiery Co. v. F.T.C., 272 Fed. 957, 960 (2d Cir., 1921); Blumenstock Bros. Advertising Co. v. Curtis Publishing Co., 252 U.S. 436 (1920); F.T.C. v. Winsted Hosiery Co., 258 U.S. 483 (1922).

6. Regulating Unions

1. Norman Stone, *Europe Transformed, 1878–1919* (London, 1983), p. 91; David Montgomery, *The Fall of the House of Labor: The Workplace, the State, and American Labor Activism, 1865–1925* (Cambridge, 1987), p. 1. See also Christopher L. Tomlins, *The State and the Unions: Labor Relations, Law, and the Organized Labor Movement in America, 1880–1960* (Cambridge, 1985).

2. Larry Peterson, "The One Big Union in International Perspective: Revolutionary Industrial Unionism, 1900–1925," *Labour*, 7 (1981), 41–66; David Montgomery, "The 'New Unionism' and the Transformation of Workers' Consciousness in America, 1900–22," *Journal of Social History*, 7 (1974), 509–535; John H. M. Laslett, *Labor and the Left: A Study of Socialist and Radical Influences in the American Labor Movement, 1881–1924* (New York, 1970); on the UMW, *Pol Sci Q*, 27 (1912), 365.

3. Victor S. Yarros, "The Labor Question's Newer Aspects," *American Monthly Review of Reviews*, 31 (1905), 591; William E. Walling, "British

and American Trade Unionism," *Annals*, 26 (1905), 721–739; idem, "The New Unionism—The Problem of the Unskilled Worker," *Annals*, 24 (1904), 296–315; George E. Barnett, "The Dominance of the National Union in American Labor Organization," *Q J Ec*, 27 (1912–13), 455–481.

4. Irene Van Kleeck, "How Women Wage Earners Fare," *World's Work*, 15 (1907–08), 9683–9690; Alvin H. Hansen, "Industrial Class Alignments in the United States," *Journal of the American Statistical Association*, n.s., 17 (1920–21), 417–425; Alba M. Edwards, "Social-Economic Groups of the United States," ibid., 15 (1916–17), 643–646; John R. Commons, "Is Class Conflict in America Growing and Is It Inevitable?" *American Journal of Sociology*, 13 (1907–08), 756–783.

5. George E. Barnett, "Growth of Labor Organization in the United States, 1897–1914," *Q J Ec*, 30 (1915–16), 780–795, 838–846; Andrew Dawson, "The Paradox of Dynamic Technological Change and the Labor Aristocracy in the United States, 1880–1914," *Labor History*, 20 (1979), 325–351.

6. Quoted in R. F. Hoxie, "Why Organized Labor Opposes Scientific Management," *Q J Ec*, 31 (1916–17), 72; *HS*, p. 177.

7. Hoxie, "Organized Labor," p. 73; Carroll D. Wright, "Strikes in the United States," *NAR*, 174 (1902), 766–767.

8. John A. Fitch, "Unionism in the Iron and Steel Industry," *Pol Sci Q*, 24 (1909), 57–59; H. E. Haigland, "Trade Unionism in the Iron Industry: A Decadent Organization," *Q J Ec*, 31 (1916–17), 674–689; John R. Commons, "Labor Conditions in Meat Packing and the Recent Strike," *Q J Ec*, 19 (1904–05), 1–32.

9. "The Coal Miners' Strike," *Gunton's Magazine*, 19 (1900), 316–323; E. Dana Durand, "The Anthracite Coal Strike and Its Settlement," *Pol Sci Q*, 18 (1903), 385–386.

10. Baer quoted in Frederick W. Unger, "George F. Baer: Master-Spirit of the Anthracite Industry," *American Monthly Review of Reviews*, 33 (1906), 547; in "The Great Coal Strike and Its Lessons," *Arena*, 29 (1903), 8; and in Edwin Maxey, "Private Property and Public Rights," *Arena*, 28 (1902), 561–562. See also B. O. Flower, "Promoters of Anarchy and Social Disorder," ibid., pp. 424–428.

11. *Tribune* quoted in "Public Concern in the Coal Strike," *Outlook*, 71 (Aug. 30, 1902), 1035; Robert J. Cornell, *The Anthracite Coal Strike of 1902* (New York, 1957); Durand, "Anthracite Coal Strike," pp. 387–414.

12. *Gunton's Magazine*, 23 (1902), 385–390. See also Bruno Ramirez, *When Workers Fight: The Politics of Industrial Relations in the Progressive Era, 1898–1916* (Westport, Conn., 1978), pt. 1.

13. Charles E. Strangeland, "The Preliminaries to the Labor War in Colorado," *Pol Sci Q*, 23 (1908), 5; Laslett, *Labor and the Left*, chap. 7. See also Louis Levine, "The Development of Syndicalism in America," *Pol Sci Q*, 28 (1913), 451–479.

14. Henry Bedford, *Socialism and the Workers in Massachusetts, 1886–1912* (Amherst, 1966), chap. 8; Melvyn Dubofsky, *We Shall Be All: A History of the Industrial Workers of the World*, 2d ed. (Urbana, 1988), chaps. 2, 10, 11.

15. Irwin Yellowitz, *Labor and the Progressive Movement in New York State, 1897–1916* (Ithaca, 1965); Melvyn Dubofsky, *When Workers Organize: New York City in the Progressive Era* (Amherst, 1968); Laslett, *Labor and the Left*, chap. 4.

16. Thomas W. Page, "The San Francisco Labor Movement in 1901," *Pol Sci Q*, 17 (1902), 664–688.

17. Michael Kazin, *Barons of Labor: The San Francisco Building Trades and Union Power in the Progressive Era* (Urbana, 1987), chap. 2; Walton Bean, *Boss Ruef's San Francisco* (Berkeley, 1968), chaps. 1, 6.

18. John R. Commons, "The New York Building Trades," *Q J Ec*, 18 (1903–04), 409–436; David C. Hammack, *Power and Society: Greater New York at the Turn of the Century* (New York, 1982), p. 180; "Labor and Capital," *Pol Sci Q*, (1905), 368.

19. Ernest L. Bogart, "The Chicago Building Trades Dispute," *Pol Sci Q*, 16 (1901), 114–141, 222–247; J. E. George, "The Chicago Building Trades Conflict of 1900," *Q J Ec*, 15 (1900–01), 348–370.

20. Baker in *McClure's Magazine*, 21 (1903), 463; John R. Commons, "Types of American Labor Organization—The Teamsters of Chicago," *Q J Ec*, 19 (1904–05), 400–433; John Cummings, "The Chicago Teamsters' Strike—A Study in Industrial Democracy," *J Pol Ec*, 13 (1904–05), 537–573.

21. *Arena*, 28 (1902), 95–96; Robert E. Zeigler, "The Limits of Power: The Amalgamated Association of Street Railway Employees in Houston, Texas, 1897–1905," *Labor History*, 18 (1977), 71–90; Steven L. Piott, "Modernization and the Anti-Monopoly Issue: The St. Louis Transit Strike of 1900," *Missouri Historical Society Publications*, 35 (1978), 3–16.

22. "Labor and Capital," *Pol Sci Q*, 25 (1910), 375, 741–743; "The Public and Trade-Union Policy," *New Republic*, 8 (1916), 235–237.

23. Marcus A. Hanna, "Industrial Conciliation and Arbitration," *Annals*, 20 (1902), 25; Samuel Gompers, "Organized Labor and the Trusts," *Ind*, 53 (1901), 1487–88. See also M. Cokely, "The Harmonizing of Organized Labor with Organized Capital," *Engineering Magazine*, 25 (1903), 161–167.

24. Samuel Gompers, "The Limitations of Conciliation and Arbitration," *Annals*, 20 (1902), 21–22; Ralph M. Easley, "Senator Hanna and the Labor Problem," *Ind*, 56 (1904), 483–487; Graham Taylor, "Industrial Survey of the Month," *Survey*, 22 (1909), 668–671; George E. Barnett, "National and District Systems of Collective Bargaining in the United States," *Q J Ec*, 26 (1911–12), 425–429. See also Tomlins, *The State and the Unions*, chap. 3; Montgomery, *Fall*, chap. 6.

25. Carlton H. Parker, "The Labor Policy of the American Trusts," *Atl*, 125 (1920), 226; Mabel Atkinson, "Trusts and Trade Unions," *Poli Sci Q*, 19 (1904), 212.

26. Taylor quoted in R. F. Hoxie, "Why Organized Labor Opposes Scientific Management," *Q J Ec*, 31 (1916–17), 67; "Democratic Control of Scientific Management," *New Republic*, 9 (1916–17), 204–205; Daniel Nelson, "Scientific Management, Systematic Management, and Labor, 1880–1915," *Bus Hist R*, 48 (1974), 489–490; idem, "The Company Union Movement, 1900–1937: A Reexamination," *Bus Hist R*, 56 (1982), 339.

27. Parry quoted in Henry White, "The Issue of the Open and Closed Shop," *NAR*, 180 (1905), 36; Kirby quoted in Taylor, "Industrial Survey," p. 670.

28. Margaret L. Stecker, "The National Founders' Association," *Q J Ec*, 30 (1915–16), 359; "Organized Capital Challenges Organized Labor: The New Employers' Association Movement," *McClure's Magazine*, 23 (1904), 279–292; William F. Willoughby, "Employers' Associations for Dealing with Labor in the United States," *Q J Ec*, 20 (1905–06), 110–156.

29. William D. Lewis, "Some Leading English Cases on Trade and Labor Disputes," *American Law Register*, n.s., 42 (1903), 160; A. V. Dicey, "The Combination Laws as Illustrating the Relation between Law and Opinion in England during the Nineteenth Century," *Harv LR*, 17 (1903–04), 511–532. See also William H. Dawson, "The Legal Position of German Workmen," *Pol Sci Q*, 21 (1906), 264–287; R. Y. Hedges and Allan Winterbottom, *The Legal History of Trade Unionism* (London, 1930), pt. 2, chap. 1.

30. Allen v. Flood [1898] A.C. 1.

31. Taff Vale [1901] A.C. 426; Quinn v. Leathem [1901] A.C. 495.

32. J. J. Posner, "English Trade Disputes Act of 1906," *Cal LR*, 10 (1921–22), 396–397; Alfred Fellows, "The Trades Disputes Act and Freedom of Contract," *Fortnightly Review*, 88 (1907), 403–416; Henry R. Seager, "The Legal Status of Trade Unions in the United Kingdom, with Conclusions Applicable to the United States," *Pol Sci Q*, 22 (1907), 611–629. See also A. Maurice Low, "Labor and the Law in England," *Forum*, 32 (1901–02), 156–165; idem, "Labor Unions and the Law," *American Monthly Review of Reviews*, 27 (1903), 200–201; A. Ure, "The Legal Position of Trade Unions," *Juridical Review*, 16 (1904), 20–29, 135–147; Jonathan G. Steffee, "The Taff Vale Case," *Am LR*, 37 (1903), 385–394.

33. Osborne v. Amalgamated Society [1910] A.C. 87; Walter V. Osborne, "Trade Unions and the Law," *Westminster Review*, 177 (1912), 10–17; John H. Greenwood, "Trade Unions and the Law," *Westminster Review*, 176 (1911), 609–619; M. F. B. Kenney, "Trade Unions under English and American Law," *Canadian Law Journal*, 49 (1913), 256.

34. PRO, *Cab 37*, 103 (1910), no. 42; Buxton in ibid., 107 (1911), no. 98; J. Ramsay MacDonald, "The Osborne Judgement and Trade Unionism," *Contemporary Review*, 98 (1910), 535–542. See also Henry Pelling, "The Politics of the Osborne Judgment," *Historical Journal*, 25 (1982), 889–909; W. M. Geldart, "The Status of Trade Unions in England," *Harv LR*, 25 (1911–12), 579–601.

35. E. W. Huffart, "Interference with Contracts and Business in New York," *Harv LR*, 17 (1903–04), 442; Henry R. Seager, "The Attitude of American Courts towards Restrictive Labor Laws," *Pol Sci Q*, 19 (1904), 589–590; "An Important Decision," *Outlook*, 82 (1906), 51–52; Atchison, T. & St. F. R.R. v. Gee, 139 Fed. 582 (1905). See also Tomlins, *State and Unions*, pp. 83–84; and Herbert Hovenkamp, "Labor Conspiracies in American Law, 1880–1930," *Texas Law Review*, 66 (1988), 919–965.

36. Frank W. Grinnell, "An Analysis of the Legal Value of a Labor Union Contract," *Am LR*, 41 (1907), 197–214; "The Law of the 'Closed Shop,'" *Nation*, 79 (1904), 46–47; *Opinion of the Justices*, 211 Mass. 618 (1912).

37. Industrial Commission quoted in Charles J. Bullock, "The Closed Shop,"

Atl, 94 (1904), 433; Ralph F. Fuchs, "Collective Labor Agreements in American Law," *St. Louis Law Review*, 10 (1922), 1–33; Ernest L. Carman, "The Outlook for the Present Legal Status of Employers and Employees in Industrial Disputes," *Minnesota Law Review*, 6 (1922), 536–541. For a major conflict of judicial views, see Plant v. Woods, 176 Mass. 992 (1900), which refused to follow Allen v. Flood; and National Protective Association v. Cumming, 170 N.Y. 315 (1902), allowing a union to forbid its members to work with members of a rival organization.

38. On number of boycotts, David Y. Thomas, "A Year of Bench Labor Law," *Pol Sci Q*, 24 (1909), 80.

39. Francis B. Sayre, "Criminal Conspiracy," *Harv LR*, 35 (1921–22), 406; Brewer quoted in George Whitelock, "Development of the Injunction in the United States," *Am LR*, 46 (1912), 739.

40. On Omaha, *Outlook*, 74 (1903), 199–200. See also Charles R. Darling, "Recent American Decisions and English Legislation Affecting Labor Unions," *Am LR*, 42 (1908), 200–228; Carman, "Outlook for Present Legal Status," pp. 533–539.

41. "The Misuse of Injunctions," *Gunton's Magazine*, 23 (1902), 227, 229, 233; F. J. Stimson, *Labor in Its Relation to Law* (New York, 1895), p. 125. See also Francis M. Burdick, "Injunctions in Labor Disputes," *NAR*, 188 (1908), 273–284.

42. Samuel Gompers, "Attitude of Labor towards Government Regulation of Industry," *Annals*, 32 (1908), 78; George G. Groat, "The Courts' View of Injunction in Labor Disputes," *Pol Sci Q*, 23 (1908), 408–439; Carl H. Mote, "Some Phases of Injunction Legislation, 1913–14," *American Political Science Review*, 9 (1915), 93–97; Bogni v. Perotti, 112 N.E. 853 (Mass., 1916).

43. George W. Alger, *The Old Law and the New Order* (Boston, 1913), chap. 4.

44. "Incorporation of Trade Unions," *Ind*, 54 (1902), 3038–39; Lindley D. Clark, "The Present Legal Status of Organized Labor in the United States," *J Pol Ec*, 13 (1904–05), 173–200.

45. Adair v. U.S., 208 U.S. 161 (1908); Loewe v. Lawlor, 208 U.S. 274 (1908); Gompers v. Bucks Stove and Range Co., 221 U.S. 418 (1911); Coppage v. Kansas, 236 U.S. 1 (1915); Hitchman Coal and Coke Co. v. Mitchell, 245 U.S. 229 (1917); James Boyle, "Organized Labor and the Court Decisions," *Forum*, 42 (1909), 535–551.

46. Richard Olney, "Discrimination against Union Labor—Legal?" *Am LR*, 42 (1908), 161–167.

47. Theodor Megaarden, "The Danbury Hatters Case—Its Possible Effect on Labor Unions," *Am LR*, 49 (1915), 417–428; "Danbury Hatters' Homes Placed on Sale," *Survey*, 38 (1917), 262.

48. Barry F. Helfand, "Labor and the Courts: The Common-Law Doctrine of Criminal Conspiracy and Its Application in the Buck's Stove Case," *Labor History*, 18 (1977), 91–114. See also Morton Keller, *In Defense of Yesterday* (New York, 1958), pp. 73–74.

49. Forrest R. Black, "How Far Is the Theory of Trust Regulation Applicable

to Labor Unions?" *Washington University Studies*, 11 (1924), 371; Burton J. Hendrick, "The Battle against the Sherman Law," *McClure*, 31 (1908), 665–680; Edward Berman, *Labor and the Sherman Act* (New York, 1930), pp. 4, 6, 11–26, 103; Alpheus T. Mason, *Organized Labor and the Law with Especial Reference to the Sherman and Clayton Acts* (Durham, N.C., 1925), pp. 192–193, 244.

50. Thomas R. Powell, "Collective Bargaining before the Supreme Court," *Pol Sci Q*, 33 (1918), 429. See also George G. Groat, *Attitudes of American Courts in Labor Cases* (New York, 1911).

51. William E. Walling, "Why American Labor Unions Keep out of Politics," *Outlook*, 80 (1905), 183–185. See also Sydney Brooks, "Is an American Labor Party a Likelihood?" *Harper's Weekly*, 52 (Nov. 14, 1908), 13; Marc Karson, *American Labor Unions and Politics, 1890–1918* (Carbondale, Ill., 1958).

52. Morton Keller, *Affairs of State: Public Life in Late Nineteenth Century America* (Cambridge, Mass., 1977), pp. 397–400.

53. "Trade Unions and Politics," *Ind*, 54 (1902), 1496–97; Alfred T. Howe, "Connecticut's Labor Mayors," *Ind*, 55 (1903), 1259–64; M. G. Cunniff, "Labor in Politics," *World's Work*, 12 (1906), 8130–35.

54. Henry J. Gibbons, "The Labor Vote in Philadelphia's Political Upheaval," *Charities*, 15 (1905–06), 588–590.

55. Gwendolyn Mink, *Old Labor and New Immigrants in American Political Development: Union, Party, and State, 1875–1920* (Ithaca, 1986), chaps. 5, 6; Gerald Rosenbloom, *Immigrant Workers: Their Impact on American Labor Radicalism* (New York, 1973). The increasing moderation of the German Socialists, culminating in their support of war in 1914, has been attributed in part to the social fragmentation of the German working class—among Ruhr miners, by the influx of Polish workers and Catholic-Protestant divisions; Stephen Hickey, "The Shaping of the German Labour Movement: Miners in the Ruhr," in *Society and Politics in Wilhelmine Germany*, ed. Richard J. Evans (London, 1978), pp. 215–240.

56. "Organized Labor in Politics," *Ind*, 61 (1906), 175; Cunniff, "Labor in Politics," pp. 8130–35.

57. Graham Taylor, "The Industrial Viewpoint," *Charities*, 17 (1906–07), 101–106.

58. Henry White, "The Labor Unions in the Presidential Campaign," *NAR*, 188 (1908), 372–382; Graham Taylor, "Organized Labor and the Elections," *Charities*, 21 (1908–09), 274–276; Philip G. Wright, "The Contest in Congress between Organized Labor and Organized Business," *Q J Ec*, 29 (1914–15), 235–261; "Navy Yard Politics," *Sci Am*, 105 (1911), 570; William B. Wilson, "The Job, the Worker, and the Government," *Ind*, 83 (1915), 48–49; *Proceedings of the Academy of Political Science*, 4 (1914), 246–308; A. T. Lane, "American Trade Unions, Mass Immigration, and the Literacy Test, 1900–1917," *Labor History*, 25 (1984), 5–25.

59. Mink, *Old Labor and New Immigrants*, chap. 7. See William M. Dick, *Labor and Socialism in America: The Gompers Era* (Port Washington, N.Y., 1972), for a more favorable view.

60. William Z. Ripley, "Race Factors in Labor Unionism," *Atl*, 93 (1904), 299–300; Jane Addams, "The Present Crisis in Trades-Union Morals," *NAR*, 178 (1904), 189–193; John A. Ryan, "The Morality of the Aims and Methods of the Labor Union," *American Catholic Quarterly*, 29 (1904), 326–355.

61. Leonard W. Hatch, *Government Industrial Arbitration*, U.S. Bureau of Labor Bulletin no. 60 (Washington, D.C. 1905); David A. McCabe, "Federal Intervention in Labor Disputes under the Erdman, Newlands, and Adamson Acts," *Proceedings of the Academy of Political Science*, 7 (1917–18), 94–107.

62. S. N. D. North, "The Industrial Commission," *NAR*, 168 (1899), 209–219; "The Report of the Industrial Commission," *Yale Review*, 11 (1902–03), 229–296; Graham Adams, *Age of Industrial Violence, 1910–15* (New York, 1966); *Pol Sci Q*, 30 (1915), 719–720.

63. Sumner H. Slichter, "The Current Labor Policies of American Industries," *Q J Ec*, 43 (1918–19), 393–395; Ruth Pickering, "Sudden Spread of the Eight-Hour Day," *Survey*, 36 (1916), 5–7; "Capital and Labor," *Pol Sci Q*, 31 (1916), 34.

64. L. C. Marshall, "The War Labor Program and Its Administration," *J Pol Ec*, 26 (1918), 447. See also Robert D. Cuff, "The Politics of Labor Administration during World War I," *Labor History*, 21 (1980), 546–569; John S. Smith, "Organized Labor and Government in the Wilson Era, 1913–1921: Some Conclusions," *Labor History*, 3 (1962), 265–286.

65. Paul B. Johnson, *Land Fit for Heroes: The Planning of British Reconstruction, 1916–1919* (Chicago, 1968), pp. 186–187; Arthur Greenwood, "Development of British Industrial Thought," *NAR*, 124 (1919), 106–115.

66. "The Destruction of the Trade Boards," *Nation* (GB), 29 (1921), 882–883; "The Attack on the Trade Boards," *New Statesman*, 17 (1922), 665–666; Edwin E. Witte, "British Trade Union Law since the Trade Disputes Act and Trade Union Act of 1927," *American Political Science Review*, 26 (1932), 345–351; A. L. Goodhart, "The Legality of the General Strike in England," *Yale LJ*, 36 (1926–27), 464–485.

67. "The Class War in America," *New Statesman*, 14 (1919), 760–761.

68. "The Labor Crisis and the People: What Does the Present Industrial Crisis Mean?" *Outlook*, 123 (1919), 223; Robert L. Friedheim, *The Seattle General Strike* (Seattle, 1964). See also Montgomery, *Fall*, chap. 8.

69. James A. Burran, "Labor Conflict in Urban Appalachia: The Knoxville Streetcar Strike of 1919," *Tennessee Historical Quarterly*, 38 (1979), 62–78; on Chicago and Landis, "Capital and Labor," *Pol Sci Q*, 36 (1921), 50–55, and 37 (1922), 52–59.

70. Ordway Tead, "Labor and Reconstruction," *Yale Review*, 7 (1918), 529–542.

71. Haggai Hurvitz, "Ideology and Industrial Conflict: President Wilson's First Industrial Conference of October, 1919," *Labor History*, 18 (1977), 509–524; Gary Dean Best, "President Wilson's Second Industrial Conference, 1919–1920," ibid., 16 (1975), 505–520; "A National Court for Labor," *Lit Dig*, 64 (Jan. 10, 1920), 14–15.

72. Robert H. Zieger, "Herbert Hoover, the Wage Earner, and the 'New Economic System,' 1919–1929," *Bus Hist R*, 51 (1977), 161–189; M. B. Hammond, "The Coal Commission Reports and the Coal Situation," *Q J Ec*, 38 (1924), 541–581.

73. Ronald Radosh, "Labor and the American Economy: The 1922 Railroad Shop Crafts Strike and the 'B&O Plan,'" in *Building the Organizational Society*, ed. Jerry Israel (New York, 1972), pp. 73–87; Clyde O. Fisher, "The Railroad Labor Board: An Appraisal," *South Atlantic Quarterly*, 24 (1925), 1–15.

74. "Legality of Strikes to Enforce Awards of Tribunal for Arbitration of Jurisdictional Labor Disputes," *Harv LR*, 39 (1925–26), 101–106; O'Brien v. Fackenthal, 5 Fed. 2d 389 (6th Cir., 1925).

75. Nelson, "Company Union Movement," pp. 335–337; NICB, *The Growth of Works Councils in the United States* (New York, 1925).

76. Kim McQuaid, "Young, Swope, and General Electric's 'New Capitalism': A Study in Corporate Liberalism," *American Journal of Economics and Sociology*, 36 (1977), 322–334; David Brody, *Workers in Industrial America* (New York, 1980), chap. 2.

77. Carlton H. Parker, "The Labor Policy of the American Trusts," *Atl*, 125 (1920), 233–234; Abraham Epstein, "Outwitting American Unionism," *New Republic*, 50 (1927), 192. See also Magnus W. Alexander, "Employers' Associations in the United States," *National Labour Review*, 25 (1932), 605–620; Sumner H. Slichter, "The Current Labor Policies of American Industries," *Q J Ec*, 43 (1928–29), 400–435.

78. Herbert Rabinowitz, "The Kansas Industrial Court Act," *Cal LR*, 12 (1923–24), 1–16; Henry J. Allen, *The Party of the Third Part: The Story of the Kansas Industrial Relations Court* (New York, 1921). See also John H. Bowers, *The Kansas Court of Industrial Relations* (Chicago, 1922); NICB, *The Kansas Court of Industrial Relations* (New York, 1924); H. W. Humble, "The Court of Industrial Relations in Kansas," *Mich LR*, 19 (1920–21), 675–689. On a flurry of other, less prominent postwar attempts at compulsory arbitration, see John A. Fitch, "Government Coercion in Labor Disputes," *Annals*, 90 (1920), 74–82; "State Control of Strikes," *Ind*, 108 (1922), 192–193.

79. George W. Wickersham, "Recent Extension of the State Police Power," *Am LR*, 54 (1920), 819; "Coal Mining Affected with a Public Interest," *Yale LJ*, 31 (1921–22), 75–78.

80. Frederick M. Davenport, "Freedom of Speech and Freedom to Work," *Outlook*, 132 (1922), 331–333; William Allen White, *Autobiography* (New York, 1946), pp. 611–614.

81. Rabinowitz, "Kansas Industrial Court Act," pp. 4n, 5; Wolff Packing Co. v. Court of Industrial Relations, 262 U.S. 522 (1923). See also Herbert Feis, "The Kansas Court of Industrial Relations, Its Spokesmen, Its Record," *Q J Ec*, 37 (1922–23), 705–733; Edward Berman, "The Present Status of the Kansas System of Compulsory Arbitration," *Illinois Law Review*, 23 (1928–29), 30–44.

82. Lewis quoted in *Lit Dig*, 63 (Nov. 22, 1919), 11–14; Gompers in ibid., 70

(July 9, 1921), 6. Victor S. Yarros, "The 'Intellectuals' and the Labor Movement," *American Federationist,* 28 (1921), 743–746; "Labor Leaders and Direct Action—A Contrast,"; *Outlook,* 126 (1920), 276–277; "The Truth about Soviet Russia and Bolshevism," ibid., 127 (1920), 167.

83. Mollie R. Carroll, *Labor and Politics* (Boston, 1923), pp. 89, 105–106.

84. Gompers quoted in Charles R. Walker, "The Fight to Keep Labor in Politics," *Ind,* 113 (1924), 499; Erik Olssen, "The Making of a Political Machine: The Railroad Unions Enter Politics," *Labor History,* 19 (1978), 373–396; William E. Walling, "Labor's Attitude toward a Third Party," *Current History,* 21 (1924–25), 32–40.

85. On immigration, William E. Walling, *American Labor and American Democracy* (New York, 1926) I, 222; Gompers in "America Must Not Be Overwhelmed," *American Federationist,* 31 (1924), 313–317; on Green, Benjamin Stolberg, "The End of the Gompers Tradition," *Ind,* 114 (1925), 185–187; "Statutes Restricting the Sale of Convict-Made Goods," *Harv LR,* 44 (1930–31), 846–850.

86. Harwood L. Childs, *Labor and Capital in National Politics* (Columbus, 1930), pp. 237–238. See also Robert H. Zieger, *Republicans and Labor, 1919–1929* (Lexington, Ky., 1969).

87. Horace B. Davis, "The German Labor Courts," *Poli Sci Q,* 44 (1929), 418; Ernest C. Carman, "The Outlook for the Present Legal Status of Employers and Employees in Industrial Disputes," *Minnesota Law Review,* 6 (1922), 550; "Strikes and Boycotts," *Harv LR,* 34 (1920–21), 883–884.

88. William G. Rice, Jr., "Collective Labor Agreements in American Law," *Harv LR,* 44 (1930–31), 604; Morris L. Ernst, "The Development of Industrial Jurisprudence," *Col LR,* 21 (1921), 155–161; Tomlins, *State and Unions,* pt. 2. See also "Collective Labor Agreements," *Col LR,* 31 (1931), 1156–62.

89. Brandeis in Dorchy v. Kansas, 272 U.S. 306 (1927); Sutherland in Bedford Cut Stone Co. v. Journeyman Stone Cutters' Assn., 274 U.S. 37 (1927).

90. American Steel Foundries v. Tri-City Trades Council, 257 U.S. 184 (1921); Duplex Printing Press Co. v. Deering, 254 U.S. 443 (1921); Truax v. Corrigan, 257 U.S. 312 (1921); Coronado Coal Co. v. U.M.W., 259 U.S. 295, 268 U.S. 295 (1925); Murray T. Quigg, "Trade Union Activities and the Sherman Law," *Annals,* 147 (1930), 51–60. See also Stanley I. Kutler, "Chief Justice Taft, Judicial Unanimity, and Labor," *Historian,* 24 (1961), 68–83; Richard Boeckel, "Labor Loses the Right to Strike," *Ind,* 105 (1921), 283–284, 299–302; "The 'Law' and Labor," *New Republic,* 25 (1921), 245–248; Alpheus T. Mason, "The Right to Strike," *U Pa LR,* 77 (1928–29), 59–60.

91. Berman, *Labor and the Sherman Act,* p. 128; on yellow dog contracts, "The Yellow Dog Device as a Bar to the Union Organizer," *Harv LR,* 41 (1927–28), 770–775; Homer F. Cary and Herman Oliphant, "The Present Status of the Hitchman Case," *Col LR,* 29 (1929), 442–460; Alpheus T. Mason, "Organized Labor as Party Plaintiff in Injunction Cases," *Col LR,* 30 (1930), 469.

92. Amidon in Great Northern Ry. v. Brosseau, 286 Fed. 414, 415 (D.N.D., 1923); Robert Kingsley, "Labor Injunctions in Illinois," *Illinois Law Re-*

view, 23 (1929), 529–555; Berman, *Labor and the Sherman Act,* pp. 211, 218–219.

93. P. F. Brissenden and C. O. Swayze, "The Use of the Labor Injunction in the New York Needle Trades," *Pol Sci Q,* 44 (1929), 548–568, and 45 (1930), 87–111; "Peaceful Picketing in New York, 1912–1926," *Yale LJ,* 36 (1926–27), 557–564; Wagner in Schlesinger v. Quinto, 192 N.Y. Supp. 564 (1922); Texas & New Orleans R.R. v. Brotherhood of Ry. Clerks, 281 U.S. 548 (1930); Edward Berman, "The Supreme Court Moves to the Left," *World Tomorrow,* 13 (1930), 411–412; Interborough v. Green, 227 N.Y. Supp. 258, 247 N.Y. 65 (1928).

94. On the IWW, "Equality before the Law," *Ind,* 108 (1922), 30–31; Edwin E. Witte, "Labor's Resort to Injunctions," *Yale LJ,* 39 (1929–39), 374–387; Alpheus T. Mason, "Labor Turns to the Injunction," *NAR,* 231 (1931), 246–250.

95. Felix Frankfurter and Nathan Greene, *The Labor Injunction* (New York, 1930), pp. 197–198; Thomas J. Donnelly, "Ohio's First Anti-Yellow-Dog Contract Law," *American Federationist,* 38 (1931), 929–935.

96. Ralph E. Flanders, "The Tariff and Social Control," *Atl,* 148 (1931), 384.

97. Edwin E. Witte, "The Federal Anti-Injunction Bill," *Minnesota Law Review,* 16 (1931–32), 638–658; P. F. Brissenden, "The Labor Injunction," *Pol Sci Q,* 48 (1933), 413–450.

98. H. A. Marquand, "American Trade Unionism and the Roosevelt Regime," *Political Quarterly,* 4 (1933), 482–503; "Labor Injunctions since the NRA," *Yale LJ,* 43 (1933–34), 625–640.

99. William W. Stafford, "Disputes within Trade Unions," *Yale LJ,* 45 (1935–36), 1248–71; Henry C. Johnson, "An Analysis of the Present Legal Status of the Collective Bargaining Agreement," *Notre Dame Lawyer,* 10 (1934–35), 413–443; Tomlins, *State and Unions,* pts. 2, 3.

7. Regulating the Countryside

1. Charles D. Warner, *My Summer in a Garden* (Boston, 1871), p. 5.

2. Murray R. Benedict, *Farm Policies of the United States, 1790–1950* (New York, 1953), chap. 7; Richard Hofstadter, *The Age of Reform: From Bryan to F. D. R.* (New York, 1955), chap. 3; Charles W. Dahlinger, *The New Agrarianism* (New York, 1913). See also Grant McConnell, *The Decline of Agrarian Democracy* (Berkeley, 1953).

3. Thomas C. Jackson, *The Agricultural Holdings Acts, 1908–14,* 3d ed. (London, 1917), p. 3 ; C. R. Fay, "Small Holdings and Agricultural Co-operation in England," *Q J Ec,* 24 (1909–10), 499–514; Peter Clarke, *Liberals and Social Democrats* (Cambridge, 1978), p. 162.

4. "The State and Agriculture," *Saturday Review* (GB), 95 (1903), 579–580.

5. Sir Horace Plunkitt, "Better Farming, Better Business, Better Living," *Outlook,* 94 (1910), 497; Edward Porritt, "Agricultural Education in the United States," *Quarterly Review,* 228 (1917), 315–332; Carl Vrooman, "The Agricultural Revolution," *Century Magazine,* 93 (1916–17), 111–123.

6. Wilson quoted in Benedict, *Farm Policies*, p. 140; ibid., pp. 112–156; Myron T. Herrick, "Farmers and the Government," *Nation*, 105 (1917), 49–51; Robert J. Bulkley, "The Federal Farm Loan Act," *J Pol Ec*, 25 (1917), 129–147.

7. Benjamin H. Hibbard, *Effects of the War upon Agriculture in the United States and Great Britain* (New York, 1919), pt. 1; James L. Guth, "Herbert Hoover, the U.S. Food Administration, and the Dairy Industry, 1917–1918," *Bus Hist R*, 55 (1981), 170–187.

8. E. H. Whetham, "The Agriculture Act, 1920, and Its Repeal—the 'Great Betrayal,'" *Agricultural History*, 22 (1974), 36–49; Christopher Turner, "Politicians and Agriculture," *Nineteenth Century*, 98 (1925), 657–665; "The Difficulties of Agricultural Cooperation," *New Statesman*, 22 (1923–24), 751–752.

9. Henry Rew, "The Agricultural Problem and Its Solution," *Nineteenth Century*, 102 (1927), 465–478; David Rolf, "The Politics of Agriculture: Farmers' Organizations and Parliamentary Representation in Herefordshire, 1909–1922," *Midland History*, 2 (1974), 168–186.

10. Kenyon Butterfield, *The Farmer and the New Day* (New York, 1919); on cotton acreage reduction, Henry L. Moore, "Empirical Laws of Demand and Supply and the Flexibility of Prices," *Pol Sci Q*, 34 (1919), 546–567; Gilbert C. Fite, *George Peek and the Fight for Farm Parity* (Oklahoma City, 1954), p. 14; Charles W. Holman, "The Cure for Rural Unrest," *Outlook*, 129 (1921), 566–567.

11. G. O. Virtue, "Legislation for the Farmers: Packers and Grain Exchanges," *Q J Ec*, 37 (1922–23), 703; G. C. Henderson, "The Agricultural Credits Act of 1923," *Q J Ec*, 37 (1922–23), 518–522; A. G. Black, "The Provision for Agricultural Credit in the United States," *Q J Ec*, 43 (1928–29), 94–131; Board of Trade v. Olsen, 261 U.S. 1 (1923); Stafford v. Wallace, 258 U.S. 495 (1922).

12. Ralph H. Gabriel, "The Farmer in the Commonwealth," *NAR*, 213 (1921), 585; Gustavus Myers, "The Organized Farmer Steps Forth," *Century Magazine*, 103 (1921–22), 20–27; McConnell, *Decline of Agrarian Democracy*, chap. 5.

13. John K. Barnes, "The Man Who Runs the Farm Bloc," *World's Work*, 45 (1922–23), 51–59; John D. Black, "The McNary-Haugen Movement," *American Economic Review*, 18 (1928), 405–427; Fite, *George Peek*, chaps. 11–12.

14. Lawrence Goodwyn, *Democratic Promise: The Populist Movement in America* (New York, 1976); Frank Parsons, "Co-operative Undertakings in Europe and America," *Arena*, 30 (1903), 159–167.

15. James A. Everitt, "The New Farmers' Movement," *Ind*, 62 (1907), 1221; Paul R. Fossum, *The Agrarian Movement in North Dakota* (Baltimore, 1925), pp. 80–88; McConnell, *Decline of Agrarian Democracy*, pp. 41–42; Benedict, *Farm Policies*, pp. 134–135.

16. "Kentucky's Anarchists," *Ind*, 64 (1908), 646; Anna Youngman, "The Tobacco Pools of Kentucky and Tennessee," *J Pol Ec*, 18 (1910), 34–49; John L. Mathews, "Agrarian Pooling in Kentucky," *Charities*, 20 (1908), 192–

196; idem, "The Farmers' Union and the Tobacco Pool," *Atl*, 102 (1908), 482–491, 192–196; Everitt, "New Farmers' Movement," pp. 1197–99; Charles V. Tevis, "A Ku-Klux Klan of To-day: The Red Record of Kentucky's 'Night Riders,'" *Harper's Weekly*, 52 (Feb. 8, 1908), 14–16, 32.

17. Fred W. Powell, "Co-operative Marketing of California Fresh Fruit," *Q J Ec*, 24 (1909–10), 417. See also Edwin G. Nourse, *The Legal Status of Agricultural Co-operation* (New York, 1927), chaps. 3, 4.

18. Carl C. Plehn, "The State Market Commission of California," *American Economic Review*, 8 (1918), 1–27; Grace Larsen, "A Progressive in Agriculture: Harris Weinstock," *Agricultural History*, 32 (1958), 187–193; Nourse, *Legal Status*, chap. 5.

19. Grace H. Larsen and Henry R. Erdman, "Aaron Sapiro: Genius of Farm Co-operative Promotion," *Mississippi Valley Historical Review*, 49 (1962), 242–268. See also Stanley M. Arndt, "The Law of California Co-operative Marketing Associations," *Cal LR*, 8 (1919–20), 281–299, 384–403, and 9 (1920–21), 44–55; Theodore R. Meyer, "The Law of Co-operative Marketing," *Cal LR*, 15 (1927), 85–112; Mansel G. Blackford, *The Politics of Business in California, 1890–1920* (Columbia, Mo., 1977), chap. 2.

20. Aaron Sapiro, "The Law of Cooperative Marketing," *Kentucky Law Journal*, 15 (1926), 12, 14; idem, "True Farmer Cooperation," *World's Work*, 46 (1923), 84–96.

21. Robert H. Montgomery, *The Cooperative Pattern in Cotton* (New York, 1929), pp. 106–111. On the co-op movement in western Canada, see C. R. Fay, "The Canadian Wheat Pools," *Economic Journal*, 35 (1925), 26–29; and Ian MacPherson, "Selected Borrowings: The American Impact upon the Prairie Co-operative Movement, 1920–39," *Canadian Review of American Studies*, 10 (1979), 137–151.

22. E. C. Lindeman, "Sapiro, the Spectacular," *New Republic*, 50 (1927), 217; Larsen and Erdman, "Aaron Sapiro," p. 265; Walton H. Hamilton, "Judicial Tolerance of Farmers' Cooperatives," *Yale LJ*, 38 (1928–29), 951; Gerard C. Henderson, "Cooperative Marketing Associations," *Col LR*, 23 (1923), 112; John K. Barnes, "An Even Break for the Farmer," *World's Work*, 44 (1922), 612–622.

23. James L. Guth, "Farmer Monopolies, Cooperatives, and the Intent of Congress: Origins of the Capper-Volstead Act," *Agricultural History*, 56 (1982), 67–82; Nourse, *Legal Status*, chap 11.

24. Liberty Warehouse Co. v. Burley Tobacco Growers Assn., 276 U.S. 71 (1928); Abe D. Waldauer, "The Tobacco Growers Association Case," *Tennessee Law Review*, 5 (1926–27), 123–132.

25. Larsen and Erdman, "Aaron Sapiro," p. 265; William R. Camp, "Agricultural Pools in Relation to Regulating the Movement and Price of Commodities," *Proceedings of the Academy of Political Science*, 11 (1926), 735–788; R. Fay, "The Farmers and the Grain Trade in the United States: An Interpretation of the Present Pooling Movement," *Economic Journal*, 35 (1925), 11–12; "Sapiro and Ford," *Outlook*, 145 (1927), 388.

26. Frost v. Corporation Commission, 278 U.S. 515 (1929). See also John Hanna, "Cooperative Associations and the Public," *Mich LR*, 29 (1930–

31), 148–190; Milton J. Keegan, "Power of Agricultural Co-Operative Associations to Limit Production," *Mich LR*, 26 (1927–28), 648–673; Matthew O. Tobriner, "The Constitutionality of Cooperative Marketing Statutes," *Cal LR*, 17 (1928), 20–34.

27. New State Ice Co. v. Liebmann, 285 U.S. 262, 277 (1932); Ernest Hopkins, "Farm Relief or Bank Relief?" *New Republic*, 61 (1929), 134–136; A. C. Hoffman, "After Two Years of Farm Relief," *New Republic*, 67 (1931), 168–170; "Competition and Monopoly under the Agricultural Marketing Act," *Yale LJ*, 41 (1932), 888–894.

28. Paul J. Kern, "Federal Farm Legislation: A Factual Appraisal," *Col LR*, 33 (1933), 984–1012; Farnsworth L. Jennings and Robert C. Sullivan, "Legal Planning for Agriculture," *Yale LJ*, 42 (1932–33), 878–918.

29. On tenantry, Howard A. Turner, "Farm Tenancy Distribution and Trends in the United States," *Law and Contemporary Problems*, 4 (1937), 424–433; A. B. Book, "A Note on the Legal Status of Share-Tenants and Share-Croppers in the South," ibid., pp. 539–545; Clarence J. Foreman, *Rent Liens and Public Welfare* (New York, 1932); Isaacs' Trustee v. Hobbs, 282 U.S. 734 (1931).

30. H. Don Scott, "Governmental Action on Farm Mortgage Foreclosures," *George Washington Law Review*, 1 (1932–33), 500–507; Clifford C. Hynning, "Constitutionality of Moratory Legislation," *Chicago-Kent Law Review*, 12 (1933–34), 182–211; Home Building and Loan Association v. Blaisdell, 290 U.S. 398 (1934).

31. Theodore Roosevelt, *Autobiography* (New York, 1913), chaps. 9, 11; D. Jerome Tweton, "Theodore Roosevelt and Land Law Reform," *Mid-America*, 49 (1967), 44–54. On the aesthetic and use strands of conservationism see, respectively, Roderick Nash, *Wilderness and the American Mind* (New Haven, 1967); and Samuel P. Hays, *Conservation and the Gospel of Efficiency* (Cambridge, Mass., 1959). See also "Conservation of Natural Resources," *Annals*, 33, no. 3 (1909); C. R. Van Hise, *The Conservation of Our Natural Resources* (New York, 1910).

32. Clayton Ellsworth, "Theodore Roosevelt's Country Life Commission," *Agricultural History*, 34 (1960), 155–172; "Country Life," *Annals*, 40 (1912); William L. Bowers, "Country-Life Reform, 1900–1920: A Neglected Aspect of Progressive Era History," *Agricultural History*, 45 (1971), 211–221.

33. Morton Keller, *Affairs of State: Public Life in Late Nineteenth Century America* (Cambridge, Mass., 1977), p. 393.

34. "A Waning Nuisance," *Saturday Evening Post*, Jan. 24, 1925, p. 24; Chauncy S. Goodrich, "Billboard Regulation and the Aesthetic Viewpoint with Reference to California Highways," *Cal LR*, 17 (1928–29), 121n; *Spectator*, 135 (1925), 440.

35. "The National Trust and Public Amenities," *Quarterly Review*, 214 (1911), 159, 157; Timothy O'Riordan, "Public Interest Environmental Groups in the United States and Britain," *Journal of American Studies*, 13 (1979), 409–438.

36. Donald Fleming, "Roots of the New Conservation Movement," *Perspectives in American History*, 6 (1972), 7–91; John R. Ross, "Man over Nature: Origins of the Conservation Movement," *American Studies*, 16 (1975), 49–62; Mary Douglas, "Purity and Danger Revisited," *Times Literary Supplement*, Sept. 19, 1980, pp. 1045–46.

37. Albert E. Cowdrey, "Pioneering Environmental Law: The Army Corps of Engineers and the Refuse Act," *Pacific Historical Review*, 44 (1975), 331–349.

38. B. N. Baker, "Conservation, Our Nation's New Patriotism," *World Today*, 17 (1909), 1174–75; Lane quoted in William E. Colby, "The New Public Land Policy with Special Reference to Oil Lands," *Cal LR*, 3 (1915), 270n; on Newell, Donald J. Pisani, "Reclamation and Social Engineering in the Progressive Era," *Agricultural History*, 57 (1983), 46–63. See also George L. Knapp, "The Other Side of Conservation," *NAR*, 191 (1910), 468–481; J. R. McKee, "The Public and the Conservation Policy," *NAR*, 192 (1910), 493–503.

39. James Penick, Jr., *Progressive Politics and Conservation: The Ballinger-Pinchot Affair* (Chicago, 1968); Elmo R. Richardson, *The Politics of Conservation: Crusades and Controversies, 1897–1913* (Berkeley, 1962). See also Leslie M. Scott, "Why East and West Differ on the Conservation Problem," *Ind*, 68 (1910), 697–699.

40. J. Leonard Bates, "Fulfilling American Democracy: The Conservation Movement, 1907 to 1921," *Mississippi Valley Historical Review*, 44 (1957), 29–57.

41. James P. Kimball, "Aggressive Forest Reservation," *NAR*, 177 (1903), 210; Sherry H. Olson, *The Depletion Myth* (Cambridge, Mass., 1971); Mansel G. Blackford, *The Politics of Business in California, 1890–1920* (Columbus, 1977), chap. 4.

42. Holmes in Hudson County Water Co. v. McCarter, 209 U.S. 349, 355 (1908); *Lit Dig*, 47 (1913), 1103–04; O. L. Waller, "Right of State to Regulate Distribution of Water Rights," *Am LR*, 49 (1915), 577–592. See also Samuel C. Weil, "Public Control of Irrigation," *Col LR*, 10 (1910), 506–519; Moses Lasky, "From Prior Appropriation to Economic Distribution of Water by the State—Via Irrigation Administration," *Rocky Mountain Law Review*, 1 (1928–29), 161–216, 238–270, and 2 (1929–30), 35–58; Dwight Williams, "The Power of the State to Control the Use of Its Natural Resources," *Minnesota Law Review*, 11 (1926–27), 139–140; Arthur Maass and Hiller B. Zobel, "Anglo-American Water Law: Who Appropriated the Riparian Doctrine?" *Public Policy*, 10 (1960), 109–156; Ira G. Clark, "The Elephant Butte Controversy: A Chapter in the Emergence of Federal Water Law," *Journal of American History*, 61 (1975), 1006–33.

43. Donald J. Pisani, "Water Law Reform in California, 1910–1913," *Agricultural History*, 54 (1980), 295–317; Clesson S. Kinney, "Beneficial Use as the Basis for Greater Uniformity of State Laws Governing Water," *Cent LJ*, 77 (1913), 3–9.

44. Phelan quoted in Kendrick A. Clements, "Politics and the Park: San Fran-

cisco's Fight for Hetch Hetchy, 1908–1913," *Pacific Historical Review,* 48 (1979), 185; "The Hetch Hetchy Valley," *Nation,* 88 (1908), 60–61; William L. Kahrl, "The Politics of California Water: Owens Valley and the Los Angeles Aqueduct, 1900–1927," *California Historical Quarterly,* 55 (1976), 2–25, 98–121.

45. John A. Fairlie, "Public Regulation of Water Power in the United States and Europe," *Mich LR,* 9 (1911), 463–483; W. A. Coutts, "Eminent Domain under the Early Mill Acts and Modern Electrical and Water Power Acts," *Cent LJ,* 68 (1909), 303–311.

46. Judson C. Welliver, "The National Water Power Trust," *McClure's Magazine,* 33 (1909), 35–39; Rome G. Brown, "The Conservation of Water-Powers," *Harv LR,* 26 (1912–13), 601–630; idem, "The Water-Power Problem in the United States,"*Yale LJ,* 24 (1914–15), 12–33; Harley W. Nehf, "The Concentration of Water Powers," *J Pol Ec,* 24 (1916), 775–793; F. Darlington, "Water Power Laws and Their Relation to Industry and Progress," *Engineering Magazine,* 50 (1916), 722–733. See also Harry W. Laidler, "The Water-Power Fight in California," *Nation,* 121 (1925), 508–510.

47. Robert E. Cushman, *The Independent Regulatory Commissions* (New York, 1941), pp. 275–294.

48. L. Ward Bannister, "The Colorado River Compact," *Cornell LQ,* 9 (1924), 388–401; Wayne C. Williams, "The Colorado River and the Constitution," *ABA Journal,* 12 (1926), 839–841; Russell D. Niles, "Legal Background of the Colorado River Controversy," *Rocky Mountain Law Review,* 1 (1929–30), 73–101.

49. Arizona v. California, 283 U.S. 423 (1931). See also Norris Hundley, Jr., *Water and the West* (Berkeley, 1975).

50. Gardner S. Williams, "The Sanitary District of Chicago in the Supreme Court of the United States," *Mich LR,* 28 (1929–30), 1–25; Cornelius Lynde, "The Controversy concerning the Diversion of Water from Lake Michigan by the Sanitary District of Chicago," *Illinois Law Review,* 25 (1930–31), 243–266; Missouri v. Illinois, 200 U.S. 518 (1903).

51. United States v. Sanitary District, 266 U.S. 405 (1925), 278 U.S. 367 (1929), 281 U.S. 179 (1930).

52. Connecticut v. Mass., 282 U.S. 660 (1931); New Jersey v. New York, 283 U.S. 336 (1931).

53. Ernest C. Carman, "Is There a New Era in the Law of Interstate Waters?" *Southern California Law Review,* 5 (1931–32), 25–35; Samuel C. Wiel, "Administrative Finality," *Harv LR,* 38 (1924–25), 447–481.

54. John S. Wise, "The Game Law Problem," *Outing,* 38 (1901), 46–50; Geer v. Connecticut, 161 U.S. 519 (1896).

55. Missouri v. Holland, 252 U.S. 416 (1920).

56. Edward S. Corwin, "Game Protection and the Constitution," *Mich LR,* 14 (1915–16), 613–625; John C. Phillips, "The Missouri Campaign," *Outing,* 69 (1916), 77–78; Michael J. Hickey and Noel Sargent, "State Legislation on Industrial Pollution of Streams," *Cent LJ,* 94 (1930), 205–211, 221–229. See also Thomas A. Lund, *American Wildlife Law* (Berkeley, 1980).

57. Westmoreland & Cambria Gas and Oil Co. v. DeWitt, 130 Pa. 235 (1889). See also Peoples Gas and Oil Co. v. Tyner, 131 Ind. 277 (1892).

58. Parish Fork Oil Co. v. Bridgewater Gas Co., 51 W. Va. 583 (1902).

59. Ohio Oil Co. v. Indiana, 177 U.S. 190 (1900); Oklahoma v. Kansas Natural Gas Co., 221 U.S. 229 (1911); "The Legal Status of Oil and Natural Gas," *Cent LJ*, 60 (1905), 465–468.

60. "Regulating the Use of Subterranean Waters and Gases under the Police Power," *Cent LJ*, 68 (1909), 1–2. See also W. L. Summers, "Property in Oil and Gas," *Yale LJ*, 29 (1919–20), 175–187; James A. Veasey, "The Law of Oil and Gas," *Mich LR*, 18 (1919–20), 445–469, 652–668, 749–773; and 19 (1920–21), 161–189; Donald H. Ford, "Controlling the Production of Oil," *Mich LR*, 30 (1931–32), 1170–92.

61. United States v. Midwest Oil, 236 U.S. 458 (1915); William E. Colby, "The New Public Land Policy with Special Reference to Oil Lands," *Cal LR*, 3 (1915), 272–291.

62. J. Leonard Bates, *The Origins of Teapot Dome: Progressives, Parties, and Petroleum, 1909–1921* (Urbana, 1963); Gary D. Libecap, "The Political Allocation of Mineral Rights: A Re-Evaluation of Teapot Dome," *Journal of Economic History*, 44 (1984), 381–391; Burl Noggle, *Teapot Dome* (Baton Rouge, 1962); Gerald Nash, *United States Oil Policy, 1890–1964* (Pittsburgh, 1968), chap. 4.

63. "The World Race for Oil," *Lit Dig*, 65 (June 12, 1920), 23–24; Gregory Mason, "America's Empty Oil Barrel," *Outlook*, 124 (1920), 549–550; William Hard, "Oil-Burning Politics," *Nation*, 116 (1923), 167–169; E. H. Davenport and Sidney R. Cooke, *The Oil Trusts and Anglo-American Relations* (New York, 1924).

64. "Dear Old Private Initiative," *Nation*, 123 (1926), 390; Ralph Arnold, "Oil: The Menaced Resource," *New Republic*, 42 (1925), 176–178.

65. James J. Hayden, *Federal Regulation of the Production of Oil* (Washington, D.C., 1929), p. 102; "A Glut of Oil," *Nation*, 124 (1927), 574; *Lit Dig*, 93 (May 28, 1927), 5–7; John Ise, *The U.S. Oil Policy* (New Haven, 1928), p. 453; Nash, *Oil Policy*, chap. 5.

66. Hubert Work, "Conservation's Need for Legal Advice," *ABA Reporter*, 52 (1927), 566; Edward M. Barrows, "Oil: An Industry Drowning in a Flood of Laws," *American Monthly Review of Reviews*, 84 (1931), 58–63; Leonard M. Logan, Jr., *Stabilization of the Petroleum Industry* (Norman, 1930).

67. Bandini Petroleum Co. v. Superior Court, 284 U.S. 8 (1931). See also Nash, *Oil Policy*, chap. 6.

68. Donald Ford, "Controlling the Production of Oil," *Mich LR*, 30 (1931–32), 1196; Charles E. G. Haglund, "The New Conservation Movement with Respect to Petroleum," *Kentucky Law Journal*, 22 (1933–34), 543–581.

69. Ford, "Controlling Production," p. 1196; *Lit Dig*, 110 (Aug. 15, 1931), 6; ibid. (August. 29, 1931), pp. 3–4; "Legislative Stabilization of the Oil Industry," *Col LR*, 31 (1931), 1170–83; J. Howard Marshall and Norman L. Meyers, "Legal Planning of Petroleum Production," *Yale LJ*, 41 (1931–32), 33–39, 52–54.

70. Champlin Refining Co. v. Corporation Commission, 286 U.S. 210 (1932); Sterling v. Constantin, 287 U.S. 378 (1932); Andrew A. Bruce, "The Oil Cases and the Public Interest," *ABA Journal,* 19 (1933), 82–86, 168–172.

8. Regulating the City

1. Avner Offer, *Property and Politics, 1870–1914: Landownership, Law, Ideology, and Urban Development in England* (Cambridge, 1981). See also J. E. Hogg, "The Present Complexity of Land Law, and Its Remedy," *London Quarterly Review,* 20 (1904), 292–299.
2. Offer, *Property and Politics,* pt. 1; J. E. Hogg, "The Breakdown of the Land Transfer Acts System in England," *London Quarterly Review,* 20 (1904), 74–80.
3. R. R. A. Walker, "The English Property Legislation of 1922–6," *J Comp Leg,* 3d ser., 10 (1929), 1–13, 173–185; John J. Johnson, "The Reform of Real Property Law in England," *Col LR,* 25 (1925), 609–627; W. S. Holdsworth, "The Reform of the Land Law: An Historical Retrospect," *London Quarterly Review,* 42 (1926), 158–183; H. J. Randall, "The Spirit of the New Property Legislation," *Edinburgh Review,* 246 (1927), 125–133.
4. Percy Bordwell, "English Property Reform and Its American Aspects," *Yale LJ,* 37 (1927–28), 1; Frederick B. McCall, "The Torrens System—After Thirty-Five Years," *North Carolina Law Review,* 10 (1931–32), 330; Morton Keller, *Affairs of State: Public Life in Late Nineteenth Century America* (Cambridge, Mass., 1977), p. 392; Tyler v. Judges, 179 U.S. 405 (1900).
5. Dorr Viale, "The Problem of Land Titles," *Pol Sci Q,* 44 (1929), 421–434.
6. Arthur Bassin, *The British Government in Housing: A Study of Housing in England and Wales under the Housing Acts of 1861–1935* (Washington, D.C., 1937); W. Ivor Jennings, "Courts and Administrative Law—The Experience of English Housing Legislation," *Harv LR,* 49 (1936), 426–454. See also Richard L. Reiss, *British and American Housing* (New York, 1937); R. Vladimir Steffel, "The Slum Question: The London County Council and Decent Dwellings for the Working Class, 1880–1914," *Albion,* 5 (1973), 314–325; for a comparative survey, Hollis Godfrey, "The Problem of City Housing," *Atl,* 105 (1910), 404–413, 548–558.
7. George M. Koher, *The History and Development of the Housing Movement in the City of Washington, D.C.,* 3d ed. (Washington, D.C., 1927); Lawrence Friedman and Michael J. Spector, "Tenement House Legislation in Wisconsin: Reform and Reaction," *American Journal of Legal History,* 9 (1965), 41–63.
8. Roy Lubove, "Lawrence Veiller and the New York State Tenement House Commission of 1900," *Mississippi Valley Historical Review,* 47 (1961), 659–677.
9. Thomas L. Phillpott, *The Slum and the Ghetto: Neighborhood Deterioration and Middle-Class Reform, Chicago, 1890–1930* (New York, 1978), pp. 101–103. See also Lawrence M. Friedman, *Government and Housing: A Century of Frustration* (Chicago, 1968), chap. 2; Roy Lubove, *The Pro-*

gressives and the Slums (Pittsburgh, 1962); Anthony Jackson, *A Place Called Home: A History of Low-Cost Housing in Manhattan* (Cambridge, Mass., 1976), chap. 10.

10. "Twenty-one—and Half-Starved," *Survey,* 51 (1923–24), 384.

11. Archibald A. Hill, "The Rental Agitation on the East Side," *Charities,* 12 (1904), 396–398; Jackson, *A Place Called Home,* chap. 11.

12. Emily W. Dinwiddie, "The Rent Strike In New York," *Charities,* 19 (1907–08), 1312; William Mailly, "The New York Rent Strike," *Ind,* 64 (1908), 148–152; Victor Rousseau, "'Low Rent or No Rent': The Tenement Dwellers' Rebellion in New York," *Harper's Weekly,* 52 (Jan. 25, 1908), 16–17.

13. Grimmer v. Tenement House Department, 97 N.E. 884 (N.Y., 1912); "Another Bad Decision," *Survey,* 27 (1911–12), 1895–96; Friedman, *Government and Housing,* p. 38.

14. Robert G. Barrows, "Beyond the Tenement: Patterns of American Urban Housing, 1870–1930," *Journal of Urban History,* 9 (1983), 402; Charles B. Ball, "The New Tenement in Chicago," *Charities,* 17 (1906–07), 90–96; on Philadelphia, H. L. Parrish, "One Million People in Small Houses— Philadelphia," *Survey,* 26 (1911), 229–232.

15. Rufus E. Miles, "The Boston Housing Situation," *Survey,* 26 (1911), 96–99; Gabriell Farrell, "Housing in Massachusetts Towns," *American City,* 15 (1916), 265–272.

16. *Opinion of the Justices,* 211 Mass. 632 (1912); "Good Housing and Legal Restraints," *Chautauquan Magazine,* 68 (1912), 253–254.

17. "The State a Landlord by Its Own Vote," *Survey,* 35 (1915–16), 228; Jackson, *A Place Called Home,* p. 171.

18. "Uncle Sam's Wooden Cities," *Lit Dig,* 60 (Feb. 22, 1919), 28–29; Curtice N. Hitchcock, "The War Housing Program and Its Future," *J Pol Ec,* 27 (1919), 241–279.

19. George F. Kearney, "How Philadelphia Tenants Curbed the Landlords," *Forum,* 63 (1920), 90–99; Charles W. Collins, "The Regulation of Rentals during the War Period," *J Pol Ec,* 28 (1920), 1–45.

20. *Outlook,* 126 (1920), 222–223; George Soule, "The Building Scandal," *Nation,* 111 (1920), 560–561.

21. Samuel M. Lindsay, *Some Economic Aspects of the Recent Emergency Housing Legislation in New York* (New York, 1924), pp. 5, 57, 61; Harold G. Aron, "The New York Landlord and Tenant Laws of 1920," *Cornell LQ,* 6 (1920), 1–35.

22. W. F. Dodd, "Housing Legislation in Illinois," *Survey,* 47 (1921–22), 115; on Wisconsin, *American Political Science Review,* 14 (1920), 696–700; on New York, Jackson, *A Place Called Home,* pp. 170, 172; see also Henry R. Brigham, "How to Meet the Housing Situation," *Atl,* 127 (1921), 404–413.

23. Alan W. Boyd, "Rent Regulation under the Police Power," *Mich LR,* 19 (1920–21), 606; Durham Realty Co. v. La Fetra, 230 N.Y. 429 (1921); "Constitutionality of the New York Emergency Housing Laws," *Harv LR,* 34 (1920–21), 426–430. See also Charles K. Burdick, "Constitutionality of the New York Rent Laws," *Cornell LQ,* 6 (1920–21), 310–317.

24. McKenna in Block v. Hirsch, 156 U.S. 135, 162–163 (1921); "The President vs. the Landlords," *Outlook*, 139 (1925), 208. See also Walter F. Dodd and Carl H. Zeiss, "Rent Regulation and Housing Problems," *ABA Journal*, 7 (1921), 5–12; Walter F. Dodd, "Constitutionality of Emergency Rental Regulation," *West Virginia Law Review*, 28 (1921–22), 125–132; F. R Aumann, "Some Constitutional Aspects of War Rent Regulation Measures," *Kentucky Law Journal*, 18 (1929–30), 354–372.

25. Ernest M. Fisher, "Housing Legislation and Housing Policy in the United States," *Mich LR*, 31 (1932–33), 332; "Municipal Tax Exemption Stimulates Home Building," *American City*, 26 (1922), 10; on Smith, " 'Paternalism'—or Slums?" *New Republic*, 45 (1926), 230–231; *Lit Dig*, 88 (March 13, 1926), 5–7.

26. Jackson, *A Place Called Home*, chap. 13; Lawson Purdy, "New York's New Dwellings Bill," *Survey*, 59 (1927–28), 615–617; Raymond H. Harkrider, "Tort Liability of a Landlord," *Mich LR*, 26 (1927–28), 260–289, 383–414, 531–544; William H. Lloyd, "The Disturbed Tenant—A Phase of Constructive Eviction," *U Pa LR*, 79 (1930–31), 727. See also Gerald Fetner, "Public Power and Professional Responsibility: Julius Henry Cohen and the Origins of Public Authority," *American Journal of Legal History*, 21 (1977), 15–39.

27. William L. Prosser, "The Minnesota Mortgage Moratorium," *Southern California Law Review*, 7 (1934), 368; Home Building and Loan Association v. Blaisdell, 290 U.S. 398 (1934).

28. "Judicial and Legislative Aid for the Mortgage Debtor," *U Pa LR*, 82 (1933–34), 261–269; *HS*, p. 651; "Mortgage Relief during the Depression," *Harv LR*, 47 (1933), 299–307.

29. Murray Seasongood, Lawrence Veiller, and Newman Baker, "Some Legal Aspects of the Problem of Blighted Areas and Slums," *American City*, 46 (1932), 96–98.

30. Fisher, "Housing Legislation," pp. 344–345; idem, "Federal Housing and Home Loan Legislation and Its Consequences," *Mich LR*, 32 (1933–34), 946–947.

31. Fisher, "Federal Housing," pp. 948–967; Harold Robinson, "Some Problems Confronting the Public Works Emergency Housing Corporation," *Cornell LQ*, 19 (1933–34), 548–579; Bennett D. Brown, "The Power of Eminent Domain in Slum-Clearance and Low-Cost Housing Projects," *St. John's Law Review*, 10 (1936), 280–291; United States v. Certain Lands in the City of Louisville, 78 Fed. 684 (6th Cir., 1935); Jackson, *A Place Called Home*, p. 205.

32. E. H. Foley, Jr., "Legal Aspects of Low Rent Housing in New York," *Fordham Law Review*, 6 (1937), 1–17; William Karlin, "New York Slum Clearance and the Law," *Pol Sci Q*, 52 (1937), 241–258; New York City Housing Authority v. Muller, 270 N.Y. 333 (1936).

33. "Validity of State Condemnation for Low-Cost Housing," *Yale LJ*, 45 (1936), 1519–23.

34. "City Congestion and City Planning," *Outlook*, 92 (1909), 341; Clinton R. Woodruff, "City Planning in America," *Atl*, 101 (1908), 721–727.

35. Charles A. Beard, "Conflicts in City Planning," *Yale Review,* 17 (1927), 67. See also Mel Scott, *American City Planning since 1890* (Berkeley, 1969), chap. 2; John W. Reps, *The Making of Urban America: A History of City Planning in the United States* (Princeton, 1965), chap. 18.

36. Norwood v. Baker, 172 U.S. 269 (1899); "The Fourteenth Amendment and Special Assessments on Real Estate," *Yale LJ,* 11 (1901–02), 210–212; Robert L. McWilliams, "The Malicious Use of One's Property," *Cent LJ,* 67 (1908), 23–28; H. A. de Colyar, "Notes on the Easement of Light in England and Elsewhere," *J Compar Leg,* 7 (1906), 298–322.

37. "Unsightly Advertising," *Law Journal,* 18 (1929), 21; "A Law to Suppress Ugliness," *Outlook,* 86 (1907), 492–493; W. J. Barnard Byles, "Foreign Law and the Control of Advertisements in Public Places," *J Compar Leg,* 7 (1906), 323–329.

38. Commonwealth v. Boston Advertising Co., 74 N.E. 601, 602–603 (Mass., 1905).

39. Robert E. Edgar, "Legal Aspect of Municipal Aesthetics," *Case & Comment,* 18 (1911), 362; Passaic v. Paterson Bill Posting Co., 62 Atl. 267, 268 (N.J., 1905). See also Wilbur Larremore, "Public Aesthetics," *Harv LR,* 20 (1906–07), 35–45; Newman F. Baker, "Municipal Aesthetics and the Law," *Illinois Law Review,* 20 (1925–26), 546–572.

40. "Billboards versus Beauty," *Chautauquan Magazine,* 51 (1908), 19–81; Charles M. Robinson, "The Abuses of Public Advertising," *Atl,* 93 (1904), 289–299; Harry F. Lake, "The Billboard Nuisance," *American City,* 3 (1910), 219–224.

41. Gunning v. St. Louis, 137 S.W. 929, 942 (Mo., 1911); Gunning v. Kansas City, 144 S.W. 1099, 1102 (Mo., 1912).

42. George K. Gardner, "The Massachusetts Billboard Decision," *Harv LR,* 49 (1936), 902; General Outdoor Advertising Co. v. Dept. of Public Works, 193 N.E. 799 (Mass., 1935).

43. Frank B. Williams, *The Law of City Planning and Zoning* (New York, 1922), pp. 397–399; "Zoning in the United States," *Annals,* 155, pt. 2 (1931), 1–15.

44. Welch v. Swasey, 214 U.S. 91 (1909); Eubank v. Richmond, 226 U.S. 137 (1912); Howard L. McBain, "Law-Making by Property Owners," *Pol Sci Q,* 36 (1921), 617–641.

45. Newman F. Baker, "Zoning Ordinances," *Iowa Law Review,* 11 (1925–26), 172–173; "Zoning in the United States," pp. 15–33; Lawrence Veiller, "Protecting Residential Districts," *American City,* 10 (1914), 525–529.

46. George B. Ford, "City Planning by Coercion or Legislation," *American City,* 14 (1916), 328–333; Robert H. Whitten, "The Building Zone Plan of New York City," *National Municipal Review,* 6 (1916), 325–326; Lubove, *Progressives and Slums,* 229–39, 238–45.

47. Gerald Wellesley, "British and American Cities Compared," *Spectator,* 135 (1925), 227; "Zoning Progress in the United States," *Sci Am,* 128 (1923), 390; Anne Lloyd, "Pittsburgh's 1923 Zoning Ordinance," *Western Pennsylvania Historical Magazine,* 57 (1974), 289–305; on Portland, Charles H. Chenery, "Removing Social Barriers by Zoning," *Survey,* 44

(1920), 275–278; Newman F. Baker, "The Zoning Board of Appeals," *Minnesota Law Review,* 10 (1926), 277–308; Bradley v. Boston, 255 Mass. 160 (1926).

48. Alfred Bettman, "Constitutionality of Zoning," *Harv LR,* 37 (1923–24), 836; Thomas R. Powell, "The Police Power in American Constitutional Law," *J Comp Leg,* 3d ser., 1 (1919), 168; "The Constitutionality of Zoning Laws," *U Pa LR,* 63 (1923–24), 421–423.

49. Baker, "Municipal Aesthetics," p. 569; Newman F. Baker, "Zoning Legislation," *Cornell LQ,* 11 (1925–26), 170.

50. People v. Friend, 261 Ill. 16, 21 (1913); Ware v. Wichita, 214 Pac. 99 (Kans., 1923); George W. Meuth, "Constitutionality of Zoning Ordinances," *Kentucky Law Journal,* 14 (1925–26), 23–35.

51. Youngstown v. Kahn Building Co., 148 N.E. 842, 844 (Ohio, 1925); "Are Apartments Necessary?" *Survey,* 44 (1920), 412; State v. Houghton, 176 N.W. 158 (Minn., 1920).

52. "Municipal Zoning," *Mich LR,* 19 (1920–21), 196–197; Miller v. Board, 234 Pac. 381, 386–87 (Cal., 1925); Thomas A. Byrne, "The Constitutionality of a General Zoning Ordinance," *Marquette Law Review,* 11 (1926–27), 208–209.

53. State v. Harper, 196 N.W. 451, 455 (Wisc., 1925); "Constitutionality of Zoning Laws," *Harv LR,* 24 (1924), 642.

54. Edward M. Bassett, "Fundamentals of American Zoning," *American City,* 33 (1925), 179; "Constitutionality of Zoning Laws," *U Pa LR,* 63 (1923–24), 423; Eugene McQuillin, "Constitutional Validity of Zoning under the Police Power," *St. Louis Law Review,* 11 (1926), 97–106. See also Newman F. Baker, "The Constitutionality of Zoning Laws," *Illinois Law Review,* 20 (1925), 236.

55. E. F. Roberts, "The Demise of Property Law," *Cornell LQ,* 57 (1971), 11.

56. E. W. Morehouse, "Validity of Comprehensive Zoning," *J Land PU Ec,* 3 (1927), 111–112; Baker quoted in Charles P. Light, Jr., "Aesthetics in Zoning," *Minnesota Law Review,* 14 (1930), 110.

57. Ambler v. Euclid, 297 Fed. 307, 313 (1924); Sutherland in Euclid v. Ambler, 272 U.S. 359, 365, 394 (1926).

58. Edward D. Landels, "Zoning: An Analysis of Its Purposes and Its Legal Sanctions," *ABA Journal,* 17 (1931), 165–167; M. T. Van Hecke, "Zoning Ordinances and Restrictions in Deeds," *Yale LJ,* 37 (1928), 407–409.

59. Robert M. Haig, "Toward an Understanding of the Metropolis," *Q J Ec,* 40 (1925–26), 181; Landels, "Zoning," p. 165; Scott, *American City Planning,* chap. 4.

60. Michael Simpson, "Meliorist versus Insurgent Planners and the Problems of New York, 1921–1941," *Journal of American Studies,* 16 (1982), 220.

9. Regulating Trade, Capital, and Revenue

1. Percy Ashley, *Modern Tariff History: Germany, United States, France,* 3d ed. (New York, 1926); Michael S. Smith, *Tariff Reform in France, 1860–1900: The Politics of Economic Interest* (Ithaca, 1980); Eugene O. Golub,

The Méline Tariff: French Agriculture and Nationalist Economic Policy (1944; reprint, New York, 1968); H. Dietzel, "The German Tariff Controversy," *Q J Ec*, 17 (1902), 365–416; N. I. Stone, "How the Germans Revised their Tariff," *American Monthly Review of Reviews*, 32 (1905), 719–721.

2. PRO, *Cab 37*, 66 (1903), no. 55; Alan Sykes, *Tariff Reform in British Politics, 1903–1913* (Oxford, 1979). For antiprotectionist arguments, see Anthony Pulbrook, "Some Results of Free Trade in England and Protection in the United States," *Westminster Review*, 163 (1905), 126–131; Yves Guyot, *The Comedy of Protection* (London, 1906).

3. Morton Keller, *Affairs of State: Public Life in Late Nineteenth Century America* (Cambridge, Mass., 1977), pp. 376–380. See also Bennett D. Baack and Edward J. Ray, "The Political Economy of Tariff Policy: A Case Study of the United States," *Explorations in Entrepreneurial History*, 20 (1983), 73–90.

4. Frederic A. Ogg, "Europe's Tariff Laws and Policies," *American Monthly Review of Reviews*, 39 (1909), 427–432; Norman Stone, *Europe Transformed, 1878–1919* (Cambridge, Mass., 1984), pp. 104–105.

5. Quoted in W. L. Saunders, "American Tariff Policy Now Shutting the Open Door," *Engineering Magazine*, 21 (1901), 28.

6. F. W. Taussig, "The Present Position of the Doctrine of Free Trade," *American Economic Association Publications*, 3d ser., 6 (1905), 29–65; Edward Atkinson, "Occupations in Their Relation to the Tariff," *Q J Ec*, 17 (1902), 280–292.

7. "Tariff Revision in the United States," *Edinburgh Review*, 209 (1909), 72; Jesse F. Orton, "Tariff Revision and the Consumer," *Ind*, 66 (1909), 524–528; H. E. Miles, "Why Manufacturers Want Tariff Revision," *NAR*, 187 (1908), 34–45; idem, "An Argument for a Permanent Expert Tariff Commission," *Annals*, 32 (1908), 434–439.

8. "The Revision of the United States Tariff," *Edinburgh Review*, 210 (1909), 269–302; F. W. Taussig, "The Tariff Debate of 1909 and the New Tariff Act," *Q J Ec*, 24 (1909–10), 1–38; George M. Fisk, "The Payne-Aldrich Tariff," *Pol Sci Q*, 25 (1910), 35–68.

9. Francis G. Newlands, "A Solution of the Tariff Question," *Ind*, 70 (1911), 334–336; Albert J. Beveridge, "A Permanent Tariff Commission," ibid., pp. 409–428.

10. James D. Whelpley, "The Tariff out of Politics," *Century Magazine*, 66 (1914), 308.

11. Roy G. Blakey, "The Proposed Sugar Tariff," *Pol Sci Q*, 28 (1913), 230–248; "Tariff Rebellion in the Sugar and Wool States," *Lit Dig*, 46 (1913), 931–933.

12. "The Long Struggle with the Tariff Comes to an End," *Current Opinion*, 55 (1913), 221–222; Henry R. Mussey, "The New Freedom in Commerce," *Pol Sci Q*, 29 (1914), 600–625; "A New Era of Industrial Efficiency," *World's Work*, 26 (1913), 380–381.

13. Whelpley, "Tariff out of Politics," p. 303; E. Pendleton Herring, "The Political Context of the Tariff Commission," *Pol Sci Q*, 49 (1934), 421–425.

14. *HS*, p. 887; Paul S. Pierce, "American Trade-Promoting Activities," *South Atlantic Quarterly*, 16 (1917), 118–132.

15. On the AIC, *Lit Dig*, 51 (1915), 1333–37. See also William H. Becker, *The Dynamics of Business-Government Relations: Industry and Exports, 1893–1921* (Chicago, 1982).

16. Henry R. Mussey, "The New Freedom in Commerce," *Pol Sci Q*, 29 (1914), p. 624.

17. Democritus, "The Future Tariff Policy of the United States," *Annals*, 141 (1929), 257n; Robert P. Pettengill, "The United States Copper Industry and the Tariff," *Q J Ec*, 46 (1931–32), 141–157; Becker, *Dynamics*, p. 158.

18. William S. Myers, "The Republican Party and the Tariff," *Annals*, 141 (1929), 246; William R. Allen, "Issues in Congressional Tariff Debates, 1890–1930," *Southern Economic Journal*, 20 (1953–54), 354; F. W. Taussig, "The Tariff Act of 1922," *Q J Ec*, 37 (1922–23), 1–28; Stephen Bell, "Our New Tariff Law," *Outlook*, 132 (1922), 180–181. On the limits of the Commission, see T. W. Page, *Making the Tariff in the United States* (New York, 1924); and Herring, "Political Context," p. 426.

19. Catherine Hackett, "The Failure of the Flexible Tariff: 1922–1927," *New Republic*, 51 (1927), 244–247; Herring, "Political Context," pp. 427–432.

20. George Crompton, *The Tariff* (New York, 1927); J. M. Keynes, "Free Trade," *Nation* (GB), 34 (1923–24), 302–303, 335–336; Myers, "Republican Party," p. 245; H. N. Brailsford, "Free Trade Ebbs in England," *New Republic*, 63 (1930), 359–361. See also R. W. D. Boyce, "America, Europe, and the Triumph of Imperial Protectionism in Britain, 1929–30," *Millennium*, 3 (Spring 1974), 53–70.

21. "The Tariff Crime Complete," *Nation* (GB), 130 (1930), 72; on poll, William O. Scruggs, "Revolt against the Tariff," *NAR*, 230 (1930), 18–24.

22. F. W. Taussig, "What the Tariff Has Done to Us," *Atl*, 148 (1931), 669–675; idem, "The Tariff, 1929–30," *Q J Ec*, 44 (1929–30), 175–204; idem, "The Tariff Act of 1930," *Q J Ec*, 45 (1930–31), 1–21; "The American Tariff," *New Statesman*, 33 (1929), 462–463; J. N. Aiken, "National Realignment on the Tariff Issue," *Current History*, 23 (1925–26), 49–55.

23. Keller, *Affairs of State*, pp. 380–384.

24. *HS*, pp. 994, 1023.

25. John A. James, "The Development of the National Money Market, 1893–1911," *J Ec Hist*, 36 (1976), 878–897; Eugene N. White, "The Political Economy of Banking Regulation, 1863–1933," *J Ec Hist*, 42 (1982), 33–52; idem, *The Regulation and Reform of the American Banking System, 1900–1929* (Princeton, 1983), chap. 1; James Livingston, *Origins of the Federal Reserve System* (Ithaca, 1986), chap. 4; F. W. Taussig, "The Currency Act of 1900," *Q J Ec*, 14 (1900), 394–415; R. P. Faulkner, "The Currency Law of 1900," *Annals*, 16 (1900), 33–55.

26. Morton Keller, *The Life Insurance Enterprise, 1885–1910* (Cambridge, Mass., 1963), chaps. 8–10; Vincent P. Carosso, *Investment Banking in America: A History* (Cambridge, Mass., 1970), chaps. 3, 4; Charles J. Bullock, "The Concentration of Banking Interests in the United States," *Atl*,

92 (1903), 183–192; Alexander D. Noyes, "The Trust Companies: Is There Danger in the System?" *Pol Sci Q*, 16 (1901), 248–261.

27. H. W. Magee, *A Treatise on the Law of National and State Banks, Including the Clearing House and Trust Companies* (Albany, 1906); U.S. National Monetary Commission, *Digest of State Banking Laws* (Washington, D.C., 1910); Pierre Jay, "Recent and Prospective State Banking Legislation," *Q J Ec*, 23 (1908–09), 233–250; Mansel G. Blackford, *The Politics of Business in California, 1890–1920* (Columbus, Ohio, 1977), chap. 6; Keller, *Life Insurance Enterprise*, chap. 12.

28. Eugene N. White, "State-Sponsored Insurance of Bank Deposits in the United States, 1907–1929," *Journal of Economic History*, 41 (1981), 537–557; idem, *Regulation and Reform*, chap. 4; Thornton Cooke, "The Insurance of Bank Deposit in the West," *Q J Ec*, 24 (1909–10), 85–108, 327–391; Noble State Bank v. Haskell, 219 U.S. 104 (1911); Thornton Cooke, "Four More Years of Deposit Guaranty," *Q J Ec*, 28 (1913–14), 69–114.

29. E. W. Kemmerer, "The United States Postal Savings Bank," *Pol Sci Q*, 26 (1911), 462–499; idem, "Six Years of Postal Savings in the United States," *American Economic Review*, 7 (1917), 46–90; George E. Roberts, "Objections to a Postal Savings-Bank," *NAR*, 184 (1907), 364–370.

30. George E. Roberts, "Financial Legislation," *NAR*, 185 (1907), 33–43; Ernest Howard, "The Money Inflation and the Future of Prices," *Pol Sci Q*, 22 (1907), 74–82.

31. On Aldrich, Robert C. West, *Banking Reform and the Federal Reserve, 1863–1923* (Ithaca, 1977), pp. 69–70; U.S. National Monetary Commission, *Report on the Fiscal Systems of the United States, England, France, and Germany*, 61st Cong., 2d. sess., Senate Doc. 403 (Washington, D.C., 1910).

32. J. Laurence Laughlin, "The Aldrich-Vreeland Act," *J Pol Ec*, 16 (1908), 513; Livingston Origins, p. 221; Arthur Link, *Woodrow Wilson and the Progressive Era, 1910–1917* (New York, 1954), pp. 43–53; White, *Regulation and Reform*, chap. 2. But see also Gabriel Kolko, *The Triumph of Conservatism* (New York, 1963), pp. 146–158; and Livingston, *Origins*, which attribute the creation of the Federal Reserve System to a class-conscious group of bankers and businessmen seeking to make the banking and monetary system safe for corporate capitalism.

33. John J. Broesamle, "The Struggle for Control of the Federal Reserve System, 1914–1917," *Mid-America*, 52 (1970), 280–297; White, *Regulation and Reform*, chap. 3.

34. H. Parker Willis, "The Federal Reserve System—A Retrospect of Eight Years," *Pol Sci Q*, 37 (1922), 553–584; Samuel Crowther, "Who Owns the United States?" *World's Work*, 40 (1920), 377–383, 495–596; W. H. Allen, "Concentration of Money at New York," *Moody's Magazine*, 19 (1916), 641–644.

35. Henry W. Macrosty, "Inflation and Deflation in the United States and the United Kingdom, 1919–23," *Journal of the Royal Statistical Society*, 90 (1927), 45–122; Carosso, *Investment Banking*, chap. 12; "We Become a

Nation of Savers," *Lit Dig*, 84 (Jan. 3, 1925), 68; Robert W. Dunn, *American Foreign Investments* (New York, 1926); Charles E. Persons, "Credit Expansion, 1920 to 1929, and Its Lessons," *Q J Ec*, 45 (1930–31), 94–130; H. Parker Willis, "Politics and the Federal Reserve System," *Bankers' Magazine*, 110 (1925), 13–20.

36. William L. Crow, "Legislative Control of Commercial Banking in Wisconsin," *Marquette Law Review*, 17 (1933), 241–269; "Bad Check Laws," *Harv LR*, 44 (1930–31), 451–456; "The Federal Reserve System against the Country Banks of the South: The Struggle for Par Clearance," *Harv LR*, 37 (1923–24), 133–136; *HS*, p. 1038.

37. Joseph S. Lawrence, "Problem of Banking Concentration," *Bankers' Magazine*, 121 (1930), 299–302, 447–451, 598–602; Thornton Cooke, "The Collapse of Bank-Deposit Guaranty in Oklahoma and Its Position in Other States," *Q J Ec*, 38 (1923–24), 108–139; Charles M. Harger, "An Experiment That Failed," *Outlook*, 143 (1926), 278–279.

38. Helen M. Burns, *The American Banking Community and New Deal Banking Reform, 1933–1934* (Westport, Conn., 1974).

39. Harry C. Emery, "Ten Years' Regulation of the Stock Exchange in Germany," *Yale Review*, 17 (1908), 5–23.

40. Keller, *Affairs of State*, pp. 415–416.

41. Carl Parker, "Government Regulation of Speculation," *Annals*, 38 (1911), 444–472; G. Wright Hoffman, "Governmental Regulation of Exchanges," *Annals*, 155 (1931), 39–55; Board of Trade v. Christie, 198 U.S. 236 (1905). See also Jonathan Lurie, *The Chicago Board of Trade, 1859–1905: The Dynamics of Self-Regulation* (Urbana, 1979).

42. Hill v. Wallace, 259 U.S. 44 (1922); Board of Trade v. Olsen, 262 U.S. 1 (1923); Telford Taylor, "Trading in Commodity Futures—A New Standard of Legality?" *Yale LJ*, 43 (1933–34), 63–106.

43. *HS*, p. 1007.

44. Quoted in Hoffman, "Governmental Regulation," p. 43.

45. R. S. Spilman, "The Constitutionality of 'Blue Sky' Laws," *Am LR*, 49 (1915), 389–416; *Lit Dig*, 48 (1914), 367; Robert R. Reed, " 'Blue Sky' Laws," *Annals*, 88 (1920), 177–181; Hall v. Geiger-Jones Co., 242 U.S. 539 (1917).

46. Forrest B. Ashby, *The Economic Effect of the Blue Sky Laws* (Philadelphia, 1926), pp. 40–43; Keyes Winter, "State Regulation of Corporations by Policing Sales of Securities," *Annals*, 129 (1927), 149–155; Watson Washburn and Olga M. Steig, "Control of Securities Selling," *Mich LR*, 31 (1932–33), 780–781.

47. Reed, " 'Blue Sky' Laws," pp. 181–187; swindles estimate in Winter, "State Regulation," p. 152; Forrest B. Ashby, "Federal Regulation of Securities Sales," *Illinois Law Review*, 22 (1927–28), 635–645. See also Michael E. Parrish, *Securities Regulation and the New Deal* (New Haven, 1970), chaps. 1, 2.

48. George E. Barnett, "The Securities Act of 1933 and the British Companies Act," *Harv Bus R*, 13 (1934), 1–14; Friedrich Kessler, "The American Se-

curities Act and Its Foreign Counterparts: A Comparative Study," *Yale LJ,* 44 (1934–35), 1133–65.

49. William O. Douglas and George E. Bates, "The Federal Securities Act of 1933," *Yale LJ,* 43 (1933–34), 171–217; Parrish, *Securities Regulation,* chap. 3; Thomas K. McCraw, *Prophets of Regulation* (Cambridge, Mass., 1984), chap. 5.

50. *HS,* pp. 1122, 1126; on late nineteenth-century background, see Keller, *Affairs of State,* pp. 307–309, 322–327, 331–332, 339–340; Carolyn Webber and Aaron Wildavsky, *A History of Taxation and Expenditure in the Western World* (New York, 1986), chap. 7; Edwin R. A. Seligman, "Recent Tax Reforms Abroad," *Pol Sci Q,* 27 (1912), 454–469, 577–604.

51. Edwin R. A. Seligman, "Newer Tendencies in American Taxation," *Annals,* 58 (1915), 1–11; Albert Jay Nock, series on tax abuses, in *American Magazine,* 71 (1910–11); Carl C. Plehn, "The Nature and Causes of the Tax Reform Movement in the United States," *Economics Journal,* 20 (1910), 1–12.

52. Howard L. McBain, "Taxation for a Private Purpose," *Pol Sci Q,* 29 (1914), 185–213; Harry Hubbard, "The Fourteenth Amendment and Special Assessments in Real Estate—Norwood v. Baker, 172 U.S. 269 (1900)," *Harv LR,* 14 (1900–01), 1–19, 98–115.

53. On Chicago, John R. Commons, "Some Taxation Problems and Reforms," *American Monthly Review of Reviews,* 27 (1903), 205–206; Edwin R. A. Seligman, "Recent Reports on State and Local Taxation," *Pol Sci Q,* 22 (1907), 298; idem, "The New York Income Tax," *Pol Sci Q,* 34 (1919), 525–545.

54. Shelby M. Harrison, "The Disproportion of Taxation in Pittsburgh," *Annals,* 58 (1915), 168–182.

55. Charles J. Bullock, *General Property Tax in the United States* (Columbia, Mo., 1908); Keller, *Affairs of State,* pp. 323–324.

56. Brewer in Metropolitan Street Rlway Co. v. New York State Board, 199 U.S. 1, 39 (1905) (quoting Adams Express Co. v. Ohio, 166 U.S. 185, 218 [1897]); Joseph H. Beale, Jr., "The Taxation of Foreign Corporations," *Harv LR,* 17 (1903–04), 248–265.

57. H. A. Millis, "The Inheritance Tax in the American Commonwealths," *Q J Ec,* 19 (1904–05), 288–301; Solomon Huebner, ibid., pp. 529–550; Max West, *The Inheritance Tax* (New York, 1908).

58. James H. Gilbert, "Single-Tax Movement in Oregon," *Pol Sci Q,* 31 (1916), 250–252; A. A. Young, "The Vote on the Single Tax in Missouri," *American Economic Review,* 3 (1913), 203–206.

59. Delos O. Kinsman, "The Present Period of Income Tax Activity in the American States," *Q J Ec,* 23 (1908–09), 296–306; W. Elliot Brownlee, Jr., "Income Taxation and the Political Economy of Wisconsin, 1890–1930," *Wisconsin Magazine of History,* 59 (1976), 299–313; J. H. Gilbert, "The Significance of the Wisconsin Income Tax," *Pol Sci Q,* 28 (1913), 569–585.

60. Charles J. Bullock, "The Taxation of Property and Income in Massachusetts," *Q J Ec,* 31 (1916–17), 46–50; idem, "The Operation of the Massa-

chusetts Income Tax," *Q J Ec*, 32 (1917–18), 525–532; Seligman, "New York Income Tax," pp. 521–524.

61. Frank A. Fetter, "Changes in the Tax Laws of New York State in 1905," *Q J Ec*, 20 (1905–06), 151–156; Howard L. McBain, "The Increase in Inheritance Taxes in New York," *Col LR*, 14 (1914), 229–240; Seligman, "Recent Reports," pp. 310–314.

62. Richard L. McCormick, *From Realignment to Reform: Political Changes in New York State, 1893–1910* (Ithaca, 1981), pp. 161–162.

63. Bullock, "Taxation of Property and Income," pp. 32–34.

64. Commons, "Some Taxation Problems," pp. 202–204.

65. William Carpenter, "An Experiment in Equalization, and Its Result," *Mich LR*, 8 (1909–10), 374–385.

66. Oliver C. Lockhart, "Recent Developments in Taxation in Ohio," *Q J Ec*, 29 (1914–15), 480–521.

67. "Tax Legislation," *American Political Science Review*, 6 (1912), 74–83; Edwin R. A. Seligman, *The Income Tax* (New York, 1911), pp. 202–213, 250–272, 306–328; Kossuth K. Kennan, *Income Taxation: Methods and Results in Various Countries* (Milwaukee, 1910); Stephen W. Owen, "The Politics of Tax Reform in France, 1906–1926" (Ph.D. diss., University of California at Berkeley, 1983); "Mr. Roosevelt's New Tax Plans," *Ind*, 61 (1906), 1432–33; X, "An Appeal to Our Millionaires," *NAR*, 182 (1906), 801.

68. William H. Dunbar, "The Constitutionality of the United States Inheritance Tax," *Q J Ec*, 15 (1901), 292–298; Henry L. West, "American Politics," *Forum*, 41 (1909), 513–520.

69. Aldrich quoted in Jerold Waltman, "Origins of the Federal Income Tax," *Mid-America*, 62 (1980), 156; Arthur W. Machen, Jr., *Treatise on the Federal Corporation Tax Law of 1909* (Boston, 1910), p. 2; Flint v. Stone Tracy Co., 220 U.S. 107 (1911). Sidney Ratner, *American Taxation: Its History as a Social Force in Democracy* (New York, 1942), chap. 14; and John F. Witte, *The Politics and Development of the Federal Income Tax* (Madison, 1985), chap. 4, are standard accounts. See also Albert B. Cummins, "The Reasons for the Income Tax," *Ind*, 67 (1909), 178–182; Charles A. Conant, "The New Corporation Tax," *NAR*, 190 (1909), 231–240; Harold M. Bowman, "Congress and the Supreme Court," *Pol Sci Q*, 25 (1910), 20–34; Ralph W. Aigler, "The Constitutionality of the Federal Corporation Tax," *Mich LR*, 8 (1909–10), 206–220.

70. *Wall Street Journal* quoted in Ratner, *American Taxation*, p. 298; Frederic D. Bond, "Income Tax versus Tariff," *Bankers' Magazine*, 83 (1911), 615–618; "The Income-Tax Amendment," *Nation*, 92 (1911), 414.

71. John D. Buenker, "Urban Liberalism and the Federal Income Tax Amendment," *Pennsylvania History*, 36 (1969), 192–215; idem, "Progressivism in Practice: New York State and the Federal Income Tax Amendment," *New York Historical Society Quarterly*, 52 (1968), 139–160. See also Edwin R. A. Seligman, "The Income-Tax Amendment," *Pol Sci Q*, 25 (1910), 193–219.

72. Edwin R. A. Seligman, "The Federal Income Tax," *Pol Sci Q*, 29 (1914), 1–27.

73. Hull quoted in "Now for the Income Tax," *Hearst's Magazine*, 23 (1913), 672–674; "The Income Tax," *Nation*, 96 (1913), 432; "American Incomes," *Nation*, 103 (1916), 534.

74. Link, *Wilson and Progressive Era*, pp. 192–196; Edwin R. A. Seligman, "The Excess-Profits Tax," *Nation*, 106 (1918), 365–366; on comparative rates, *Lit Dig*, 58 (Sept. 14, 1918), 14–15.

75. W. Elliot Brownlee, "Wilson and Financing the Modern State: The Revenue Act of 1916," *American Philosophical Society Proceedings*, 129 (1985), 173–210.

76. Webber and Wildavsky, *Taxation and Expenditure*, pp. 436–451; Herbert W. Horwill, "Problems of Local Taxation in England," *Pol Sci Q*, 36 (1921), 561–571; John A. Hobson, *Taxation in the New State* (London, 1919), pp.1–2.

77. Webber and Wildavsky, *Taxation and Expenditure*, p. 451; NICB, *State Income Taxes* (New York, 1930), I, 4.

78. H. Larry Ingle, "The Dangers of Reaction: Repeal of the Revenue Act of 1918," *North Carolina Historical Review*, 44 (1967), 72–88.

79. "The Growing Tax Burden," *Nation*, 115 (1922), 681–682. See also Edward B. Rosa, "Expenditures and Revenues of the Federal Government," *Annals*, 95 (1921), 1–113.

80. Lawrence L. Murray, "Bureaucracy and Bi-partisanship in Taxation: The Mellon Plan Revisited," *Bus Hist R*, 52 (1978), 200–225.

81. Herbert Stein, *The Fiscal Revolution in America* (Chicago, 1969), pp. 9–11.

82. *HS*, p. 1122.

83. K. M. Williamson, "The Literature on the Sales Tax," *Q J Ec*, 35 (1920–21), 618–633.

84. Roswell Magill, "The Taxation of Unrealized Income," *Harv LR*, 39 (1925–26), 100; Towne v. Eisner, 245 U.S. 418 (1918), Eisner v. Macomber, 252 U.S. 189 (1920); Witte, *Federal Income Tax*, p. 93; Thomas R. Powell, "Stock Dividends, Direct Taxes, and the Sixteenth Amendment," *Col LR*, 20 (1920), 536–549.

85. Robert M. Haig, "Tax-Exempt Securities *vs.* Progressive Income Tax," *NAR*, 217 (1923), 423–432; Fabian Franklin, "Income Taxation and Tax-Exempt Securities," *Ind*, 110 (1923), 17–18; Albert W. Atwood, "The Rich Man and His Taxes," *Saturday Evening Post*, May 3, 1924, pp. 433–438.

86. Joseph J. Klein, *Federal Income Taxation* (New York, 1929), p. xiv.

87. *HS*, pp. 1126, 1127, 1129–30; "Growing Tax Burden," p. 682; L. R. Gottlieb, "Post-War Local Burdens," *J Pol Ec*, 32 (1924), 226–235; idem, "Growth in Local Tax Burdens," *Q J Ec*, 37 (1922–23), 374–382.

88. George Vaughan, "The Increasing Importance of Special Taxes," *Cent LJ*, 89 (1925), 223–230; Commonwealth of Massachusetts, Special Commission on Taxation, *Report* (Boston, 1928). See also Rodman Sullivan, "The Development of Transfer Taxes in the United States in the Twentieth

Century," *Tax Magazine*, 13 (1935), 389–397, 436–437; NICB, *State and Local Taxation of Business Corporations* (New York, 1931), p. 133; Jens P. Jensen, *Property Taxation in the United States* (Chicago, 1931), pp. 17–18.

89. Joseph H. Beale, "Taxation: The Progress of the Law, 1923–1924," *Harv LR*, 38 (1924–25), 283.

90. Harley L. Lutz, "The Progress of State Income Taxation since 1911," *American Economic Review*, 10 (1920), 66–91; *Lit Dig*, 84 (Jan. 3, 1925), 69; Henry Rottschaefer, "State Jurisdiction of Income for Tax Purposes," *Harv LR*, 44 (1930–31), 1075–1101.

91. Bowman v. Continental Oil Co., 256 U.S. 642 (1921); Pierce Oil Co. v. Hopkins, 264 U.S. 137 (1924); "The Constitutionality of Gasoline Taxes in Light of Their Current Operation," *Yale LJ*, 41 (1932), 763–768.

92. *HS*, p. 1129.

93. "Taxation Directed against the Chain Store," *Yale LJ*, 40 (1930–31), 431–441; "Chain Store Taxation," *U Pa LR*, 80 (1931–32), 289–295; Indiana v. Jackson, 283 U.S. 527 (1931); Fredrick K. Hardy, "Legal and Economic Aspects of Chain Store Taxation in Wisconsin," *Wisconsin Law Review*, 9 (1933–34), 382–387.

94. Edwin Kessler, Jr., "Some Legal Problems in State Personal Income Taxation," *Yale LJ*, 34 (1924–25), 759–764, 862–878; "Interstate Allocation of Corporate Income for Taxing Purposes," *Yale LJ*, 40 (1931), 1273–83.

95. Thomas R. Powell, "Due Process Tests of State Taxation, 1922–1925," *U Pa LR*, 74 (1925–26), 423–451, 573–600; Frick v. Pennsylvania, 268 U.S. 473 (1925); "A New Era in State Inheritance Taxes," *U Pa LR*, 74 (1925–26), 73–77.

96. *HS*, p. 1133; NICB, *State and Local Taxation of Property* (New York, 1930), p. v.

97. Ralph T. Compton, *Fiscal Problems of Rural Decline* (Albany, 1929); Eric Englund, "The Trend of Real Estate Taxation in Kansas, 1910–1923," *J Land PU Ec*, 1 (1925), 444–458.

98. C. E. Rightor, "Comparative Tax Rates of 290 Cities, 1931," *National Municipal Review*, 20 (1931), 707; Simeon E. Leland, "Breakdown of Personal Property Tax in Illinois and Its Solution," *National Income Tax Magazine*, 7 (1929), 266–271, 288–289.

99. Herbert D. Simpson, *Tax Racket and Tax Reform in Chicago* (Chicago, 1930); Blake E. Nicholson, *Collection of Taxes in Pennsylvania* (Philadelphia, 1932), pp. 47–48, 269. See also "Local Taxation in the United States of America," *Justice of the Peace*, 95 (1931), 795–796.

100. Harold M. Groves, "Recent State Tax Legislation in the United States," *Tax Magazine*, 10 (1932), 405; Roy O. Blakey and Gladys C. Blakey, *The Federal Income Tax* (New York, 1940), p. 306.

101. Mark H. Leff, *The Limits of Symbolic Reform: The New Deal and Taxation, 1933–39* (Cambridge, 1984).

102. Herbert D. Simpson, "Tax Delinquency," *Illinois Law Review*, 28 (1933–34), 148; Earl H. De Long, "The Illinois Tax Receivership Act," ibid., pp. 379–395; Robert C. Brown, "State Taxation of Interstate Commerce, and

Federal and State Taxation in Intergovernmental Relations—1930–1932," *U Pa LR*, 81 (1932–33), 247–266.

103. "Taxpayer Rebellions," *Lit Dig*, 112 (Jan. 9, 1932), 11; N.Y. Laws 1933, chap. 815.

104. "The Search for New Sources of Revenue," *Harv LR*, 47 (1934), 503–510; Carl Shoup and Louis Haimoff, "The Sales Tax," *Col LR*, 34 (1934), 809–830; James W. Martin and William A. Tolman, "Recent State Gross Sales Tax Legislation," *Tax Magazine*, 11 (1933), 449–454, 477–481; "The Sales Tax," *Harv LR*, 47 (1934), 860–870; "Taxation—Constitutional Limitations on Sales Taxes," *Mich LR*, 33 (1934–35), 614–627. See also Murray Haig and Carl Shoup, *The Sales Tax in the American States* (New York, 1934).

105. *HS*, p. 1129.

Index

298 · Index

Jeff Brady 293-2770